C++ for Scientists and Engineers

C++ for Scientists and Engineers

James T. Smith

San Francisco State University

Intertext Publications
McGraw-Hill Book Company

New York St. Louis San Francisco Auckland Bogotá
Hamburg London Madrid Mexico Milan Montreal
New Delhi Panama Paris São Paolo
Singapore Sydney Tokyo Toronto

Library of Congress Catalog Card Number 91-71590

10 9 8 7 6 5 4 3 2 1

ISBN 0-07-059180-6

Intertext Publications/Multiscience Press, Inc.
One Lincoln Plaza
New York, NY 10023

McGraw-Hill Book Company
1221 Avenue of the Americas
New York, NY 10020

Composed in Ventura Publisher by High Text Corp., Colleyville, TX.

This book is dedicated to my students.
My Malaysian students are taking advantage
of expanding educational opportunities.
I hope my students in California don't see the collapse of theirs.

Acknowledgments

San Francisco State University encouraged me to undertake this project and provided a realistic workload while I carried it out. My colleagues Dr. David Ellis and Dr. David Meredith provided essential advice on some of the mathematics and programming techniques used or described in this book. In addition, Dr. Meredith provided constant access to the most current versions of his *Calculus Calculator* (CC) mathematical desktop software (Reference [31]), a wonderful tool for scientific and engineering computation. Finally, I want to thank all my university colleagues and my wife Helen, who tolerated my preoccupation and neglect while this project was under way.

Contents

Preface

This book describes the design, construction, and use of a numerical analysis software tool kit. It's written in C++, Version 2.0, and makes essential use of that language's Object Oriented Programming (OOP) features. Its development environment is the Borland International, Inc. Turbo C++ compiler, Version 1.00, for IBM compatible personal computers. But the book describes few features specific to that product.

The tool kit and its description and background discussions cover the most fundamental aspects of numerical analysis. At the heart of most scientific or engineering applications programs lie some of the concepts and techniques presented here. The most basic include details of computation with floating point real and complex numbers, mathematical functions in the C++ Library, and a general OOP framework for vector, polynomial, and matrix algebra. On this foundation are constructed routines for solving nonlinear equations, for linear and nonlinear systems of equations, and for eigenvalue problems.

The book is heavily weighted toward software development. What's new here is the emphasis on software tools and on OOP techniques for handling vectors, polynomials, and matrices. Rather than describing programs implementing specific numerical techniques to solve specific applications problems, the book constructs reusable tools with which you can implement many techniques for solving broad classes of problems. Examples are included to demonstrate their use. The tools are organized into layers. The deepest is formed by the C++ Library functions for computing with real and complex numbers. The entire package is constructed so that it's easy to select real or complex scalars. Resting on these scalar routines is vector algebra software. Vectors are implemented as OOP objects, and a program can handle vectors of any dimension simultaneously. This feature is critical for manipulating polynomial objects, which inherit properties of vectors, but boast specific properties of their own. For example, you can add polynomials of different degrees, handling them as vectors of different dimensions; you can multiply polynomials, but that operation isn't useful for vectors in general. Many higher level numerical analysis tools can be built on the vector and polynomial algebra routines. For others, however, another software layer for defining and handling matrix objects is built atop the vector class.

While it emphasizes OOP features in implementing vector, polynomial, and matrix algebra, this book actually steers a middle course in using OOP techniques. The organization of higher mathematics into the theories of vector spaces, polynomial and matrix algebras, etc., is the product of many decades of work ultimately aimed at scientific and engineering applications problems. It's an efficient, elegant, and highly successful methodology. Through similar organizational devices, OOP is beginning to let developers attain comparable generality and grace in software tool kits. This book employs OOP techniques only where they obviously further that goal. *Here, OOP is used to organize numerical application programs and make them look like the mathematics they represent.*

It's possible to write C++ numerical software *entirely* in an OOP framework, where *every* computational entity is an object of some class. Turbo C++ is shipped with a "Class Library" to encourage that process. But those techniques are under current development. For example, the *Annotated C++ Reference Manual,* by C++ designer Bjarne Stroustrup [13], describes experimental features that *may* be built into the next C++ version. These include fundamental constructs that would make it possible for C++ programs to parallel underlying mathematics even closer. *C++ for Scientists and Engineers* keeps to the middle course, using OOP techniques just for vector, polynomial, and matrix algebra, because it's not now clear what further steps would take it *closer* to the *goal: making programs easier to construct, understand, and maintain.*

An optional diskette containing the source code for all the tools described in this book is available at modest cost from the author. For your convenience, an order card is included at the back of this book.

1

Introduction

This book is an introduction to C++ techniques for scientific and engineering applications software development. It will show you how to use C++ Object Oriented Programming (OOP) methods to define and work with classes of mathematical structures, or objects, commonly involved in these applications — vectors, matrices, polynomials, and complex numbers. C++ ultimately gives you more freedom than most other languages in handling objects like these, but at considerable cost: You yourself must provide the underlying software that constructs, maintains, manipulates, and dismantles these structures. The book concentrates on these matters, and implements the basic algorithms of vector, matrix, and polynomial algebra and analysis. It shows how to base powerful applications software on this foundation.

The compiler used for all the work in the book is *Turbo C++*, Version 1.00, by Borland International, Inc. (Reference [5]), for IBM compatible personal computers. Most of the language and C++ Library features used here are included in C++ Version 2.0, developed at AT&T Bell Laboratories (Reference [13]). C++ includes a version of the C language, differing only slightly from ANSI C as described in American National Standard X3.159-1989. Turbo C++ departures from the standards are noted.

This book is really a report on a research project: How can you use C++ OOP techniques to facilitate scientific and engineering applications software development? How can they enhance the quality of your software? The project required restricting the scope of the software considered. This book describes in detail the implementation of software for these areas of numerical analysis:

- real and complex arithmetic,
- elementary functions,
- vector and matrix algebra,
- polynomial algebra,
- solution of transcendental and polynomial equations,
- solution of linear systems of equations,
- eigenvalue problems,
- solution of nonlinear systems of equations.

Most of this software applies equally well to real and complex scalars. In addition, the book explores standard C and specific Turbo C++ programming methods for reacting to arithmetic and library function error situations.

A comprehensive introduction to scientific and engineering applications software would cover several other areas, too. But this book stresses software development problems more than a comprehensive introduction would. You'll meet the major OOP software development problems while implementing algorithms in the areas just listed. Once you can manage those, C++ OOP based implementation of algorithms in other areas — for example, integration and initial value problems — should be straightforward. In fact, most really complicated programming problems in numerical analysis occur in the areas covered in this book. Constraints of time and size limit it to these central themes.

The book is built around a Mathematical Software Package called MSP that the author is developing to study C++ OOP implementation of numerical analysis algorithms. Typical applications problems are sketched to show why the algorithms are needed in scientific and engineering practice. The underlying mathematics is discussed as required. It's emphasized mainly where an understanding of the algorithms requires mathematics beyond the usual introductory courses. MSP routines are discussed in detail in the text, and much of the source code is displayed, with profuse documentation. Example test programs and output show how MSP is used in practice.

All of the source code is available on an optional diskette from the author at nominal cost. To obtain it, send the coupon in the back of the book directly to him.

This introductory chapter describes the book, its purpose, and its audience in greater detail. It considers general software tool kit methodology and pros and cons of C++ and Turbo C++ for scientific and engineering applications software development. Finally, it lists a number of references and resources for further work in this subject.

1.1 Who Needs This Book?

Who needs this book? You do, if you're developing scientific or engineering applications software and must use C++ to remain compatible with some other software. Or perhaps you want to experiment with C++ Object Oriented Programming (OOP) techniques to facilitate software development, or to see how they can enhance software quality in this area.

AT&T Bell Laboratories extended the popular commercial systems programming language C to form C++, a language designed to foster the use of OOP techniques in diverse applications. Thus, C++ is a compromise. OOP techniques restrict programming practices to enhance the efficiency of program development and to insure program robustness. On the other hand, freedom from such restrictions had been a major aim in designing C.

OOP techniques for defining classes of data objects parallel the organization of higher mathematics. When you study mathematical structures, you consider the operations on the data together with the data themselves. For example, in studying a vector space, you consider the vector addition and scalar multiplication operations along with the vectors themselves. Moreover, you regard some structures as particular instances of others, perhaps enhanced by additional features. For example, a polynomial algebra is a vector space with some additional operations, including polynomial multiplication and evaluation. This mathematical organization was refined over decades to handle some deep mathematical and logical problems that arose originally in applications. If it is applied in programming practice, OOP will exert a strong influence on mathematical software development. In particular, it will facilitate construction of very general routines that are easily adaptable to specific situations, and the relationship between the software and the mathematics will be transparent.

Many, but not all, OOP techniques are implemented in C++. This, plus the widespread dissemination of the Turbo C++ compiler, and the extreme flexibility of the underlying C language, make it an ideal vehicle for OOP experimentation in mathematical software development. This book's MSP software package represents the current status of such an experiment.

This book is an argument for incorporating OOP techniques in scientific and engineering applications software development, but it does not push for adoption of C++ as a standard language for developing production software. Twenty-five years from now, the next generation of programmers will view OOP as ordinary, common sense applications programming methodology. But C++ will be remembered as a curious language that grafted OOP features onto a host of another species to produce a vehicle for experimental development in a commercial environment. This book is written to help you carry on those experiments.

C++ requires you to provide software to create, maintain, manipulate, and dismantle the mathematical data structures needed for your application. Applications programmers using other languages don't encounter so many low-level tasks. The book's MSP modules for vector, matrix, and polynomial algebra allow you to perform these tasks easily, usually with efficient grace. Its higher level modules for solving equations and systems of equations show you how to build powerful applications software based on the low level OOP routines.

You see here just a snapshot of the ongoing MSP project. This package, and your own MSP modifications and enhancements, will continue to evolve. Moreover, C++ will change, probably quite rapidly. In *The Annotated C++ Reference Manual* (Reference [13]), C++ designer Bjarne Stroustrup devotes two chapters to experimental techniques — class templates and exception handling — that go beyond the language and compiler used for this book. Both of these new concepts are directly relevant to scientific and engineering applications programming. Had they been available, this book's MSP software would have been designed differently. Finally, OOP itself is an area of active computer science research. During the next few years, new ideas there will result in new and modified languages, and ultimately produce major trends in commercial software development.

Thus, you should approach C++ applications software development with enthusiasm, but with caution, too. The language, its OOP techniques, and this book will allow you to write programs more effectively and gracefully, and to easily implement algorithms that would present major difficulties with other languages. On the other hand, your programs won't remain current for long. Your new techniques will be supplanted with newer ones soon, you'll develop even greater power as a programmer, and you'll soon want to redo your work to achieve the ultimate in effectiveness and grace. But that won't be the end, either.

The evolution of C++ as a research tool notwithstanding, this language *will* be used for developing some production applications software. The widespread availability of Turbo C++ and Borland's continued support of this powerful and convenient compiler will ensure that. Therefore, you may well need to develop scientific or engineering applications software in C++ to maintain compatibility with other C++ software. If that's the case, this book will clarify the issues and help you get started with an exciting programming project.

Prerequisites

What must you know *before* reading this book? It assumes you are a skilled programmer in some higher level language, and you are familiar with Turbo C. Most C++ features that go beyond the C language are described in this text, but not in complete detail. You'll need a C++ manual. With general hardware concepts you need only minimal acquaintance: There's occasional reference to memory organization, the stack, and registers. To become adept with Turbo C++, you should be familiar with the various hardware components of IBM compatible PCs, and with DOS user services. Finally, to understand the numerical analysis algorithms covered in this book, you should have mastered university level mathematics through multivariable calculus and elementary linear algebra.

Turbo C++ can easily overtax the speed and memory capabilities of a computer. The system the author used to produce the MSP software and write this book is described in Section 1.4.

1.2   Working with Software Tools

C++ requires you to provide software to create, maintain, manipulate, and dismantle the mathematical data structures needed for your application: for example, vectors, matrices, and polynomials. Applications programmers using other languages don't encounter so many low-level tasks. As a C++ programmer, you'll need a tool kit of routines for performing these tasks. This can be expanded to include routines for real and complex arithmetic and elementary functions, vector and matrix algebra, and polynomial manipulation. The resulting low-level tool kit can be expanded further with higher level routines for more complicated tasks like computing determinants, solving equations or systems of equations, computing integrals, etc. The higher level routines can be organized like the theory and algorithms presented in numerical analysis texts. Your tool kit contains known solutions to common problems, so you can concentrate on new problems as they arise in your work.

The Turbo C++ Library is organized as a tool kit. You'll need its functions occasionally for the services it offers to programmers in all applications areas, particularly for input/output, string handling, mathematical functions, etc. You should become familiar with its organization — see its *Reference guide*, Reference [5] — else you may waste time trying to solve programming problems for which the Library provides convenient solutions. The Library consists of about five hundred service functions covering the following programming areas:

manipulating memory areas	memory management
text string processing	executing separate programs
text mode screen handling	time calculations
keyboard input	mathematical functions
file input/output	error handling
directory management	low-level graphics output.

Many of these services are specified by the ANSI C standard, so are available for other C compilers. Most of them, except for the last three categories, are described in great detail in the author's earlier book (Reference [37]). The present book covers the Library's mathematical functions and much of its error handling capability.

Although the Turbo C++ Library is comprehensive and professionally implemented, it falls short of your needs in some areas. One is, of course, numerical analysis. That's the main reason for this book. Others that may be critical for your work are asynchronous communication, interactive input/output and high-level graphics output. Many commercial products can provide further support for your work in these areas. Some are mentioned in Section 1.6.

What principles should govern tool kit development? First, *isolate mathematical and programming problems,* and attack them independently while they occupy your entire attention. That's a much more likely way to produce useful tools than *ad hoc* solutions by a programmer really interested only in getting some particular application to work. Second, *strive for generality.* Each application will differ a little from earlier ones. A tool that's too particular will need modification again and again, and may lose a little robustness each time. Next, *test the code!* Have others use it in as many different situations as possible. Finally, *write readable, understandable, trustable code and documentation.* Programmers who can't understand how a tool works may not want to use it in products on which their jobs depend.

The tools in the Turbo C++ Library and in its commercial supplements were generally written with those guidelines in mind. The tools in this book's MSP package were, too, but there's a difference.

The commercial products are intended to assist in building production software, and were tested and modified accordingly over a long period of time. MSP is an experimental tool kit, with no such history.

1.3 This Book's Structure

This book's chapters are organized into three groups:

Introduction
> 1 Introduction
> 2 Software organization

MSP and Turbo C++ Library foundation
> 3 Introduction to MSP
> 4 Computing with real and complex numbers

High-level MSP routines
> 5 Solving real and complex equations
> 6 Matrix computations
> 7 Iterative solution of systems of equations

Chapter 2 considers programming fundamentals. It discusses first the layers of software that are simultaneously active when an applications program is executing — from the program itself down through layers of tools like this book's MSP software, through Turbo C++ and DOS layers, to the bottom layer, your machine's BIOS. The remainder of Chapter 2 is devoted to OOP and C++ fundamentals on which are based the data structures — complex numbers, vectors, matrices, and polynomials — used in this book.

The middle chapters consider the low-level MSP routines and the mathematical and error handling features of the Turbo C++ Library. The low-level MSP routines construct, maintain, manipulate, and dismantle the fundamental structures, and carry out algebraic computations with complex numbers, vectors, matrices, and polynomials. Chapters 3 and 4 could have been presented in either order. The present order resulted from a decision to keep Chapters 2 and 3 in succession.

The final chapters are more typical of books on scientific and engineering applications programming. They describe various algorithms, based on calculus and linear and polynomial algebra, for solving common mathematical problems arising in applications. These methods are then implemented in C++, based on the low-level routines in the middle chapters. The algorithms in the three final chapters were selected for two reasons:

- they are fundamental ideas of numerical analysis;
- they provide a test bed for the low-level routines: Major design and implementation problems should surface here, if at all.

The high-level material was limited to these chapters solely for reasons of space and time.

Most scientific and engineering applications programming books concentrate on the high-level algorithms and their implementations, de-emphasizing or ignoring low-level aspects. But the main reason for using C++ must be to construct the data structure classes and their low-level maintenance routines to allow the use of OOP techniques in applications. Therefore, the book must emphasize those aspects. Once you have mastered the techniques for implementing the high-level algorithms in the final three chapters, applying them in other areas of numerical analysis should be straightforward.

What Would Come Next?

In this book you see a snapshot of the MSP software package in a particular state of development. Were the book to continue with additional chapters on high-level algorithms, it would include chapters on

- interpolation and approximation,
- numerical integration and differentiation,
- ordinary differential equation initial value problems.

You can see that there's no obvious place to draw the line. Moreover, by the time the subjects just mentioned are covered, C++ may have evolved further. That would call for a reassessment of the foundations, in order to improve some MSP features which aren't ideal in the current version.

Optional Diskette

While most MSP routines are discussed in detail in the text, not all the source code could be included. For that reason, and for your convenience in modifying and enhancing MSP for your own use, all the source code is available on an optional diskette. Its directory is listed in Appendix A.6. The diskette is available at modest cost. To obtain it, send the coupon at the back of the book directly to the author.

1.4 C, C++, and Turbo C++

This section discusses some of the benefits and costs of programming in C and C++, and the benefits of using the Turbo C++ compiler. It concludes with a brief description of the hardware and software used to produce this book and its MSP software.

Why Use C++?

Since C++ is an extension of C, reasons for and against using those languages for software development are closely related. In the programming literature, several standard arguments are often recited in favor of C:

- C is a high-level language, well suited to expressing algorithms of all sorts.
- C fosters writing elegant, readable programs.
- C programs are portable to many computer systems.
- Excellent compilers are available.
- Excellent software tools are available in many areas.
- C compilers produce small, fast executable code.
- C lets you access and control hardware features.
- C programming makes you consider low-level details.

How do these statements apply to C++? They're considered now one by one, both as stated, and as extended to apply to C++. The author does not agree fully with all of them. The first and the last are even contradictory.

Is C++ a High-Level Language?

The original C language is really *not* a high-level language. With C you're constantly forced to consider low-level address details. Unless you become a C specialist, you'll be an inefficient C programmer, because those details are often very difficult to get right. Even if you manage to avoid most addressing problems in a simple program, during debugging you'll usually need to confront them to figure out what really happened when your program didn't do what you expected. C is not particularly well suited to expressing most algorithms, except for those explicitly involved with addressing. Low-level concerns often predominate, and the resulting C programs don't look like the algorithms. Thus, the contradiction between the first reason for choosing C and the last is resolved in favor of the last.

C does foster writing elegant, readable programs. But it's really *neutral*: it also fosters writing inelegant, unreadable programs. If anything, the scale tips negative on this criterion.

Most of the enhancements that transform C to C++ support high-level language features. Here are the chief examples:

- *The class concept* As in higher mathematics, you can *encapsulate* the definition of a data structure with the definitions of its operations.
- *Regarding a particular class K as an instance of a general class G* You can write routines to manipulate all objects in *G*, and apply them to particular instances in *K*, which may have more elaborate data structures and additional or more specialized operations.
- *Overloading function names and operators* You can use similar, intuitive notation for like operations on objects of different classes.
- *Reference parameters* You can pass function parameters by reference instead of value, without explicitly referring to their addresses.
- *Parameter initialization* You can assign default values to some function parameters, and omit them from calling sequences unless you want to give them special values.
- *Stream input/output* The C++ Library includes input/output operations that are somewhat less awkward than the standard input/output functions in the C Library.

If you use these features systematically, you can produce elegant, readable programs much more readily in C++ than in C. In fact, a major object of this book's MSP software tool kit is to enable you to write applications programs that look like the mathematical descriptions of the algorithms they implement. The cost of employing these C++ features is the requirement for elaborate underlying software, like the low-level MSP routines, to construct, maintain, manipulate, and dismantle the data structures you want to use.

One aspect of the OOP data encapsulation technique is defeated in C++. A class definition can declare *private* some components of its data structures, so that only designated *member* and *friend* functions can access them. That should make debugging easier, since only a limited number of functions can change private data. However, the libertarian design of C allows easy circumvention of this restriction through low-level maneuvers.

Two other C++ features are awkward. First, one aspect of the class concept is a mandatory syntax for the principal arguments of member functions, which conflicts with standard mathematical notation and discourages their use. (For example, the real and imaginary components of the **complex** data structure are private; if the function **real** that returns the real component of a **complex** argument z were a member function, you'd have to invoke it with the expression **z.real( )**. To permit the standard notation **real(z)** it's declared a **friend**. But definitions of **friend** functions aren't encapsulated with the data structure definition.) Second, the parameter initialization feature invites class design errors that make it collide with overloading, and produces bugs that are difficult to identify. Moreover, those design problems are hard to resolve.

As remarked in Section 1.1, some of the high level aspects of C++ are still under development. For example, there are already two different versions of stream input/output. The concept of a class *template* is being refined for inclusion in a later version of C++. That will make it possible to define gracefully a general vector class, for example, and then instances like vectors of integers, vectors of complex numbers, and vectors of polynomials. When the new feature is available, MSP will need a major revision. Similarly, C++ error handling mechanisms are under development for the next version, and will probably spur another major revision of MSP.

With a language undergoing current development, you gain access to improved programming techniques quickly, but you may lose stability.

In summary, C++ consists of some very powerful, still evolving, high-level features grafted onto a low-level base language. There's little reason to use C++ if you're not going to rely on those features. If you prepare the low-level foundation of your programs properly, you can write elegant, readable high-level applications programs that clearly reflect the underlying mathematics. However, the debugging and program maintenance process will continually force you to face lower level details to find out what a misbehaving program is actually doing.

Software Tools

Excellent software tools are available for C programmers. The Turbo C++ Library and some commercial supplements were described briefly in Section 1.2. The author's earlier book *Advanced Turbo C* (Reference [37]) is an extremely detailed description of most of the Turbo C Library and one commercial supplement.

Of course, C tools all work with C++. Software tool kits specifically for C++ are beginning to appear. This book's MSP is one such. You should approach such products with caution. They're generally libraries of class definitions and code for member functions and friends and related functions. Since OOP is an active research area and C++ is still evolving, any such tools — particularly MSP — are experimental. The best ways to use OOP to solve common programming problems haven't necessarily been discovered yet.

Minor Considerations

You can write C programs that are portable to many environments, and excellent C compilers are available for many machines. C++ programs are somewhat less portable, and fewer C++ compilers are available, simply because it's a younger language. As remarked earlier, C++ was designed as a vehicle for research in programming language design. That may restrict the number of compilers available. (On the other hand, you could make the same statement about C.) Turbo C++ is an excellent compiler for both C and C++ programs. Its specific qualities are considered later. Almost all of its nonportable features are found in its Library.

C compilers generally produce small, fast executable code. Too few C++ compilers have been studied in detail to make such a statement about C++. Assessment will be difficult, because C++ is designed to enhance the efficiency of the program development and maintenance processes, and that may be a conflicting goal. This book emphasizes the development process completely. It reports the results of an experiment in software design, for which program speed and size were irrelevant.

The last reason given earlier for choosing C as a development language is that it lets you access and control hardware features. That's certainly true for C++ as well (and for some other high-level languages). It's irrelevant for most scientific and engineering applications programming, unless your project involves reading data from sensors or communication lines, or controlling some piece of equipment.

Turbo C++

Why should you use the Turbo C++ compiler? Here, the arguments are less controversial:

- Turbo C++ has a *wonderful* user interface.
- You can configure most features to fit your habits.
- Syntax errors are immediately flagged in the editor.
- The editor will emulate popular word processors.
- From the editor you can control a powerful source code debugger.
- Its Library is comprehensive, well documented, and reliable.
- Turbo C++ includes standard features that facilitate development of very large software systems.
- It will use expanded memory to edit, compile, and link large files.
- The newest version, called *Borland C++*, runs under Microsoft Windows and contains a tool kit for developing Windows applications.

The latest version was not available for this project. The author has only a few criticisms of Turbo C++:

- The early version used for producing this book contained a few bugs, which Borland acknowledged via the *CompuServe* information service and is presumably correcting.
- Passing parameters by reference is either extremely delicate or else imperfectly implemented. It invites problems that the author has been unable to identify. These reveal either a compiler bug or a C++ design flaw that renders this feature less useful than it should be. In any case, the faulty programs tended to crash the Turbo C++ system, and often required rebooting.
- The debugger didn't allow inspection of temporary variables, nor most parameters passed by reference.
- Compilation was somewhat slow. Part of the problem was the extremely long header files; the latest version of the compiler has apparently improved performance there.

In summary, Turbo C++ is generally a delight to use.

Producing This Book

A 33 MHz Taiwanese 80386 system was used to develop the software for this book and to write the text. It was equipped with an 80 MB fixed disk, and a 40 MB streaming tape unit for backup. The low average disk access time — 20 msec — was essential. No numeric coprocessor was installed. The original 4 MB memory proved inadequate, so it was doubled. This memory was managed by Quarterdeck Software's *QEMM* and *DESQview 386* products. Six DESQview windows were simultaneously active:

IBM DOS	Version 4.01,
F	a shareware directory management program,
WordPerfect	Version 5.1,
CC	a Prentice-Hall mathematical desktop program (Reference [31]),
PCFile+	Version 2.0, a ButtonWare database product — the author's personal information manager,
Turbo C++	Version 1.00.

A 1 MB disk cache was loaded before DESQview, and the Word-Perfect screen grabber was loaded first as a memory resident utility in the CC window. DESQview was used constantly to copy text from the Turbo C++ or DOS window to WordPerfect. CC drew the graphic figures, and the screen grabber copied them for WordPerfect. Super-VGA graphics and a color display were very important for editing.

This system's speed was critical, both for Turbo C++ and for Word-Perfect. The author would not look forward to Turbo C++ software development on a system much slower than this one.

The test programs for the low-level MSP functions were compiled with the C++ *small* memory model. This was essential, because sub-scripting and other pointer errors are common when working at that level. Those often cause your program to commit **NULL pointer assignment** errors, which Turbo C++ will identify after a test run terminates, if it's compiled with the small model. Test programs for higher level routines required both data and code space larger than 64 K, so at that point the author switched to compiling with the *large* model.

1.5 This Book's MSP Software Tool Kit

This book reports on a research project: How can you use C++ Object Oriented Programming (OOP) techniques to facilitate scientific and engineering applications software development? It's centered around a software tool kit called MSP (Mathematical Software Package) that was constructed to test these ideas. Its chief design goal was to lay the required software foundation so that client programmers using this tool kit can write elegant, readable programs that mirror the mathematical descriptions of the algorithms they implement.

OOP techniques permit encapsulation of definitions of classes of data structures with definitions of the operations on them, just as higher mathematics is organized. Moreover, you can regard some classes as particular instances of more general ones, just as polynomial algebras are particular types of vector spaces. Finally, you can overload operators and function names so that similar operations on different structures are notated similarly, just as the same mathematical notation denotes multiplication of polynomials and multiplication of vectors by scalars.

Implementing this scheme in C++ requires more attention to low-level details than most applications programmers enjoy. You must provide software to construct, maintain, manipulate, and dismantle the data structures you'll use, like complex numbers, vectors, matrices, and polynomials. The first task of the MSP is to define those classes of data structures and provide that low-level support. Next, MSP includes routines to perform basic algebraic operations on these objects. On this foundation are built the high-level MSP routines that implement specific numerical analysis algorithms for solving applications problems.

MSP consists of nine *modules*. The first two offer general and mathematical support for all the others:

General   General support for all other modules.

RealFunc   Real functions supplementing those in the Turbo
              C++ **Math.H** Library.

Most of the features in **General** and **RealFunc** could have been included with the Turbo C++ Library, but weren't. The next module determines whether you'll be computing with real or complex scalars:

Scalar   Basic functions supporting scalar arithmetic.
              There are two versions, for real and complex sca-
              lars.

You can use either version. The other modules adjust automatically to computing with real or complex scalars. The same code works for both cases. The next three modules complete the low-level part of MSP:

Vector   Matrix   Polynom.

Each of these contains the routines that support the corresponding data structures and the fundamental algebraic operations. For example, **Vector** contains routines that construct, copy, and output vectors, and **Polynom** contains routines that multiply and divide polynomials. The last four modules are higher level:

Equate1   Solve equations in a single real or complex un-known.

GaussEl   Solve systems of linear equations through Gauss elimination. Compute determinants and invert matrices.

Eigenval   Construct the characteristic polynomial of a matrix and find its eigenvalues.

Equate2   Solve systems of linear and nonlinear equations by iterative methods.

These routines implement fundamental algorithms of numerical analysis.

A comprehensive numerical analysis software tool kit would contain further modules for interpolation and approximation, numerical integration and differentiation, initial value problems, etc. However, this book emphasizes software development, and the major programming questions are encountered in constructing the high-level modules included here. Once you've understood these, implementing further numerical analysis algorithms should be straightforward. Time and space required stopping here.

The use of two versions of the **Scalar** module is neat, and demonstrates the benefits of operator overloading. However, there's a disadvantage. Programs built on MSP must use one or the other. It's awkward to deal with both kinds of scalars at once. The need to perform a *single* complex calculation may require *all* data structures to be stored with complex scalars, and those need twice as much space as real scalars. Although it would have been possible to design MSP to use space more efficiently, that would make its client programs much less readable, and client programmers would have to tend to more low-level details. The appropriate solution to this problem is the C++ *template* concept, which is still under development, and not yet included in Turbo C++. (See Reference [13, Chapter 14].) When that feature becomes available, MSP will be due for revision.

MSP should also have a more systematic means for reporting and handling arithmetic error situations, like overflow and attempts to divide by zero. It provides some capability, and this book describes in detail the methods available through the Turbo C++ Library. But error handling techniques are also under development (see Reference [13, Chapter 15]), and what's implemented now by Turbo C++ may not be supported in the future. A major change in this area would also spur revision of MSP.

1.6   References and Further Topics

To do serious scientific and engineering applications software development in Turbo C++ you need to find answers to hardware, software, and mathematical questions that arise constantly. This book covers only a small fraction of that material. This section, however, indicates a number of references that will help you. Some are immediately relevant — even indispensable — to this type of programming. Others provide background information, and some are commercial packages that extend the tool kit concept to other areas mentioned in Section 1.2. Numbers in brackets refer to the Bibliography at the end of the book.

This book assumes you're basically familiar with Turbo C and its use in applications programming. That involves both general knowledge of C and particular knowledge of its Borland implementation. You need access to Turbo C++, but need not have previous experience with it. And you must be quite familiar with IBM compatible hardware and the DOS operating system.

The original C reference, Kernighan and Ritchie [27], is not a good tool for learning C, but is referred to so frequently and religiously that you should have it. The reference work by Harbison and Steele [18] is quite useful. The original C++ reference, Stroustrup [39], has been supplanted by his authoritative *Annotated Reference Manual* [13]. A number of text and trade books are available that introduce C, C++, and object oriented programming techniques. The author finds most of them tedious and nearly useless for an experienced programmer. They often avoid discussing delicate questions that might give you trouble in programming. The best is Lippman's book [29], but even he buries good information inside irrelevant case studies.

Two trade books, Norton [33] and Sargent and Shoemaker [36], discuss IBM compatible hardware thoroughly. You may need to consult your system's technical reference manual to ascertain how its components conform with or depart from the standards that these books describe. Good luck: Many such manuals seem to be written by illiterates! Some of the best information is in the IBM *Technical Reference* manuals [24], even for non-IBM systems.

If you need detailed information on your CPU's machine language, or on your numeric coprocessor, consult the Intel 80286-80287 manual [22]. Similar volumes are available for the 80386 and 80486. They may refer to the 80287 manual for information about their coprocessors.

For information on DOS, its manuals [23] are, of course, important. The ones delivered with the software are essential but inadequate for advanced programming use. The advanced IBM manuals have generally been overly expensive. But they have been mostly supplanted by the wonderful, inexpensive, and indispensable Microsoft *MS-DOS Encyclopedia* [32]. That covers DOS 3.3; you may have to dig to find information on special features of later versions. Trade books by Norton [34] and Duncan [12] cover some of that material in a less formal style. (Duncan is the *Encyclopedia* editor.)

Turbo C++ comes with a four-volume set of manuals [5]. Its "professional" version comes with three more for the *Turbo Assembler* [3], one for the stand-alone *Turbo Debugger* [6], and one for the *Turbo Profiler* [7]. The next version of Turbo C++, called *Borland C++*, combines all these in one package. The organization of the manuals is somewhat frustrating, but that's understandable since the product changes so fast. You'll need to become very familiar with the Turbo C++ manuals; the other three products are not directly relevant to this book.

The author's earlier book *Advanced Turbo C* [37] is a thorough description of Turbo C and most of its Library. The expensive Turbo C Library source code [4] is perhaps *too* helpful. If you can't gain understanding of a routine through its documentation, you must conduct experiments or analyze its source code. The author spends *too much* time in both activities. For this book, the major problem of this type was the error handling routines discussed in Section 4.5; those will probably change with later versions of Turbo C++.

Excellent software tools compatible with Turbo C++ are available in several other areas. Scientific and engineering applications programmers occasionally venture there, particularly to construct interactive user interfaces, to handle serial communication with data sensors, computers, or other equipment, and to display graphical output. A comprehensive and highly reliable tool kit specially suited for building interfaces is the Blaise Computing Inc. product, *Turbo C TOOLS* [2], described in detail in the author's earlier book [37]. Another Blaise Product, *C ASYNCH MANAGER* [1], provides reliable low-level C language support for interrupt driven serial communications. Several tool kits are available that extend the low-level graphics capabilities of Turbo C++, but the author is unfamiliar with them. For further information on such products, consult the advertisements and frequent survey articles in the trade journals.

Scientific and engineering applications programmers encounter mathematical questions as often as questions about hardware or software. The author uses Courant's [11] and Hille's [19] classic volumes for reference on calculus and related topics. For advanced calculus and algebraic matters, Wylie [45] and Uspensky [40] are rich sources. The author can't recommend any linear algebra text: The readable ones too often ignore questions that arise in computation. Knuth's books [28] are a surprisingly good source of information on all kinds of mathematics related to computation. Of the many numerical analysis texts, two are specially good references: Burden and Faires [8], and Maron and Lopez [30]. The former is elegant; the latter has an incredible number of examples. The *Numerical Recipes* book [35] by Press *et al.* is not a textbook, but a useful compendium of numerical methods, discussed from a computational viewpoint.

Finally, you should become familiar with a new development in scientific and engineering computing: *mathematical desktop software.* Several products are now available to make computations on demand. You enter the problem via the keyboard, in notation approximating standard mathematics, and read the answer immediately from the display. Some products display two- and three-dimensional graphs and use graphics techniques to display formulas in true mathematical notation. Mathematical desktop products can handle problems that formerly required complicated programs in high-level languages. Most of these products can even be programmed. Programming in a specialized mathematical desktop language is much simpler than struggling with a general purpose language like C++. The most noted desktop software now is the expensive *Mathematica* system [43, 44], which excels in symbolic algebra computations. Not needing the algebra features, the author used Meredith's inexpensive but powerful *Calculus Calculator* [31] program (CC) for all incidental computations involved with developing and testing this book's MSP software, and for drawing all the graphs shown in this book. (The latest, yet unpublished, version of CC incorporates linear algebra capabilities, and, in fact, can perform most of the computations that this book's MSP software can do.)

2

Software Organization

This chapter first presents an overview of the layers of software present and running in your machine when you're executing a C++ application program. Even a high-level application program will interact with several of these layers, so you need to become familiar with them.

Sections 2.2 to 2.7 then discuss many new C++ features that play a role in this book's Mathematical Software Package (MSP). This chapter assumes that you're familiar with C, and uses basic C concepts with little remark. Neither is it a general introduction to C++. For that, please consult a text devoted to the language, as well as the Turbo C++ manual (Reference [5]). Rather than discuss new C++ features haphazardly in the order that they appear in MSP, this chapter considers some general C++ principles systematically. You may use it as a guide through a C++ text — for example, Reference [29] — or the Turbo manual. What's mentioned here you need to understand the low-level MSP routines. What's not, you can safely ignore. Later, as you read Chapter 3, a detailed description of the lower levels of the MSP, you'll often want to refer back to this chapter to review the fundamental concepts.

2.1 Software Layers

If you're a scientific applications programmer interested in C++ programming, you're probably considering a project that involves software beyond that directly concerned with numerical analysis.

Actually, any project does to some extent, particularly when implemented on a personal computer. Arguments for selecting C++ usually cite the appropriateness of the C language and its offspring for detailed interaction with underlying hardware and systems software, and the potentiality of C++ object oriented programming techniques for organizing complex applications.

Thus, it's important to gain an overview of the full ensemble of software present and running in your machine when your own numeric computations are executing. This software is organized into layers, with detailed hardware conscious systems software at the bottom, and an application program at the top, possibly modeling a real-world problem and written with no consideration of hardware. Here are the most apparent layers, when you're running an application program that uses this book's MSP numerical analysis software:

Top: Client program
             Mathematical Software Package (MSP)
             Turbo C++ Library and run time support
             DOS operating system
Bottom: Basic Input/Output System (BIOS).

Your application program is called an MSP *client* because the MSP provides needed mathematical *services*. Each of the upper tiers, in fact, is a client of the next lower one. This section will describe the layers, starting with the BIOS at the bottom, and explain their roles in making your application run.

Basic Input/Output System (BIOS)

Built into your PC hardware, this program starts the bootstrap process and provides low-level input/output and memory control. It's stored in Read-Only Memory (ROM) chips on your motherboard and on some optional controller boards. The hardware starts the BIOS executing when you turn on the power. Its first task is to check all your memory. This causes a pronounced delay for slow machines with large memories. The BIOS checks a few more motherboard components and initializes some tables in the low address part of memory that describe the hardware configuration. Optional BIOS components perform similar checking and initialization on some controller boards that may be plugged into the motherboard.

Once this Power-On Self Test (POST) checking and initialization is complete, the BIOS transfers control to a tiny program that must occupy a specific place on your fixed disk. This *bootstrap* program loads the DOS operating system software into memory and transfers control to it. DOS performs a few more initializations, then transfers control to its command interpreter — usually the **Command.Com** program — which displays a familiar prompt and awaits your command. The difficulty of designing this start-up process seemed comparable to that of lifting yourself by your own bootstraps, and gave rise to the "booting" terminology.

Once your computer is booted, the BIOS assumes a background role, providing low level input/output and memory control services. Here are three typical BIOS services:

- *Disk read* Read *n* sectors, starting at sector *s* on disk *d* and continuing on the same track, into memory starting at address *a*. Parameters *n*, *s*, *d*, and *a* are specified by the (assembly language) commands that request the service.
- *Keyboard status* Ascertain whether the <CapsLock> key is toggled on, and whether the <LeftShift> or <RightShift> key is down. The BIOS places a coded answer in a CPU register, to which the client program has access. The code also includes answers to several similar questions about other keys.
- *Display character* Display character *c* at the current cursor location. Parameter *c* is specified by the command that requests the service.

Other typical services include reading and removing a character from the queue in memory that records recent keystrokes, setting the background color of a location on the display, and clearing the display entirely.

Most BIOS services are tied closely to standard PC hardware components. IBM designed the BIOS for the original PC and published the program listing in the PC manual (Reference [24]). Reading it is an adventure, and a wonderful way to learn Intel 8086 family assembly language programming! Now, alternative BIOS chips are marketed by several companies for installation in IBM compatible PCs. They must respond to the same commands in compatible ways. Generally, this cloning is successful, but compatibility problems do arise, particularly with the BIOS components of optional controllers for which no strong standards emerged early in market history. A mathematical applications programmer is unlikely to encounter these problems except perhaps in attempting to use very high resolution displays.

DOS Operating System

Once loaded and initialized during the bootstrap process, the operating system has charge of your machine. You request it to execute operating system commands or programs. After a program terminates, control returns to the operating system. A PC operating system has three major roles:

- organizing and maintaining the file system, and providing file input/output services for clients;
- supervising the program execution process;
- providing other input/output and memory control services, much like the BIOS, but in a more general form, more convenient for client programs.

The Microsoft Corporation developed DOS from the earlier CP/M operating system. Microsoft licenses manufacturers to adapt and sell DOS for various computers. Adaptation consists mainly in tailoring it to interface with a specific BIOS. If suitably adapted, DOS can run on machines whose BIOS is nothing like the PC's. IBM sells its version, called IBM DOS or PC DOS. Others are generally shipped with their machines. The ability to run IBM DOS is generally regarded as the criterion for IBM PC compatibility. Microsoft and IBM periodically upgrade DOS. The most common versions now are probably 3.3 and 4.0. This book's programs were developed with IBM DOS 4.01.

Occupying one of the lower tiers of the software hierarchy in your machine, DOS is itself divided into three levels:

top:	command interpreter (usually the **Command.Com** program)
middle:	DOS core (IBM DOS file **IBMDOS.Com**)
bottom:	BIOS interface (IBM DOS file **IBMBIO.Com**)

The BIOS interface may also include optional *device driver* programs. These are commonly supplied by other sources, to manage your equipment in specific ways. You can adjust the bootstrap process (via the **Config.Sys** file) to load them into memory with DOS and initialize them.

The interpreter (often called a *shell*) is a program with the same status in the software hierarchy as a client program. After initialization, the DOS core starts the interpreter, which displays a prompt and awaits your call. You can request various DOS services like directory listings, or command DOS to execute another program. When you command it to execute program P, the command interpreter suspends its own operation temporarily and requests the core to find, load, and execute P. When P terminates, control passes back to the core, which performs some housekeeping tasks and then reactivates the interpreter.

Since the command interpreter is relatively independent of the rest of DOS, it can be replaced by an alternative program. Several are available commercially, including one shipped with IBM DOS version 4.0. These often provide more powerful DOS commands and more elaborate user interfaces: for example, *sorted* directory listings and control via a mouse.

Most of DOS' work is done by the core. It accepts service requests from the command interpreter and other programs. In turn, the core may request attention from the BIOS interface. That lower level component reformulates requests as required for a particular BIOS, obtains the service, and passes results back to the core.

Here are four typical DOS services:

- *Open file* Locate a file named F, set the file pointer at its start, and provide an integer h for later use as its *handle*. The service request command must specify the memory address of the character string F. DOS places h in a CPU register to which the client program has access.
- *Read file* Read n bytes from the file with handle h, starting at the file pointer, into memory starting at address a. Parameters n, h, and a are specified by the service request command.
- *Input character* Read one character from the standard input device, waiting, if necessary, for an input to appear. DOS places the input in a CPU register to which the client program has access.
- *Output character* Send character c to the standard output device.

DOS' file system supervisor maintains directories of all disks in use by the executing software. *Locating a file* means using the directory to find the disk sectors where the file is stored. Once this information is available, DOS can translate a *read file* request into a *disk read* request as described earlier, and pass it on to the BIOS. *Standard input* and *standard output* are usually associated with keyboard and display, but you can reassign them at run time to other devices or files by using DOS' redirection symbols < and > in your program execution command. DOS translates standard input/output commands into proper form for the associated device and generates appropriate BIOS service requests. For example, "send character c to the display" means "display c at the current cursor location."

Programmers using assembly language or software tools like the Turbo C++ Library can write DOS or BIOS service requests. Often they may choose between nearly equivalent DOS and BIOS services, like requesting DOS to send a character to standard output or asking the BIOS to display it at the current cursor location. There's a trade-off:

* BIOS service is faster and may provide closer control, but works only on machines whose BIOS is IBM PC compatible.
* DOS service works on a greater variety of machines.

Formulating BIOS disk service requests is complicated, and testing them risks loss of stored data. Moreover, using BIOS disk services directly provides little gain in speed. Thus, application programmers virtually always use DOS disk services. For certain keyboard services, however, it's necessary to use the BIOS: For example, DOS provides no equivalent of the keyboard status request described earlier. Few incompatibility problems arise, because virtually all BIOS keyboard components work similarly in this regard.

Programming for display control presents a major problem when speed is important. It usually doesn't matter when output is presented just once at the end of a computation. But if an interactive application program must display data at specific screen locations, perhaps in distinctive colors, and expects quick user response, display speed has considerable psychological impact. DOS' display services are generally slow, and its color control is primitive and even slower. The problem is particularly severe on older, slower machines. Thus, most applications and Turbo C++ Library functions bypass DOS and use the BIOS directly. They pay the price of decreased portability to computers incompatible with IBM. This isn't a complete solution, however. Different display controllers may vary considerably in speed, and the slower ones can present the same psychological problems for users. Thus, many applications and some Turbo C++ Library functions even bypass the BIOS and control the display hardware directly. Such software is even less portable.

Further discussion of DOS and BIOS services is beyond the scope of this book. Readers may consult works by Norton (References [33, 34]), Sargent and Shoemaker (Reference [36]), and this author (References [37,38]) for further information.

Turbo C++ Library and Run-Time Support

A C++ program **P** consists of some functions, including one called **main**. Each function can invoke any function except **main**. Source code for the functions can be apportioned among any number of files, each of which is compiled into a separate object code file. The object code files are linked into an executable file **P.Exe**. Here's the flow of control when DOS loads and executes this file:

        DOS
⇒   C++ entrance routine
⇒   **main**
        :
⇒   (depends on code in **main** and the other functions)
        :
⇒   C++ exit routine
⇒   DOS.

The entrance and exit routines are provided by the C++ compiler. They take care of housekeeping details that applications programmers don't need to know about.

The functions that make up this program don't all have to be part of the project at hand. Usually, many are utility routines completed long before, whose object codes are stored in a *library*. Turbo C++ is distributed with a vast library of such functions, which provides these categories of services:

- manipulating memory areas
- character string manipulation
- keyboard and display input/output
- file input/output and file system maintenance
- memory management
- execution of DOS commands and other programs
- timer input and time calculations
- calculation of mathematical functions like square root, sine, and exponential
- error handling.

The C++ entrance and exit routines and the first few categories of Library functions constitute an interface — a software layer — between the BIOS and DOS and all C++ application programs. The string and mathematical functions constitute an underlying layer, as well. Except for the mathematical and error handling functions, these services fall outside the scope of this book. They will be used occasionally in its programs, with little comment. For further information, consult the Turbo C++ Library reference manual (Reference [5]) and the author's book (Reference [37]).

The Library was developed originally by AT&T Bell Laboratories and adapted by Borland International, Inc. for the DOS and IBM PC compatible environments. Many Library functions are portable to any C++ system; most work on any DOS system. Some of the display output functions, however, require an IBM compatible BIOS, and others expect even greater display controller compatibility. By using the more specific display functions, you gain control and speed, but lose some portability. All Library functions that require DOS or the BIOS will be identified when used in this book.

Mathematical Software Package (MSP)

The numerical analysis software described in this book — the Mathematical Software Package (MSP) — is also organized in layers. Its lowest layer, the **Scalar** module, overlaps with mathematical services provided by the Turbo C++ Library to provide all the required operations on *scalars*: real or complex numbers. The top layer contains what most professionals regard as numerical analysis tools: routines for solving linear and nonlinear equations and systems of equations, computing eigenvalues, etc. In between are layers that provide the necessary logical and algebraic manipulation of vectors, matrices, and polynomials.

Figure 2.1.1 provides an informal overview of the MSP structure. The middle part comprises three modules: **Vector**, **Matrix**, and **Polynom**. The Vector module is itself divided into two parts, logical and algebraic. The *logical* part handles vector manipulation: creation, input/output, copying, equality, and destruction. The *algebraic* part is concerned with vector norms, addition, scalar multiplication, inner product, etc. The **Matrix** module treats matrices as arrays of vectors and is split along similar lines. Polynomials are handled by module **Polynom**. Since they're really vectors of coefficients, their algebra is essentially an adaptation of vector algebra. However, polynomial evaluation, multiplication, differentiation, and integration are also implemented.

High-level numerical analysis routines may use the Turbo C++ Library directly, as well as any functions in the **Scalar**, **Vector**, **Matrix**, and **Polynom** modules.

Client Programs

MSP client programs translate real-world problems and data into the MSP mathematics, then use MSP functions for solution. In some cases, client software might best be organized in layers, too. For

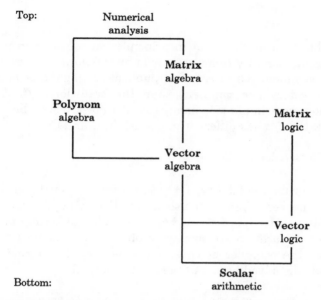

Top:　Numerical analysis

Matrix algebra

Polynom algebra

Matrix logic

Vector algebra

Vector logic

Bottom:　Scalar arithmetic

Figure 2.1.1 MSP layers

example, this book doesn't directly handle approximation of data y_j at points x_j for $j = 0, ..., m$ by a least squares polynomial p of degree n. The coefficients of p are the solutions of a system of linear equations constructed from the x_j and y_j values. (See Reference [45, Section 4.6].) If your project requires this technique, you should write a general function that constructs the polynomial coefficients, given the x_j and y_j values and the degree m. This would invoke MSP routines to handle matrices and compute determinants. You should test it first on simple problems, then more realistic ones. Finally, you can build a client program that uses this "underlying" routine to solve your real problem.

2.2　C++ Minor Features

C++ is a major extension of C, a remarkable feat of grafting onto an older design a number of powerful new features based on a programming philosophy very different from the original C paradigm. This extension also includes a number of minor changes — some useful in their own right, others needed just to clear away obstacles to the major goal. Several of these, frequently used in MSP, are discussed in this section.

// comments

One change that's inconsequential in principle but effective in practice is the introduction of // comments: whatever follows that symbol on a line is a comment. On a crowded publication page, this allows two more characters per comment than the traditional /*...*/ C comments. (However simple this change is, it's not trivial: The code **a = b //*check this*/c** has different meanings in C and C++!)

Local Variable Declarations

To improve program readability, C++ now permits you to declare local variables nearer where you use them. For example, you can usually write **for (int i = 0; i <= n; ++i)**. The rules governing placement of the **int** declaration are somewhat obscure, and invite annoying errors that the compiler catches. For example, they forbid the first line of code displayed here, but permit the second:

```
if (condition) for (int i = 0; i <= n; ++i);      // Error!
if (condition) { for (int i = 0; i <= n; ++i); } // OK!
```

New and Delete Operators

The C++ **new** and **delete** operators are used in MSP where Library functions **malloc** and **free** would have occurred in C code. Their syntax is simpler and less redundant.

Mandatory Function Prototypes

There are three important changes in function parameter syntax and semantics. First, prototypes are no longer optional: You *must* use one unless you include the complete function definition before all its invocations, in the same compilation unit. Although major in principle, this change is minor in practice, because well-written C programs always used prototypes — that's now part of the ANSI C standard.

Initialized Parameters

Second, you may give *default values* to the last one or more formal parameters in a function signature, and you may omit these parameters from the invocation. You may place the initialization in a prototype; if so, it may not occur in the function definition. Here's an example:

```
void f(int i = 0);      // Prototype
void f(int i) { ... ; }  // Definition
void main( ) {          // All these invocations
   f( ); f(0); f(1); }   // are OK.
```

Placing the initialization in a header allows a client to change it. *Caution:* An initialization in a header affects only those invocations in the same compilation unit! On the other hand, you can hide an initial value by placing it in the definition and distributing only object code for **f**. MSP uses initialized parameters to simplify common invocations. *Warning:* This practice tends to collide with function overloading, and invites errors that are hard to find! Refer to the discussion of overloading in Section 2.6.

Reference Parameters

The third change relating to parameters is the use of *reference* parameters. A function signature like

```
int f(int& p)
```

specifies that formal parameter **p** will be passed by reference. That is, the caller passes the *address* of the actual parameter, not its *value*. This is a standard feature of other languages. (In FORTRAN, for example, it's the *only* way to pass parameters.) You can use a reference parameter **p** to transmit a result back to the caller. If **p** were a large structure instead of an integer, passing by reference would be much more efficient than passing the structure itself. That leads to a problem when **p** isn't intended to convey results back: **f** may inappropriately change the value of **p** (one of the most common errors in FORTRAN programming). To counter this danger, you may declare **p** *constant*:

```
int f(const int& p)
```

The compiler will then catch any attempt to change **p**. Finally, a function may also *return* a reference:

```
int& f(const int& p) .
```

Instead of pushing a result onto the stack for the caller to pop, **f** pushes its address. In this case the result must be stored in static or free memory: A local variable would disappear before the address could be used to refer to it. You can achieve most of the effects of reference parameters by using pointers. But reference parameters allow the calling program to avoid pointers, a major source of error.

Passing parameters by reference is either too delicately designed or else imperfectly implemented in Turbo C++. It invites problems that the author has been unable to identify. These reveal either a compiler bug or a C++ design flaw that renders this feature less useful than it should be. In any case, faulty programs tend to crash the Turbo C++ system, and that often requires rebooting. Moreover, the Turbo C++ debugger doesn't allow inspection of most parameters passed by reference.

C++ Version 2 Stream Input/Output

Each C version seems to have new input/output conventions. They're implemented in the Library, so aren't officially part of the language. The authoritative *Annotated C++ Reference Manual* (Reference [13]) doesn't even mention them! Input/output routines constitute a *utility package*, distributed with the compiler. You may use it, or undertake the formidable task of writing your own custom input/output package. The input/output functions for previous C and C++ versions are distributed with Turbo C++, but its manual recommends that you use *C++ Version 2 streams*. This facility was developed at AT&T Bell Laboratories, and adapted by Borland International, Inc. It's implemented via a clever overloading (extended definition) of the C operators >> and <<. As such, it falls outside the established structure of the Turbo C++ Library documentation. (You can't find stream functions in the alphabetical listing.) They're discussed elsewhere in the Turbo C++ manuals, but not as thoroughly as you might like. Lippman's book (Reference [29, App. A]) includes a readable, but also incomplete, account. This section will cover only those aspects of stream input/output that are actually used in MSP.

To use Version 2 stream input/output, your program must include the Turbo C++ header file **IOStream.H**. To use the stream *manipulator* features, also include **IOManip.H** *after* that file. **IOStream.H** defines types **istream** and **ostream**. These correspond to streams of data coming from or going to a memory buffer, which may be associated with a device or a file, or just used as temporary storage. **IOStream.H** declares some standard objects — called *streams* — of these types, and associates them with standard DOS file handles; in turn, DOS associates the handles with devices:

Stream	Type	File handle	Default device
cin	istream	standard input	CON keyboard
cout	ostream	standard output	CON display

At run time, you can use the DOS < or > operator to redirect standard input or output to a file or another device, such as a parallel port. Your programs can also declare **istream** or **ostream** objects and associate them with files or other devices. See Lippman's book (Reference [29, App. A]) for examples.

C++ stream input/output syntax is best illustrated by example. To prompt a user, then input **int** and **double** values on separate lines, and display it, use statements like

```
int i; double x;
cout << "Enter integer, real values i,x on separate lines:\n";
cin >> i >> x;
cout << "i = " << i << " and x = " << x;
```

Operator **>>** automatically flushes **cout** before pausing for **cin** input, so the prompt is guaranteed to be displayed.

Be careful of the somewhat illogical appearance of the input statement **cin >> i >> x** : you might think that **x** is input first, since it's farthest removed from **cin**, but that's not so. This anomaly is due to the fact that **>>** is the C right shift operator, overloaded to apply to arguments of these types. An unparenthesized multiple **>>** expression is evaluated from left to right, and **>>** returns as a value its left operand. Thus, the statement is interpreted as **(cin >> i) >> x**, and **i** is input first.

The output operator **<<** is treated similarly. You can also overload these operators to provide stream input/output for user-defined types. Examples are discussed in Chapter 3.

The standard streams use default formats to input or output the various built-in types. You can change format — for example, field width, justification, scientific, or fixed point notation — by inserting a *manipulator* in the input/output stream. For example, the statements

```
cout << 17;
cout << setw(10) << 17;
```

will display the two-digit numeral 17 twice: The first exactly occupies a two-digit field (default format); the second is right justified in a

ten-digit field. *Warning:* The field width changes for *one output only!*
As another example, the statement **cout << endl** uses the manipulator **endl** to trigger a new line and flush the **cout** output stream.
MSP uses some additional manipulators with file input/output
streams. See Lippman's book (Reference [29, App. A]) for those.

The stream output format manipulators for **double** values are not
quite as general as the corresponding **StdIO** format features for C.
MSP requires the omitted detail, so it uses **StdIO** function **sprintf**
to convert numerical output first to an output string **S**. Then it executes **cout << S** to output the string.

Text output shown in this book was produced first on the author's
display. It's rendered machine readable by one of two methods. When
it fills one screen only, it's copied into a file **F** by a memory resident
screen capture utility. To capture more than one screen of output
from a program **P**, the **P.Exe** file is executed with DOS command
P > F, which redirects standard output to **F**. Neither method is
ideal. With a capture utility it's awkward to copy multiple screens.
On the other hand, redirection fails to reproduce **cin** input echoes,
because they go to the display directly, not via DOS standard output.
After **P** terminates, the output file **F** is imported into WordPerfect
and edited with care to preserve the exact appearance of the display.

2.3   Abstract Data Types and Classes

C++ was developed by grafting onto the C language some new features that support implementation of Abstract Data Types (ADTs)
and use of Object Oriented Programming (OOP) techniques. This
book doesn't attempt to sketch all the notions underlying ADTs and
OOP. But their effect on the design of the mathematical software
presented here is important. Thus, this section will describe some
ADT and OOP concepts that played major roles in that design.

Abstract Data Types (ADTs)

The ADT concept developed as a way of modularizing software design and limiting the effect of programming errors. When software
uses ADTs strictly, processes may not access data unless an ADT
declaration *explicitly* permits. Thus, changing the design of software
implementing an ADT can affect only an explicit list of processes.
Moreover, if data become corrupted while you are executing this

software, the definition narrows the field where you must search for the error.

The C language programming paradigm, however, conflicts with the ADT restriction. C programmers don't like to be told *no*. Therefore, ADT notions were incorporated into C++ only loosely, so that unless an ADT explicitly allows access by a C++ function **f**, it's just *difficult*, but not impossible, for **f** to access the data. Unauthorized access should be the result of a conscious (therefore relatively safe?) effort, and should involve conspicuous programming ploys that a maintenance programmer can easily detect and understand.

The ADT concept is so general that it's hard to describe: To avoid writing something obviously false, you tend to write as little as possible. An ADT consists of a (small) set F of (related) function prototypes, and a data structure definition D. D defines the set of all data that are handled interchangeably by the functions in F. The definition normally specifies the organization of the memory allocated to store each instance of D. (If you have to bring in further conditions — for example, conditions on what bit patterns are allowable — you probably haven't selected the set F appropriately.) The only aspect of the ADT that is shown to client programs is the set F of prototypes. The data structure definition and the implementation of the functions in F are hidden. A client program has no access to the data except by invoking functions in F. The client never knows how the data are stored in memory nor how the functions in F manipulate them, except as revealed by the prototypes.

For example, consider an ADT for vector algebra. F will contain prototypes of functions for vector addition, scalar multiplication, etc., and D will define structures called vectors. Clients know — through the addition prototype — that the sum of two vectors is a vector. But they needn't know *how* vectors are stored nor *how* addition is performed. Conventional vector algebra software might store vectors as arrays of scalars, but software for handling very long sparse vectors (mostly zero entries) might store them as linked lists. The corresponding addition algorithms are quite different.

Parallel with Higher Mathematics

This example shows how closely the ADT notion parallels modern higher mathematics. You study vector algebra by considering *vector spaces*. A vector space consists of a set $D = \{\alpha, \beta, \ldots\}$ of vectors and a (small) set F containing the addition and scalar multiplication operators $+$ and $\cdot$. A short list of axioms like $t\cdot(\alpha + \beta) = t\cdot\alpha + t\cdot\beta$ tells what rules these vectors and operators obey. Vector space theory derives theorems from these axioms. Some of them are very deep and involved. Many different vector spaces arise in practical mathematics. Numerical analysis considers spaces whose vectors are n-tuples of real numbers, n-tuples of complex numbers, polynomials, integrable functions, power series, matrices, etc. A vector algebra ADT as described in the previous paragraph defines a vector space if its addition and scalar multiplication operations obey the axioms. By presenting vector algebra in the abstract context of vector space theory, we *modularize* the mathematics: We ensure that the theorems you learn about vector spaces apply equally well to *all* those concrete examples. Virtually all of modern higher mathematics uses this modularization technique.

The previous two paragraphs skirted a conflict in terminology that perplexes a mathematician. In mathematical language, a set D has *members*: The vectors of a vector space or a vector algebra ADT D are members of D. In C++ terminology, however, the functions in F are called members of the ADT. This collision hampers discussion and understanding. The author chooses to retain some C++ usage by calling the functions in F *member* functions: They do *apply* to members. But the *instances* of a data structure definition D are called just that. Vectors will be called *instances*, not members, of D. Mathematicians developed abstract mathematics terminology over decades, with time to reflect on its side effects. After decades, ADT and OOP terminology will mature, too. By that time, C++ will be just a historical curiosity.

As mentioned earlier, the ADT concept was built into C++ only loosely. The data structure definition isn't hidden; it lies bare for all clients to admire. (Or to scoff at, if that's warranted.) It may have several components, some of which are private, accessible only through member functions, and some public, available to all clients for use or abuse. The member function prototypes are public, of course. But their implementations can be public or compiled separately, giving clients access only to object code. Finally, there are provisions for giving specific nonmember functions access to private data and for making specific member functions private. The private functions can be invoked only by other member functions. (They're for the dirty work that the public must never see!)

C++ Classes and Objects

The C++ adaptation of the ADT is the *class*. The declaration of a class called **ClassC** looks like this:

```
class ClassC {
  public:
    :
    Declarations of public data structure components, and
    prototypes or definitions of public member functions
    :
  private:
    :
    Declarations of private data structure components, and
    prototypes or definitions of private member functions
    :}
```

Once declared, **ClassC** is a type with the same status as **char, int, double,** etc. The term **ClassC** *object* is used for *instance of the data structure defined by* **ClassC.**

The name of a member function **f** isn't meaningful without some clue to the class name. Usually this is given through the types of its arguments. When that's not appropriate, you may use a class name qualifier like this: **ClassC::f.**

Member Functions

Design of the public and private member functions of a class is complicated by two demands. First, as already mentioned, client programs must be able to carry out all object manipulations through the public member functions. Second, objects of a class often have varying size. Those of a polynomial class, for example, might include coefficient arrays for polynomials of various degrees. In such cases, the components of indeterminate size are generally represented by pointers to storage areas in free memory. You must provide public functions for creating, destroying, duplicating, comparing, and input/output of these components.

To satisfy these requirements, several kinds of public member functions — constructors, assignment, selectors, etc. — frequently occur in class declarations. Moreover, some syntax considerations affect all member functions. Sections 2.4 to 2.6 consider these topics.

2.4 Member and Friend Functions

Principal Argument Syntax

C++ has adopted a new syntax for declaring and evaluating member functions of a class **ClassC.** Since they're used in the beginning to define its data components, member functions must have some argument of type **ClassC**. One is called the *principal* argument. Traditional function evaluation syntax is used for the other arguments, but the principal argument is omitted in the declaration of a member function. For example, this class definition fragment declares member functions **f** and **g** with principal arguments of type **ClassC**:

```
class ClassC {
  :
  int f(int i);
  ClassC& g( );
  : }.
```

f also has an **int** argument and returns an **int** value; **g** returns a reference to a **ClassC** object. If **X** is a **ClassC** object, then the expression **X.f(17)** evaluates **f** with arguments **X** and **17**. Function **g** returns a reference to a **ClassC** object, which can be passed as principal argument to another member function. This kind of function composition has a new *concatenation* syntax: **X.g( ).f(17)** indicates that **g** is evaluated with principal argument **X**, producing a **ClassC** value stored in a temporary variable **T**, then **f** is evaluated with arguments **T** and **17**.

The principal argument of a member function is always passed by reference. You may want to indicate that the argument's value is not changed. You can't place the **const** qualifier before the parameter as you would for a nonmember function, so place it after the parameter list. For the example function **f** in the previous paragraph, you would declare **int f(int i) const**.

Within the definition of a member function, the principal argument is anonymous. It doesn't appear in the formal parameter list. Occasionally a name is necessary, though. To that end, C++ provides the pronoun **this***. Actually, within a member function definition, **this** is the name of a pointer to the principal argument, so **this*** is the argument itself. The programs in this book use the abbreviation **This** for **this***. It's not necessary to write **this*.f(17)** to send **this*** to member function **f** as its principal argument: Just write **f(17)**.

Selectors

Declaring public a data component of a class permits unlimited public access: A client program can use or change it at will. If you want to provide limited access — for example, to prevent changing a variable or to check array indices before granting access, you must use public member functions called *selectors*. A selector that provides read-only access is usually a member function with no nonprincipal arguments. It returns the desired component of the principal argument. The index checking facility is usually provided by overloading the subscripting operator **[ ]**. Overloading is discussed later in Section 2.6.

Operator Functions

It's also possible to declare class member *operators*. Briefly, singulary and binary operators like **!** and **==** are equivalent to certain *operator* functions. If these are declared as member functions, the corresponding single or left-hand operand becomes the principal argument and is omitted in certain syntactic constructs. This is all an aspect of overloading and is discussed in Section 2.6.

Membership Criteria

While designing a class **ClassC**, you'll often ask whether a function **f** should be a member function. The answer must be *yes* if

1. some C++ rule explicitly says so, or
2. **f** *must* have access to private components of **ClassC**, or
3. you want to use the principal argument syntax for evaluating **f**.

The author suggests applying Ockham's razor: *No other* functions should be member functions.

Friend Functions

Since the principal argument syntax is mandatory for member functions, (2) and (3) sometimes collide. What if a function **h** must have access to private components of **ClassC** but you don't want to use the principal argument syntax? In that case declare **h** a *friend* of **ClassC**, and use traditional syntax, like this:

```
class ClassC {
  :
  friend int h(int i, ClassC X);
  : }.
```

You must declare **h** in the same compilation unit with the **ClassC** declaration. Rely on friendship, for example, when **h** must have access to the private components of two different classes.

2.5 Constructors and Destructors

Default Constructor

When a class has a data component of large or indeterminate size, such as a long vector or a polynomial of varying degree, you normally store the data in free memory space allocated by the **new** operator; the class component is really a *pointer* to the data. When you declare an object as a global or local variable, the compiler will allocate space for the pointer in static memory or on the stack. You must provide code to allocate free memory storage for the data itself. This requires a *constructor*, a public member function that shares the class name and returns no value: for example,

```
Declaration            Definition
class ClassC {     ClassC::ClassC( ) {
public:          :
ClassC( );         Code to allocate free memory, etc.
: }          : }
```

There are different kinds of constructors; this example is called a *default* constructor. Its execution syntax is like that for a traditional declaration: The statement **ClassC X** constructs a **ClassC** object **X**, and **ClassC Y[7]** constructs an array of seven **ClassC** objects **Y[0]**, ..., **Y[6]**. The first declaration executes your constructor once; the second, seven times.

A default constructor provides no flexibility: You can't specify how much memory to allocate. Fortunately, though, a constructor may have arguments to specify size, initial value, etc. For example, a constructor **ClassC(int n)** might allocate free memory for an **n** dimensional vector. To declare such a vector **V**, you might compute **n**, then declare **ClassC V(n)**. You can't directly declare an *array* of such vectors, however: The syntax **ClassC V(n)[7]** is illegal.

Instead, you may define a member function **ClassC& SetUp(int n)** to do the work of **ClassC(int n)**. To declare an array of 7 vectors of length **n**, you would declare an array **ClassC V[7]** using the default constructor, then execute **SetUp** on each entry of **V**:

```
for (int I = 0; i < 7; ++i) V[i]. SetUp(n)
```

If you need this **SetUp** facility, you'll probably want to define

```
ClassC::ClassC(int n) { SetUp(n); }
```

to emphasize the relationship of the constructor and the **SetUp** function.

Copy Constructor

Occasionally you need to construct a new **ClassC** object that's an exact copy of an existing **ClassC** object X. For this, you use a *copy* constructor, which you must declare as **ClassC(const ClassC& X)**. It should determine the size of **X** if necessary, use the **SetUp** function to allocate sufficient space, then copy **X** into the new object. You can create a new copy Y of object X by executing **ClassC X(Y)** or **ClassC X = Y.**

The compiler also generates code that invokes your copy constructor whenever appropriate to make *temporary* copies. This occurs if you pass a **ClassC** argument by value to a function, or a function returns such a value. To invoke function **ClassC f(ClassC X)**, for example, the caller will use your copy constructor to copy X onto the stack as the actual parameter **TempX** for f. Then f is invoked, and uses **TempX** in place of X in its computations. **TempX** disappears when f terminates. One **TempX** component is probably a pointer to the free memory storage allocated earlier by your copy constructor. Unless you make some provision to destroy it, that storage will persist, allocated but inaccessible because its pointer has disappeared. This provision is described later, under the heading "Destructors."

The return value computed by f can't remain in place on the stack, because it's a local variable for f, and would also disappear when f terminates. Therefore, the compiler generates code that uses your copy constructor to copy the return value into a temporary local variable for the caller. If your function call has the form Y = f(X), you'll assign this temporary value immediately to another variable, and the temporary variable isn't really needed. (Assignment is discussed in a later paragraph.) However, the compiler must also let you pass the return value immediately as an argument to another function g — to evaluate g(f(X)), for example. To accommodate that, a temporary variable is required.

When an argument or a function value is passed by reference, no temporary copies are needed, and your copy constructor is not involved.

Converters

Closely related to the copy constructor for a class **ClassC** is the function you'd need to convert to **ClassC** a variable of a related type **SourceType**. For example, you might want to convert a scalar to a polynomial with degree 0. You need to define a *converter*: a public **ClassC** member function **ClassC(const SourceType& X)** that returns no value. It should allocate — probably via the **SetUp** function — sufficient space for the **ClassC** object, then enter into the **ClassC** components the appropriate data from X. The implementation and invocation syntax is just like that of the copy constructor. Moreover, you can use ordinary function evaluation syntax: **ClassC(X)** is simply the **ClassC** object obtained by converting X from type **SourceType**.

The reverse conversion, *from* **ClassC** *to* some type **TargetType**, requires defining a public **ClassC** member operator function

```
operator TargetType( ) const
```

Although the special syntax doesn't so indicate, this function must return a **TargetType** value. The syntax for invoking this converter is exactly the same as that for converting in the opposite direction.

Assignment Operator

If you use a class **ClassC** with a pointer component, you must provide code to perform assignments X = Y between existing **ClassC** objects X and Y. This will resemble the code for your copy constructor, except that it doesn't have to set up X in free memory: X is already there. You'll have to decide what to do if X and Y may point to free memory areas of different sizes. That may indicate an error, or you may want to copy part of Y into a smaller X or all of Y into part of a larger X. To provide this enhanced assignment facility, you overload the assignment operator = by declaring = a public member operator

```
ClassC& operator=(const ClassC& Source)
```

Its definition looks like this:

```
ClassC& ClassC::operator=(const ClassC& Source) {
    :
    Code to adjust the memory allocated to the principal argument
    This if necessary, and to copy Source to This.
    :
    return This; }
```

Overloading will be discussed in general in Section 2.6.

If a program includes an assignment statement with mismatched types, and you provide the appropriate converter, the compiler will automatically generate code to invoke it before executing the assignment. Similarly, if you pass an argument of the wrong type by value when invoking a function, and you provide the converter, the compiler will generate code to call it. This makes programs more readable, but also more hazardous. If the type conflict was unintentional and the converter doesn't transform the offending object into an exactly equivalent form, your program can appear to execute correctly but actually give incorrect results. One way to detect such an error during debugging is to insert an output statement in the converter to announce its execution.

Destructors

C++ programmers have great flexibility in choosing processes to be carried out by constructors. In the examples under the previous heading, the constructors allocated free memory storage. When OOP techniques are used for input/output programming, for example, they might also open a file or open a screen window corresponding to a file buffer or a window image in memory. You must generally provide some code to do housekeeping when the constructed objects pass away: release free memory storage, close a file, redraw the screen, etc. Otherwise, free memory might remain allocated but inaccessible because its pointer has disappeared, a file might remain open with buffer unflushed, or an inactive window might remain on the screen. To take care of such matters, C++ invites you to place such housekeeping tasks in a class *destructor* function. The compiler generates code to execute it whenever an object X passes away. This occurs when you explicitly destroy X by executing **delete X**, but more frequently whenever execution control leaves the block in which X was defined. The syntax is simple: The destructor for a class **ClassC** is simply a public member function named ~**ClassC( )** with no non-principal argument and no return value.

2.6 Overloading

As mentioned earlier, a major goal of this book's MSP software is to let C++ scientific and engineering application programs look like the mathematical descriptions of the corresponding algorithms. This will make programs more understandable, and consequently less prone to error, in both the development and maintenance phases. The two major OOP techniques that contribute to this goal are the use of classes and overloading. *Overloading* refers to use of the same function name or operator symbol to denote various functions or operators that differ in the types of their arguments. By overloading functions and operators, you can use familiar short names for mathematical processes. For example, the addition operators for scalars, vectors, polynomials, and matrices can all be represented by the familiar **+** sign, and the equality tests by **==**. The value of polynomial **p** at scalar argument **x** can still be represented by **p(x)** even though **p** is stored as an array of coefficients.

C++ enables overloading through two simple devices. First, in encoding a function name, the compiler considers the entire function signature, or list of types of arguments. Functions with the same name that differ in signature have different name codes, so the compiler can ascertain which to apply in a given situation. Second, operators are equivalent to C++ *operator functions*: **int** operator **+**, for example, corresponds to function **int operator+(int i, int j)**. Thus, any function overloading technique applies to operators, too.

The dot, .***, ::**, and **?:** operators cannot be overloaded. The singulary ***** and **&** operators and the binary comma operator are so tied to C++ syntax that overloading them would be inadvisable. Others, like the binary **( )**, **[ ]**, and **=** operators, are delicate. MSP does overload these last three, following strict C++ guidelines.

Overloading sometimes conflicts with the provision for default function parameters. Providing default parameters really creates a second form of a function with a different (shorter) signature. The compiler will flag as an error a subsequent attempt to implement the same signature through overloading.

You've already seen some examples of overloading. A single class usually has several constructors, all with the same name — that of the class itself — but varying signatures. Converters also overload these same functions. Assignment of an object to a class variable is an example of operator overloading.

The best way to grasp the overloading strategy is to see it in action. The low-level MSP modules contain many examples, and are discussed in detail later in Chapter 3.

2.7 Derived Classes

The algebraic structures of higher mathematics are organized into an elaborate hierarchy. Here's a part of it that's heavily used in numerical analysis:

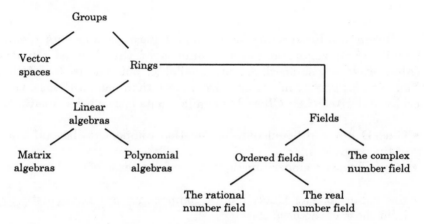

Each kind of structure inherits qualities from those above it. Vector spaces and rings are special kinds of groups; linear algebras inherit properties of both vector spaces and rings, etc. At the lowest level, these structures become more nearly concrete: The real number field in which we commonly perform arithmetic is an example of an ordered field. Computer arithmetic works with numbers that belong to the rational field. Symbolic algebra packages like *Mathematica* (References [43, 44]) also do arithmetic in the rational number field. At the upper levels are structures that you rarely see mentioned in numerical analysis texts; they are used to describe qualities shared by widely differing concrete examples. The properties of addition shared by rational numbers and matrices are studied in group theory, for instance.

Various programming specialties use similar hierarchies. For example, a display software package may define a structure called a window, of which there are several types, including menu. In turn, there may be several types of menu.

Experience with hierarchies like these led to development of the OOP class inheritance technique. In C++ you can define a class **ClassD** so that it inherits qualities from a base class **ClassB**. **ClassD** is said to be *derived* from **ClassB**. Its declaration looks like this:

```
class ClassD public ClassB {
  :
  Declarations of additional ClassD components and of
  member functions that differ from those of ClassB
  : }
```

The token **public** specifies that public **ClassB** components remain public when regarded as components of the derived **ClassD**. (Alternative access specifiers are available, but not used in MSP.) You can also specify inheritance from more than one base class. Generally, a derived class **ClassD** is similar to its base class **ClassB**, but

- **ClassD** has additional data or function components beyond those of the base class, or
- some **ClassD** member functions differ from those of the base class, or
- the values of the **ClassD** data components are more restricted than those of the base class.

The third provision is usually carried out by modifying **ClassB** member functions: You restrict those that construct or alter the data components.

Class inheritance is the basic OOP technique least used in MSP. Although it seems appropriate to use inheritance to model the part of the higher mathematics structure hierarchy used in numerical analysis, considerable overhead — intellectual as well as programming overhead — is incurred. Classes would need to be declared for each type of structure used, and for structures like groups that are not used per se but would serve as common base structures. Many of these classes would require their own constructors, destructors, etc., and the conversions between the large number of resulting types would have to be analyzed in detail for consistency and for conformity with mathematical usage. In the author's opinion, this design could be useful if the result was a software package that was so easy to describe and so like ordinary mathematics that client programmers could ignore virtually all of the class structure details. Unfortunately, that's impossible with C++. There are two reasons.

First, C++ programming still retains that troubling quality of C: you just can't ignore details. A seemingly trivial error can have far-flung effects. Sorting these out during debugging requires facility with the dirtiest aspects of the language. (Comparable facility with English sometimes helps, too.)

Second, some aspects of the mathematical hierarchy can't be modeled neatly with C++ classes. In higher mathematics you study the properties of vector spaces, matrix algebras, and polynomial algebras over an unspecified field of scalars. The theories are general, and apply equally whether the scalars are real, complex, or rational numbers, for example. The appropriate class structure for modeling mathematics would include, for instance, a class of vectors with entries of an unspecified scalar type. The vector class member functions would include vector addition and multiplication of vectors by scalars. Their implementations would refer to the addition and multiplication operations of the unspecified scalar class. This structure can be implemented in C++, but at the cost of much low-level programming. If vectors are implemented essentially as arrays of scalars, then the implementations of vector operations must have access to the details of the scalars — but in this scheme they wouldn't have access. Alternatively, vectors could be implemented as arrays of pointers to scalars. In that case, it's not clear that the resulting vector class could be used by client programs without continually manipulating pointers and other details. Freeing client programs from that mess is a major MSP goal.

An extension is planned for C++ that would handle this problem more neatly. The *Annotated C++ Reference Manual* (Reference [13]) includes a chapter on *templates*, an experimental feature that may, indeed, allow for graceful modeling of all the mathematical structures used in numerical analysis. Unfortunately, this has not yet been implemented in Turbo C++.

Thus, it seemed inadvisable for the MSP to rely heavily on class inheritance. The technique is used to derive a polynomial class from the vector class: Polynomials are regarded as vectors of coefficients, and new member functions are added for polynomial multiplication and evaluation. The discussion of class **Polynom** in Section 3.7 will give you an idea of the power of the inheritance technique.

Class inheritance was not used in MSP to model the dependence of vector or polynomial operations on the scalar type. Instead, a header file with a preprocessor definition specifies whether the scalars are real, complex, or some other type. This has a major fault: In a client program, all scalars must have the same type.

3

Introduction to MSP

The numerical analysis routines described in this book are organized into a Mathematical Software Package (MSP). Its components are C++ functions for manipulating numbers, vectors, matrices, and polynomials, and for solving equations and systems of equations frequently encountered in science and engineering. Many of these routines — for example, the data handling functions — are individually quite simple, while others, like some of the polynomial equation and linear algebra routines, are quite intricate. A major MSP design goal is to make the individual functions as simple as possible, while enabling client programmers to easily build very powerful and complicated applications programs.

A second design guideline is flexibility. MSP uses very general structures for scalars, vectors, matrices, and polynomials, and provides a comprehensive set of general functions for manipulating them. Because of their generality and simplicity, client programmers can adapt them easily to build programs to solve problems in various application contexts.

The third design goal is to enable client programmers to write programs that resemble mathematics. As much as possible, software intricacies are handled by the low-level MSP routines discussed in this chapter, so that client programmers may concentrate on the mathematics. The more a program resembles the mathematical description of the algorithm it implements, the less likely it is to contain errors, and the easier it is to maintain and adapt to related problems.

A fourth goal, minor from a scientist's or engineer's point of view, but major for writing this book, is to show how the flexibility and power of C++ can be harnessed to help solve mathematical problems of major scientific and engineering interest.

This chapter describes in great detail the lower levels of MSP software: its modules for manipulating scalars, vectors, matrices, and polynomials. While the mathematical aspects of these modules are generally inconsequential, their programming features are quite the opposite. In fact, MSP is designed to separate these qualities: Where the mathematics is complicated, the programming should be simple.

Using C++ emphasizes this distinction. One of its major features is its facility for overloading arithmetic operator symbols like **+**, **−**, and ***** to denote operations on data types like vectors and matrices. Using C++ you can compute a product of the sum of vectors **V** and **W** by the difference of matrices **A** and **B**, for example, by writing (**V** + **W**)*(**A** − **B**). Awkward and verbose function call syntax disappears, and you don't have to declare temporary variables to store intermediate results like **V** + **W** and **A** − **B**. Another C++ feature, its inheritance mechanism, enables MSP programmers to refer to polynomials in the manner common in mathematics: as the vectors of their scalar coefficients. Vector operations can be adapted for some aspects of polynomial algebra, and new features added to implement others.

C++ attains flexibility and power at a cost. The mathematical programming features just mentioned are *not part of* the language; C++ merely *enables* a programmer to implement them. That programmer must be familiar with many sophisticated programming concepts, including some normally regarded as belonging to systems programming. The low-level MSP modules described in this chapter concentrate this kind of programming in one place, so that client programmers using the modules can concentrate on the mathematics.

Thus, the programming in this chapter is far more intricate than what you'll meet in the rest of the book. If you're interested in *developing* this kind of software, you'll want to read this chapter in detail, try alternative approaches, find out where the difficulties lie, and try to develop better modules that are still usable by applications programmers. But if you're one of the latter class, mainly interested in *using* MSP to solve scientific and engineering problems, you'll want to read it more quickly, to find out what's here, what it does, and how to use it. You can then proceed to the descriptions of the more mathematical functions later in the book, and use the examples there to guide you in writing your own applications programs. But you should anticipate reading parts of this chapter again — perhaps several times — to figure out what's going on when your programs malfunction.

This book's approach to C++ numerical analysis programming isn't meant to be definitive, nor even to set a precedent. It's aim is more modest: to show that the major MSP goals can be attained effectively by using C++. There's no aim to show that C++ is the best possible language for this work. (In fact, the author would probably disagree with such a claim.)

Nor is there even a concerted attempt to find the best possible C++ techniques. Here are several features of C++ that ensure that the MSP, in its present design, is only a brief stopping point in a much broader flow of numerical analysis software development.

- C++, like its ancestor C, was developed to enhance effectiveness in systems programming, not specifically to facilitate scientific applications programming.
- Some of the Object Oriented Programming (OOP) goals of C++ are inconsistent with some of the original goals of the C language design. This results in awkwardness in some parts of C++, regardless of the type of program under development.
- Some C++ features, particularly the principal argument syntax, which are intended to enforce the OOP paradigm, actually contravene some mathematical practices developed over decades to handle gracefully some commonplace but logically complex mathematical notions.
- C++ is changing. It was not designed as a major objective in the development of programming languages, but as an experimental tool in this field. Some features, particularly *templates*, scheduled for implementation in future versions of C++, will have major impact on numerical analysis programming techniques.

Finally, before you plunge into this chapter's details, you should consider briefly the process of *testing* these low-level routines. Once the overall organization and the catalog of MSP functions was determined, and their prototypes designed, test routines were written. These exercise every function in every module in ways commonly required in scientific applications programming. The functions were tested as they were written. This was the main test bed, but many additional routines were used to verify correct operation for special inputs. (For example, does the **MaxNorm** function correctly give the norm 0 for the empty vector?) Actually, this description of the testing process is idealized. Frequent minor design changes made the development of the test bed more gradual and more chaotic. It's too long, boring, and messy to include in this book. It's certainly *incomplete*: Additional bugs will come to light. If you need to test an MSP function further or modify it or build a new one, you should replicate part of the original testing process. You'll find in Section 3.7 some neat test bed fragments involving Legendre polynomials, and many of the examples in later chapters can be used to test low-level functions. The best organized parts of the test bed code are included in subdirectory **Tests** of the optional diskette. (See Appendix A.6.)

3.1 General Module

The MSP **General** module contains some macros and functions used by all other MSP modules and by client programs. They're somewhat unrelated, but are rather simple. This module is the natural place to begin, if you want to understand any aspect of the lower levels of the MSP. Like the other modules, it has a header file **General.H**, and a source code file **General.CPP** that implements the functions defined in the header. You'll find these files on the optional diskette. The first parts of these files are displayed in Figures 3.1.1 and 3.1.2. **General.H** must be included in every MSP and client source code file. It causes several C++ Library header files to be included as well; therefore, client programs don't need to include those headers explicitly.

#ifndef and #endif

The first **General.H** header feature is a set of C++ preprocessor directives:

```
#ifndef General_H
#define General_H
  :
The rest of the header file
  :
#endif
```

Each time the preprocessor encounters the directive **#include** "General.H" in a source code file and starts reading the header file, it first asks if **General_H** has been entered in its list of defined tokens. If not (**#ifndef**), it makes the definition (**#define**) and reads the rest of the header file. But if the token is defined, the preprocessor has already read the file, so it skips to the end (**#endif**). This is a standard C technique to avoid duplicate definitions and declarations, which are usually illegal.

```
//***********************************************************
//                          General.H

#ifndef      General_H
#define      General_H

#include     <ConIO.H>
#include  <IOStream.H>
#include  <IOManip.H>
#include    <Limits.H>
#include    <StdLib.H>

//***********************************************************
//  General programming aids

#define This (*this)            // Shorthand for the target
                                // of a class' self pointer.

#define Boolean int             // These constitute an approxi-
#define True    1               // mation of the two valued
#define False   0               // Boolean data type.

#define StrEmpty(S) (*(S) == 0) // Is string  S  empty?

void Pause(char* Prompt = ""); // Display the prompt, then
                                // await and discard a charac-
                                // ter from the keyboard.

#define Inspect Pause("\nPress any key...\n\n")

int Digits(int x);              // Number of characters in the
                                // shortest numeral for  x .

int Sign(double x);             // Return  -1 , 0 ,  or  1
                                // when  x < , = ,  or  > 0 .

//***********************************************************
//  Maxima and minima

#undef    max
#undef    min
int       max(int    x, int    y); // Return the larger  of  x,y .
int       min(int    x, int    y); // Return the smaller of  x,y .
double fmax(double x, double y); // Return the larger  of  x,y .
double fmin(double x, double y); // Return the smaller of  x,y .

//..continued
```

Figure 3.1.1 MSP header file General.H (Part 1)

Definition of This

The first macro in **General.H** defines **This** to stand for (this*). Described in Section 2.4, **this** points to the principal argument of a class member function. The author found that the abbreviation helped avoid many trivial syntax errors. The parentheses prevent possible operator misassociation when **This** occurs in a compound expression.

```
//***********************************************************
//                        General.CPP

#include "General.H"
#include   <ConIO.H>

void Pause(char* Prompt) {       // Display the prompt, then
  cout << Prompt << flush;       // await and discard a charac-
  getch(); }                     // ter from the keyboard.

int Digits(int x) {              // Return the number of
  int p = 1;  long n = 10;       // characters 0 , .. , 9 , -
  while (abs(x) >= n) {          // in the shortest numeral
    ++p;  n *= 10; }             // for  x .
  if (x < 0) ++p;
  return p; }

long double Factorial(int n) {   // Return n! .
  long double f = 1;             // Return 1 if  n < 0 .
  for (int k = 1; k <= n; ++k)   // This overflows for
    f *= k;                      // n > 1754 .
  return f; }

int Sign(double x) {             // Return -1 , 0 , or -1
  if (x <  0) return -1;         // when  x < , = , or  > 0 .
  if (x == 0) return  0;
  else        return  1; }

int max(int x, int y) {          // Return the larger  of
  return (x < y ? y : x); }      // x  and  y .
int min(int x, int y) {          // Return the smaller of
  return (x < y ? x : y); }  .   // x  and  y .
double fmax(double x, double y) {// Return the larger of
  return (x < y ? y : x); }      // x  and  y .
double fmin(double x, double y) {// Return the smaller of
  return (x < y ? x : y); }      // x  and  y .

//..continued
```

Figure 3.1.2 MSP source code file General.CPP (Part 1)

Identifier Capitalization

The **This** definition illustrates this book's capitalization convention: Capitalized identifiers don't occur in C++ or its Library (except for a few written entirely in upper case). On the other hand, most MSP identifiers are capitalized. The major exception to that rule is an occasional generic variable of a built-in or the **complex** type, for which traditional mathematics notation uses lower case.

The Boolean Type

C++ has no official two valued Boolean type. **if** statements and various operators regard the **int** value zero as representing falsehood and any other **int** value as truth. (It's easier to say *yes* to a C programmer than to say *no!*) Actually, most Turbo C++ operators return the value 1 to represent truth. This situation distresses the author, so **General.H** includes definitions that make **int** the **Boolean** type for MSP and give the values 0 and 1 the names **False** and **True**. This rarely conflicts with Turbo C++ conventions, and helps eliminate logical errors. MSP could use a **typedef** here, but that would cause the compiler to generate a warning every time a Boolean function returns a value like (**x < 0**); it might also cause actual syntax errors.

Empty Strings

C++ strings are **char** arrays terminated by the null character, the one with ASCII code zero. An empty string consists of the terminator alone. Since a string variable **S** is a pointer to the beginning of the corresponding array, you can check whether **S** is empty by asking whether ((***S**) **== 0**). This occurs frequently enough — in constructing output captions — that **General.H** defines the macro **StrEmpty(S)** to stand for this condition. The outer parentheses prevent operator misassociation when **StrEmpty(S)** occurs in a compound expression.

The empty string has a simple name: " ".

Pausing to Inspect Output

Occasionally you want to stop execution to inspect the display and prompt for any keystroke to resume computation. The **General** module supports this requirement with function

```
void Pause(const char* Prompt = "") .
```

You may specify the prompt or accept the empty string (no prompt) as the default. Further, a macro **Inspect** invokes **Pause** with a familiar prompt, surrounded by newlines to make it particularly visible. Since the default **Pause** prompt and the **Inspect** prompt are specified in the header, you can change them without altering source code. **Pause** sends the stream manipulator **flush** to **cout** after the prompt to ensure that it's displayed. **Pause** calls the C Library ConIO function **getch** to input a character, which it ignores. In turn, **getch** calls for a BIOS service, so this code might not be portable to incompatible systems. **Pause** didn't use **cin** stream nor StdIO input because they often have undesirable effects on the display.

The Digits and Sign Functions

MSP must be able to determine the smallest number of digits required to display an **int** value X. (This is used to make neat subscripts.) Although that information is provided by Library function **sprintf** or **itoa**, these are inconvenient, so MSP includes its own function **int Digits(int X)**.

The MSP function **int Sign(double x)** returns −1, 0, or 1 to indicate that **x < 0, = 0, or > 0**. It's used later in several numerical analysis routines. It works for arguments **x** of other numerical types, too, because the compiler will cast them automatically to type **double**.

Maximum and Minimum

Library header file **StdLib.H** defines macros **max(x,y)** and **min(x,y)** for the maximum and minimum operations. These work whenever operator < is defined for the types of **x** and **y**. Unfortunately, each one mentions its arguments twice: For instance, **x** occurs twice in the **StdLib.H** definition of **max(x,y)**. This can cause side effect errors. For example, suppose function **int f(int x)** beeps (a side effect), then returns some value. Executing **max(f(x),y)** will cause two beeps, not one as the notation suggests. In practice, side effects might involve memory allocation or file manipulation, so the error could be more serious.

To eliminate this hazard, **General.H** uses preprocessor directive **#undef** to "undefine" **max** and **min**, and module **General** includes *functions* **max** and **min** to perform the same services properly for **int** arguments. Functions **fmax** and **fmin** work for **double** arguments. This notation agrees with that for the absolute value macros **abs** and **fabs** defined in Library files **StdLib.H** and **Math.H** for **int** and **double** arguments.

MSP Error Handling

Error reporting and handling is a tedious and delicate subject, because of the wide variety of error sources. DOS has some standard methods for dealing with errors from sources within its sphere. C++ has some inadequate facilities, discussed in detail in Section 4.5. More elaborate ones are planned: See the chapter on error handling in the *Annotated C++ Reference Manual* (Reference [13]).

MSP needs a basic error reporting system. It should permit a client program to try to stop gracefully and display a message when an inconsistent error situation occurs. Stopping *ungracefully* means crashing or leaving the computer in an inconsistent state for DOS or some other software that will assume control next. Displaying no message at all is worse: The program may produce erroneous output in misleadingly proper format, even though it knew something was wrong.

Designing — or even describing — a comprehensive error handling system is beyond the scope of this book. It's a systems programming task, not numerical analysis. Therefore, MSP implements only a minimal system. Whenever an MSP routine detects an error, it sets a global variable called an *error signal,* and attempts to return to the caller without further action that might cause a crash. MSP provides functions for client programs to inspect the error signal and reset it.

The source code for the MSP error handling system is contained in Figures 3.1.3 and 3.1.4, which conclude the display of files **General.H** and **General.CPP** begun in Figures 3.1.1 and 3.1.2. The error signal itself is static variable **ErrorSignal**, declared and initialized in **General.CPP**. Function **GetError( )** returns its value. Thus, the signal itself can be hidden from a client: If **General.CPP** is not distributed, **ErrorSignal** can be read easily but not altered directly. The signal has values of an enumerated type **ErrorType** that's defined in **General.H**. MSP functions assign these values to **ErrorSignal** to reflect the type of error. One is **NoError**, the initial **ErrorSignal** value. Another variable "hidden" in **General.CPP** is an array of English names for the **ErrorType** values, for producing legible output. Clients are provided two more functions:

```
void SetError          // Set ErrorSignal = E .
  (ErrorType E);
char* ErrorName( );     // Return the current error name
                        // and set ErrorSignal = NoError .
```

According to the design of the last of these functions, you can sprinkle **cout << ErrorName( )** statements through a misbehaving program, and each one after the first will report what happened since its predecessor.

Random Number Generation

Many scientific applications must use sequences of numbers that approximate measurements of random phenomena. Being computer generated, the sequences are not really random. But if they pass sufficiently many of the randomness tests devised by statisticians, these sequences deserve to be called *pseudorandom*. A good pseudorandom number sequence will have these qualities:

• tested randomness,
• ease of generation,
• amenability to mathematical analysis,
• reproducibility, for study and debugging.

There's a large amount of literature devoted to pseudorandom number sequences. The standard summary is Knuth (Reference [28], Chapter 3).

The Turbo C++ Library contains several functions for random number generation, constructed according to Knuth's guidelines. Unfortunately, they contain errors, and do not perform according to the published documentation. The MSP **General** module redefines these functions to conform with the documentation. The corresponding parts of the header and source code files are shown in Figures 3.1.3 and 3.1.4.

Definitions like **#define rand( ) MSPrand( )** in **General.H** ensure that all later references to function **rand** — including its redefinition in **General.CPP** — are translated into references to function **MSPrand**. Thus, the new function replaces Library function **rand**. References in this text to **rand** and the other redefined functions **random, randomize,** and **srand** are to the new functions, unless otherwise noted.

rand generates a pseudorandom sequence of **long** values x_0, x_1, $x_2, \neg$ ... in the range $0 \leq x \leq$ **RAND_MAX**. Another **General.H** definition makes this last constant equal to **LONG_MAX**, the largest **long** value, which is defined in Library header file **Limits.H**. The x values are generated according to the formula

$$x_0 = 1$$
$$x_{n+1} = (ax_n + 1) \bmod m,$$

where $a = 3 \times 7^2 \times 61 \times 2531$ and $m = 2^{32}$. You can execute **srand(n)** to make the sequence start with $x_0 = $ **n**, or **randomize( )** to make it start with a random value derived from the time. Reduction mod m

```
//*******************************************************************
// MSP  error handling facilities

typedef enum ErrorType              // Error signal codes.
  { NoError,      BadFormat,
    IndexError,   OutOfMemory,
    DivideError };
void        SetError(ErrorType E);  // Set error signal.
ErrorType GetError();               // Return error signal.
char*       ErrorName();            // Return error name, turn
                                    // off error signal.

//*******************************************************************
//  Random number generation

#undef  RAND_MAX                    // Redefine  StdLib.H
#define RAND_MAX    LONG_MAX        // random number
#define RandMaxP1   double(RAND_MAX) + 1  // generator to
#define rand()      MSPrand()       // correct errors.
#define random(n)   MSPrandom(n)
#define randomize() MSPrandomize()
#define srand(Seed) MSPsrand(Seed)

long rand();                        // Return a random number.
long random(long n);                // Return random  x ,  0 ≤ x < n .
void randomize();                   // Restart random numbers randomly.
void srand(long n);                 // Restart random numbers at  n .

#endif
```

Figure 3.1.3 MSP header file General.H (Part 2)

is implicit in C++ integer arithmetic: The arithmetic operations often produce results too large for **long** variables, and **long** arithmetic overflow on an Intel 8086 family CPU results in arithmetic mod 2^{32}.

The formula for the x values is called a *linear congruential* algorithm. Knuth proves that with these particular values of a and m, the pseudorandom sequence has the maximum possible period: x_0, ..., x_{m-1} are all distinct.

To generate a random **long** value x in the interval $0 \le x < $ **n**, where **n** is a specific **long** value, execute **random(n)**. This function simply obtains a random value from **rand** and transforms it linearly to fit the specified interval.

The original Turbo C++ Library functions had two defects. Although **rand** used the same method to compute pseudorandom x values, it converted them to type **int** return values. This destroyed the long period of the sequence: If you started with $x_0 = 1$, ..., 9, the first $k > 0$ such that $x_k = x_0$ could be as small as 1434; the average k value is 11705. (These statistics were computed by program **TestRand.CPP**, which you'll find on the accompanying diskette.) The second fault was an error in **random**: Borland used **RAND_MAX** instead of **RAND_MAX + 1** in the formula.

```
//*******************************************************************
//  MSP  error handling facilities

ErrorType ErrorSignal    = NoError;
char*      ErrorString[] =
  { "No Error",    "Bad Format",        // Error signal
    "Index Error", "Out of Memory",     // output names.
    "DivideError" };

void SetError(ErrorType E) {            // Set error signal.
  ErrorSignal = E; }
ErrorType GetError() {                  // Return error signal.
  return ErrorSignal; }
char* ErrorName() {                     // Return error name and
  ErrorType E = ErrorSignal;            // turn off error signal.
  ErrorSignal = NoError;
  return ErrorString[E]; }

//*******************************************************************
//  Random number generation

long Seed = 1;                          // Current random number.
long rand() {                           // Generate and return a
  return Seed = 22695477 * Seed + 1; }  // new random number.
long random(long n) {                   // Return a random number
  double x = (RandMaxP1 + rand()) * n   // x  in the interval
    / (2 * RandMaxP1);                  // 0 ≤ x < n .
  return long(x); }
void randomize() {                      // Restart the random num-
  srand(time(NULL)); }                  // ber sequence randomly.
void srand(long n) {                    // Restart the random num-
  Seed = n; }                           // ber sequence with  n .
```

Figure 3.1.4 MSP source code file General.CPP (Part 2)

3.2   Scalar Module: Double Version

The MSP **Scalar** module defines the type of the numbers with which this book's numerical analysis calculations are performed. In mathematical terms, these are normally real or complex, though for some computations, members of other number fields, such as rational numbers, could be used. The corresponding C++ data types used in this book are **double** and **complex**. The former is a built-in type; the latter is defined in the C++ Library as a class. The less precise **float** or more precise **long double** type could have been used for **real** numbers, but then it would have been necessary to define a new complex number type with the same precision.

To conform with ideal C++ programming style, this module should define a new class **real** corresponding to the **double** type, with features analogous to those of the Library class **complex**. Clients should then be able to build vectors, matrices, and polynomials, etc., with entries or coefficients of type **real** or **complex** at will. As discussed in Section 2.7, that isn't practical with the present version of Turbo C++.

Instead, MSP provides two alternative modules, which define **Scalar** to mean **double** or **complex**, respectively. Client programs must include one or the other. This is convenient, but has an unfortunate consequence: In a client program, *all* scalars are **double**, or *all* are **complex**.

The **Scalar** modules have three purposes:

- to define the **Scalar** type;
- to provide a few rudimentary services not offered by Library functions;
- to ensure that the **double** and **complex** versions are equivalent, so that higher level MSP software and clients can ask for and receive equivalent services in either case.

Each module consists of a header file and a source code file. On the optional diskette, they're named

ScDouble.H
ScDouble.CPP
ScCmplex.H
ScCmplex.CPP

You must rename one set as **Scalar.H** and **Scalar.CPP** for use with MSP. The **double** versions are shown in Figures 3.2.1 and 3.2.2 and described in this section. The **complex** versions are described later, in Section 4.6.

Scalar.H includes the MSP header file **General.H**, and with it the C++ Library headers mentioned in Section 3.1. The first feature in **Scalar.H** is the type definition:

```
#define Scalar double   or   #define Scalar complex
```

The remaining features are divided into *logical* and *mathematical* groups. Logical features are required by any data type, not just one designed for mathematical applications. The logical features of this module are concerned with output. Its mathematical features provide a few generally useful services that the C++ Library omitted.

Displaying Scalars

The **Scalar** module provides two functions for standard scalar output:

```
//*****************************************************************
//                          Scalar.H
//           double   version, also stored as   ScDouble.H

#ifndef    Scalar_H
#define    Scalar_H

#include "General.H"

#define Scalar double

//*****************************************************************
// Logical features

#define DefaultScalarFormat "% -#9.2g" // Shortest general form.

char* ForShow(const double& x,          // Convert  x  to a string
                const char* Format =    // for standard output.
              DefaultScalarFormat);     // Use  printf  Format .

int   Show   (const double& x,          // Standard output;  re-
                const char* Format =    // turn output length.
              DefaultScalarFormat);

//*****************************************************************
// Mathematical features

double real(double x);                  // Return  x = real part.
double imag(double x);                  // Return  0 = imaginary part.
double conj(double x);                  // Return  x = conjugate.
double Norm(double x);                  // Return  |x| = abs(x) .
double Random();                        // Random  x ,  0 ≤ |x| < 1 .

#endif
```

Figure 3.2.1 MSP header file Scalar.H

```
char* ForShow(const double& x, const char* Format =
   DefaultScalarFormat);
int   Show   (const double& x, const char* Format =
   DefaultScalarFormat);
```

ForShow invokes the StdIO Library function **sprintf** to convert scalar **x** to a string **S**, which it returns, ready for output by the caller. The **Format** code that governs the conversion is described later. **ForShow** allocates free memory storage for **S**. If allocation fails, **ForShow** sets the MSP error signal. If it succeeds, the caller must deallocate that memory when **S** is no longer needed. If the **Format** code is bad, **sprintf** returns a constant **EOF** defined in the StdIO header file and **ForShow** sets the error signal. In either error situation, **ForShow** returns a **NULL** pointer, since it must return a string, and strings are pointers. The second output function **Show** calls **ForShow** to prepare an output string **S**, then outputs it with

```
//**********************************************************************
//                          Scalar.CPP
//          double version, also stored as   ScDouble.CPP

#include    "Scalar.H"
#include    <Math.H>
#include    <StdIO.H>
#include    <String.H>

//**********************************************************************
// Logical features

char* ForShow(const double& x,          // Convert  x  to a string
              const char* Format) {     // S  for standard output.
  char* S = new char[80];               // Use  printf  Format .
  if (S == NULL)
    SetError(OutOfMemory);                    // 80  characters
  else if (sprintf(S,Format,x) == EOF) {  // should be long
    SetError(BadFormat);                  // enough for  S .
    S = NULL; }
  return S; }

int Show(const double& x,               // Standard output; re-
         const char* Format) {          // turn output length.
  char* S = ForShow(x,Format);          // Prepare output.  This
  int n = 0;                            // allocates  S .
  if (S != NULL) {                      // n = output length.
    n = strlen(S);
    cout << S;                          // Output.
    delete S; }
  return n; }

//**********************************************************************
// Mathematical features

double real(double x) {                 // Return the real part of  x :
  return x; }                           // this is just  x .
double imag(double x) {                 // Return the imaginary part of
  return 0; }                           // x :  this is  0 .
double conj(double x) {                 // Return  x  conjugate:  this
  return x; }                           // is just  x .
double Norm(double x) {                 // Return the norm of  x
  return fabs(x); }                     // --i.e. its absolute value.
double Random() {                       // Return a random  x  such
  return (RandMaxP1 + rand())           // that  0 <= |x| < 1 .
    / (2 * RandMaxP1); }
```

Figure 3.2.2 MSP source code file Scalar.CPP

the statement **cout << S**. If **ForShow** encounters an error, there's
no output. After output, **Show** frees the memory allocated to **S** and
returns the length of **S**. The length is calculated by StdIO Library
function **strlen**.

If you invoke **ForShow** or **Show** to output a scalar x without
specifying a **Format** code, or with an empty code string, MSP will
use the default scalar format "**% –#9.2g**" defined in the **Scalar**
header file. This code produces the shortest string **S** which displays

two significant digits as well as the order of magnitude of x. Like all format codes, it begins with %. **#9.2g** signifies that **S** should contain eight characters, including a decimal point and two significant digits, in floating point format if $.0001 \leq |x| < 100$, and in scientific notation outside that range. The blank and minus after the initial % indicate that the numeral should begin with a blank if $x > 0$, then it should be left justified in **S** and padded on the right with blanks if necessary. You can inspect some output samples in Figure 3.2.3.

This format code ensures that output columns will align nicely. You can find all possible format codes in the Turbo C++ reference guide (Reference [5]), in the discussion of function **printf**.

Although C++ Version 2 stream input/output includes fairly elaborate formatting conventions, it doesn't support all the features used in the **DefaultScalarFormat** code, hence doesn't let you line up columns so nicely. That's why MSP uses **sprintf**.

Consistency Between Double and Complex Scalars

To enforce consistency, the **Scalar** module defines functions **real, imag, conj**, and **Norm** for both the **double** and **complex** versions. For a complex operand $z = x + iy$,

$$\text{real}(z) = x$$
$$\text{imag}(z) = y \qquad \text{Norm}(z) = \| z \| = \sqrt{x^2 + y^2}$$
$$\text{conj}(z) = \bar{z} = x - iy$$

For the real operands **x** in this version of **Scalar**, however, these operations are redundant: **real(x) = conj(x) = x, imag(x) = 0**, and **Norm(x) = abs(x)**. (This use of the word *Norm* differs from that in the Turbo C++ manual, but is consistent with mathematical convention.)

Scalar	MSP output
.0000765	7.7e–05
.000765	0.00076
77.5	78.
–66.5	–66.
–675	–6.8e+02

Figure 3.2.3 Sample MSP scalar output

Random Scalars

The fundamental MSP random number generator is the function **rand( )** described in Section 3.1. A statement **long k = rand( )** produces a pseudorandom integer **k** in the interval $0 \leq k < 2^{32}$. Usually, the intended application must use a different interval. To generate a pseudorandom integer **k** in the interval $0 \leq k < n$, where **n** is a specified **long** value, you can use the statement **long k = random(n)**, also described in Section 3.1. The function **random** merely calls **rand**, then scales the return value linearly to fit the specified interval. (These MSP functions are redefinitions of the Turbo C++ functions, which return **int** values and do not perform according to their documentation.)

Often, an application needs a pseudorandom scalar value x in a specified region R. Since R varies so much in practice, the **Scalar** module provides function **Random( )**, which returns a **Scalar** value t in the half-open unit interval $0 \leq t < 1$ (or the half-open unit square $0 \leq$ Real z, Imag $z < 1$, in the **complex** version). Client programs can then manipulate t as desired to cover a different region. For example, to generate a pseudorandom real x in an interval $a \leq x < b$, compute $x = a + (b - a)\, t$.

3.3   Handling Vector Objects

The MSP **Vector** class implements an abstract data type for vector algebra, and is also the underlying structure for matrix and polynomial computations. Thus, it has many applications, which can place widely differing requirements on the data structure. No single class definition can possibly meet all these demands. This implementation is merely an example, showing how C++ can be used to tailor numerical analysis software to general or particular needs. It provides for

- vectors with varying starting indices,
- vectors of varying dimension,
- real or complex vectors,
- bounds checking.

The first provision means, for instance, that you can use vectors $x = [x_1, x_2, ...]$ and $a = [a_0, a_1, ...]$ in the same program. This is particularly convenient in polynomial algebra applications, where the use of the zero subscript for the constant coefficient often collides with other notation. Other first index choices are possible, too. Although you can use vectors with various index bounds at will, you cannot use both real and complex vectors in the same program. The **Vector** class provides an intermediate level of bounds checking: Most vector operations check their operands for consistency of lower and upper index bounds. However, to avoid loss of speed, in individual references to vector entries x_k, index k is not checked against the index bounds for vector x. Most client program references to entries x_k are found, nevertheless, in the algorithms for operations which do check for overall consistency.

The MSP functions that manipulate vectors can be classified as *logical* or *mathematical*. Counterparts of the logical functions would be defined for most any class that has a data component of indeterminate size. The logical functions are described in detail in this section. The mathematical functions implement vector algebra; they're discussed in Section 3.4.

Like other MSP modules, this one has a header file **Vector.H**. The source code is so long, however, that it was split into two files, **VectorL.CPP** and **VectorM.CPP**, for logical and mathematical functions. You'll find these files on the accompanying diskette. The logical part of the header file is shown in Figures 3.3.1 and 3.3.2. It automatically includes the MSP header file **Scalar.H** and other header files that **Scalar.H** loads. (See Section 3.2.) Parts of **VectorL.CPP** are displayed later in this section. The mathematical part of the header file, and its corresponding source code, will be discussed in Section 3.4.

The Vector Data Structure

The **Vector** module is designed to handle vectors whose **Scalar** entries have varying low and high indices. To facilitate ascertaining the lower and upper index bounds of a vector, they are data components of the **Vector** class. Vector entries are stored in an array of scalars. Since the size of this array is indeterminate, it must be stored in free memory. In order to enforce the intermediate level of bounds checking described earlier, the index bounds and array must be private components, and member functions must be provided to manipulate them as needed. In designing the class, no other private components proved necessary. Thus, the private part of class **Vector** is

```
private:
    int Low;          // Index bounds for the
    int High;         // vector entries.
    Scalar* Array;    // Storage for entries.
```

```
//*****************************************************************
//                 Vector.H  (Logical components, Part 1)

#ifndef    Vector_H
#define    Vector_H

#include "Scalar.H"

class Vector {                      // The private parts of
                                    // class  Vector  are its
    private:                        // data components.
      int     Low;                  // Index bounds for the
      int     High;                 // vector entries.
      Scalar* Array;                // Storage for entries.

    public:

      //*****************************************************
      //  Selectors

      int LowIndex () const;        // Selectors for the index
      int HighIndex() const;        // bounds.
      Scalar& operator             // Vector entry selector
         [](int k) const;           // (overloaded  [] ).

      //*****************************************************
      //  Constructors and destructor

      Vector();                     // Default constructor.
      Vector& SetUp(int Hi,         // Set the index bounds
               int Lo = 1);         // and allocate storage.
      Vector(int Hi,                // Construct a vector with
             int Lo = 1);           // specified index bounds.
      ~Vector();                    // Destructor.

      //*****************************************************
      //  Copiers and assignment

      Vector(const Vector& Source); // Copy constructor.
      Vector& operator             // Assignment.
         =(const Vector& Source);
      Vector& Copy(int     Lo,      // Copy  Source[SourceLo]
              const Vector& Source,  // ..Source[SourceHi]  to
                   int     SourceLo, // target starting at
                   int     SourceHigh); // index  Lo .
```

Figure 3.3.1 MSP header file Vector.H (logical components, Part 1)

The **Array** component is *not* the array itself, but merely a *pointer* to its first entry in free memory.

MSP uses a standard representation for *empty* vectors: **Low = 0**, **High = –1**, and **Array = NULL**.

According to the overview given in Sections 2.3–2.6, the functions necessary for logical manipulation of these components include

- *selectors*, to provide limited access to the data components;
- *constructors*, to initialize the index bounds and the array pointer, and — usually — to set up the array in free memory;

```
//*********************************************************************
//              Vector.H  (Logical components, Part 2)

    //*****************************************************************
    //  Input/output

    Vector& KeyIn(char* Name);            // Prompted keyboard input.
    Vector& Show(
       char*    Format    = DefaultScalarFormat,   // Standard
       Boolean RowFormat = True,                    // display
       char*    Name      = "") const;              // output.
    friend istream& operator
       >>(istream& Source,                          // Stream input.
          Vector& Target);

    //*****************************************************************
    //  Here are declared several member functions that implement
    //  parts of vector algebra.  They're described in §3.4.

    };               // End of the definition of class  Vector .

//*********************************************************************
//  Related non-member logical functions

Boolean  operator==(const Vector& V,      // Equality.
                    const Vector& W);
Boolean  operator!=(const Vector& V,      // Inequality.
                    const Vector& W);
istream& operator>>(      istream& Source,  // Stream input:  a
                    Vector& Target);  // friend.
ostream& operator<<(      ostream& Target,  // Stream output.
                    const Vector& Source);

//*********************************************************************
//  Here are declared the remaining vector algebra functions.
//  They're described in §3.4.

#endif
```

Figure 3.3.2 MSP header file Vector.H (logical components, Part 2)

- a *destructor*, to deallocate the array when a vector is deleted or passes out of scope;
- a *copy constructor*, for the compiler to use when temporary copies are needed for function calls;
- an overloaded *assignment* operator, to copy the array during assignment;
- a general *copier*, for manipulating pieces of vectors;
- overloaded *equality* and *inequality* operators, to compare the index bounds and arrays;
- *keyboard input* and *display output* functions;
- *stream input/output* functions.

These features are described in detail in the rest of this section. Sometimes, source code is given here in the text. For the display and stream input/output functions, you're referred to Appendices A.1 and A.2. The code for the remaining functions is generally described with just a few words, because it's trivial or repetitive. You'll find it on the accompanying diskette.

Selectors

Selectors are public member functions that provide limited access to private data components. For instance, function **LowIndex** merely returns the **Low** component of its principal argument:

```
int Vector::LowIndex( ) const { return Low; }
```

The **const** qualifier is included because the overloaded operator doesn't change the value **This** of its principal argument. This provision allows the principal argument to be a **Vector** *constant*. The **Low** component can be changed only in a very controlled way, by other member functions. Function **HighIndex** is similar.

Since vector entries are stored in a private array in free memory, they can't be accessed directly by the subscript operator **[ ]**. Instead, this must be overloaded so that if **V** is a **Vector** object and **k** an **int** value within the **V** index bounds, then **V[k]** is a reference to the appropriate **Array** entry in free memory. The overloaded **[ ]** operator must return the *reference to*, not the value of, the entry because it must be usable on the left-hand side of an assignment. (In C++ terminology, it must be an *lvalue*.) Since the **V** and **Array** indices range over different intervals, starting with **Low** and zero, respectively, the appropriate **Array** entry has index **k – Low**. The source code is quite simple:

```
Scalar& Vector::operator[ ](int k) const {
   return Array[k-Low]; }
```

Constructors

According to Section 2.5, the **Vector** class needs a default constructor that the compiler will call *n* times whenever you declare an array of *n* vectors. It needn't do much; the MSP function just initializes an empty vector:

```
Vector::Vector( ) { Low = 0; High = -1; Array = NULL; }
```

When you declare a vector, however, you usually want to set up specific index bounds, and allocate the storage array in free memory. Section 2.5 gives a good reason for placing this code in a separate public function **SetUp**: It needs to be invoked in several different situations. Here's the source code:

```
Vector& Vector::SetUp(int Hi,      // Set index bounds and
                      int Lo) {    // allocate storage.
   Low = Lo; High = Hi;
   int n = High - Low + 1;         // Allocate n entries.
   Array = new Scalar[n];
   if (n > 0 && Array == NULL) {   // If free memory is
      SetError(OutOfMemory);       // exhausted, set the
      Low = 0; High = -1; }        // error signal and set
   return This; }                  // up an empty vector.
```

Operator **new** returns the **NULL** pointer if it allocates no storage. That indicates an error if you asked for some, so **SetUp** reports the error and sets up an empty vector. Otherwise, **new** returns a pointer to the allocated space. **SetUp** returns the value of its principal argument, to permit operator concatenation.

Ignoring the error signal after an attempt to construct a vector **V** fails sometimes results in the Turbo C++ **Null pointer assignment** error message when the program terminates. Unfortunately, this error may cause a system crash before that point. If you attempt to assign a value to an entry of an empty vector **V**, C++ will follow its **NULL** pointer and store the value *somewhere*. If your program was compiled under a small memory model, that's in a memory region reserved for storing DOS and BIOS constants. If the resulting corruption doesn't cause a crash before your program terminates, Turbo C++ will then check whether that area has changed since your program started. If so, you'll see the error message.

Client programs use the constructor **Vector(int Hi, int Lo = 1)** most often. This merely calls **SetUp(Hi,Lo)** to set up the index bounds and allocate the memory. For example, you may invoke it with its last parameter defaulted by declaring **Vector V(3)** to set up a vector with three entries [**V[1]**, ..., **V[3]**], as is customary in analytic geometry. Alternatively, you can include the last parameter explicitly: For example, declaring **Vector V(3,-1)** sets up a vector [**V[-1]**, **V[0]**, ..., **V[3]**].

To construct an array of **n** vectors (of possibly varying dimensions), execute the default constructor **n** times by declaring **Vector V[n]**, then call **SetUp** in a **for** loop **n** times to set the index bounds and allocate the memory. The vectors are then **[V[0], ..., V[n-1]]**, and — for example — **V[0][1]** is the entry of **V[0]** with index **1**.

Destructor

When you construct a local **Vector** object **V** by declaring **Vector V**, the three components **V.Low, V.High**, and **V.Array** are stored on the stack. The last is the address of an array in free memory. When control passes out of the block where **V** was declared, these three components are destroyed. You must provide a way to release the array storage in free memory. Otherwise, it will constitute unusable storage, because it's allocated but no pointer points to it. The mechanism is the *destructor* for class **Vector**. If you provide the function, the compiler will arrange to execute it at the proper time. The source code is simple:

```
Vector::~Vector( ) { delete [High-Low+1] Array; }
```

The compiler will also execute this to destroy temporary **Vector** objects that it constructs for passing function parameters and return values, and to complete the destruction when you execute **delete V** for a **Vector** object **V**.

Copiers and Assignment

According to Section 2.5, class **Vector** needs a copy constructor and an overloaded assignment operator. The former, declared as **Vector(const Vector& Source)**, constructs a new vector identical to **Source**. The compiler will invoke it automatically to make temporary copies for passing function parameters and return values, and you can use it explicitly in declarations like **Vector V(Source)** or **Vector V = Source**. The overloaded assignment operator must be declared as

```
Vector& operator=(const Vector& Source).
```

These two features function alike except that the assignment operator has a principal argument when it's invoked, and should return that argument. The copy constructor has no principal argument and returns no value.

Here's the copy constructor source code:

```
Vector::Vector(const Vector& Source) {    // Copy constructor.
  SetUp(Source.High,Source.Low);          // Set index bounds,
  if (GetError( )) return;                 // allocate storage
  int n = High - Low + 1;                  // for, and copy n
  memcpy(Array,Source.Array,              // vector entries.
    n * sizeof(Scalar)); }
```

Since the **Source** index bounds are presumably consistent, an error signal after **SetUp** probably indicates that free memory is exhausted; copying is then impossible, so the function returns without completing its task. Library function **memcpy(Target,Source,n)** copies **n** bytes from **Source** to **Target**. Its prototype is in Library header file **Mem.H**. It's implemented with a single machine language instruction, so is very fast.

In designing the overloaded assignment operator, you have to decide what to do when source and target vectors have different index bounds. MSP regards this as normal; it simply makes the target an exact copy of the source. Its code is identical to that of the copy constructor, except that it first deletes the **Array** component of its principal argument, and it returns **This**. The deletion would be disastrous if the source were the same as the target (that is, **&Source == this**). In that case, which results from assigning a vector to itself, the routine terminates immediately, returning **This**. Its source code is on the optional diskette.

Another copy function is necessary if you ever want to manipulate parts of vectors — for example, in assembling a matrix for Gauss elimination or disassembling one after LU factorization. The source code documentation in Figure 3.3.3 explains the details. The function copies a specified piece of the source vector to the target vector starting at a specified index. It first ensures that the specified piece is consistent with the source vector bounds, then trims it, if necessary, so that the copy doesn't overflow the target bounds. The copy operation is performed by **Mem.H** function **memmove**, which is a little more elaborate (hence slower) than **memcpy**. **memmove** adjusts its operation if the source and target arrays overlap, which is possible in this case. **memcpy** takes no such precaution, and could yield an incorrect result.

Equality and Inequality

A software package that enables you to copy data structures and thus *make* them equal should also enable you to ascertain whether

```
Vector& Vector::Copy(int Lo,              // Copy  Source[SourceLo]
            const Vector& Source,         // .. Source[SourceHi]  to
                   int SourceLo,          // the target starting at
                   int SourceHi) {        // index  Lo .
    Lo        = max(Lo,Low);              // Ensure reasonable
    SourceLo = max(SourceLo,Source.Low);  // indices.
    SourceHi = min(SourceHi,Source.High);
    int n     = min(High-Lo ,SourceHi-SourceLo) + 1;
    memmove(&This[Lo],&Source[SourceLo],
      n * sizeof(Scalar));                // n = the number of
    return This; }                        // entries to move.
```

Figure 3.3.3 MSP function Copy(Lo,Source,SourceLo,SourceHi)

two structures *are* in fact equal. Deciding what *equal* means is sometimes a problem, since measurements in nature — even of the same phenomenon — are rarely exactly equal. There are vector algebra tools for dealing with that sort of problem. MSP provides overloaded equality and inequality operators == and != that test whether two vectors are *exactly* equal:

```
Boolean operator==(const Vector& V, const Vector& W);
Boolean operator!=(const Vector& V, const Vector& W);
```

Their code is straightforward; you'll find it on the accompanying diskette. Operator == checks first whether the V and W index bounds agree, and if so compares their entries. The inequality operator simply returns !(V == W). According to the criteria in Section 2.4, there's no good reason why these should be member functions, so they aren't.

Keyboard Input and Display Output

An important first step in numerical software development is to construct convenient and reliable keyboard input and display output routines for scalars, vectors, matrices, etc. If you try to make do with poorly conceived input/output, you'll find yourself mistaking bugs in that design for bugs in what really counts — the computational software.

The **cin** input stream provides appropriate keyboard input for scalars. The **Scalar** module includes function **Show** for standard display output. The latter is especially flexible: One of its arguments specifies the output format, and a default is provided. The default format displays the minimum precision necessary for debugging and for tabulating approximation errors. A second aspect of output flexibility is that **Show** uses DOS standard output, so results can be redirected to a file or a printer with some ease.

For vector input/output there are a few more considerations. Entering several scalars in succession on a keyboard is awkward: A prompt should be displayed before each one. Moreover, an output routine should provide for displaying a vector as a row or as a column. In the former case, the scalar format length is important, to control wrapping at the end of a screen row. In the latter, the routine should provide optional labels for the output vector entries, since the client program can't intervene to do so.

The **Vector** module includes a simple prompted keyboard input function:

```
Vector& Vector::KeyIn(              // Prompted key-
    char* Name) {                   // board input. A
    for (int i <= Low; i <= High; ++i) {   // prompt consists
        cout << Name << '['<< < i   // of the specified
            << "] : ";              // vector name and
        cin >> This[i]; }           // corresponding
    return This; }                  // entry index.
```

For example, if **V** is a vector with entries **V[0]**, ..., **V[n]**, then executing **V.KeyIn("V")** will display V[0] :   , with two spaces after the colon : , and await input of that vector entry. Users can backspace if necessary to edit the input, then accept it by pressing the <ENTER> key. DOS provides this rudimentary input editing facility via its standard input file and input stream **cin**. With care, you can redirect the input to come from a file. (*Caution*: Handling the end of the file sometimes presents a puzzle.) **KeyIn** returns **This** to permit member function concatenation.

The standard MSP **Vector** display output function is

```
Vector& Show(char* Format       = DefaultScalarFormat,
             Boolean RowFormat  = True,
             char* Name         = "") const;
```

It calls **Scalar** function **Show** to display each entry of its principal argument vector, and uses the **printf** string argument **Format** in the same way. **DefaultScalarFormat** is described in Section 3.2. With parameter **RowFormat** you can select row or column format; the former is the default. With row format, a specified **Name** is displayed at the left. Unless it's the empty string (the default), it will be followed automatically by the four character string " :   ". Row entries are separated by two blanks. With column format, every output line is prefixed with **Name**. Unless it's empty, it will be followed by the entry index enclosed by brackets and the string " :   ". Here are sample row and column outputs in the default scalar format, with the statements that produced them:

Row format	**Column format**

```
                                         Name&
    Name   ____.........__.........      index  ____.........
  Solution  :  1.2e+03    -4.5e-67       D[ 8]  :  -1.2
                                         D[ 9]  :  0.3
                                         D[10]  :  -4.0
Show("",True,"Solution");               Show("",False,"D");
```

As usual for functions of this sort, the source code for **Vector** function **Show** is uninstructively complicated. In fact, it took longer to write than any other function in this book. It's included in Appendix A.1 for your convenience.

Stream Input/Output

The last two logical functions of the **Vector** module are straightforward stream input/output operators intended for use with files. Their implementation requires a file format for a **Vector** object **V**. MSP uses a very simple record, reflecting the data structure definition: the **int** values **V.Low** and **V.High**, followed by the entries of **V.Array**, in order. For the individual items, MSP outputs ASCII numerals. It uses the minimum number of characters for the integers; for the scalars, it uses scientific notation with maximum, 15 significant digit, precision. All items are followed by newline characters.

These operators, like all C++ Version 2 stream input/output routines, overload the << and >> operators. They return their left-hand arguments, to permit concatenation. The declarations are shown in Figure 3.3.2; the source code is in Appendix A.2.

For production software, you should use various C++ Version 2 stream input/output features resources to handle exceptional situations like an unexpected end of file, improper format, media failure, etc. Numerical analysis software that seriously supports file input/output needs much more consideration of those problems than this book includes. That's really a systems programming task, however, and you should consider sources like Lippman's book (Reference [29, Appendix A]) that give it more attention.

3.4   Vector Algebra Functions

This section details the MSP functions that implement vector algebra. They constitute the mathematical part of module **Vector**. Its logical functions were discussed in the previous section. Individually, the vector algebra functions aren't very complicated or interesting. But their overall organization is important, because so much of this book's numerical analysis software, especially the matrix algebra functions, is based on them. The vector algebra functions are listed in Figure 3.4.1, which is part of the MSP **Vector.H** header file. Their source code constitutes the MSP file **VectorM.CPP** on the accompanying diskette. The source code for a few of the functions will be discussed in detail here. For others, which are generally very similar, you may consult the diskette.

A standard notation for vectors is introduced here. When no confusion with matrix notation arises, they will be denoted by upper case Latin italic letters, and their entries by the corresponding lower case letters, usually with subscripts. Sometimes this is emphasized by writing an equation like $V = [v_k]$. **Boldface** is used instead of italic in C++ expressions and in reproducing screen displays. Unless explicitly stated otherwise, the lower index bound is assumed to be 1.

In a matrix algebra context, vectors are generally regarded as column matrices, and denoted instead by lower case Greek italic letters. (See Section 3.6.)

Constructing Special Vectors

Module **Vector** includes member functions

```
MakeRandom( )
MakeZero( )
AllEntries(const Scalar& x)
MakeUnit(int i)
```

for constructing special vectors. **MakeRandom** initializes its principal argument to a pseudorandom vector by executing **This[k]** = **Random( )** for each appropriate index **k**. **AllEntries(k)** sets all entries **This[k]** of its principal argument equal to **x**. **MakeZero** makes its principal argument a zero vector by executing **AllEntries(0)**.

MakeUnit(k) initializes its principal argument as the **k**th unit vector, provided **k** lies within bounds. Otherwise, it merely sets the error signal. Here's its source code:

```
//**********************************************************************
//                 Vector.H  (Mathematical components)
//
//  Member functions of class  Vector :

Vector& MakeRandom();              // Set = a random vector.
Vector& AllEntries(               // Set all entries = x .
  const Scalar& x);
Vector& MakeZero();                // Set all entries = 0 .
Vector& MakeUnit(int k);           // Set = kth  unit vector.
Vector& operator                   // Add  V .
  +=(const Vector& V);
Vector& operator                   // Subtract  V .
  -=(const Vector& V);
Vector& operator                   // Multiply by scalar  t .
  *=(const Scalar& t);
Vector& operator                   // Cross multiply by the  3D
  %=(const Vector& V); };          // vector  V .

//**********************************************************************
//  Non-member functions:

double   MaxNorm   (const Vector& V);    // l_∞  norm.
double   Euclid    (const Vector& V);    // l_2  norm.
double   CityNorm  (const Vector& V);    // l_1  norm.
Vector   operator -(const Vector& V);    // Negative.
Vector   operator +(const Vector& V);    // No effect.
Vector   conj      (const Vector& V);    // Conjugate.
Vector   operator +(const Vector& V,     // Vector sum.
                    const Vector& W);
Vector   operator -(const Vector& V,     // Vector difference.
                    const Vector& W);
Vector   operator *(const Vector& V,     // Right scalar multiple.
                    const Scalar& t);
/*                                       // Left scalar multiple.
Vector   operator *(const Scalar& t,     // A Turbo C++ bug keeps
                    const Vector& V);    // this from compiling!
*/
Scalar   operator *(const Vector& V,     // Scalar product.
                    const Vector& W);
Scalar   operator |(const Vector& V,     // Inner product:
                    const Vector& W);    // V * conj(W) .
Vector   operator %(const Vector& V,     // 3D  cross product.
                    const Vector& W);
Scalar   Triple    (const Vector& U,     // 3D  triple product:
                    const Vector& V,     // U * (V % W) .
                    const Vector& W);
```

Figure 3.4.1 MSP header file Vector.H (mathematical components)

```
Vector& Vector::MakeUnit(int k) { // Set = the kth
  if ( Low <= k && k <= High) {   // unit vector.
      MakeZero( );
      This[k] = 1; }
    else                          // Do nothing if k
      SetError(IndexError);       // is out of bounds.
  return This; }
```

An alternative design would make these functions all constructors. However, that would involve overloading and complicated syntax conventions to specify or default the various parameters. It seemed more natural to separate the construction and initialization operations, and to implement the latter as member functions. They can be invoked quite naturally. For example, this code constructs unit vector $U = [0, 0, 1, 0, 0]$:

```
Vector U(5); U.MakeUnit(3);
```

These member functions all return their principal argument, so they permit concatenation. In the previous example, for instance, you could display U by substituting **U.MakeUnit(3).Show( )** for the second statement.

Vector Norms

One of the fundamental vector algebra operations is computing the magnitude of a vector V. There are several definitions of this concept. When it's used in a mathematical text, it's denoted by $\| V \|$, called the *norm* of V; somewhere in the text you'll find which type of norm, or magnitude, is intended. Here are the three norms of a vector $V = [v_1, \ldots, v_n]$ that are most common in numerical analysis:

$$max\ (l_\infty)\ \text{norm} = \| V \| = \max_{i=1}^{n} |v_i|$$

$$Euclidean\ (l_2)\ \text{norm} = \| V \| = \sqrt{\sum_{i=1}^{n} v_i^2}$$

$$city\ (l_1)\ \text{norm} = \| V \| = \sum_{i=1}^{n} |v_i|$$

The *max* norm of vector V is simply the largest of the norms $|v_k|$ of its scalar entries. (If v_k is real, $|v_k|$ is its absolute value.) This is certainly the easiest vector norm to compute, and the one most frequently used in numerical analysis. The *Euclidean* norm is defined by the formula commonly used in calculus and analytic geometry for the distance to a point V from the origin. Because the square root takes relatively long to compute, this norm is generally used only when it's necessary to maintain a theoretical connection with the

standard geometric distance concept. The least used of the three is
the *city* norm, the sum of the norms of the scalar entries. (Its name
was chosen because in a city with numbered east-west streets and
north-south avenues the city norm of vector V = [7, 11] is the number of blocks you walk from the origin to the intersection of 7th
Street and 11th Avenue.) It's listed here mainly because it's closely
related to a matrix norm discussed later in Section 3.6. The max,
Euclidean, and city norms also arise in higher mathematics in the
study of normed linear spaces, where they are called the l_∞, l_2, and l_1
norms. (See Reference [8, Section 7.1], for a discussion of vector
norms in general.)

These vector norms all satisfy three rules that underlie computations and theoretical considerations in this book:

1. $\|V\| = 0 \leftrightarrow V = 0$
2. $\|t\,V\| = |t|\ \|V\|$
3. $\|V + W\| \leq \|V\| + \|W\|$ (the *triangle* inequality).

The name of inequality (3) stems from the fact that if V and W are
points in a Cartesian coordinate system, and Δ is the triangle with
vertices O, V, and $-W$, then the Euclidean norm $\|V + W\|$ is the
length of the side of Δ opposite O.

The max, Euclidean, and city norms are implemented in MSP via
functions **MaxNorm**, **Euclid**, and **CityNorm**. They're not member
functions, because principal argument notation is inappropriate.
Here's the source code for **MaxNorm**:

```
double MaxNorm(const Vector& V) {        // l∞ norm.
   int Low = V.LowIndex( );
   int High = V.HighIndex( );            // Treat an empty
   if (Low > High) return 0;             // vector like 0 .
   double N = Norm(V[Low]);              // Compute the larg-
   for (int k = Low+1; k <= High; ++k)   // est of the norms
     N = fmax(N,Norm(V[k]));             // of the entries.
   return N; }
```

Function **Norm** is defined in the **Scalar** module: It's the absolute
value for a real scalar, and the complex norm for complex scalars.
Function **fmax** is defined in the **General** module for **double** arguments. Function **Euclid** merely returns the square root of the inner
product of **V** with itself; the product is discussed later in this section.
For function **CityNorm** you may consult the accompanying diskette.

Plus, Minus, and Conjugate

MSP overloads the singulary C++ operators **+** and **−** to implement the corresponding vector operations. In the latter case, it constructs a new vector **W** of the same dimension as the operand **V**, computes the entries, then returns **W**. It passes parameter **V** by reference, for efficiency in case **V** is large. It must return **W** by value, however, since **W** would disappear before the caller could use a returned address. Here's the source code for operator −:

```
Vector operator-(const Vector& V) {        // Negation:
   int Low = V.LowIndex( );                 // overload singu-
   int High = V.HighIndex( );               // lary - .
   Vector W(High,Low);                      // Construct the
   for (int k = Low; k <= High; ++k)        // negative, entry
      W[k] = -V[k];                         // by entry, and
   return W; }                              // return it.
```

Operator **+** is simpler: It just returns its argument **V**. There was no reason to make operator **+** or **−** a member function.

MSP uses a similar technique to implement the complex conjugation operation on vectors: It overloads Library function **conj** to take a **Vector** parameter V. The source code is very similar to that of operator −: Instead of computing the negative of each **V** entry, it computes the conjugate.

Addition and Subtraction

Implementing vector addition requires a design decision: What should you do if the addends' index limits disagree? In some cases you might regard this as an error. But when you use vectors to represent polynomials, you'll often want to add vectors with different upper limits: They just stand for polynomials of different degree. In other cases — for example, initial segments of Laurent series — you might want to allow different lower limits, too. It seems reasonable, therefore, not to signal an error when index limits differ, but to pad the vectors with zeros to make their limits match. For example, consider the sum $U = [u_k]$ of these two vectors $V = [v_k]$ and $W = [w_k]$ whose lower and upper index limits both differ:

k:	−2	−1	0	1	2
v_k:	6	8	1	1	
w_k:		2	7	4	5
u_k:	6	10	8	5	5

```
Vector operator+(const Vector& V,           // Vector addition:
                 const Vector& W) {         // overload binary
   int J = V.LowIndex();                    // + . Regard each
   int K = W.LowIndex();                    // addend as padded
   int i = min(J,K);                        // with zeros, if
   int M = V.HighIndex();                   // necessary, so
   int N = W.HighIndex();                   // that they begin
   int L = min(M,N);                        // and end with the
   Vector Sum(max(M,N),i);                  // same indices.
   if (GetError()) return Sum;              // If memory is ex-
   for (; i <  J; ++i) Sum[i] = W[i];       // hausted, return
   for (; i <  K; ++i) Sum[i] = V[i];       // the sum empty.
   for (; i <= L; ++i) Sum[i] = V[i] + W[i]; // Otherwise, com-
   for (; i <= M; ++i) Sum[i] = V[i];       // pute it, entry
   for (; i <= N; ++i) Sum[i] = W[i];       // by entry, and
   return Sum; }                            // return it.
```

Figure 3.4.2 MSP vector addition operator

MSP implements this operation by overloading the C++ binary operator **+**. The source code is shown in Figure 3.4.2. It just constructs a new vector **Sum** of the appropriate dimension, computes its entries, and returns it. For efficiency, the addends are passed by reference. **Sum** must be returned by value, however, because it would disappear before the caller could use a returned address. If free memory is exhausted, this operator signals an error and returns an empty vector.

Vector subtraction could be implemented like vector addition. However, it seems best to deal with the upper bound problem only once. Therefore, the MSP vector subtraction operator

```
Vector operator-(const Vector &V, const Vector& W)
```

merely computes and returns V + (–W).

There was no reason to make vector addition or subtraction a member function.

Scalar Multiplication

There's no complication at all in the MSP implementation of its right scalar multiplication operator,

```
Vector operator*(const Vector& V, const Scalar& t) .
```

The source code is structured like that of the singulary – operation already discussed: It just constructs a vector **P** of the same dimension as **V**, computes its entries $P[k] = V[k]*t$, and returns **P**. The *left* scalar multiplication operator

```
Vector operator*(const Scalar& t, const Vector& V) ,
```

which is much more commonly used in mathematics, should be similar. However, at the time this paragraph was written, a bug in Turbo C++ prevented compilation of *any* operator with this declaration. Borland International, Inc. had acknowledged the bug, but hadn't yet provided a correction. Thus, all MSP programs requiring scalar multiplication use the right-hand version. This contravenes standard mathematical notation, but not very seriously.

Scalar and Inner Products

There are two common methods for multiplying two vectors $V = [v_1, ..., v_n]$ and $W = [w_1, ..., w_n]$ to get a product p that is a scalar. The simplest method yields a product, called the *scalar* product, of the same scalar type as the vector entries:

$$p = V * W = \sum_{i=1}^{n} v_i w_i \ .$$

MSP also implements this operation by overloading *:

```
Scalar operator*(const Vector& V, const Vector& W) .
```

If the index bounds agree, this operator computes and returns the product. If not, it sets the error flag and leaves the return value undefined. The source code is straightforward; you'll find it on the accompanying diskette.

The scalar product satisfies several *linearity* rules often used in numerical analysis computations: for all vectors V, W, X, and scalars t,

1. $V * W = W * V$
2. $V * (W + X) = V * W + V * X$
3. $(t V) * W = t (W * V)$
4. $0 * V = 0.$

Many other similar rules can be derived from these.

The second kind of product of two vectors is the *inner* product

$$V \mid W = V * \overline{W} \ .$$

This is used in place of the scalar product in many aspects of complex linear algebra, especially when there's a theoretical connection with the notion of distance. The inner product satisfies some *semilinearity* rules somewhat like those for the scalar product: for all vectors V, W, X, and scalars t,

1. $V \mid W = \overline{W \mid V}$
2. $V \mid (W + X) = V \mid W + V \mid X$
3. $(tV) \mid W = t(V \mid W)$
4. $V \mid (Wt) = (V \mid W)\bar{t}$
5. $0 \mid V = 0$
6. $V \mid V \geq 0$
7. $V \mid V = 0 \leftrightarrow V = 0$

MSP implements the inner product by overloading the C++ *inclusive or* operator $|$:

```
Scalar operator|(const Vector& V, const Vector& W) .
```

This function simply returns $V * conj(W)$.

The Euclidean norm, described earlier, is closely related to the inner product. In fact, function **Euclid** simply returns $sqrt(V \mid V)$.

Cross and Triple Products

Two further kinds of products are commonly used in three-dimensional vector algebra: the *cross product* $U \% V$ and *triple product* $U * (V \% W)$ of vectors U, V, and W. If the vector indices range from 1 to 3, then the cross product is a vector $P = [p_1, p_2, p_3]$ defined by equations

$$p_1 = v_2 w_3 - v_3 w_2$$
$$p_2 = v_3 w_1 - v_1 w_3$$
$$p_3 = v_1 w_2 - v_2 w_1.$$

You'll find various notations for these products in the literature — none is standard. The use of $\%$ here is bizarre: It seemed the only alternative for MSP. In vector calculus texts you can find a number of computational rules governing these products — for example, the triple product can also be expressed as the determinant of the matrix consisting of the three columns U, V, and W. (See Reference [45, Chapter 13].)

MSP implements the cross product by overloading C++ operator %:

```
Vector operator%(const Vector& V, const Vector& W) .
```

This function returns the vector computed as described above if the indices range from 1 to 3, or an analogous one if they range from 0 to 2. In other cases, it sets the error signal and leaves the return value undefined. The triple product function

```
Scalar Triple(const Vector& U, const Vector& V, const Vector& W)
```

simply returns U * (V % W). You'll find the source code for these functions on the accompanying diskette.

Replacement Operators

MSP implements four vector algebra replacement operators: **+=**, **-=**, **%=**, and ***=**. If V and W are vectors, then V **+=** W adds W to V, V **-=** W subtracts W from V, and V **%=** W cross multiplies V by W. If **t** is a scalar, then V ***=** **t** replaces V by V*t. C++ requires that these replacement operators be implemented with member functions that return references to their principal arguments. Here's the source code for **+=**:

```
Vector& Vector::operator+=(const Vector& V) {
   return This = This + V; }
```

The other functions are similar.

3.5 Handling Matrix Objects

The MSP **Matrix** class implements an abstract data type for matrix algebra. It's based on the **Vector** class, and provides for

• matrices with varying starting indices,
• matrices of varying dimensions,
• real or complex matrices,
• bounds checking.

The first provision means, for instance, that you can use matrices

$$A = \begin{bmatrix} a_{00} & a_{01} & \cdots \\ a_{10} & a_{11} & \cdots \\ \vdots & \vdots & \end{bmatrix} \qquad B = \begin{bmatrix} b_{11} & b_{12} & \cdots \\ b_{21} & b_{22} & \cdots \\ \vdots & \vdots & \end{bmatrix}$$

in the same program. However, the rows and columns of a given matrix must start with the same index, so that the diagonal entries have equal row and column indices. Although you can use matrices with various index bounds at will, you cannot use both real and complex matrices in the same program. The **Matrix** class provides an intermediate level of bounds checking: most matrix operations check their operands for consistency of lower and upper index bounds. However, to avoid loss of speed, in individual references to entries a_{ij} of matrix A, index j is not checked against the column index bounds for A. Most client program references to entries a_{ij} are found, nevertheless, in the algorithms for operations which do check for overall consistency.

MSP functions that manipulate matrices are classified as *logical* or *mathematical*. The logical matrix functions, described in Section 3.5, almost exactly parallel the logical vector functions described earlier in Section 3.3. The mathematical functions implement matrix algebra; they're discussed in Section 3.6.

Like other MSP modules, this one has a header file **Matrix.H**. The source code is so long, however, that it was split into two files, **MatrixL.CPP** and **MatrixM.CPP**, for logical and mathematical functions. You'll find these files on the accompanying diskette. The logical part of the header file is shown in Figures 3.5.1 and 3.5.2. Parts of **MatrixL.CPP** are displayed later in this section. The mathematical part of the header file, and its corresponding source code, are discussed in Section 3.6.

The Matrix Data Structure

The **Matrix** module is designed to handle matrices of varying dimensions. To facilitate ascertaining the lower and upper row and column index bounds, they are data components of the class. Moreover, it was decided that a matrix should be stored as an array of vectors, so that the extensive MSP vector handling features could be used for matrices, too. Since the size of this array is indeterminate, it must be stored in free memory. In order to enforce the intermediate level of bounds checking described earlier, the index bounds and array must be private components, and member functions must be pro-

```
//*****************************************************************
//              Matrix.H  (Logical components, Part 1)

#ifndef Matrix_H
#define Matrix_H

#include "Vector.H"

class Matrix {                          // The private parts of
                                        // class  Matrix  are its
   private:                             // data components.
      int    Low;                       // Index bounds for the
      int    HighRow;                   // matrix entries.
      int    HighCol;
      Vector* Row;                      // Row vector storage.

   public:

      //*********************************************************
      //  Selectors

      int LowIndex()      const;        // Selectors for the index
      int HighRowIndex()  const;        // bounds.
      int HighColIndex()  const;
      Vector& operator[](int i) const;  // Matrix row selector:
                                        // overloaded  [] .
      Vector  Col(int j) const;         // Column selector.

      //*********************************************************
      //  Constructors and destructor

      Matrix();                         // Default constructor.
      Matrix& SetUp(int HiRow,          // Set the index bounds
                    int HiCol,          // and allocate storage.
                    int Lo = 1);
      Matrix(int HiRow,                 // Construct a matrix with
             int HiCol,                 // specified index bounds.
             int Lo = 1);
      ~Matrix();                        // Destructor.

      //*********************************************************
      //  Converters to and from type  Vector

      Matrix(const Vector& V);          // Vector to row matrix.
      operator Vector();                // Row, column to vector.
```

Figure 3.5.1 MSP header file Matrix.H (logical components, Part 1)

vided to manipulate them as needed. In designing the class, no other
private components proved necessary. Thus, the private part of class
Matrix is

```
   private:
      int    Low;           // Index bounds for the
      int    HighRow;       // matrix entries.
      int    HighCol;
      Vector* Row;          // Row vector storage.
```

```
//**********************************************************************
//              Matrix.H  (Logical components, Part 2)

    //******************************************************************
    //  Copiers and assignment

    Matrix(const Matrix& Source);        // Copy constructor.
    Matrix& operator                     // Assignment.
      =(const Matrix& Source);
    Matrix& Copy(int      LoRow,         // Copy the source matrix
                 int      LoCol,         // rectangle with indicat-
          const Matrix&   Source,        // ed corner indices to
                 int      SourceLoRow,   // the target matrix so
                 int      SourceLoCol,   // that its  Lo  corner
                 int      SourceHiRow,   // falls at target posi-
                 int      SourceHiCol);  // tion  (LoRow,LoCol) .

    //******************************************************************
    //  Input/output
                                         // Prompted keyboard
    Matrix& KeyIn(char* Name);           // input.
    Matrix& Show(
      char* Format = DefaultScalarFormat,  // Standard display
      char* Name   = "") const;          // output.
    friend istream& operator
      >>(istream& Source, Matrix& Target);  // Stream input.

    //******************************************************************
    //  Here are declared several member functions that implement
    //  parts of matrix algebra.  They are described in §3.6.

    };                  // End of the definition of class  Matrix .

//**********************************************************************
//  Related non-member logical functions

Matrix     operator~ (const Vector& V);   // Vector to column.
Boolean    operator==(const Matrix& A,    // Equality.
                      const Matrix& B);
Boolean    operator!=(const Matrix& A,    // Inequality.
                      const Matrix& B);
istream&   operator>>(istream& Source,    // Stream input:  a
                      Matrix& Target);    // friend.
ostream&   operator<<(    ostream& Target, // Stream output.
                      const Matrix& Source);

//**********************************************************************
//  Here are found most declarations of matrix algebra functions.
//  They are described in  §3.6.

#endif
```

Figure 3.5.2 MSP header file Matrix.H (logical components, Part 2)

The **Row** component is *not* the array itself, but merely a *pointer* to its first entry in free memory. If m = **HighRow** − **Low** + 1, then vectors **Row[0]**, ..., **Row[m]** represent the rows of the matrix. A row's memory image consists of its lower and upper index bounds, and a pointer to another array in free memory that stores its **Scalar** entries. Duplicating the index bounds **Low** and **HighRow** in each row vector is an inefficient use of memory. In view of the overall goal of making numerical analysis programs easier to read, however, this was judged an acceptable cost.

MSP uses a standard representation for *empty* matrices: **Low** = **0**, **HighRow** = **HighCol** = **–1**, and **Row** = **NULL**.

It's sometimes more convenient mathematically to regard a matrix as an array of *column* vectors instead of row vectors. Unfortunately, in defining the structure, you have to choose one or the other, and C++ array indexing conventions make the row vector array, chosen for MSP, easier and more efficient to program. As you'll see, operations with column vectors are consequently somewhat clumsy and inefficient.

An alternative MSP design strategy would make *matrices* basic, rather than vectors. The matrix data structure would consist of the three index bounds and a pointer to a two dimensional array of scalars in free memory. Vectors could be defined and manipulated as matrices with a single row or a single column, as appropriate for an application. That would save storage space, and some of the code in the **Vector** module could be eliminated. The cost is the disappearance of the data structure corresponding to a *row of a matrix*. The row structures wouldn't be available in that format in the matrix structure, and would have to be created whenever an application needed them.

According to the overview given in Sections 2.3–2.6, the functions necessary for logical manipulation of matrices include

- *selectors*, to provide limited access to the data components;
- *constructors*, to initialize the index bounds and the row array pointer, and — usually — to set up the rows in free memory;
- a *destructor*, to deallocate the row vectors when a matrix is deleted or passes out of scope;
- *converters*, to convert row and column matrices to and from vector format;
- a *copy constructor*, for the compiler to use when temporary copies are needed for function calls;
- an overloaded *assignment* operator, to copy the row vectors during assignment;
- a general *copier*, for manipulating pieces of matrices;
- overloaded *equality* and *inequality* operators, to compare the index bounds and row vectors;
- *keyboard input* and *display output* functions;
- *stream input/output* functions.

These features are described in detail in the rest of this section. Sometimes, source code is given here in the text. For the display output and stream input/output functions, you're referred to Appendix A. The code for the remaining functions is generally described with just a few words, because they're trivial or repetitive. You'll find it on the accompanying diskette.

Selectors

Selectors are public member functions that provide limited access to private data components. For instance, the **Matrix** class provides functions **LowIndex**, **HighRowIndex**, and **HighColIndex** to return the **Low**, **HighRow**, and **HighCol** components.

Since a matrix' row vectors are stored in a private array in free memory, they can't be accessed directly by the subscript operator **[ ]**. Instead, this must be overloaded so that if **A** is a **Matrix** object and **i** an **int** value within the **A** row index bounds, then **A[i]** is a reference to the appropriate **Row** entry in free memory. Since the **A** and **Row** indices range over different intervals, starting with **Low** and zero, respectively, the appropriate **Row** entry has index **i** − **Low**. Here's the source code:

```
Vector& Matrix::operator[ ](int i)    // Row selector:
    const {                           // overload [ ] .
  int iOld = i;                       // Ensure i is in
  i = min(max(Low,i),HighRow);        // bounds.
  if (i != iOld)                      // Signal if it wasn't.
    SetError(IndexError);             // Adjust for lower
  return Row[i-Low]; }                // index c 0 .
```

This function sets the error signal if row index **i** is out of bounds. In that error situation, it must return a reference to *some* row, so it selects the nearest: the first or last, as appropriate. It returns a null pointer if the matrix is empty.

The matrix row selector lets you use the standard C++ double subscripting technique to access matrix entries: **A[i][j]** is the **j**th entry of the **i**th row of **A**, provided **i** and **j** fall within bounds.

Unfortunately, it's impossible to use in C++ the more conventional double subscripting notation **A[i,j]**. The reason is that the *comma* is a C++ operator: It is used in multivariable function invocations. Invoking a function **void f(int i, int j)**, for example, applies the comma to operands **i** and **j**. Interpreting an operator, the C++

compiler looks no farther than the type of its operands, so it can't distinguish a comma in **A[i,j]** from one in a function invocation. It would misinterpret the former. If you overloaded the comma to implement conventional double subscript notation, you'd disable the use of commas in function calls.

The matrix *column selector* is a member function **Col** with one parameter, the column index. Thus, the vector **A.Col(j)** is the jth column of matrix **A**, provided **j** falls within bounds. In an error situation, **Col** behaves like the row selector: It sets the error signal and returns the nearest column — first or last — as appropriate. Here's the source code. It's less efficient than the row selector, since it must build a new vector:

```
Vector Matrix::Col(int j) const {        // Column selector.
  int jold = j;                          // Ensure j is
  j = min(max(Low,j),HighCol);           // in bounds.
  if (j != jold)                         // Signal if it
    SetError(IndexError);                // wasn't.
  Vector V(HighRow,Low);                 // Allocate space
  for (int i = Low; i <= HighRow; ++i)   // for the vector
    V[i] = This[i][j];                   // and set each
  return V ; }                           // entry.
```

Constructors

The **Matrix** class needs a *default constructor* that the compiler will call *n* times whenever you declare an array of *n* matrices. It needn't do much; the function just initializes an empty matrix by setting **Low = 0, HighRow = HighCol = –1**, and **Row = NULL**.

When you declare a matrix, however, you usually want to set up specific index bounds and allocate the storage arrays in free memory. Code for this is placed in a separate public function **SetUp** because it's invoked in several different situations. It's shown in Figure 3.5.3. **SetUp** first allocates space for the row vectors by invoking the default **Vector** constructor. That initializes them as empty rows. Then **SetUp** calls its counterpart function **Vector::SetUp** to set the row index limits properly and allocate free memory storage for the matrix entries. An error is signalled, and the process terminated, if the **new** operator or **Vector::SetUp** reports that free memory is exhausted.

Client programs use the constructor

```
Matrix(int HiRow, int HiCol, int Lo = 1)
```

```
Matrix& Matrix::SetUp(int HiRow,        // Set the index bounds
                      int HiCol,        // and allocate storage.
                      int Lo) {
   Low  = Lo;  HighRow = HiRow;  HighCol = HiCol;
   int m = HighRow - Low + 1;
   Row  = new Vector[m];                 // Allocate  m  row
   if (m > 0 && Row == NULL)             // vectors.
      SetError(OutOfMemory);
   for (int i = Low;                     // For each row, set
        i <= HighRow && !GetError(); ++i) // the index bounds
      This[i].SetUp(HighCol,Low);        // and allocate
   return This; }                        // storage.
```

Figure 3.5.3 MSP function Matrix::SetUp

most often. It merely calls **SetUp(HiRow,HighCol,Lo)** to set up the index bounds and allocate the memory. For example, you may invoke it with the last parameter defaulted by declaring **Matrix A(2,3)** to set up matrix **A** as shown on the left:

$$A = \begin{bmatrix} a_{11} & a_{12} & a_{13} \\ a_{21} & a_{22} & a_{23} \end{bmatrix} \quad B = \begin{bmatrix} b_{00} & b_{01} & b_{02} \\ b_{10} & b_{11} & b_{12} \end{bmatrix}$$

Alternatively, you can include the last parameter explicitly: Declaring **Matrix B(1,2,0)** sets up a matrix **B** as shown on the right.

To construct an array of **k** matrices (possibly of varying dimensions), execute the default constructor **k** times by declaring **Matrix A[k]**, then call **SetUp k** times to set the index bounds and allocate the memory. The matrices are then **A[0]**, ..., **A[k-1]**, and — for example — **A[0][1][1]** is top left entry of **A[0]**.

Destructors

When you construct a local **Matrix** object A by declaring **Matrix A**, the four components **A.Low**, **A.HighRow**, **A.HighCol**, and **A.Row** are stored on the stack. The last is the address of an array of vectors in free memory. Each of these vectors, in turn, includes a pointer to another array — of scalars — in free memory. When control passes out of the block where **A** was declared, the first four components are destroyed. But you must provide a *destructor* to release the free memory areas. The compiler will arrange to execute the destructor at the proper time. The source code is simple:

```
Matrix::~Matrix( ) { delete [HighRow-Low+1] Row; }
```

This deletes the entire array of **HighRow – Low + 1** = m row vectors; during that process, it invokes the class **Vector** destructor m times implicitly to release the corresponding scalar arrays.

Converters

Matrix algebra is often applied to a vector by regarding it as a matrix with a single row or column. Thus, MSP should include functions to convert a vector to a row or column matrix and back again. The first of these is implemented simply as a **Matrix** constructor:

```
Matrix::Matrix(const Vector& V) {      // Convert vector
  int Lo = V.LowIndex( );              // V to a matrix
  int Hi = V.HighIndex( );             // with one row.
  SetUp(Lo,Hi,Lo);
  This[Lo] = V; }
```

For converting a vector to a column matrix, however, it seemed appropriate to overload the ~ operator, which is used in another context to represent transposition. Thus, if **V** is a vector with lower index bound 1, then ~V is a column matrix, and (~V)[i,1] = V[i] for each index i. The parentheses are necessary because operator ~ has lower precedence than [ ]. Here's the source code:

```
Matrix operator~(const Vector& V) {    // Convert a vector
  int Lo = V.LowIndex( );              // to a column.
  int Hi = V.HighIndex( );             // Allocate storage
  Matrix C(Hi,Lo,Lo);                  // for one column.
  for (int i = Lo; i <= Hi; ++i)       // Insert its
    C[i][Lo] = V[i];                   // entries, one
  return C; }                          // by one.
```

This operator is not a member function.

To convert a row or column matrix to a vector, MSP provides the conversion operator **Matrix::Vector( )** :

```
Matrix::operator Vector( ) {    // Convert a row or column
  if (HighCol = = Low)          // matrix to a vector. If
    return Col(Low);            // there's only one column,
  else {                        // return that. Otherwise,
  if (HighRow != Low)           // return the first row,
    SetError(IndexError);       // but signal an error if
  return This[Low]; }}          // there's more than one.
```

Copiers and Assignment

The copy constructor and overloaded assignment operator for class **Matrix** are much like their **Vector** counterparts. Here's the copy constructor source code:

```
Matrix::Matrix(const Matrix& Source) {      // Copy
   SetUp(Source.HighRowIndex( ),            // constructor.
      Source.HighColIndex( ),               // Set the index
      Source.LowIndex( ));                  // bounds, allo-
   for (int i = Low; i <= HighRow; ++i)     // cate storage.
      This[i] = Source[i]; }                // Copy rows.
```

Since the **Source** index bounds are presumably consistent, an error signal after **SetUp** would probably indicate that free memory is exhausted. **SetUp** would initialize **This** as the empty matrix, and the attempted assignment to **This[i]** would trigger the C++ **Null pointer assignment** error message.

The overloaded assignment operator makes the target an exact copy of the source. Its code is identical to that of the copy constructor, except that it first executes **delete [HighRow–Low+1] Row** to destroy the old target value, and it returns **This**. The deletion would be disastrous if the source were the same as the target (**&Source == this** — assigning a matrix to itself). In that case the routine should terminate immediately, just returning **This**.

Another copy function is necessary for manipulating parts of matrices — for example, to assemble a matrix for Gauss elimination or disassemble one after LU factorization. The source code documentation in Figure 3.5.4 explains the details. The function copies a specified piece of the source matrix to the target matrix starting at a given location. It first ensures that the specified piece is consistent with the source matrix bounds, then trims it, if necessary, so that the copy doesn't overflow the target bounds. The copy operation is performed by repeated application of the analogous **Vector** function.

Equality and Inequality

As in the **Vector** module, MSP provides overloaded equality and inequality operators == and != that test whether two matrices are *exactly* equal:

```
Boolean operator==(const Matrix& A, const Matrix& B);
Boolean operator!=(const Matrix& A, const Matrix& B);
```

```
Matrix& Matrix::Copy(int      TargetLoRow,    // Copy the source
               int      TargetLoCol,    // matrix, between
         const Matrix& Source,          // indicated corners,
               int      SourceLoRow,    // to the target
               int      SourceLoCol,    // matrix:  the Lo
               int      SourceHiRow,    // corner falls at
               int      SourceHiCol) {  // (LoRow,LoCol) .
  TargetLoRow = max(TargetLoRow,Low);
  TargetLoCol = max(TargetLoCol,Low);                  // Ensure
  SourceLoRow = max(SourceLoRow,Source.Low);           // reason-
  SourceLoCol = max(SourceLoCol,Source.Low);           // able
  SourceHiRow = min(SourceHiRow,Source.HighRow);       // indices.
  SourceHiCol = min(SourceHiCol,Source.HighCol);
  int iS = SourceLoRow;
  int iT = TargetLoRow;
  while (iS <= SourceHiRow && iT <= HighRow) {          // Copy
     This[iT].Copy(TargetLoCol,Source[iS],             // each
       SourceLoCol,SourceHiCol);                        // row.
     ++iS;   ++iT; }
  return This; }
```

Figure 3.5.4 MSP function Matrix::Copy

Their code is straightforward; you'll find it on the accompanying diskette. Operator **==** checks first whether the **A** and **B** index bounds agree, and if so compares their entries. The inequality operator simply returns !(**A == B**). These are not member functions.

Keyboard Input and Display Output

The **Matrix** module includes a simple keyboard input member function **Matrix& KeyIn(char* Name)**. If you've declared **Matrix A(2,2)**, then executing **A.KeyIn("A")** prompts the user for input:

```
i  j  A[i, j]
1  1  ...
1  2  ...
2  1  ...
2  2  ...
```

The user, of course, supplies input where the dots appear here. There's room for one- or two-digit indices **i** and **j**. Here's the source code:

```
Matrix& Matrix::KeyIn(                    // Keyboard
    char* Name) {                         // input,
  cout << " i j " < Name < "[i, j]";      // prompted
  for (int i = Low; i <= HighRow; ++i) {  // by matrix
    cout << endl;                         // name.
```

```
    for (int j = Low; j <= HighCol; ++j) {      // Enter each
        cout << setw(2) << i << setw(3) << j     // input on a
            << " ";                              // new line.
        cin >> This[i][j]; }}                    // Skip be-
    return This; }                               // tween rows.
```

Users can backspace to edit the input, then accept it by pressing the
<ENTER> key. With care, you can redirect the input to come from a
file. (*Caution*: Handling the end of the file sometimes presents a puzzle.)

The standard MSP **Matrix** display output function is

```
Matrix& Show(char* Format = DefaultScalarFormat,
             char* Name = "") const;
```

It calls **Vector** function **Show** to display each row of its principal
argument matrix, and uses the **printf** string argument **Format** in
the same way. The default scalar format was described in Section
3.2. The specified **Name** is displayed before each row, at the left
margin. Unless it's the empty string (the default), it's followed
automatically by the row index, enclosed by brackets [ ], then the
four characters " : ". Row entries are separated by two blanks. If
you've declared **Matrix** A(2,3), for example, then **A.Show(" ","A")**
might produce output like this:

```
----...-.------------.----------..---------
A[1] :     3.0       -0.3        4.7
A[2] :    -6.7        7.6       -5.1
```

The dots and dashes are not part of the output; they just help you
ascertain the spacing specified by the **DefaultScalarFormat** code.
Show will align the row indices, using the minimum possible space.
Its source code is included in Appendix A.1 for your convenience.

Stream Input/Output

The last two logical functions of the **Matrix** module are stream
input/output operators intended for use with files. Their implementation
requires a file format for a **Matrix** object A. MSP uses a record
that reflects the data structure definition: the **int** values A.**Low**,
A.**HighRow**, and A.**HighCol**, followed by the vectors A[Low] to
A[HighRow], in order. Each vector is stored in the format described
in Section 3.3: the **int** values of its index bounds **Low** and **High**,

followed by its array of **Scalar** values. For the individual items, MSP outputs ASCII numerals. It uses the minimum number of characters for the integers; for the scalars, it uses scientific notation with maximum, 15 significant digit, precision. All items are followed by newline characters.

These operators, like the analogous **Vector** stream input/output routines, overload the << and >> operators. They return their left-hand arguments, to permit concatenation. The declarations are shown in Figure 3.5.2; the source code is in Appendix A.2.

3.6   Matrix Algebra Functions

This section details the MSP functions that implement matrix algebra. They constitute the mathematical part of module **Matrix**. Its logical functions were discussed in the previous section. Individually, the matrix algebra functions aren't very complicated or interesting. But their overall organization is important, because so much of this book's numerical analysis software is based on them. The matrix algebra functions are listed in Figure 3.6.1, which is part of the MSP **Matrix.H** header file. Their source code constitutes the MSP file **MatrixM.CPP** on the accompanying diskette. The source code for a few of the functions will be discussed in detail here. For others, which are generally very similar, you may consult the diskette.

A standard notation for matrices is introduced here. They will be denoted by upper case Latin letters, and their entries by the corresponding lower case letters, usually with subscripts. Sometimes this is emphasized by writing an equation like $A = [a_{ij}]$. **Boldface** is used instead of *italic* in C++ expressions. Unless explicitly stated otherwise, the lower row and column index bound is assumed to be 1.

When vectors are regarded as *column* matrices, they're denoted by lower case Greek letters, and their entries by the corresponding lower case Latin letters. Sometimes this is emphasized by writing an equation like $\xi = [x_k]$. The transposition sign ~ is used to indicate the corresponding row matrix: $\xi^{\sim}$.

Constructing Special Matrices

The **Matrix** module includes member functions

```
MakeRandom( )
MakeZero( )
AllEntries(const Scalar& x)
MakeIdentity( )
```

```
//*****************************************************************
//                Matrix.H  (Mathematical components)
//
// Member functions of class  Matrix :

    Matrix& MakeRandom();              // Set  = a random matrix.
    Matrix& AllEntries(               // Set all entries  = x .
       const Scalar& x);
    Matrix& MakeZero();               // Set all entries  = 0 .
    Matrix& MakeIdentity();           // Set  = identity matrix.
    Matrix& operator                  // Add  A .
·      +=(const Matrix& A);
    Matrix& operator                  // Subtract  A .
       -=(const Matrix& A);
    Matrix& operator                  // Multiply by scalar  t .
       *=(const Scalar& t);
    Matrix& operator                  // Postmultiply by
       *=(const Matrix& A);  };       // matrix  A .

//*****************************************************************
// Non-member functions

double   RowNorm    (const Matrix& A);     // Row norm.
double   ColNorm    (const Matrix& A);     // Column norm.
Matrix   operator -(const Matrix& A);      // Negative.
Matrix   operator +(const Matrix& A);      // No effect.
Matrix   conj       (const Matrix& A);     // Conjugate.
Matrix   operator ~(const Matrix& A);      // Transpose.
Matrix   operator !(const Matrix& A);      // Conjugate transpose.
Matrix   operator +(const Matrix& A,       // Matrix sum.
                    const Matrix& B);
Matrix   operator -(const Matrix& A,       // Matrix difference.
                    const Matrix& B);
Scalar   Trace      (const Matrix& A);     // Trace.
Matrix   operator *(const Matrix& A,       // Right scalar
                    const Scalar& t);      // multiple.
/*
Matrix   operator *(const Scalar& t,       // Left scalar multiple.
                    const Matrix& A);      // A Turbo C++ bug keeps
*/                                         // this from compiling!
Vector   operator *(const Vector& V,
                    const Matrix& B);      // Row vector * matrix.
Matrix   operator *(const Matrix& A,       // Matrix * matrix.
                    const Matrix& B);
Vector   operator *(const Matrix& A,       // Matrix * column
                    const Vector& W);      // vector.
Vector& operator*=(      Vector& V,        // Postmultiply a vector
                    const Matrix& B);      // by a matrix.
```

Figure 3.6.1 MSP header file Matrix.H (mathematical components)

for constructing special matrices. **MakeRandom** initializes its principal argument to a pseudorandom matrix by executing **This[i].MakeRandom( )** (the corresponding **Vector** function) for each row index **i**. In the same way, **AllEntries** sets all entries of its principal argument equal to the **Scalar** value **x**. **MakeZero** makes its principal argument a zero matrix by executing **AllEntries(0)**.

MakeIdentity initializes its principal argument as the identity matrix of the same dimensions, by executing **This[i].MakeUnit(i)**

for each row index **i**. This produces the familiar square identity matrices, as well as rectangular ones, which are also useful. For example, if you've declared **Matrix I(2,3)**, then executing **I.MakeIdentity( )** sets

$$I = \begin{bmatrix} 1 & 0 & 0 \\ 0 & 1 & 0 \end{bmatrix} .$$

An alternative design would make these functions all constructors. However, as in the **Vector** module, that would involve overloading and complicated syntax conventions to specify or default the various parameters. It seemed more natural to separate the construction and initialization operations, and to implement the latter as member functions. These member functions all return their principal argument, so they permit concatenation.

Matrix Norms

Corresponding to each vector norm is a *matrix norm*: a measure $\| A \|$ of the magnitude of a matrix A. This concept is defined by the equation

$$\| A \| = \inf_{\xi \neq 0} \frac{\| A \xi \|}{\| \xi \|} .$$

The right-hand side stands for the *infimum*, or greatest lower bound, taken over all nonzero vectors ξ.

In general, matrix norms are difficult to compute. They're the subject of an extensive theory. However, those corresponding to the l_∞ and l_1 vector norms — the max and city norms — are easy to compute. They're called the *row* and *column norms* of A. Short arguments show that for an $m \times n$ matrix A,

$$\text{Row norm } \| A \| = \max_{i=1}^{m} \sum_{j=1}^{n} | a_{ij} |$$

$$\text{Column norm } \| A \| = \max_{j=1}^{n} \sum_{i=1}^{m} | a_{ij} | .$$

Thus, the row norm of a matrix A is the maximum city norm of its rows, and the column norm is the maximum city norm of its columns. The connection between these corresponding vector and matrix norms is even closer:

- if A is a column matrix, then its row norm is the max norm of the corresponding vector;
- if A is a row matrix, then its row norm is the city norm of the corresponding vector.

For the column norm, you must reverse these two statements. Because the row and column norms are so similar, there's rarely a need for both. Therefore, for the remainder of this book, the notation $\|A\|$ *stands for the row norm of matrix A*. For a vector ξ (regarded as a column matrix) $\|\xi\|$ automatically indicates the max norm, and $\|\xi^-\|$ denotes the city norm of the corresponding row vector.

The row norm satisfies four rules that underlie computations and theoretical considerations in this book:

1. $\|A\| = 0 \leftrightarrow A = 0$
2. $\|tA\| = |t| \; \|A\|$
3. $\|A + B\| \le \|A\| + \|B\|$ (the *triangle* inequality)
4. $\|AB\| \le \|A\| \; \|B\|$.

The name of inequality (3) stems from the analogous one for vector norms.

The row and column norms are implemented in MSP via functions **RowNorm** and **ColNorm**. They're not member functions, because principal argument notation is inappropriate. Here's the source code for **RowNorm**:

```
double RowNorm(const Matrix& A) {          // Return the
   int    Low     = A.LowIndex( );         // row norm:
   int    HighRow = A.HighRowIndex( );     // the larg-
   double N       = CityNorm(A[Low]);      // est city
   for (int i = Low+1; i <= HighRow; ++i)  // norm of
     N = fmax(N,CityNorm(A[i]));           // the matrix
   return N; }                             // rows.
```

Plus and Minus

MSP overloads the singulary C++ operators **+** and **−** to implement the corresponding matrix operations. In the latter case, it constructs a new matrix **B** of the same dimension as the operand **A**, computes the entries, then returns **B**. It passes parameter **A** by reference, for efficiency in case **A** is large. It must return **B** by value, however, since **B** would disappear before the caller could use a returned address. Here's the source code for operator **−**:

```
Matrix operator-(const Matrix& A) {        // Negation:
   int Low     = A.LowIndex( );            // overload singu-
   int HighRow = A.HighRowIndex( );        // lary - .
   int HighCol = A.HighColIndex( );        // Construct the
   Matrix B(HighRow,HighCol,Low);          // negative, row
   for (int i = Low; i <= HighRow; ++i)    // by row, and
      B[i] = -A[i];                        // return it.
   return B; }
```

Operator **+** is simpler: It just returns its argument **A**. There was no reason to make operator **+** or **−** a member function.

Conjugate and Transpose

MSP uses a similar technique to implement the complex conjugation operation on matrices: It overloads Library function **conj** to take a **Matrix** parameter **A**. The source code is very similar to that of operator **−**: instead of computing the negative of each **A** row, it computes the conjugate.

In Section 3.5 the C++ operator ~ was overloaded to convert a vector to a column matrix: that is, ~**V** was defined for a **Vector** operand **V**. MSP further overloads ~ to implement the matrix transposition operator. The operator must be placed *before* its **Matrix** operand, although in mathematical formulas, this book will continue to use the more conventional postfix notation:

MSP notation ~**A**   mathematics A^-.

The source code is similar to that for the negation operation:

```
Matrix operator~(const Matrix& A) {        // Trans-
   int Low     = A.LowIndex( );            // position:
   int HighRow = A.HighRowIndex( );        // overload ~
   int HighCol = A.HighColIndex( );        // Construct
   Matrix T(HighCol,HighRow,Low);          // the trans-
   for (int i = Low; i <= HighCol; ++i) {  // pose T ,
      for (int j = Low; j <= HighRow; ++j) // entry by
         T[i][j] = A[j][i]; }              // entry, and
   return T; }                             // return it.
```

In complex matrix algebra, the *conjugate transpose* operator plays a more important role. It's implemented in MSP by overloading the C++ operator ! :

```
Matrix operator!(const Matrix& A) { return conj(~A); }
```

Unfortunately, this notation differs widely from standard mathematics:

MSP notation !A   mathematics A^*

Nothing can be done about that, because overloading the C++ singulary operator * would interfere with its use in manipulating pointers.

Addition and Subtraction, Trace

Although MSP permits vector addition when addends' index limits disagree, it regards the analogous situation as an error for *matrix* addition. MSP implements this operation by overloading the C++ binary operator +. The source code is shown in Figure 3.6.2. It first checks whether the index limits agree. If so, it constructs a new vector **Sum** of the appropriate dimension, computes its entries, and returns it. If not, it sets the error signal and returns an empty matrix. For efficiency, the addends are passed by reference. **Sum** must be returned by value, however, because it would disappear before the caller could use a returned address.

Matrix subtraction could be implemented like matrix addition. However, it seems better to deal with index compatibility only once. Therefore, the MSP matrix subtraction operator

```
Matrix operator-(const Matrix &A, const Matrix& B)
```

merely computes and returns A + (−B).

```
Matrix operator+(const Matrix& A,          // Matrix addition:
                 const Matrix& B) {        // overload
    int Low     = A.LowIndex();            // binary  + .
    int HighRow = A.HighRowIndex();        // Declare and ini-
    int HighCol = A.HighColIndex();        // tialize an empty
    Matrix Sum;                            // matrix for the
       if ( Low      == B.LowIndex()       // sum.  If the index
       && HighRow == B.HighRowIndex()) {   // bounds agree, con-
          Sum.SetUp(HighRow,HighCol,Low);  // construct the sum,
          for (int i = Low; i <= HighRow; ++i)  // row by row and
             Sum[i] = A[i] + B[i]; }       // return it.  Other-
       else                                // Otherwise, signal
          SetError(IndexError); .          // an error & return
       return Sum; }                       // the empty matrix.
```

Figure 3.6.2 MSP matrix addition operator

The *trace* of an $m \times n$ matrix A is the sum of its diagonal entries:

$$\text{tr}A = \sum_{k=1}^{\min(m,n)} a_{kk}$$

This notion is implemented by MSP function **Scalar Trace(const Matrix& A)**. Its code is straightforward; you'll find it on the diskette.

Scalar Multiplication

There's no complication at all in the MSP implementation of its right scalar multiplication operator,

Matrix operator*(const Matrix& V,const Scalar& t) .

The source code is structured like that of the singulary – operation already discussed. The *left* scalar multiplication operator

Matrix operator*(const Scalar& t, const Matrix& A) ,

which is much more commonly used in mathematics, should be similar. However, at the time this paragraph was written, a bug in Turbo C++ prevented compilation of *any* operator with this declaration. Borland International, Inc. had acknowledged the bug, but hadn't yet provided a correction. Thus, all MSP programs requiring scalar multiplication use the right-hand version. This contravenes standard mathematical notation, but not very seriously.

Matrix Multiplication

MSP implements three related forms of matrix multiplication by overloading the C++ binary * operator:

$1 \times m$ row vector **V**	*	$m \times n$ matrix **B**
$l \times m$ matrix **A**	*	$m \times n$ matrix **B**
$m \times n$ matrix **A**	*	$n \times 1$ column vector **W** .

The first form is regarded as the most basic: For each index j, the jth entry of the product **V*B** is the scalar product of **V** by the jth column of **B**. The second form is computed row by row: For each row index i, the ith row of the product $A*B$ is the product of the ith row of A by the matrix B. The third form is computed as a special case of the

```
Vector operator*(const Vector& V,        // Row vector * Matrix.
                 const Matrix& A) {
  int Low = V.LowIndex();                // Think of  V ,  A  and
  int n   = A.HighColIndex();            // their product  P  as
  Vector P(n,Low);                       // 1xm , mxn ,  and  1xn .
  for (int j = Low; j <= n; ++j)         // Construct  P  entry by
    P[j] = V * A.Col(j);                 // entry. (This  *  is
  return P; }                            // the scalar product.)

Matrix operator*(const Matrix& A,        // Matrix * Matrix.
                 const Matrix& B) {
  int Low = A.LowIndex();                // Think of  A , B ,  and
  int L   = A.HighRowIndex();            // their product  P  as
  int n   = B.HighColIndex();            // Lxm , mxn ,  and  Lxn .
  Matrix P(L,n,Low);
  for (int i = Low; i <= L; ++i)         // Construct  P  row by
    P[i] = A[i] * B;                     // row. (This  *  is row
  return P; }                            // vector * matrix.)

Vector operator*(const Matrix& A,        // Matrix * column vector.
                 const Vector& W) {
  return A * (~W); }                     // (Matrix * matrix.)
```

Figure 3.6.3 MSP matrix multiplication operators

second. The source codes are shown in Figure 3.6.3. There's no need
to check index bound compatibility in these routines, because that's
done by the scalar multiplication operator.

MSP also overloads the ^ operator to compute integral powers M^n
of a square matrix M. Its definition for $n \geq 0$ could be discussed here,
but for $n < 0$ that requires the notion of inverse matrix. Therefore,
the power operation is considered later, in Section 6.6.

Replacement Operators

MSP implements five matrix algebra replacement operators: **+=, -=**,
and three forms of ***=**. If A and B are matrices, then A **+=** B adds B
to A, A **-=** B subtracts B from A, and A ***=** B postmultiplies A by B.
If **t** is a scalar, then A ***=** t replaces A by A*t. If V is a vector, then
V ***=** B postmultiplies V (regarded as a row matrix) by B. (*Caution*:
this can change the dimension of V.) The source code for each of
these operators is like that of the analogous **Vector** operators.

3.7 Polynomials

One of the major MSP features is the generality of the **Vector** class.
You've seen it used to implement vector algebra in Section 3.4
and matrix algebra in Section 3.6. In this section, a module for

polynomial algebra is based on the **Vector** class. Whereas matrices were implemented as arrays of **Vector** objects, polynomials are represented as objects of a class **Polynom** that is *derived* from class **Vector** through the C++ inheritance mechanism.

In general, you derive a new class from a base class by adding new data components and adding or modifying member functions. In this case, no new data components are necessary: in higher mathematics, a polynomial

$$P(x) = p_0 + p_1 x + p_2 x^2 + \cdots + p_n x^n$$

is regarded simply as the vector $P = [p_k]$ of its scalar coefficients. Trailing zero coefficients are banned: for instance, the polynomial $P(x) = x^2$ is regarded as the vector [0,0,1] of coefficients of $0 + 0x + 1x^2$, *not* as the vector [0,0,1,0,0] of coefficients of $0 + 0x + 1x^2 + 0x^3 + 0x^4$. The zero polynomial is represented by the *empty* vector. Some new member functions are clearly necessary. For example, one must evaluate a polynomial $P(x)$, given its coefficient vector $[p_k]$ and a scalar argument x. Also, some familiar **Vector** functions must be specialized to work on polynomials. For example, when you construct a polynomial, the index lower bound will always be zero. And when you add or subtract polynomials, you remove any trailing zero coefficients from the sum vector.

This section considers first the logical aspects of class **Polynom**: how some logical features of the **Vector** class must be specialized for polynomials. Then it describes a few necessary modifications to the addition and subtraction operations. Finally, it discusses in detail some new mathematical functions, including polynomial multiplication, division, and evaluation. As a concluding example, it computes the Legendre polynomials and verifies some of their complicated properties, demonstrating how easy the MSP is to use.

Like other MSP modules, this one has a header file **Polynom.H**, shown in Figures 3.7.1 and 3.7.2, and a source code file **Polynom.CPP**. You'll find those on the accompanying diskette. Most of the source code is listed later in this section, and described in detail.

Logical Features

Since MSP represents a polynomial $P(x) = p_0 + p_1 x + p_2 x^2 + \cdots + p_n x^n$ as the vector $P = [p_k]$ of its coefficients, most of the logical features of the **Vector** class should apply to polynomials. Since a few modifications and additions are necessary, polynomials should be objects of a

```
//*******************************************************************
//                            Polynom.H

#ifndef   Polynom_H
#define   Polynom_H

#include "Vector.H"

class Polynom: public Vector {
  public:

      //*************************************************************
      //  Logical functions

      Polynom();                    // Construct a zero polynomial.
      Polynom& SetUp(int n);        // Set degree, allocate memory.

      #ifdef Complex_H
      Polynom(const double& t);     // Construct constant polynomial.
      #endif

      Polynom(const Scalar& t);     // Construct constant polynomial.
      Polynom(const Vector& V);     // Copy a vector to a polynomial.

      //*************************************************************
      //  Polynomial algebra member functions

      Polynom& operator+=           // Add  P .
        (const Polynom& P);
      Polynom& operator-=           // Subtract  P .
        (const Polynom& P);
      Polynom& operator*=           // Multiply by  P .
        (const Polynom& P);
      Polynom& operator/=           // Divide by  P .
        (const Polynom& P);
      Polynom& operator%=           // Reduce modulo  P .
        (const Polynom& P);
      Scalar   operator()           // Evaluate polynomial
        (const Scalar& x) const; }; // at  x .
```

Figure 3.7.1 MSP header file Polynom.H (Part 1: the class Polynom)

class **Polynom** derived from **Vector**. This requires a definition
starting with the phrase

```
class Polynom: public Vector {
```

as in Figure 3.7.1. The word **public** specifies that the public components of class **Vector** remain public when regarded as components of
class **Polynom**. After this phrase are listed the new and modified
class components.

C++ requires you to define a default constructor **Polynom( )**. This
should construct the empty, or *zero*, polynomial. (The zero polynomial has no coefficients at all.) This is already done by the default
Vector constructor (see Section 3.3), which is invoked automatically
whenever an object of a derived class is constructed. Therefore,

```
//*****************************************************************
//        Polynom.H  (Part 2:  Related non-member functions)
//
//  Logical functions

Polynom xTo(int n);              // Construct polynomial  xⁿ .
int Degree(const Vector& V)      // Return the index of the
  const;                         // last nonzero coefficient.

//*****************************************************************
//  Polynomial algebra functions

Polynom operator+               // Polynomial addition.
 (const Polynom& P,
  const Polynom& Q);
Polynom operator-               // Polynomial subtraction.
 (const Polynom& P,
  const Polynom& Q);
Polynom operator*               // Polynomial multiplication.
 (const Polynom& P,
  const Polynom& Q);
Polynom operator^(Polynom P,    // Return  P(x)ⁿ .
             int   n);
void Divide(Polynom  F,         // Divide  F  by  G ,  getting
         const Polynom& G,      // quotient  Q  and remainder
               Polynom& Q,      // R .  Set the error signal if
               Polynom& R);     // G = 0 .
Polynom operator/(Polynom& F,   // Divide  F  by  G  and return
          const Polynom& G);    // the quotient.
Polynom operator%(Polynom& F,   // Divide  F  by  G  and return
          const Polynom& G);    // the remainder.
Polynom GCD(Polynom& P,         // Return a greatest common di-
            Polynom& Q,         // visor of  P , Q .  Assume
            double   T = 0);    // norm ≤ T -> polynomial = 0 .
Polynom LCM(Polynom& P,         // Return a least common mul-
            Polynom& Q,         // tiple of  P , Q .  Assume
            double   T = 0);    // norm ≤ T -> polynomial = 0 .
Polynom Deriv(const Polynom& P);  // Return derivative  P'(x) .
Polynom Integ(const Polynom& P);  // Return the integral of  P(x)
                                // with const. coefficient  0 .
Scalar  Horner(Polynom& Q,      // Divide  P(x)  by  x - t ,
          const Polynom& P,     // getting the quotient  Q(x)
          const Scalar& t);     // and returning the remainder.
Polynom Legendre(int n);        // Return the  nth  degree
                                // Legendre polynomial.
#endif
```

Figure 3.7.2 MSP header file Polynom.H (Part 2: related nonmember functions)

Polynom( ) needn't do anything at all: Its code is just **Polynom::Polynom( ) { }**.

For more serious construction tasks, class **Polynom** needs a function **SetUp(int n)** to set the index bounds and allocate memory for the coefficients. It's like the corresponding **Vector** function (see Section 3.3), but specialized to ensure that the lower index bound is zero. Here's its code. It merely calls the **Vector** function, then adjusts the type of the return value.

```
Polynom& Polynom::SetUp(int n) {      // Set the degree and
   return (Polynom&)                  // allocate memory:
      Vector::SetUp(n,0); }           // set up a vector and
                                      // call it a polynomial.
```

This function is invoked, for example, when you construct a *constant* polynomial. For that, MSP provides the constructor **Polynom(const Scalar& t)**. Here's its code:

```
Polynom::Polynom            // Construct a constant
   (const Scalar& t) {      // polynomial.
   if (t = = 0)             // The zero polynomial
      SetUp(-1);            // is the empty vector.
   else {                   // Any other constant
      SetUp(0);             // has degree 0 and
      This[0] = t; }}       // one entry.
```

For example, you can construct polynomials $Q(x) = 2.1$, $P(x) = 2$, and $O(x) = 0$ by declaring **Polynom Q(2.1)**, **Polynom P(2)**, and **Polynom O(0)**. In the second example, C++ automatically converts the **int** constant **2** to type **Scalar** before it invokes the constructor. The third declaration could have been written just **Polynom O**, which invokes the default constructor, not the **SetUp** function; but that's cryptic.

For a technical reason, it's necessary to include another constant polynomial constructor when you use the **complex** version of the **Scalar** module:

```
Polynom(const double& t).
```

(That version is discussed in detail in Section 4.6.) The problem stems from the way C++ interprets a declaration **Polynom P(1)**, intended to construct a polynomial with constant value 1. Without the additional constructor, this declaration would be ambiguous. C++ wouldn't know whether to execute **Polynom(const Scalar& t)**, or to execute **Vector(int Hi, int Lo = 1)**, then convert the constructed vector to type **Polynom**. (The **Vector** to **Polynom** converter is described later in this section.) You could resolve the ambiguity by removing the parameter **Lo** default value, but that would be inconvenient for many client programs. Another solution would be to omit the **Vector** to **Polynomial** converter, but that has a definite use. It wouldn't help to use only declarations like **Polynom P(1.0)**, because C++ would first cast **1.0** to type **int** implicitly. Therefore, an additional constructor seems the best solution. You must enclose it in **#ifdef Complex_H** ... **#endif** brackets to avoid including it twice when you use the **double** version of the **Scalar** module. The source code for the additional constructor is exactly the same as that for the original one.

More complicated polynomials are constructed in stages, as in mathematics: First construct some powers x^n, then perform scalar multiplications to get the terms $p_n x^n$, then add and subtract these and constant polynomials. The multiplication, addition, and subtraction operators are discussed later, with examples. To construct the polynomial $P(x) = x^n$, call the MSP function **xTo(int n)** like this: **Polynom P = xTo(n)**. Here's its source code:

```
Polynom xTo(int n) {              // Construct the
   Polynom xn;                    // polynomial xⁿ.
   xn.SetUp(n).MakeUnit(n);
   return xn; }
```

This function calls **Polynom::SetUp**, too. It's not a member function because the principal argument syntax is inappropriate.

When **Polynom** objects are manipulated by a **Vector** operator, the result has type **Vector**, and must be converted back to **Polynom**. This requires removing trailing zero entries from the resulting coefficient vector. That is, you must ascertain the degree of the corresponding polynomial, and copy the appropriate initial coefficients to a **Polynom** object. This process is implemented by the last two logical member functions of class **Polynom**: the **Degree** selector and a **Vector** converter/copier. The former is straightforward:

```
int Degree(const Vector& V) {     // Return the index
   int n = V.HighIndex( );        // of the last non-
   while (n >= 0 && V[n] = = 0) --n;  // zero coefficient.
   return n; }
```

(The order of the conditions in the **while** statement is critical!) The declaration of the converter/copier allows the compiler to call it implicitly:

```
Polynom::Polynom(const Vector& V) {  // Copy a vector
   int n;                            // to a polynomial.
   if (V.LowIndex( ) != 0) {         // Its lower index
      SetError(IndexError);          // must be zero.
      n = -1; }                      // If so, set the
```

```
    else n = Degree(V);           // degree, allocate
SetUp(n);                         // memory, and copy
if (GetError( )) return;          // the entries. In
for (int i = 0; i <= n; ++i)      // case of error,
  This[i] = V[i]; }               // set up 0
                                  // polynomial.
```

If it's asked to convert a vector whose lower index bound is not zero, or if it runs out of memory, this function sets the error signal and constructs the zero polynomial.

Addition and Subtraction

Polynomials are added and subtracted like vectors, but the converter/copier just described must be applied to the result, to remove trailing zero entries. Here's the addition operator:

```
Polynom operator+(const Polynom& P,    // Polynomial
                  const Polynom& Q) { // addition.
  return Vector(P) + Vector(Q); }
```

Subtraction is similar. These operators are designed to force the compiler to call the converter/copier implicitly to convert the return value to type **Polynom**. The explicit **Vector** converters in the source code ensure that the **Vector** addition or subtraction operator is invoked; without them, calling the **Polynom** operator would result in endless recursion.

The addition and subtraction replacement operators are implemented similarly, except that C++ requires them to be member functions. Here's addition:

```
Polynom& Polynom::operator+=        // Add polynomial
    (const Polynom& P) {            // P . Use Vector
  return Polynom(                   // operator, and
    Vector(This) + Vector(P)); }    // convert back to
                                    // type Polynom.
```

You might think this code could be simpler: just return **This = This + P**, like the analogous **Vector** operator. (See Section 3.4.) However, that wouldn't work, for an obscure reason: In interpreting a statement **Q += 1**, where **Q** is a **Polynom** object, the compiler searches for the proper type to which it should cast the constant **1**.

The intended process — casting first to a **Scalar**, then to a **Polynom** — is too indirect. Instead, the constructor **Vector(int Hi, int Lo = 1)** would be invoked with the second parameter defaulted, and the resulting uninitialized vector would be added to **Q**. The MSP operator is written to force the compiler to cast the **1** to a **Polynom**. This species of bug is all too common when you use derived classes, overloaded functions, and default parameters all at once. With the Turbo C++ integrated debugger, you can step through a program and ascertain which functions are being executed. Without it, you'd have to insert trace output statements, and sift through mountains of confusing data.

Multiplication and Powers

Multiplication of two polynomials

$$P(x) = \sum_{i=0}^{m} p_i x^i \quad Q(x) = \sum_{j=0}^{n} q_j x^j$$

is based on the formula

$$P(x) \, Q(x) = \sum_{i+j=k=0}^{m+n} p_i \, q_j \, x^k = \sum_{k=0}^{m+n} \sum_{i=max(0,k-n)}^{min(m,k)} p_i \, q_{k-i} \, x^k$$

Its MSP implementation is shown in Figure 3.7.3. There was no reason to make it a member function. The corresponding replacement operator simply returns **This = This * P**.

Due to a technicality in its implicit typecasting criteria, C++ interprets expressions **a*P** and **P*a**, where **a** is a **Scalar** and P a **Poly-**

```
Polynom operator*(const Polynom& P,          // Polynomial
                  const Polynom& Q) {        // multiplication.
  Polynom Zero(0);
  if (P == Zero || Q == Zero) return Zero;   // Special cases.
  int m = Degree(P);                         // A nonzero product
  int n = Degree(Q);                         // must have degree
  Polynom Product;  Product.SetUp(m+n);      // m + n .
  for (int k = 0; k <= m+n; ++k) {           // Compute each
    Product[k]   = 0;                        // coefficient, in
    for (int i   = max(0,k-n);               // turn.
             i <= min(m,k); ++i)
      Product[k] += P[i]*Q[k-i]; }
  return Product; }
```

Figure 3.7.3 MSP polynomial multiplication operator

nom, as products of *two polynomials.* That is, it first casts **a** to a polynomial, then multiplies. While this is less efficient than multiplying the corresponding vector **P** by **a,** it's inoffensive, handles zero properly, and is unaffected by the Turbo C++ bug that prevents left scalar multiplications.

MSP overloads C++ operator ^ to compute nonnegative integral powers of polynomials. *Danger!* Operator ^ has lower precedence than accorded exponentiation in conventional mathematical notation. For example, to get **(P^2) + 1,** you *must* use the parentheses! The conventional algorithm $P(x) \cdot P(x) \cdot \ldots \cdot P(x)$ with $n - 1$ multiplications is inefficient, so MSP uses a faster one, which is implemented recursively. Here's the source code:

```
Polynom operator^(Polynom P, int n) { // Return P(x) .
  if (n < 0) {
    SetError(DivideError); return 0; }
  if (n = = 0) return 1;                // Recursion: P$ = 1;
  if (n % 2 != 0) return P*(P^(n-1)); // if n is odd, then
  Polynom Q = P^(n/2);                  // P = PP^(n-1) ;
  return Q*Q; }                         // else P = (P^½n).
```

P is a value parameter because of its role in the recursion. It seems that parameter **P** should be declared as **const Polynom&,** but the author couldn't get that to work properly.

You can follow the source code to see, for example, that for $n = 15$ it computes

$$
\begin{aligned}
P(x)^{15} &= P(x) \cdot P(x)^{14} \\
&= P(x) \cdot (P(x)^7)^2 \\
&= P(x) \cdot (P(x) \cdot P(x)^6)^2 \\
&= P(x) \cdot (P(x) \cdot (P(x)^3)^2)^2 \\
&= P(x) \cdot (P(x) \cdot (P(x) \cdot P(x)^2)^2)^2,
\end{aligned}
$$

using six, rather than $n - 1 =$ fourteen multiplications. This method is certainly more efficient, but it's not the fastest. In fact, you can compute $P(x)^{15}$ with only five multiplications: First compute $y = P(x) \cdot P(x)^2$, then $P(x)^{15} = y \cdot (y^2)^2$. An algorithm that computes every integral power the fastest way would be more complicated, so MSP uses a compromise. There's a large literature on efficient power algorithms: Knuth (Reference [28, Section 4.6.3]) gives it 25 pages!

MSP also implements the corresponding replacement operator ^=, which simply returns **This = This^n.**

Division

When you divide a polynomial $F(x) = a_0 + a_1x + \cdots + a_mx^m$ of degree m by a nonzero polynomial $G(x) = b_0 + b_1x + \cdots + b_nx^n$ of degree n, you get *quotient* and *remainder* polynomials $Q(x)$ and $R(x)$ such that

$$\frac{F(x)}{G(x)} = Q(x) + \frac{R(x)}{G(x)} \qquad i.e., \quad F(x) = Q(x)\,G(x) + R(x)$$

and degree(R) < degree(G). If $G(x)$ is just the constant b_0, this is scalar multiplication by $1/b_0$, and $R(x) = 0$. If degree(F) < degree(G), then $Q(x) = 0$ and $R(x) = F(x)$. In other cases, you can compute $Q(x)$ and $R(x)$ by the recursive algorithm you learned in an algebra class:

$$\frac{a_m}{b_n} x^{m-n} + \cdots \qquad = Q_1(x) + \cdots$$

$$G(x) = b_n x^n + \cdots \overline{\left| \begin{array}{l} a_m x^m + \cdots \\ a_m x^m + \cdots \\ \qquad \cdots \end{array} \right.}
\begin{array}{l}
= F(x) \\
= Q_1(x)\,G(x) \\
= F(x) - Q_1(x)\,G(x) \\
= R(x) \text{ or new } F(x)
\end{array}$$

The first term $Q_1(x)$ of the quotient is $(a_m/b_n)\,x^{m-n}$; you multiply the divisor $G(x)$ by that term and subtract the product from the dividend $F(x)$. If the remainder $R(x) = F(x) - Q_1(x)G(x)$ has degree less than n, you can stop with $Q(x) = Q_1(x)$; otherwise, make $R(x)$ the new dividend, divide by $G(x)$ and add the quotient to the term you've already computed. This familiar algorithm is implemented by MSP function **Divide**, shown in Figure 3.7.4. F is a value parameter because of its role in the recursion.

MSP also includes operators **/** and **%** for dividing a polynomial F by a nonzero polynomial G and reducing F modulo G: Executing **F/G** or **F%G** invokes **Divide(F,G,Q,R)**, then returns **Q** or **R**. The corresponding replacement operators **/=** and **%=** are implemented too.

The concept of *greatest common divisor*, GCD, of two polynomials is used in Chapter 5 to expedite solution of polynomial equations. It's only slightly more involved than the corresponding notion for integers. $D(x)$ is a GCD of polynomials $P(x)$ and $Q(x)$ if $D(x)$ divides them both (with remainder 0) and any other divisor has degree less than or equal to that of $D(x)$. Thus, the GCDs of $P(x)$ and $Q(x)$ consist of any single GCD and all its scalar multiples. Under this definition, $P(x)$ is a GCD of $P(x)$ and the zero polynomial. But if $P(x)$ and $Q(x)$

```
void Divide(Polynom F,              // Divide F by G ,
       const Polynom& G,            // getting quotient Q
            Polynom& Q,             // and remainder R . Set
            Polynom& R) {           // the error signal if
   Polynom Zero(0);                 // G = 0 .
   int m = Degree(F);
   int n = Degree(G);
   if (G == Zero)                   // Division by zero is not
      SetError(DivideError);        // permitted.
    else if (n == 0) {              // Division by a constant
      Q = (1/G[0])*F;               // c is scalar multipli-
      R = Zero; }                   // cation by 1/c .
    else if (m < n) {               // Division by a polynomi-
      Q = Zero;                     // of larger degree gives
      R = F; }                      // only a remainder. Com-
    else {                                // pute first term
      Polynom Q1 = (F[m]/G[n])*xTo(m-n);  // of quotient. Mul-
      F -= Q1*G;                          // tiply it by G ,
      if (Degree(F) == m)           // subtract to get a new divi-
         F -= F[m]*xTo(m);          // dend F , and continue re-
      Divide(F,G,Q,R);             // cursively. Make sure that
      Q += Q1; }}                   // the degree of F decreases.
```

Figure 3.7.4 MSP function Divide

are both zero, their GCD must be specially defined as the zero polynomial. It's easy to find a GCD $D(x)$ if you consider *prime decompositions* of $P(x)$ and $Q(x)$ as in Figure 3.7.5 — *i.e.*, write them as products of powers of polynomials $p_0(x)$, ..., $p_n(x)$ that can't be factored further. However, factoring polynomials P and Q is not a practical way to find a GCD.

Instead, you can use an analog of Euclid's algorithm for the GCD of integers:

(0)   if either polynomial is zero, then the other is a GCD;

(1)   if either polynomial is a constant, then 1 is a GCD;

(2a)   otherwise, if degree(P) $\geq$ degree(Q), then find a GCD of P and P mod Q;

(2b)   or if degree(Q) $\geq$ degree(P), then find a GCD of Q and Q mod P.

$$P(x) = \prod_{k=1}^{n} p_j(x)^{k_j} \quad Q(x) = \prod_{j=1}^{n} p_j(x)^{l_j} \quad D(x) = \prod_{j=1}^{n} p_j(x)^{m_j} \quad m_j = \min(k_j, l_j)$$

Figure 3.7.5 GCD $G(x)$ of polynomials $P(x)$ and $Q(x)$

```
Polynom GCD(Polynom& P,          // Return a greatest com-
            Polynom& Q,          // mon divisor of  P  and
            double  T) {         // Q . Assume that a
   if (MaxNorm(P) <= T) return Q; // polynomial is  0  if
   if (MaxNorm(Q) <= T) return P; // its max norm is  <= T .
   int m = Degree(P);
   int n = Degree(Q);            // GCD(P,c) = GCD(c,Q) = 1
   if (m == 0 || n == 0) return 1; // if constant  c + 0 .
   Polynom G;                    // Euclid's recursive al-
   if (m >= n) G = GCD(Q,P%Q,T); // gorithm.  Use variable
     else      G = GCD(P,Q%P,T); // G  to avoid what seems
   return G; }                   // to be a Turbo C++ bug.
```

Figure 3.7.6 MSP function GCD

A step of type (2a) or (2b) always requires solution of a simpler problem than the original, since degree(P mod Q) < degree(Q) and degree(Q mod P) < degree(P). These conditions ensure that the recursion will terminate with a step of type of (0) or (1). The result of this version of the algorithm is often inappropriate in practice, because roundoff error makes you work with approximations of zero: polynomials whose coefficients are all very small. The recursion continues too long, because it doesn't reach an exact zero remainder when it should. Therefore, the algorithm must be modified slightly. Replace step (0) by

(0′)   if the max norm of either polynomial is less than or equal to a specified tolerance T, then the other polynomial is a GCD.

The appropriate tolerance might depend on the problem at hand, so the client is responsible for specifying it. The modified algorithm is implemented as MSP function **GCD** in Figure 3.7.6. Here's output from a test program that executed **GCD(P,Q).Show( )** for the specified polynomials **P** and **Q**:

```
P(x)    = (x² + x)³(x - 1)²
Q(x)    = (x² + x)²(x - 1)³
GCD(P,Q) = c(x² + x)²(x - 1)² = cx²(x² - 1)²:
   0.0    0.0    2.0    0.0    -4.0    0.0    2.0
```

As in this example, Euclid's algorithm usually computes a scalar multiple of the GCD you'd get by factoring. GCD could have divided the result by its leading coefficient, but there seemed no compelling reason to do so, and the division could add to roundoff error, so it was omitted. In header file **Polynom.H**, parameter **T** is initialized with default value 0.

MSP includes one more function related to division:

```
Polynom LCM(Polynom& P, Polynom& Q, double T = 0) .
```

LCM computes a *least common multiple* $L(x)$ of polynomials $P(x)$ and $Q(x)$: $L(x)$ is a nonzero multiple of both $P(x)$ and $Q(x)$, but no polynomial of smaller degree is. (If both $P(x)$ and $Q(x)$ are zero, $L(x)$ is specially defined to be zero.) The least common multiples of $P(x)$ and $Q(x)$ consist of all scalar multiples of any single LCM. If you factor $P(x)$ and $Q(x)$ into prime factors, you can easily construct a least common multiple like $D(x)$ in Figure 3.7.5: Just let $m_j = \max(k_j, l_j)$ instead of $\min(k_j, l_j)$. From this you can see how LCD was implemented: It just divides the product of $P(x)$ and $Q(x)$ by a GCD.

It seems that the GCD and LCM parameters **P** and **Q** should be declared as **const Polynom&**; but the author couldn't get that to work properly. Moreover, the clearer code

```
if (m >= n)   return GCD(Q,P%Q,T);
else          return GCD(P,Q%P,T);
```

for function **GCD** wouldn't work either.

Differentiation and Integration

MSP includes functions **Deriv** and **Integ** for differentiating and integrating a polynomial

$$P(x) = \sum_{x=0}^{n} p_k \, x^k \ .$$

Here are the differentiation and integration formulas and the corresponding implementations.

$$P'(x) = \sum_{k=1}^{n} k p_k \, x^{k-1}$$

```
Polynom Deriv(const Polynom& P) {      // Return the
  int n = Degree(P);                   // derivative
  Polynom D; D.SetUp(n-1);             // D(x) = P'(x) .
  for (int k = 1; k <= n; ++k)
    D[k-1] = k * P[k];
  return D; }
```

$$\int_0^x P(t)\, dt = \sum_{k=0}^{n} \frac{P_k}{k+1}\, x^{k+1} = \sum_{k=1}^{n+1} \frac{P_{k-1}}{k}\, x^k$$

```
Polynom Integ(const Polynom& P) {      // Return the
  int n = Degree(P);                   // integral
  Polynom J; J.SetUp(n+1);             //
  J[0] = 0;                            //
  for (int k = 1; k <= n+1; ++k)       // J(x)   =
    J[k] = P[k-1] / k;                 //
  return J; }                          //
```

$$J(x) = \int_0^x P(t)\, dt .$$

Horner's Algorithm and Evaluation

The naive way to evaluate $P(t) = a_0 + a_1 t + a_2 t^2 + \cdots + a_n t^n$ is to compute the powers $t^2, \ldots, t^n$, and the terms $a_1 t, a_2 t^2, \ldots, a_n t^n$, then add. That requires n additions and $2n - 1$ multiplications. There's a much more efficient method, called *Horner's algorithm*:

$q_{n-1} = p_n$;
for $k = n - 1$ down to 1 do
$\quad q_{k-1} = p_k + t q_k$;
$P(t) = p_0 + t q_0$.

For $n = 3$, this amounts to the computation

$$P(t) = p_0 + t\,(p_1 + t\,(p_2 + t\,p_3))$$

q_2
q_1
q_0

Horner's algorithm requires only n additions and n multiplications!

Horner's algorithm is also known as *synthetic division*, for the following reason: with its intermediate results $q_0, \ldots, q_{n-1}$ compute

$$
\begin{aligned}
P(t) &+ (x - t)(q_0 + q_1 x + \cdots + q_{n-1} x^{n-1}) \\
&= P(t) - t q_0 - t q_1 x - \cdots - t q_{n-1} x^{n-1} + q_0 x + \cdots + q_{n-2} x^{n-1} + q_{n-1} x^n \\
&= [P(t) - t q_0] + [q_0 - t p_1]\, x + \cdots + [q^{n-2} - t q^{n-1}]\, x^{n-1} \\
&= p_0 + p_1 x + \cdots + p_{n-1} x^{n-1} + p_n x^n \\
&= P(x) .
\end{aligned}
$$

```
Scalar Horner(       Polynom& Q,       // Divide  P(x)  by
             const Polynom& P,         // x - t ,  getting the
             const Scalar&  t) {       // quotient  Q(x)  and re-
   int n = Degree(P);                  // turning the remainder.
   Q.SetUp(n-1);
   if (n <  0) return 0;               // In case  P(x)  is zero.
   if (n == 0) return P[0];            // Constant  P(x) ≠ 0 .
   Q[n-1] = P[n];
   for (int i = n-1; i >= 1; --i)      // Horner's algorithm.
     Q[i-1] = P[i] + t*Q[i];
   return P[0] + t*Q[0]; }
```

Figure 3.7.7 MSP function Horner

Thus, $q_0, \ldots, q_{n-1}$ are the coefficients of the quotient polynomial $Q(x)$ in the long division

$$\frac{P(x)}{x-t} = Q(x) + \frac{P(t)}{x-t}$$

and $P(t)$ is the remainder. That is, $P(x) = (x - t) Q(x) + P(t)$.

Using the product rule to differentiate the previous equation, you get $P'(x) = Q(x) + (x - t) Q'(x)$, hence $Q(t) = P'(t)$. Thus, a polynomial $P(x)$ and its derivative can be evaluated easily for an argument t by *two* applications of Horner's algorithm: First apply it to $P(x)$, obtaining $P(t)$ and the coefficients of $Q(x)$, then apply it to $Q(x)$, obtaining $Q(t) = P'(t)$. This technique will be used in Chapter 5.

MSP includes function **Horner**, a straightforward implementation of Horner's algorithm. Its source code is shown in Figure 3.7.7.

Function **Horner**, in turn, is the basis of the overloaded ( ) operator, which is used to evaluate a polynomial at a specified **Scalar** argument **t**:

```
Scalar Polynom::operator( )       // Evaluate polynomial
    (const Scalar& t) const {     // at t . Use Horner's
   Polynom Q;                     // algorithm. Ignore
   return Horner(Q,This,t); }     // the quotient that it
                                  // returns in Q .
```

This overloading makes it possible to use the expression **P(t)** for the value of **Polynom P** at a **Scalar t**. You'll find several examples in the following paragraphs.

Polynomial evaluation is such an important feature of numerical software that much effort has been spent analyzing its efficiency. It's known that any algorithm that computes $P(x) = p_0 + p_1 x + \cdots + p_n x^n$

for all possible values of p_0, ..., p_n, and x must use at least n additions and n multiplications, and that the only one that achieves this optimality is Horner's. (See Reference [28, Section 4.6.4].)

Testing with the Legendre Polynomials

Legendre polynomials play important roles in numerical analysis. In this section, they're introduced to test and to demonstrate the power and convenience of the **Polynom** module. The test routines discussed here are typical of those actually used while developing the MSP modules.

The Legendre polynomials $L_0(x)$, $L_1(x)$, $L_2(x)$, ... are defined recursively by the equations $L_0(x) = 1$, $L_1(x) = x$, and

$$L_n(x) = \frac{2n-1}{n} \, x \, L_{n-1}(x) - \frac{n-1}{n} L_{n-2}(x) \ .$$

The degree of $L_n(x)$ increases by one with each recursion, hence $L_n(x)$ has degree n in general. Here are the next three polynomials in the sequence:

$$L_2(x) = \frac{3}{2} x^2 - \frac{1}{2} \qquad L_3(x) = \frac{5}{2} x^3 - \frac{3}{2} x \qquad L_4(x) = \frac{35}{8} x^4 - \frac{15}{4} x^2 + \frac{3}{8} \ .$$

It can be shown that $L_n(x)$ is always even if n is even and odd if n is odd.

MSP includes function **Legendre** for generating these polynomials. Its implementation, shown in Figure 3.7.8, closely follows the definition. Allocating memory for $n + 1$ Legendre polynomials is not strictly necessary, since you only need the two most current ones to

```
Polynom Legendre(int n) {            // Construct the   nth
  if (n <= 0) return 1;              // Legendre polynomial.
  Polynom* L;  L = new Polynom[n+1]; // n = 0  is a special
  L[0] = Polynom(1);                 // case.
  Polynom x = L[1] = xTo(1);         // Otherwise, use the
  for (int m = 2; m <= n; ++m) {     // recursion formula to
    Scalar M = m;                    // construct an array
    Scalar a = (2*M - 1)/M;          // consisting of Legendre
    Scalar b = (M - 1)/M;            // polynomials  L0
    L[m] =   a*x*L[m-1] - b*L[m-2]; }  // to  Ln .
  Polynom P = L[n];
  delete [n+1] L;                    // Return  Ln  and delete
  return P; }                        // the array.
```

Figure 3.7.8 MSP function Legendre

```
double LegInt(int m, int n) {        // $3.7  module  Polynom  test
  Polynom K = Legendre(m);           // routine.  LegInt  integrates
  Polynom L = Legendre(n);           // the product of Legendre
  Polynom J = Integ(K*L);            // polynomials  Lk :
  return  J(1) - J(-1); }            //
                                     //        ⌠1
void Test1() {                       // Jmn = ⎮    Lm(x) Ln(x) dx
  cout << "Enter  m  n = ";          //        ⌡-1
  int m,n; cin >> m >> n;            //
  cout << "\nJmm       = " << LegInt(m,m);
  cout << "\n2/(2m+1)  = " << 2.0/(2*m+1);
  cout << "\nJmn       = " << LegInt(m,n);
  cout << "\nJnn       = " << LegInt(n,n);
  cout << "\n2/(2n+1)  = " << 2.0/(2*n+1); }
```

Sample output

```
Enter  m  n = 9  11

Jmm       = 0.105263
2/(2m+1)  = 0.105263
Jmn       = 3.637979e-12
Jnn       = 0.086957
2/(2n+1)  = 0.086957
```

Figure 3.7.9 Polynom routine, Test 1

construct the next. But restricting the allocation to accommodate just those three would make the program more complicated.

The Legendre polynomials have many complicated (and important) properties that are easily adapted for checking numerical software. Their most important property is *orthogonality*:

$$\int_{-1}^{1} L_m(x)L_n(x)\, dx = \begin{cases} \dfrac{2}{2n+1} & \text{if } m = n \\[2mm] 0 & \text{if } m \neq n \ . \end{cases}$$

In Figure 3.7.9 is a routine that employs this property to test **Polynom** functions **Legendre** and **Integ** and the polynomial multiplication and evaluation operators. The figure includes sample test output.

A second test uses an alternative definition often given for the Legendre polynomials:

$$L_n(x) = \frac{1}{n!2^n} \frac{d^n}{dx^n} (x^2 - 1)^n \ .$$

The test routine in Figure 3.7.10 computes a Legendre polynomial according to this definition, but calls it $K_n(x)$. Then it calls function

```
void Test2() {                    // §3.7  module  Polynom  test
  cout << "Enter  n  = ";         // routine.  Compare Legendre
  int n;   cin >> n;              // polynomial  Ln  with
  Polynom Kn = (xTo(2) - 1)^n;
  for (int k = 1; k <= n; ++k)    //              1    dⁿ
    Kn = Deriv(Kn);               // Kn = ─────  ── (x² - 1)ⁿ
  Kn *= 1/(Power(2,n)*Factorial(n));  //       n!2ⁿ  dxⁿ
  Polynom Ln = Legendre(n);
  cout << "‖Kn - Ln‖ = " << MaxNorm(Kn - Ln); }
```

$$K_n = \frac{1}{n!\,2^n} \frac{d^n}{dx^n}(x^2 - 1)^n .$$

Sample output

Enter n = 13
‖Kn - Ln‖ = 4.547474e-13

Figure 3.7.10 Polynom routine, Test 2

Legendre to compute $L_n(x)$ as usual, and outputs the max norm of the difference of the corresponding coefficient vectors. Sample test output is included in the figure. This routine tests functions **Legendre** and **Deriv** and the polynomial subtraction, multiplication, and power operators.

For further information on Legendre polynomials, consult Wylie's book (Reference [45, Section 9.8]).

4

Computing with Real and Complex Numbers

The real number system that mathematicians developed over the centuries is an idealization and simplification of the numbers that you use in calculation. They make the theory easier, and that has enabled us to avoid many useless or inefficient calculations. Most calculations are performed with finite decimal expansions, which approximate the real numbers that arise through theoretical considerations.

One method of organizing such calculations is to give each expansion a fixed number n of decimal places. You add, subtract, and divide numbers p and q in that system just like you manipulate the corresponding integers $10^n p$ and $10^n q$. Multiplication is a little harder: You must round a product with $2n$ decimals back to n decimals. This system is called *fixed point* arithmetic. You use it every day, but you don't notice it, because it looks like integer arithmetic. For example, in monetary calculations, you often convert dollar figures to cents, and calculate with those.

A more flexible method gives each decimal expansion x a fixed number n of significant digits, and you use scientific notation: $x = \pm d_0.d_1 d_2 \ldots d_{n-1} \times 10^E$. In calculations, you must keep track not only of the $\pm$ sign and significand $d_0.d_1 d_2 \ldots d_{n-1}$, but also the exponent E. You can move the decimal point in x easily by changing E; for that reason, this method is called *floating point* arithmetic. It's so much more convenient for handling numbers of widely varying magnitude that it's virtually universal in scientific and engineering applications.

This chapter discusses arithmetic computation in greater depth than usual for books on scientific and engineering applications. You might place some of these basic arithmetic considerations under the category of general programming techniques. But they may be less important in more general contexts, and consequently they're not often covered by books with broader scope. For example, Section 4.1 gives a brief overview of C integer arithmetic and its implementation on the Intel 8086 CPU family; it concentrates on the use of modular arithmetic and on properties of integer division. These details arise occasionally in scientific and engineering work, and are rarely covered in programming texts. Section 4.2 describes floating point arithmetic in terms of Intel conventions and recent IEEE standards.

Sections 4.3 and 4.4 are devoted to the C++ Library functions defined in its header file **Math.H**, and to a complementary set of functions provided by this book's MSP software package. Although the algorithms are described here in considerable depth, some of their details aren't readily accessible for study. Sections 4.6 and 4.7 describe the C++ facilities for calculating with complex numbers, and the complex version of the MSP **Scalar** module. The latter lets you convert most of the higher level MSP equation solving routines to handle equations with complex roots and coefficients.

Section 4.5 is the longest and most involved part of this chapter. It describes in detail the Turbo C++ arithmetic error handling facilities. This is the least polished area covered in the book. The relevant C++ features are still being developed, the Turbo C++ facilities are rudimentary, and the error handling facilities of MSP are primitive. The Turbo C++ techniques are described here in detail because they are occasionally needed in scientific and engineering applications and information is difficult to obtain. There's no attempt to adapt them for MSP use.

4.1   Integer Arithmetic

Although this chapter is mostly concerned with real and complex numbers, it starts by considering the integers. There are three reasons. First, integers, after all, form the basis of the real number system. Second, all computations involve counting, hence integer operations, to some extent. Third, some features of integer arithmetic yield results that aren't easy to predict unless you've taken the time at least once to study them in detail. This section surveys the various integer types available to C++ programmers, stressing their similarities. It considers the standard integer operations and functions supplied with C++, and a few more that you may find useful. It concludes by mentioning some aspects of integer arithmetic that are not supported by C++ or this book's MSP software package.

C++ Integer Types

Turbo C++ provides six integer types, which you can distinguish by their ranges of values:

Type	Full Type Name	Range		Macro
char	signed char	-2^7 ... $2^7 - 1 = 127$		
int	signed int	-2^{15} ... $2^{15} - 1 = 32767$		= MAXINT
long	signed long int	-2^{31} ... $2^{31} - 1 = 2147483647$		= MAXLONG
	unsigned char	0 ... $2^8 - 1 = 255$		
	unsigned int	0 ... $2^{16} - 1 = 65535$		
	unsigned long	0 ... $2^{32} - 1 = 4294967295$		

The two macro constants are provided for your convenience in Turbo C++ header file **Values.H**. (The ranges in this table are not C++ standards, but depend on the machine on which the language is implemented.) The storage required for an integer depends on the type. For Turbo C++ the requirements are

> **char** types: 1 byte
> **int** types: 2 bytes
> **long** types: 4 bytes.

int arithmetic is generally faster than long arithmetic, but because of the architecture of the 8086 family machines on which Turbo C++ runs, it performs **char** arithmetic no faster than **int**. Most C++ programs, including virtually all in this book, use **int** arithmetic, resorting to **long** variables only when extremely large sets must be counted — for example, the number of bytes in the text files containing this chapter.

Addition, Subtraction, and Multiplication

The standard integer arithmetic operations are provided for each C++ integer type. Addition, subtraction, and multiplication are really *modular* arithmetic, with these moduli:

char types   mod 2^8
int types   mod 2^{16}
long types   mod 2^{32}.

To perform an arithmetic operation mod M, you carry out the operation as usual, obtaining an intermediate value v; then you divide v by M, return the remainder r as the result, and discard the quotient q. The following equations hold among these quantities:

$$\frac{v}{M} = q + \frac{r}{M} \qquad v = qM + r$$

r is adjusted to lie in the appropriate range: $-\frac{1}{2} M \le r < \frac{1}{2} M$ for the **signed** types, and $0 \le r < M$ for the **unsigned** ones.

For example, the program fragment

```
int i = MAXINT;
i = 2*i;
cout << "i = " << i;
```

outputs **i = –2**. (Since **MAXINT** = $2^{15} - 1$, the intermediate value v is $2(2^{15} - 1) = 2^{16} - 2 = M - 2$, so the quotient is 1 and the remainder is -2, the output.) Here's an analogous example with an unsigned type: the fragment

```
unsigned long u = MAXLONG + 2;
u = 2*u;
cout << "u = " << u;
```

outputs **u = 2**. (Since **MAXLONG** = $2^{31} - 1$, the intermediate value v is $2(2^{31} + 1) = 2^{32} + 2 = M + 2$, so the quotient is 1 and the remainder is 2, the output.) You can construct similar fragments for the other four integer types. (You'll have to output **char** values using **printf** format string "%d"; otherwise **char** output defaults to characters, not numerals.)

These examples should convince you that there's no such thing as overflow in integer arithmetic! But if the numbers get too large for the selected integer type, you may get unexpected results!

Order and Absolute Value

When you study arithmetic mod M, you generally regard the range of values as circular, like the examples of Figure 4.1.1 with $M = 12$. (Modular arithmetic is taught in grade school as *clock* arithmetic!) It

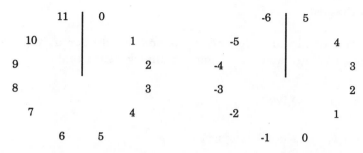

Figure 4.1.1 Circles for unsigned and signed modular arithmetic

makes no intrinsic sense to say that one value is larger than another. But the order relation < for the infinite set of integers must be imitated in modular arithmetic for each of the C++ types. In fact, given two instances j and k of an integer type, you determine whether $j < k$ by cutting the circle at the natural place, flattening out the scale, then checking as usual to see whether $j < k$. The natural cut depends on whether the type is unsigned or signed, as in Figure 4.1.1.

This seems a straightforward way to interpret the order relation $j < k$, but you should realize that, because of the circular nature of modular arithmetic and the violence done by the cut, some of the familiar order properties fail to hold in integer arithmetic. For example, the statement *if* $i < j$ *and* $j < k$ *then* $i < k$ is still true, but the statement *if* $i < j$ *then* $2i < 2j$ is false when applied to type **int** arithmetic. (Try $i = 1$ and $j = 16384$: $2i = 2$ but $2j = -32768$. Following the analysis presented under the previous heading, the modulus is $M = 2^{16}$ and $j = \frac{1}{4} M$, so the intermediate product of 2 by j is $v = \frac{1}{2} M = M - \frac{1}{2} M$; the quotient and remainder are $q = 1$ and $-\frac{1}{2} M$. The latter is the final result $2j$ in type **int**.)

The absolute value function is involved with the order relation. With the signed types you can regard j as the larger of j and $-j$: whichever one of these is ≥ 0. This operation is implemented by C++ Library routines **abs** and **labs**, which are defined in header file **StdLib.H** for types **int** and **long**. The definition just given for the absolute value doesn't work with unsigned types. Of course, there's no real need for it, but if you misapplied one of these to a parameter of an unsigned type, you'd get an incorrect result. For example, if you executed **unsigned j = 32769** then **cout << abs(j)**, C++ would automatically convert **j** to the **int** value -32767 with the same bit pattern in memory, then output **32767**. *Beware!*

Integer Division

When you divide an integer x by a nonzero divisor d, you get an integer quotient q and an integer remainder r such that

$$\frac{x}{d} = q + \frac{r}{d} \qquad x = qd + r$$

$$|r| < |d| \qquad \text{sign}(r) = \text{sign}(x) \ .$$

Since x and r have the same sign, q is also the result of truncating the exact (real) quotient x/d toward 0. The 8086 family CPUs are designed to implement this familiar process, so Turbo C++ integer division reflects these same features. For any integer type, you can obtain the quotient and remainder separately by executing

```
q = x/d;       r = x % d;
```

For the **int** type, you can get them both at once by executing the C++ Library function

```
div_t div(int x, int d) .
```

The **div_t** type is defined with **div** in header file **StdLib.H** as

```
typedef struct {long quot; long rem; } div_t;
```

An analogous function **ldiv** and type **ldiv_t** are provided for dividing long integers.

Additional Integer Operations

The MSP **General** module implements three useful integer functions:

```
int Sign(double x);     // Return -1 , 0 , or 1
                        // when x < , = , or > 0 .
int max(int x, int y);  // Return the larger of x , y .
int min(int x, int y);  // Return the smaller of x , y .
```

These were discussed earlier, in Section 3.1. Although function **Sign** takes a **double** parameter, you can use it with an integer argument; C++ does the required type conversion automatically.

The **Math.H** Library function

```
double pow(double b, double p)
```

can be invoked with **int** arguments to compute an integer power b^p. It returns a **double** value; if that's in the **int** or **long** range, you can assign it immediately to a variable of that type, and the value will be rounded correctly. More details of the function **pow** are discussed in Section 4.3. Two more functions commonly used for integer calculations are implemented in MSP module **RealFunc**:

```
long double Factorial(int    n); // Return n!
double      Binomial (double x,  // Return the binomial
                      int    n); // coefficient x
                                 // over n .
```

The **Factorial** function returns a **long double** value because n! gets so large; it overflows when **n** > 1054. **RealFunc** features are discussed in detail in Section 4.4.

Formatting Output

Formatting numerical output is often unexpectedly difficult. C++ provides comprehensive facilities for this task — too many to consider here. For integer output the questions aren't really complicated. Even so, MSP needed a new function **Digits**, already discussed in Section 3.1, to compute the minimum length of a numeral that represents a given integer. This subject is discussed in great detail in Section 3.7 of the author's earlier book, Reference [37], on Turbo C.

Integers of Arbitrary Length

Current developments are creating many applications for an integer data type that's not supported by Turbo C++, nor included in the MSP software of this book: *arbitrarily long integers*. These are normally stored as linked lists of integers or of digits. Devising efficient algorithms for their arithmetic is a major software engineering project. Some applications for this kind of programming are quite new, such as encryption methods for secure communication. Others originated decades or centuries ago — they stem from classical problems that require exact calculations with integer coefficients in problems involving polynomials and linear equations. Also, integers of arbitrary length form the numerators and denominators of rational numbers, a form of scalar that's coming into frequent use now to avoid roundoff error. These kinds of applications are increasing in importance because the hardware necessary to perform such calculations in reasonable time is now becoming affordable. One of the first steps in developing MSP beyond the scope of this book will be to implement the arithmetic of integers of arbitrary length.

4.2   Floating Point Arithmetic

Real and Floating Point Numbers

Using decimal notation you can represent a nonzero real number in the form $x = \pm 10^E \times d_0.d_1d_2...$, where the *exponent* E is an integer; the *significand* $d_0.d_1d_2...$ is an infinite sequence of digits d_k in the range $0 \le d_k < 10$, with *leading digit* $d_0 \ne 0$. The value of x is

$$x = \pm\, 10^E \sum_{k=0}^{\infty} 10^{-k}\, d_k \ .$$

For computation, you approximate x by truncating or rounding the significand to n *significant* digits:

$$x \approx \pm 10^E \times d_0.d_1...d_{n-1} = \pm 10^E \sum_{k=0}^{n-1} 10^{-k} d_k \ .$$

You choose n small enough for convenient computation, but large enough for the required precision. Approximations like this, and the number zero, are called *floating point* numbers. If you want to record floating point numbers on a physical medium, you must also limit the exponent to a specific range $E_{min} \le E \le E_{max}$. ($E_{min}$ is generally negative and E_{max} positive.)

It's instructive to contrast the sets of real and floating point numbers available for reasoning and calculating. Consider, for example, floating point numbers with 3 significant digits and exponents E in the range $-8 \le E \le 8$. The two smallest positive floating point numbers in this system are 1.00×10^{-8} and 1.01×10^{-8}; the two largest are 9.98×10^8 and 9.99×10^8. The negative floating point numbers mirror these. In contrast, real numbers can have arbitrarily large or small magnitudes. Moreover, the real numbers form a *continuum*:

There are no gaps. But the floating point numbers form a *finite discrete* set: Nonzero floating point numbers are bounded away from zero, those nearest zero are separated by at least $0.01 \times 10^{-8} = 10^{-10}$, and those largest in magnitude can be separated by as much as $0.01 \times 10^8 = 10^6$. When you use floating point numbers, be careful what you mean by precision, because attainable precision depends on the magnitude of the numbers you're using.

With a floating point system like the one just considered, you may be tempted to use numbers like $u = 0.12 \times 10^{-8}$. But u isn't admissible, because its leading digit is zero. Numbers like u convey less precision (fewer significant digits) than those that really belong to the system. Sometimes numbers like u are in fact useful; then they're called *non-normalized* floating point numbers.

Computers use binary notation, not decimal. Using binary notation for the significand, a nonzero real number has the form $x = \pm 2^E \times b_0.b_1b_2...$, where the *exponent* E is an integer; the *significand* $b_0.b_1b_2...$ is an infinite sequence of bits b_k in the range $0 \le b_k \le 1$, with *leading bit* $b_0 \ne 0$. The value of x is

$$x = \pm\, 2^E \sum_{k=0}^{\infty} 2^{-k}b_k \ .$$

For computation, you obtain a binary floating point system by restricting the significand to n significant bits and the exponent to a range $E_{min} \le E \le E_{max}$.

IEEE Binary Floating Point Standard

In the early days of computing, many different binary floating point systems were used for numerical computation, as well as some decimal systems and some others. That was awkward because results computed by a given algorithm would vary when transferred to a different computer or programming language.

The American National Standards Institute (ANSI) recently approved a floating point arithmetic standard. Languages and hardware that adhere to this standard produce the same results for the same arithmetic problem. The standard was prepared by a committee of the Institute for Electrical and Electronics Engineers (IEEE), and is described in its document, Reference [21].

The Intel 8087 numeric coprocessor family supports the IEEE standard. These chips provide the basis for most numerical computation on the IBM PC computer family, the target machines for Turbo C++. If no coprocessor is installed, PC software often emulates one.

	float	double	long double
Bytes for number	4	8	10
Bits for significand	23 (+1)	52 (+1)	63 (+1)
Bits for exponent	8	11	16
Exponent bias	127	1023	16383
Significant digits	7	15	19
Largest positive number $\approx$	3.4×10^{38}	1.8×10^{308}	1.2×10^{4932}
Smallest positive number $\approx$	1.2×10^{-38}	2.2×10^{-308}	3.4×10^{-4932}
$\varepsilon \approx$	1.2×10^{-7}	2.2×10^{-16}	1.1×10^{-19}

Figure 4.2.1 Types float, double, and long double

For example, normally compiled Turbo C++ programs will use an 8087 family coprocessor for numerical computations if one is installed; if not, a rather involved software system will perform the computations as though an 8087 were in use. The only major difference is speed: The emulated computations may take as much as 10 times as long to complete.

The IEEE standard includes definitions of three floating point data types that are implemented by the 8087 coprocessors and Turbo C++: **float**, **double**, and **long double**. (Their IEEE names are *single*, *double*, and *extended*.) They differ in the number of bytes allocated to store a number, and consequently in the number of bits allocated to exponent and significand. These and other relevant data are displayed in Figure 4.2.1. The following discussion explains the entries in this figure. Many entries and a few other related data are given with full precision by mnemonic macro constants in Turbo C++ header file **Float.H**. (These values disagree occasionally with the Turbo C++ manual. The **Float.H** constants are correct, except it gives 6 instead of 7 as the number of significant digits for **float** values.)

For example, a **double** variable requires 8 bytes — 64 bits — of storage. As shown in Figure 4.2.2, the first bit is the sign (0 for + and 1 for −). The next 11 bits store the exponent, and the final 52 store the significand. The exponent bits will accommodate up to $2^{11} = 2048$ different exponents E. They are apportioned between positive and negative E values by storing the sum e of E and the *bias* 1023. The inequality $0 \le e = E + 1023 < 2048$ implies $-1023 \le E < 1025$. But one of these bit patterns, $e = 1024$, is reserved for special use with infinities and *NaN*s (discussed later). Thus, the valid **double** exponents lie in the range $-1023 \le E \le 1023$.

The largest positive **double** value is binary $1.11\ldots1 \times 2^{1023} \approx 2 \times 2^{1023} = 2^{1024} \approx 1.8 \times 10^{308}$. The smallest positive value is binary

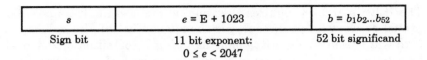

s	$e = E + 1023$	$b = b_1b_2...b_{52}$
Sign bit	11 bit exponent: $0 \leq e < 2047$	52 bit significand

Figure 4.2.2 A double variable

$1.00...01 \times 2^{-1023} \approx 2^{-1023} \approx 2.2 \times 10^{-308}$. (You'll see later that the binary value $1.00...0 \times 2^{-1023}$ isn't allowed.)

A valid nonzero floating point number is normalized: The leading bit b_0 of the significand $b_0.b_1b_2...$ is always 1. Therefore, it's not necessary to store b_0. The remaining 52 bits of a **double** variable are bits $b_1b_2...b_{52}$ of the significand. A **double** value has 53 significant bits.

Under this scheme, the value $1.00... \times 2^{-1023}$ would be stored with $s = 0$, $e = -1023 + 1023 = 0$, and $f = 00...0 = 0$ (using the Figure 4.2.2 notation). All bits would be zero. But IEEE reserves that particular bit pattern, which would otherwise have represented the smallest positive value, to represent zero. The corresponding pattern with $s = 1$ represents -0. The IEEE standard has some rules and suggestions regarding the use of -0; they're beyond the scope of this book.

The largest integer that can be represented as a **double** value without roundoff is binary $1.11...1 \times 2^{52} = 2^{53} - 1 \approx 9.0 \times 10^{15}$, a 16 digit number. Some, but not all, 16 digit numbers are representable without roundoff. That means that **double** values have 15 significant digits in general, and sometimes 16.

The first floating point number larger than 1 is $1 + \varepsilon = $ binary $1.00...01 \times 2^0$, which gives $\varepsilon = 2^{-52} \approx 2.2 \times 10^{-16}$. The number ε, tabulated in Figure 4.2.1, is sometimes used in numerical analysis calculations as a threshold: Numbers δ with magnitude $< \varepsilon$ are regarded as zero, because **double** arithmetic yields $1 + \delta = 1$.

The following table shows how all possible bit patterns of **double** variables are interpreted. Figure 4.2.2 shows a sign bit s, followed by an 11 bit exponent $e = E + 1023$, then a 52 bit significand $b = b_1b_2...b_{52}$.

e	b	Interpretation	
0	0	$(-1)^s 0$	(Zero values)
0	$\neq 0$	$(-1)^s 0.b \times 2^{-1022}$	(Non-normalized numbers)
255	0	$(-1)^s \infty$	(Infinite values)
255	$\neq 0$	NaN	(Not a Number)
All others		$(-1)^s 1.b \times 2^E$	(Normal **double** values)

The IEEE standard requires that non-normalized numbers be interpreted as shown, but discourages their use. The infinite values and *NaN*s are used in reporting and handling error situations like attempts to divide by zero or take the square root of a negative number. Their use is described in somewhat more detail later, in Section 4.5.

All entries in the **double** column of Figure 4.2.1 have been explained. You can mimic this discussion for the **float** and **long double** types.

Arithmetic and Rounding

Following the IEEE standard, an 8087 family coprocessor implements the standard arithmetic operations:

$$x + y \qquad -x \qquad x < y \qquad x \times y$$
$$x - y \qquad |x| \qquad \text{round}(x) \qquad x/y \; .$$

Further, it will extract the exponent or significand from a floating point number, and multiply by a specified power of 2 (by manipulating the exponent). Turbo C++ either uses the coprocessor to perform these operations or else invokes its own routines, which emulate the coprocessor.

In order to ensure correctness of all bits of the result of a floating point operation, the coprocessor performs every computation with some extra bits, then rounds the result. Four rounding methods are provided:

(0) round to nearest   (2) round down
(1) round up   (3) round toward zero (chop) .

If a result computed with extra bits is exactly halfway between its nearest floating point neighbors, and the coprocessor is rounding to nearest, it selects the neighbor with least significant bit zero. About half the time this rounds up, and half the time down, so some roundoff errors may cancel.

The coprocessor provides a mechanism for controlling the rounding method: You store a coded *control word* in a coprocessor register. In turn, Turbo C++ provides Library function

```
unsigned _control87(unsigned NewCW, unsigned Mask)
```

to set the control word. It will set the control word bits that correspond to the 1 bits in **Mask**. You must place the new values in the corresponding bits of **NewCW**. Any remaining **NewCW** bits are ignored. The function returns the modified control word. You'll find the **_control87** prototype in Turbo C++ header file **Float.H**, along with many mnemonic macro constants that you can use for **Mask** and **NewCW**. For example, the constant **MCW_RC** is the mask for the rounding control bits, and the constant **RC_NEAR** contains the bits to be set for rounding to nearest. To select that rounding method, execute **_control87(RC_NEAR,MCW_RC)**. Rounding to nearest is the coprocessor's default method. To select a different method, use **Float.H** constant **RC_DOWN, RC_UP,** or **RC_CHOP**.

You'll probably never have to deal with rounding problems, unless you have to troubleshoot a disagreement between results of a program when run under Turbo C++ and under another C system, or perhaps modify and extend features of the Turbo C++ floating point Library functions. So your lack of information about rounding will probably not be serious. But this information gap is more extensive. To what extent *does* the emulator produce the same results as the coprocessor?

Further, how do you *know* that the coprocessor really produces accurate results? The Intel literature — for example, Reference [22] — is comprehensive enough to let you control the coprocessor. (This requires low level C++ or assembly language techniques.) But it doesn't document the underlying algorithms or any definitive tests. A software package called *Paranoia* has been developed to test floating point arithmetic, and is available in a C version (Reference [26]). The results of a comprehensive test should be published in an accessible source. Unfortunately, that's beyond the scope of this book.

Input/Output

C++ provides several methods for inputing floating point values. They're familiar, so it's not necessary to discuss them in detail here. What's really involved in converting from a decimal floating point input to binary notation? How do you do it by hand? Consider, as an example, the input 0.123 . Write it as a ratio of two integers, first in decimal, then in binary:

$$0.123 = \frac{123}{1000} = \frac{1111011}{1111101000} \ .$$

Now do long division, in binary:

```
                    0 .000111...
1111101000 | 1111011.00000000
             111110.1000
             ─────────────
             111100 10000
             11111 01000
             ─────────────
             11101 010000
             1111 101000
             ─────────────
                 :
```

Finally, normalize: $0.123 = $ binary $0.000111\ldots = $ binary $1.11\ldots \times 2^{-4}$.

Formatting floating point *output* is often unexpectedly difficult. C++ provides comprehensive facilities for this task — too many to consider here. Unfortunately, the facilities provided by any language always seem to fall just short of what's required. For instance, it was necessary to include a special formatting routine **Show** in the MSP **Scalar** module. Output of numerical data is discussed in great detail in Section 3.7 of the author's earlier book (Reference [37]) on Turbo C.

4.3   Math.H Library Functions

This section surveys the mathematical routines declared in Turbo C++ header file **Math.H**. It discusses the underlying algorithms, and stresses the relationship of these functions to the Intel 8087 coprocessor instruction set. Unfortunately, in some cases neither the coprocessor algorithms nor those of the Turbo C++ coprocessor emulator are documented — not even in the published Turbo C++ Library source code, Reference [4]. Later in this section, some methods for testing the **Math.H** functions are considered.

Arithmetic Functions

The first two **Math.H** functions are used to extract the exponent and significand E and S of a **double** value $x = S \times 2^E$, and to assemble x from these components:

```
double frexp(double x, int* E);   // Given x, return
                                  // S and E .
double ldexp(double S, int E);    // Given S and E,
                                  // return x .
```

frexp merely arranges to execute the 8087 instruction **FXTRACT**. The next three functions are involved with rounding:

```
double ceil (double x);      // Return the smallest integer
                             // ⌈x⌉ ≥ x , in double format.
double floor(double x);      // Return the largest integer
                             // ⌊x⌋ ≤ x , in double format.
double modf (double x,       // Set c = chop(x) and
            double* c);      // return x - chop(x).
```

For example,

x	$\lceil x \rceil$	$\lfloor x \rfloor$	chop(x)	$x - $chop($x$)
1.234	2	1	1	.234
−1.234	−1	−2	−1	−.234

When x is an integer, $x = \lceil x \rceil = \lfloor x \rfloor = $ chop(x). It's always true that chop(x) and $x - $chop($x$) have the same sign as x. All three functions make essential use of the 8087 rounding instruction **FRNDINT**.

Functions **fmod** and **fabs** implement modular division and absolute value:

```
double fmod(double x,        // Divide x / d to get an
           double d);        // integer quotient; return
                             // the remainder.
double fabs(double x);       // Return x .
```

The value returned by **fmod** is determined like the remainder for integer division:

$$\frac{x}{d} = q + \frac{r}{d} \quad x = qd + r \ ,$$

q is an integer, $|r| < |d|$, and sign(r) = sign(d). Function **fmod** is built around the 8087 instruction **FPREM**.

Powers and Logarithms; Hyperbolic Functions

Several **Math.H** functions implement roots, exponentials, logarithms, and powers:

```
double sqrt (double x);      // Return √x .
double exp  (double x);      // Return eˣ .
double log  (double x);      // Return log x .
double log10(double x);      // Return log₁₀x .
```

Function **sqrt** is merely an interface to 8087 instruction **FSQRT**. The algorithm that underlies the computation of $\sqrt{x}$ is undocumented. Function **exp** is based on the 8087 instruction **F2XM1**, which computes $2^x - 1$ for x in the interval $0 \le x \le \frac{1}{2}$. The **exp** code carries out some algebraic manipulations involving the constant $\log 2$ to compute e^x after it gets $2^x - 1$ from the coprocessor. The algorithm for computing $2^x - 1$ is undocumented. Functions **log** and **log10** are based on the 8087 instructions **FYL2X** and **FYL2XP1**, which compute $y \log_2 x$ and $y \log_2(x+1)$. (FYL2XP1 is used to compute logarithms of numbers near 1, and restricts x to the interval $0 \le |x| < 1 - \frac{1}{2}\sqrt{2}$.) The **log** and **log10** codes carry out some algebraic manipulations involving the constant $\log 2$ to compute $\log x$ and $\log_{10} x$ after they get $\log 2 \log_2 x$ or $\log_{10} 2 \log_2 x$ from the coprocessor. The algorithms that underlie **FYL2X** and **FYL2XP1** are undocumented.

Two **Math.H** functions compute powers:

```
double pow  (double x,      // Return xᵖ .
             double p);
double pow10(int    p);     // Return 10ᵖ .
```

For positive integral powers, **pow** and **pow10** use the algorithm already described in Section 3.7 for polynomials. For negative integers p, they compute $x^p = 1/x^{-p}$ and $10^p = 1/10^{-p}$. When $x > 0$ and p is not an integer, **pow** computes x^p via the formula

$$x^p = 2^{p \log_2 x} .$$

It uses the coprocessor instructions mentioned earlier to compute the power of 2 and the base 2 logarithm. You can use **pow** to compute most radicals via the formula

$$\sqrt[r]{b} = b^{1/r}$$

but this won't work when $b < 0$ and r is an odd integer. MSP provides a more convenient function root that works in all cases. It is described in Section 4.4.

Three hyperbolic functions are declared in **Math.H** :

$$\sinh x = \frac{e^x - e^{-x}}{2} \qquad \cosh x = \frac{e^x - e^{-x}}{2} \qquad \tanh x = \frac{\sinh x}{\cosh x} \; .$$

Their implementations are straightforward.

Trigonometric Functions

This **Math.H** function facilitates elementary trigonometry calculations:

```
double hypot(double x,    // Return (x² + y²)^½ .
             double y);
```

Its implementation uses coprocessor instruction **FSQRT**.
Math.H declares three trigonometric functions:

```
double tan(double A);
double cos(double A);
double sin(double A);
```

The first step in their calculation uses the coprocessor division instruction **FPREM** to compute $A' = A \bmod \pi/4$. Via an undocumented algorithm, the coprocessor instruction **FPTAN** then computes values x and y such that $\tan A' = y/x$. FPREM also returns the low order three bits of the integer quotient of A by $\pi/4$. Function **tan** inspects these, and negates and/or interchanges x, y so that the resulting pair represents tan A, and x and y have the same signs as cos A and sin A. With that preparation, it's apparent how the three functions compute their values, using **hypot**:

$$\frac{y}{x} = \tan A \qquad \sin A = \frac{y}{\sqrt{x^2 + y^2}} \qquad \cos A = \frac{x}{\sqrt{x^2 + y^2}} \; .$$

Math.H also declares these inverse trigonometric functions:

```
double atan2(double y,    // Return Θ so that -π < Θ < π
             double x);   // and x , y = cos Θ, sin Θ.
double atan (double t);   // Return tan⁻¹ t .
double asin (double y);   // Return sin⁻¹ y .
double acos (double x);   // Return cos⁻¹ x .
```

Function **atan2** is based on the coprocessor instruction **FPATAN**, which requires that $0 \le y < x$. When this condition is not fulfilled, **atan2** must do some trigonometric manipulation. It handles negative x, y values with the equation $\tan^{-1}(-t) = -\tan^{-1} t$. If $0 \le x < y$, it uses

$$\tan^{-1} \frac{y}{x} = \frac{\pi}{2} - \cot^{-1} \frac{y}{x} = \frac{\pi}{2} - \tan^{-1} \frac{x}{y} \ .$$

Further trigonometric manipulations permit calculation of the remaining inverse functions, as follows. If $A = \sin^{-1} t$, then $t = \sin A$, so $\cos^2 A = 1 - t^2$. Because A is in the range of the inverse sine, $|A| < \pi/2$, so $\cos A$ is positive and

$$\tan A = \frac{\sin A}{\cos A} = \frac{t}{\sqrt{1 - t^2}}$$

Since A is also in the range of the inverse tangent, this equation and the definition of A yield

$$\sin^{-1} t = \begin{cases} -\dfrac{\pi}{2} & \text{if } -1 = t, \\[2ex] \tan^{-1} \dfrac{t}{\sqrt{1 - t^2}} & \text{if } -1 < t < 1, \\[2ex] \dfrac{\pi}{2} & \text{if } t = 1. \end{cases}$$

The inverse cosine is computed via the formula $\cos^{-1} t = \pi/2 - \sin^{-1} t$.

Testing Math.H Functions

How can you test the accuracy of the **Math.H** functions? Given the number of vital activities that depend on accurate calculations, there should be a standard way to certify the basic functions. But there's almost no literature on this subject. The Intel coprocessor manuals and the Borland Turbo C++ manuals don't even mention it. The author feels that any book on numerical analysis software should cover this topic. It was impossible to do so adequately here. Because of the lack of easily accessible material, undertaking and reporting on a certification project might justify a book in itself.

The easiest way to proceed, of course, would be to compare Turbo C++ results against some system that's already certified. Information about such systems, if they exist, is inaccessible, so this *external* validation method isn't available.

Another method would be to ascertain what algorithms are implemented by the coprocessors and the emulator software, then to certify the algorithms mathematically. It would remain to check for bugs in their implementation. Again, the information is inaccessible. Obtaining it through reverse engineering with a debugger would be feasible but very arduous. The survey under the previous heading makes a start on this method, describing the **Math.H** functions in considerable detail. But the critical information is lacking:

* description of the algorithms that underlie the coprocessor instructions **FSQRT, F2XM1, FYL2X, FYL2XP1, FPTAN,** and **FPATAN**;
* assurance that the emulator software uses the same algorithms.

Even with this information, considerable investigation would be necessary to check the implementation.

A third strategy would be to develop a new set of mathematical algorithms whose accuracy is known, and through some means certify that the implementation is bug free. Then you could compare results with those from the coprocessor and emulator. This would be a major development project, comparable to designing and validating a new emulator, except that its efficiency would be unimportant.

Centuries before computers came into use, mathematicians used yet another technique — *internal* validation — to check tables. With this method, you select algebraic or trigonometric identities that relate tabulated function values, and check that they're satisfied within acceptable roundoff error. This method is used next to check some of the **Math.H** functions.

Internal Validation Experiments

You can select many identities to check **Math.H** functions, bringing different function properties to the forefront. The program in Figure 4.3.1 uses the sine double angle formula to test **sin** and **cos**. It inputs a value x, then computes the relative error E incurred by using $2 \sin x \cos x$ in place of $\sin 2x$. If the values are accurate to 16 significant digits, then E should be approximately 10^{-16}, or larger if $\sin 2x$ is very small. The displayed output shows that E is generally smaller than this prediction.

Success for a very large sample of x values would constitute strong evidence for the validity of the **sin** and **cos** functions. Two possibilities could weaken the impact, however. First, if the double angle

```
#include "Scalar.H"
#include   "Math.H"

void main() {
  clrscr();
  cout << "          TESTING ACCURACY OF  sin(x), cos(x)  \n\n"
          "Compute relative error of the  sin 2x  formula:\n"
          "     E =  |(sin 2x - 2 sin x cos x)/sin 2x| .          ";
  for (;;) {
    cout << "\n\nEnter  x  (x = 0  to stop):  ";
    double x;  cin >> x;
    double y = sin(2*x);
    if (y == 0) return;
    double E = fabs((y - 2*sin(x)*cos(x))/y);
    cout << "E = ";  Show(E); }}
```

Output

```
          TESTING ACCURACY OF   sin(x), cos(x)

Compute relative error of the  sin 2x  formula:
     E =  |(sin 2x - 2 sin x cos x)/sin 2x| .

Enter  x  (x = 0  to stop):  .03
E =   2.7e-17

Enter  x  (x = 0  to stop):  3
E =   4.6e-17

Enter  x  (x = 0  to stop):  300
E =   7.0e-17
```

Figure 4.3.1 Testing sin and cos

formula had been heavily involved in the design of the algorithms, it might not betray systematic errors. Second, software bugs often occur at case boundaries — transitions between methods that apply to arguments x in different ranges. Without source code to identify those, a sampler would probably miss the most vulnerable regions.

If an x value failed this test, you wouldn't know whether to suspect **sin** or **cos**. You'd need to try another identity that involves only one of these functions, and you'd probably want to use as little arithmetic as possible, too.

It might be more appropriate for this program to operate entirely in binary. That would prevent confusing **sin** and **cos** phenomena with the computation of 10^{-n} and the conversion to decimal output.

Another type of internal validation applies to inverse functions. For example, the program in Figure 4.3.2 involves the square root and square functions. Given inputs x and n, it computes $y_1 = \sqrt{x}$ rounded to n decimals, and y_0, $y_2 = y \pm 10^{-n}$. Then it outputs $y_k^2 - x$ for $k = 0,1,2$. The difference for $k = 1$ should have the smallest magnitude. Sample outputs are given, showing what happens when the limit of precision is reached. In this example, function **sqrt** does achieve the maximum possible precision, because the difference for k = 1 is smallest until the y_k values become indistinguishable. A version of the Figure 4.3.2 program that tested all possible inputs would constitute a *complete* validation of the square root routine.

Analogous programs could be used to validate other inverse pairs, for example **exp, log** and **tan, atan**.

4.4 MSP Module RealFunc

Although the Turbo C++ Library includes a rich variety of real functions, some are missing, and should be included, either because of their general usefulness, or just to provide completeness. (For example, why should you have to remember which trigonometric functions are available? Why not have them all?) This book's MSP software package includes a number of additional functions of similar nature in its **RealFunc** module. Like the other modules, this one has a header file **RealFunc.H** and a source code file **RealFunc.CPP**. The header is listed in Appendix A.3; you'll find the source code file on the accompanying diskette. Most of the functions are straightforward implementations of their mathematical definitions — many consist of a single **return** statement. Therefore, source code is not discussed much in this section.

Factorials and Binomial Coefficients

Turbo C++ has no built-in factorial function, so one is provided in the **RealFunc** unit: **long double Factorial(int n)**. The return type was chosen to permit the largest possible argument n. This function causes overflow only if $n > 1054$. Don't take the result very seriously for such large values of n, however, since $n!$ has several thousand digits and this function approximates $n!$ simply by multiplying the first n positive integers, with 19 digit precision.

The binomial coefficients are usually defined by the equation

$$\binom{x}{m} = \frac{x!}{m!(x-m)!} = \frac{x(x-1)(x-2)\ldots(x-(m-1))}{m(m-1)(m-2)\ldots} \quad (1)$$

where x and m are integers, with $x \geq m \geq 0$. In Reference [28, Section 1.2.6], Knuth finds utility in allowing x to be an arbitrary real number: The right-hand side of the previous equation still makes sense. Therefore, this definition is implemented by **RealFunc** function **double Binomial(double x, int n)**.

```
#include "Scalar.H"
#include  "Math.H"

void main() {
  clrscr();
  cout << "           TESTING ACCURACY OF  sqrt(x)         \n\n"
          "Compute  y1 = sqrt(x)  rounded to  n  decimals\n"
          "and set  y0, y2 = y1 ± 10^(-n) .  Then compare\n"
          "y0², y1², and  y2²  with  x .                 ";
  for (;;) {
    cout << "\n\nEnter  x  and  n  (x = 0  to stop):  ";
    double x;  int n;  cin >> x >> n;
    if (x <= 0) return;
    double p = pow10(n);                        // p = 10ⁿ .
    double y[3];
    y[1]  = sqrt(x);
    y[1] = floor(p*y[1] + .5);                  // Round
    y[2] = (y[1] + 1)/p;                        // y0  to  y2
    y[0] = (y[1] - 1)/p;                        // to  n
    y[1] /= p;                                  // decimals.
    for (int k = 0; k <= 2; ++k) {
      cout << "\ny" << k << " = ";
      cout.setf(ios::left,ios::adjustfield);
      cout.width(n+6);
      cout << setprecision(n) << y[k] << "  y" << k
           << "² - x = ";
      Show(y[k]*y[k] - x); }}}
```

Output

```
           TESTING ACCURACY OF  sqrt(x)

      Compute  y1 = sqrt(x)  rounded to  n  decimals
      and set  y0, y2 = y1 ± 10^(-n) .  Then compare
      y0², y1², and  y2²  with  x .

      Enter  x  and  n  (x = 0  to stop):  2 15

      y0 = 1.414213562373094      y0² - x = -2.9e-15
      y1 = 1.414213562373095      y1² - x = -3.5e-16
      y2 = 1.414213562373096      y2² - x =  2.8e-15

      Enter  x  and  n  (x = 0  to stop):  2 16

      y0 = 1.4142135623730951     y0² - x =  2.7e-16
      y1 = 1.4142135623730951     y1² - x =  2.7e-16
      y2 = 1.4142135623730954     y2² - x =  9.0e-16
```

Figure 4.3.2 Testing sqrt

Functions Root and Logbase

Normally, you'd compute an rth root of a number b by regarding it as a power:

$$\sqrt[r]{b} = b^{1/r} \ .$$

In most cases, you could use the **Math.H** function **pow(b,1.0/r)**. However, there's one common situation where **pow** doesn't work: when $x < 0$ and n is an odd integer. Then, you must use the equation

$$\sqrt[r]{b} = - \sqrt[r]{-b} \qquad (b < 0, r\ odd) \ .$$

MSP provides function **Root** to handle *all* cases. Here's its source code:

```
double Root(double b,           // Return b^(1/r) .
            double r) {         // This function provides
  double* nn;                   // for odd integral (type
  if (b < 0 && modf(r,nn) = = 0 // long ) roots of a
      && fabs(*nn) <= MAXLONG   // negative b . Math.H
      && long(r) % 2 != 0)      // function pow handles
    return -exp(log(-b)/r);     // all other cases.
  else return pow(b,1/r); }
```

The left-to-right evaluation of the conjunction in the conditional statement is essential!

Often in mathematical work you need logarithms $\log_b$ relative to various bases b. The **Math.H** natural and common logarithm functions **log** and **log10** provide for bases e and 10 but others are needed, too, particularly base 2. $l = \log_b x$ means $x = b^l = e^{l \log b}$; hence, $\log x = l \log b$, and

$$\log_b x = \frac{\log x}{\log b} \ .$$

MSP implements this equation with function

```
double logbase(double b, double x)
```

(This is inefficient, since the Turbo C++ $\log x$ function first invokes the coprocessor or its emulator to compute $\log_2 x$, then converts that to $\log x$ using a similar equation. But Turbo C++ doesn't provide direct access to the $\log_2 x$ function.)

Hyperbolic Functions

Of the hyperbolic functions, **Math.H** implements only sinh, cosh, and tanh. (See Section 4.3 for their definitions.) MSP includes the hyperbolic cotangent, secant, and cosecant as well:

$$\coth x = \frac{\cosh x}{\sinh x} \qquad \mathrm{sech}\ x = \frac{1}{\cosh x} \qquad \mathrm{csch}\ x = \frac{1}{\sinh x}\ .$$

Their implementations are straightforward — one statement each.

MSP also includes the inverse hyperbolic functions. Since these are not so familiar, it's appropriate to derive one of their formulas. The inverse hyperbolic cosine ArgCosh is typical. Suppose $x = \cosh y$. Then $x \geq 1$ and

$$x = \frac{e^y + e^{-y}}{2} = \frac{(e^y)^2 + 1}{2e^y} \qquad (e^y)^2 - 2xe^y + 1 = 0\ .$$

By the Quadratic Formula,

$$e^y = \frac{2x \pm \sqrt{4x^2 - 4}}{2}\ .$$

Since the radical is $< 2x$, both signs give possible values for e^y. By mathematical convention, the + sign is used. This amounts to reflecting the graph of $x = \cosh y$ across the line $x = y$ so that the resulting catenary opens rightward, then selecting its upper half as the graph of the inverse function. The desired formula is

$$\mathrm{ArgCosh}\ x = y = \log(x + \sqrt{x^2 - 1})\ .$$

Here are the formulas for the other inverse hyperbolic functions:

$$\mathrm{ArgSinh}\ x = \log(x + \sqrt{x^2 + 1})$$

$$\mathrm{ArgTanh}\ x = \frac{1}{2}\log\frac{1 + x}{1 - x} \qquad \mathrm{ArgCoth}\ x = \frac{1}{2}\log\frac{x + 1}{x - 1}$$

$$\mathrm{ArgSech}\ x = \log\frac{1 + \sqrt{1 - x^2}}{x} \qquad \mathrm{ArgCsch}\ x = \log\frac{1 + \sqrt{1 + x^2}}{x}\ .$$

The implementations of these six functions are straightforward: one statement each.

Trigonometric Functions

Of the trigonometric functions, **Math.H** implements only **sin, cos,** and **tan.** MSP includes the cotangent, secant, and cosecant as well:

$$\cot x = \frac{\cos x}{\sin x} \qquad \sec x = \frac{1}{\cos x} \qquad \csc x = \frac{1}{\sin x} \ .$$

Their implementations are straightforward — one statement each.

Similarly, the Turbo C++ Library implements only three of the inverse trigonometric functions: $\sin^{-1}$, $\cos^{-1}$, and $\tan^{-1}$, corresponding to **Math.H** functions **asin**, **acos**, and **atan**. MSP implements $\cot^{-1}$, $\sec^{-1}$, and $\csc^{-1}$ as well, with **RealFunc** functions **acot**, **asec**, and **acsc**. Each of these has a formula in terms of $\tan^{-1}$, derived like the $\sin^{-1}$ formula in Section 4.3:

$$\cot^{-1} t = \frac{\pi}{2} - \tan^{-1} t$$
$$\csc^{-1} t = \frac{\pi}{2} - \sec^{-1} t \qquad\qquad \sec^{-1} t = \begin{cases} \tan^{-1}\sqrt{t^2 - 1} & \text{if } t \geq 1 \\ \tan^{-1}\sqrt{t^2 - 1} + \pi & \text{if } t \leq -1 \ . \end{cases}$$

Their implementations are straightforward.

The complication in the definition of the inverse secant corresponds to the choice of what to delete once you've reflected the graph of $x = \sec y$ across the line $x = y$. This particular choice seems the most common, but is no ironclad convention. The author has seen at least one other in a popular calculus text. (The other definition resulted in a simpler differentiation formula for the inverse secant.) The definition just given for $\csc^{-1}$ is intentionally tied to that of $\sec^{-1}$. It works under both conventions. *Beware!*

4.5 Turbo C++ Arithmetic and Math.H Error Handling

This section investigates how Turbo C++ programs behave when faced with error situations involving arithmetic operations and mathematical Library functions, and discusses the programming techniques necessary to alter that behavior. There are four overall questions:

• What sort of error conditions are considered?
• What does an ordinary Turbo C++ program do in those cases?
• How can you arrange to intervene in that process?
• How can you re-establish the previous error response conventions?

As an example, consider writing a calculator program that accepts user input and performs certain calculations on demand. One of its simpler services is multiplying two **double** values x, $y > 1$. Their product could *overflow* — it could be too large to store in a double variable. In that case, if you merely attempt to multiply them, your program will crash after displaying the error message

```
Floating point error: Overflow.
Abnormal program termination
```

How can you intervene in this response, and, instead, just ask the user for more appropriate input? You could first divide the largest **double** value by x and compare the result against y. But that seems roundabout and inefficient. Moreover, you'd need a more complicated test if x and y weren't necessarily > 1, and analogous protection for other arithmetic operations or Library functions might be even more involved. Is there a better way?

To approach this question, you have to consider what kinds of error situations can occur. The choice of intervention method depends on how the underlying hardware and software detects and reacts to the error. Therefore, error situations are classified not by any mathematical criterion, but according to how and when they're detected. Moreover, successful intervention depends on understanding what happens after that occurs.

When your hardware or coprocessor emulator detects an error, it executes an *interrupt*. The interrupt concept is fundamental to systems programming, but rarely encountered by scientific or engineering applications programmers. The next heading briefly describes this idea. Most of the later topics in this section are related to interrupts to some extent.

Before you consider error handling facilities more deeply, you should realize that the detailed aspects of this subject are still under development. In fact, Borland International, Inc. warns that future Turbo C++ versions may no longer support one of its major error handling features, the **matherr** function, because that doesn't comply with the ANSI standard. On the other hand, the newer error *signalling* facility, which does meet the standard, is implemented using variable argument lists, which are not standard. The authoritative *Annotated C++ Reference Manual*, by the language's developers at AT&T (Reference [13]), devotes an entire chapter to experimental work on error handling techniques.

Interrupts

When one C++ function invokes another, several actions take place automatically — that is, the compiler sets up the appropriate code without any detailed instructions from you. For example, consider what happens when function **Caller** executes a statement like z = **f(x,y)**.

First, **Caller** places the values of parameters **x** and **y** on the stack (or their addresses, if they're reference parameters). Then it stacks the return address. This is the address of the instruction in **Caller** that should be executed immediately after **f** completes its computation. That instruction will be identified by the letters RRR when it occurs later in this paragraph. Now, **Caller** executes a jump instruction, transferring control to **f**. **Caller** knows where **f** is, *because the linker inserted into the* **.exe** *file the addresses of* **Caller** *and* **f** *relative to the start of your program,* and DOS provided the starting address when it loaded the **.exe** file. At this point, **f** begins execution and computes a function value **v**, using the parameters or their addresses, which are on the stack immediately under the return address. When this computation is finished, the stack will be the same as it was when **f** began execution. Then **f** places **v** in a register (or its address, depending on its type) and jumps back to **Caller**, using the return address that's now on top of the stack. **Caller** copies the return value into **z** — this is instruction RRR. **Caller** can find the return value because it saw the **f** prototype during compilation. Moreover, **Caller** knows what it put on the stack, so it restores the stack to its status when the function call began.

The function invocation process depends on the *italicized* sentence in the last paragraph: The object codes for the functions must be *linked*.

A *system service* function **f** that provides a service to other programs is often loaded separately, in the BIOS, with DOS, or as an operating system extension. Its code isn't available to **Caller**, so you can't link them. Moreover, system designers can't give **f** a fixed address in all machines, because that would interfere with system upgrades and with the choice of optional system components. How should a function call be implemented for a system service function?

An *interrupt* is a modified function call that provides for such situations. A function **f** that's invoked via an interrupt is called an *Interrupt Service Routine* (ISR). ISRs must be coded according to special conventions, as you'll see. You must assign an ISR an *interrupt number* in the range 0...255. (Since your systems software must provide for several hundred services of this type, some ISRs merely serve as dispatchers. When you need a service you execute the ISR after assigning a service code to one of its parameters; the ISR inspects the code, then provides the appropriate service by executing an ordinary function, which is not itself an ISR.) When an ISR with number n is loaded, as a part of the BIOS of DOS, or of some other systems software package, its address must be stored in memory as *interrupt vector n*. The interrupt vectors occupy the same position in the memory of every IBM compatible PC running under DOS. To obtain the service provided by ISR number *n*, your program must execute the machine language instruction **Int n**, which operates something like a function call, except it obtains the ISR address from interrupt vector *n*. Your system's software manuals specify the parameters of the ISR.

The interrupt concept is complicated by the circumstances in which your program — function **Caller** — needs to invoke a system function. Often, these are beyond its control. For example, data might arrive on a communication line while **Caller** is performing some low-priority computation. Or a timer may signal that it's time to back up some file. At any point in function **Caller**, an unrelated event may require execution of an ISR to obtain some higher priority system service. These events are often detected by your hardware — in these examples, a serial port or the clock. These and a few other hardware components are allowed to trigger a *hardware* interrupt at any time while your program is executing. Actually, they send a signal to a hardware component called the *interrupt controller*, which checks priorities, then executes the interrupt.

How can a hardware interrupt service avoid disrupting your program? First, ISR programmers must know how to avoid conflict with other programs over use of memory and hardware components. Second, provided no such conflicts occur, execution of your program can be suspended temporarily and reactivated later if the contents of several CPU registers are saved at the instant of interruption and restored just before reactivation. The **Int n** interrupt instruction actually saves the registers in a specific order on the stack before it jumps to the ISR. Just before the ISR returns to **Caller**, it must use that data to restore the registers to their previous values.

The coprocessor emulator is driven by a hardware interrupt. If an 8086 family CPU encounters a coprocessor instruction but no coprocessor is installed, it executes an interrupt. The corresponding ISR is the emulator. The emulator uses the stacked return address to locate the preceding instruction in your program, which caused the interrupt, then inspects the stacked register images and imitates the operation that a coprocessor would have executed had it been installed.

This description of the IBM PC interrupt system has been tailored to the needs of this book, and perhaps oversimplified. If you need more detail, please consult the author's earlier books, References [37] and [38], and the Intel manual, Reference [22].

Classifying Errors

The Turbo C++ mathematical error handling facilities deal with errors of two kinds: hardware exceptions and Library function errors.

Hardware exceptions are interrupts triggered when you ask the CPU, coprocessor, or its emulator to do something it can't: for example, to

- divide an integer by 0,
- divide a floating point number by 0,
- perform a floating point operation that would cause overflow or underflow,
- calculate the square root or logarithm of a negative number.

An attempt to divide an integer by zero causes the CPU itself to execute an exception interrupt. The other exceptions all are issued by a coprocessor or emulator.

The C++ mathematical Library functions all test for input parameters that would cause hardware exceptions or other mathematical errors. In these situations, the functions don't just continue and trigger interrupts; instead, they execute specific Library functions designed to handle errors.

The coprocessor can be set to handle some error situations automatically without causing exceptions: It returns *NaN* (*Not a Number*) or ±∞ values. But it can't handle some of these values as operands in later calculations; if you ask it to do that, it *will* issue an exception. This error handling technique, called *masking*, is discussed in more detail later in this section.

Before discussing Turbo C++ error handling methods in detail, it's useful to describe briefly the structure of a Turbo C program.

Turbo C++ Initialization and Exit Routines

The object code for your Turbo C++ program consists of three main parts: the initialization routine, the code corresponding to the program itself, and the exit routines. The initialization routine, called **C0.Asm** in the published Turbo C++ Library source code (Reference [4]), installs the emulator ISR if no coprocessor is installed. (You can use a compiler switch to prevent installation if you know your program won't use the emulator.) The initialization routine also sets up the heap memory allocation scheme, and some other constants and addresses that your program code may use. In this process, **C0.Asm** saves the previous values of any interrupt vectors that it changes.

After initialization, **C0.Asm** calls function **main:** This executes your program.

If **main** returns (that is, if your program terminates normally), **C0.Asm** proceeds with its next instruction, calling Library routine **exit(int E)** with **E = 0**, which flushes all output file buffers and closes all open files. (Your program may have used Library function **atexit** to "register" some further routines for **exit** to execute.) In turn, **exit** invokes function **_exit(int E)** with the same E parameter, which restores to their previous status any interrupt vectors that **C0.Asm** may have changed earlier, then returns to DOS, setting the DOS **ErrorLevel** variable equal to E. If your program is using a small memory model, **_exit** also performs the test that reports some programming errors via the message **Null pointer assignment**. You may also call **exit** or **_exit** directly.

Hardware Exceptions

Mathematical errors that cause hardware exceptions are detected either by the CPU or the coprocessor. The CPU detects only attempted integer division by zero, and in that case it executes **Int 0**. What does the corresponding ISR do? This story is complicated, and is given here only as an indication of the care you must take in investigating such matters. When you boot your machine, the BIOS automatically installs an Int 0 ISR that does nothing but return to the interrupted program. Midway in the boot process, the BIOS installs DOS. The DOS installation routine replaces the BIOS ISR with one that prints the message

```
Divide Overflow
Exiting...
```

That is, DOS replaces interrupt vector 0 by the address of its own ISR. After this message, the DOS ISR exits from your program to DOS. When DOS loads a Turbo C++ program, it transfers control to the Turbo C++ initialization routine. That replaces the DOS **Int 0** service routine by yet another, which prints the message

```
Divide error
Abnormal program termination
```

and calls the Library routine **_exit(3)** — this sets the DOS **ErrorLevel** variable = 3 to report the error. This abnormal termination doesn't invoke function **exit:** No registered exit routines are executed, and your files may remain in disarray.

All other hardware exceptions are issued by the coprocessor. These also cause an interrupt. The details of the corresponding ISR are more complicated than those for the integer division exception handler just described; they even vary with the PC model. In short, the Turbo C++ initialization routine installs an ISR that ascertains the type of error by looking at the coprocessor registers, then prints a message and terminates by calling **_exit**. For example, if you attempt to divide a floating point number by zero, it prints

```
Floating point error: Divide by 0.
Abnormal program termination
```

As with the integer division exception, this abnormal termination may leave your files in disarray.

The previous paragraph was oversimplified. The Turbo C++ ISR actually uses the signalling process, described later in this section, to call a service function that writes the message and terminates your program. It's possible for you to substitute your own service function to avoid terminating.

Library Function Errors

Faced with input parameters that would lead to a mathematical error or a hardware exception, a **Math.H** Library function executes function **_matherr**, with parameters that identify itself and the type of error. **_matherr** in turn executes function **matherr**. The latter classifies the error and returns, reporting either that it was unable to fix the error (return 0), or that there's no problem (return 1). In the first case, **_matherr** prints an error message identifying the Library function and the type of error. In either case, **_matherr** returns to the Library function that encountered the error. (The second case — no problem — is used for some situations where the coprocessor reports an error that ANSI C doesn't object to.)

For example, if you attempt to compute **double z = sqrt(-1)**, where **sqrt** is the real square root routine (not the complex one), you'll get an error message from **_matherr**, and execution proceeds. But if you try to *do* anything with the z value, you may cause a hardware exception later. Here's an example program and its output:

```
void main( ) {
  double z = sqrt(-1);
  printf("Via printf , sqrt(-1) = %f .\n",z);
  cout << "Via cout , sqrt(-1) = " << z; }
```

Output

```
sqrt: DOMAIN error
Via  printf ,  sqrt(-1) = +NAN .
Via  cout   ,  sqrt(-1) = Floating point error: Domain.
Abnormal program termination
```

The newer **cout** stream output routine checks to avoid propagating the error, but the older StdIO function **printf** doesn't.

Borland ships with Turbo C++ the **matherr** source code, for you to modify if you want more elaborate error handling. That's discussed under the next heading.

Customizing Function Matherr

You can implement custom error handling for the Turbo C++ **Math.H** Library functions by altering function

```
int matherr(struct exception *E).
```

As mentioned under the last heading, a mathematics Library function error transfers control to **matherr**. Structure ***E** describes the situation that led to the error. It's defined in **Math.H**:

```
struct exception {
    int    type;     // Type of error.
    char*  name;     // Name of Library function in error.
    double arg1;     // First function argument.
    double arg2;     // Second function argument (if any).
    double retval; } // Return value for function.
```

(This differs from the Turbo C++ manual; the manual is wrong.) **Math.H** also defines an enumerated type that provides constants for the possible values of the **type** field:

```
typdef enum {
    DOMAIN = 1,   // Argument not in the function's domain.
    SING,         // Argument is a singularity.
    OVERFLOW,     // Argument would cause overflow.
    UNDERFLOW,    // Argument would cause underflow.
    TLOSS,        // Value would have no accurate digits.
    PLOSS }       // Not used.
    _mexcep .
```

Unless you alter the **matherr** code appropriately, the Library function that encountered the error will ultimately return **E–>retval** as function value.

As examples of **DOMAIN** and **SING** errors, Math.H cites attempts to execute **log(–1)** and **pow(0,–2)** — evidently error type **SING** takes precedence over **DOMAIN**. An attempt to compute **sin(1e70)** would cause a **TLOSS** error: The first step would be to compute 10^{70} mod $\pi/4$. For any digits to be accurate in that result, you'd have to use $\pi/4$ expanded to about 70 significant digits, which is impossible with type **double**.

If **matherr** returns 0 to function _matherr, the latter will inspect *E, write a message identifying the error type and the Library function that encountered the error, then return to the Library function. If **matherr** returns a nonzero value, _matherr skips the error message.

Figure 4.5.1 includes three pieces of code: a very short customized **matherr** function, a test program, and a declaration that sets up a long jump facility. (Long jumps are described under the next heading.) This **matherr** code supersedes the Library code because the linker finds it in the object code file in your working directory before it searches the Library for the name **matherr**. The test program — function **main** — causes an error in Library function **sqrt** and then recovers nicely, using **matherr** and the long jump facility. Function **main** merely inputs a value a, then outputs (log sin a)$^{1/2}$. This slightly complicated function was selected to emphasize that it's often difficult to decide *a priori* which values belong to the domain of a function. Programs become simpler if you let the Library functions do that job. If bad input causes an error in any of the three nested functions, the customized **matherr** code outputs an error message and jumps to the input statement in function **main**. The output displays repeated unsuccessful attempts to input an appropriate a value, then finally a success.

Since you have the original code for **matherr**, you can easily disable your custom version and return to the original at any time.

The Turbo C++ manual warns that **matherr** is not designed according to ANSI C standards, that its use is not portable, and that it may not be included in subsequent versions of Turbo C++.

Long Jumps

The C++ *long jump* facility was designed for error intervention like that shown in Figure 4.5.1. Its two functions are prototyped in Turbo C++ header file **SetJmp.H**:

```
#include "General.H"
#include    <Math.H>
#include  <SetJmp.H>

char* MathErrorName[] = {"","DOMAIN","SING","OVERFLOW",
                         "UNDERFLOW","TLOSS","PLOSS"};
jmp_buf Input;

int matherr(struct exception *E) {       // Custom mathematics
   cout << "Bad input caused  "          // Library error handler.
        << MathErrorName[E->type]
        << " error  in  " << E->name
        << " .  Try again.";
   longjmp(Input,1);                      // Parameter  1  not used.
   return 0; }                            // return  never executes.

void main() {
   clrscr();
   cout << "Testing  matherr  and the long jump facility.\n";
   setjmp(Input);  cout << "\nEnter  a = ";
   double a;        cin >> a;
   cout << "sqrt(log(2*sin(a))) = " << sqrt(log(2*sin(a)));
   Inspect; }
```

Output

```
Testing  matherr  and the long jump facility.

Enter  a = .1
Bad input caused  DOMAIN  error  in  sqrt .  Try again.
Enter  a = -.1
Bad input caused  DOMAIN  error  in  log .  Try again.
Enter  a = 1e70
Bad input caused  TLOSS  error  in  sin .  Try again.
Enter  a = 1
sqrt(log(2*sin(a))) = 0.721487
Press any key...
```

Figure 4.5.1 Customized matherr and long jump demonstration

```
int setjmp (jmp_buf Status);
voidlongjmp(jmp_buf Status, int k);
```

That header file also declares a structure type **jmp_buf**, which is only used in the parameters to these two functions. You never have to modify a **jmp_buf** structure, so it's not necessary to describe it here. In short, **setjmp** returns 0 to its caller and records in **Status** enough information about the state of the CPU at that instant to restart your program from that point. Function **longjmp** uses **Status** to do just that. Moreover, it appears to return **k** instead of 0 to the function that called **setjmp**. (If you set **k** = 0, **longjmp** will reset **k** = 1.) The **jmp_buf** structure **Status** must be declared in a scope that encompasses the calls to both **setjmp** and **longjmp**; in the Figure 4.5.1 example, that required using a global **Status** variable.

The long jump facility works only if the information on the stack at the instant **setjmp** returned is still intact when you execute **longjmp**. Therefore, the function that called **setjmp** must still be active when you execute **longjmp**; it must not have executed a **return** statement in the intervening time.

A long jump abruptly returns the stack to its status at the time you executed **setjmp**. Presumably, you wouldn't do that unless you're sure your program no longer needs access to the items stacked in the intervening time. Even in that case, though, there's a potential problem. If the items to be deleted include pointers to allocated heap storage, you'll lose the ability to deallocate it; and that can cause memory utilization problems. Before you include a long jump in your software design, you must be certain that destroying those items on the stack will really cause no problem.

Installing a Custom Hardware Exception Handler

Arithmetic errors can cause two kinds of hardware exceptions. An attempt to divide an integer by zero causes the CPU to execute **Int 0**, and several floating point error conditions described earlier cause the coprocessor or emulator to execute another interrupt. As you've seen, Turbo C++ provides minimal support in those situations. How can you arrange for your own routine to be invoked to provide more extensive service?

For the integer zero division interrupt the problem has a straightforward solution. Replacing the **Int 0** service routine by a custom ISR is a task familiar to systems programmers. See the author's earlier book, Reference [37, Chapter 9] for details. The standard techniques described there include restoring the previous ISR. The same technique would work for exception interrupts generated by an installed coprocessor. Unfortunately, implementing this technique for the coprocessor emulator would require access to the emulator source code. Since the emulator invokes the interrupt, the stacked CPU registers and return address pertain to the emulator, not to the instruction in your program that caused the error. A custom ISR would have to use emulator features to locate that instruction and decide what to do.

Turbo C++ implements the *signalling* method for customizing exception interrupt services. Signalling works for coprocessor exceptions, integer zero division, and several other interrupts triggered by hardware or software in abnormal situations. A number of Turbo C++ signalling constants and Library functions are mentioned in the following paragraphs. You'll find their definitions and prototypes in

Turbo C++ header files **Signal.H** and **Float.H**. Conceptually, there are six Turbo C++ signal *flags* that indicate the kind of exception:

SIGFPE   Int 0, IntO, or coprocessor exceptions;

SIGILL   the CPU was asked to perform an illegal operation;

SIGSEGV   the CPU detected an illegal memory address;

SIGABRT   software requested program abortion, even if that might leave files in disarray;

SIGINT   software detected a <Ctrl-C> keystroke or the equivalent;

SIGTERM   software requested normal program termination.

The signal flags are actually just integer values defined by macro constants in **Signal.H**. This discussion is mostly concerned with **SIGFPE**. This signal also triggers a service in response to the machine language instruction **IntO**, a special interrupt designed for implementing integer arithmetic features not supported directly by the machine language (for example, multiple precision arithmetic).

A service routine **Service** for a signal flag must be prototyped like this:

```
void Service(int Flag) .
```

Since the signalling facility is meant only to handle abnormal situations, the service routine should not return to its caller normally. Instead, it should call exit routine **_exit**, **exit**, or **abort**, or long jump to another routine to carry on execution of your program. To install your custom **Service** routine to respond to a signal **Flag**, execute

```
void* PreviousService = signal(Flag,Service) .
```

According to C++ conventions, the latter parameter is a pointer to the start of your **Service** routine. **signal** returns as function value a pointer to the start of the previously active service routine. Thus, you may reactivate the previous routine later by executing **signal(Flag,PreviousService)**. **signal** might also return the value

SIG_ERR, to indicate that it failed to install the specified service routine. Turbo C++ provides a default service routine **SIG_DFL,** that terminates your program.

The current service routine **Service** for signal **Flag** can be invoked explicitly or implicitly. You can raise **Flag** explicitly and patriotically by executing **raise(Flag).** The effect is to execute

```
signal(Flag,SIG_DFL); Service(Flag);
```

hence, function **raise** won't return. (Reinstalling the default service routine insures that your program will terminate if **Flag** is raised again while you're servicing the first exception. Including **Flag** as a parameter also permits one **Service** routine to handle several **Flag** values.) You can only invoke the **SIGABRT** or **SIGTERM** service routines explicitly. The **SIGINT** flag is also raised *implicitly,* by a Turbo C++ ISR in response to a <Ctrl-Break> or <Ctrl-C> keystroke. The other three flags can be raised in several different ways, as discussed next.

Flags **SIGFPE, SIGILL,** and **SIGSEGV** are associated with individual code values that identify the circumstances of their invocation:

Codes Associated with Signal Flags

Flag	Codes		
SIGFPE:	FPE_INTOVFLOW	FPE_INTDIV0	FPE_INVALID
	FPE_ZERODIVIDE	FPE_OVERFLOW	FPE_UNDERFLOW
	FPE_INEXACT	FPE_EXPLICITGEN	
SIGILL:	ILL_EXECUTION	ILL_EXPLICITGEN	
SIGSEGV:	SEGV_BOUND	SEGV_EXPLICITGEN	

Each of these flags has a code to indicate that it was raised explicitly. The **SIGFPE** codes correspond to the **IntO** interrupt, the integer zero division interrupt **Int 0,** and to five coprocessor exceptions described earlier.

When **SIGFPE** is raised implicitly, by a Turbo C++ ISR in response to **IntO** or **Int 0,** two parameters are stacked in addition to the one specified by the prototype

```
void Service(int Flag) .
```

The stack then looks as though **Service** should have been prototyped as

```
void Service(int Flag, int Code, int* Register) .
```

The first extra parameter is one of the **Code** values for **SIGFPE** tabulated earlier. The second points to an array containing the values of all the CPU registers when **SIGFPE** is raised. A later paragraph shows how to access and use the **Code** parameter. The information contained in ***Register** enables a custom **SIGFPE** service routine to analyze an integer arithmetic exception in more detail. That requires assembly language techniques, and won't be discussed further.

When **SIGFPE** is raised implicitly in response to a coprocessor exception, the extra **Code** parameter is stacked, but not the **Register** pointer. When **SIGILL** or **SIGSEGV** is raised implicitly, by a Turbo C++ ISR responding to a CPU hardware exception, the additional **Code** and **Register** parameters are both stacked.

Figure 4.5.2 displays a custom **SIGFPE** service routine, a brief test program, and its output. The test program contains a valid-input loop like that of Figure 4.5.1, implemented with a long jump. This one inputs a **double** value a and attempts to display the value $v = (1/a)^2$. That will generate an **SIGFPE** exception if $a = 0$ or v is larger than permitted for a **double** value. Once v is successfully computed, the test program raises **SIGFPE** explicitly. Function **main** never returns. Inside the input loop, **main** installs the custom service routine **FPError**. (Each time **FPError** is executed, **raise** reinstalls the default service routine **SIG_DFL** to handle further **SIGFPE** exceptions.)

FPError first displays the **Code** parameter. If **Code** == **FPE_EXPLICITGEN**, the service routine simply exits. That's why the Figure 4.5.2 test program terminates after the first valid input. Otherwise, **FPError** cues the user and resets the coprocessor using **Float.H** function void **_fpreset( )**. The latter step is necessary because the coprocessor registers may have been corrupted by an error. Finally, the service routine continues the input loop via a long jump.

You must write **FPError** according to the prototype of function **signal** in header **Float.H**, with just one parameter. The extra parameters stacked when **SIGFPE** is raised implicitly introduce a major complication in this program. There is no ANSI standard way of dealing with this. Turbo C++ uses a mechanism called a *variable argument* list, imported from UNIX C implementations. These features appear in **FPError** — see Figure 4.5.2 — as instances of macros **va_list**, **va_start**, **va_arg**, and **va_end**. They're defined in header file **StdArg.H**. Consult the corresponding entries in the Turbo C++ reference guide, Reference [5], for details of their use. (The **va_** feature isn't discussed here because it's a C mechanism of general use. But it's also a ludicrous programming method.)

```
#include "General.H"
#include   <Float.H>
#include  <SetJmp.H>
#include  <Signal.H>
#include  <StdArg.H>

char* Name[] = {"INTOVFLOW","INTDIV0","???","INVALID","???",
  "ZERODIVIDE","OVERFLOW","UNDERFLOW","INEXACT","???","???",
  "???","???","???","EXPLICITGEN" };

jmp_buf Input;

void FPError(int Flag) {              // Custom coprocessor
  va_list ap;                         // exception handler.
  va_start(ap,Flag);                  // Get the first optional
  int Code = va_arg(ap,int);          // parameter.
  cout << "FPE "
       << Name[Code-FPE_INTOVFLOW]
       << " signal. ";
  if (Code == FPE_EXPLICITGEN) exit(0);
  cout << "Bad input: try again!";
  int* Dummy = va_arg(ap,int*);       // Clean up the second op-
  va_end(ap);                         // tional parameter and
  _fpreset();                         // reset the coprocessor.
  longjmp(Input,1); }                 // Parameter 1 not used.

void main() {
  clrscr();
  cout << "Testing coprocessor error signalling.\n";
  setjmp(Input);
    signal(SIGFPE,FPError);                  // Input loop.
    cout << "\nEnter  a = ";                 // Bad input
    double a;  cin >> a;                     // raises a flag
    cout << "(1/a)² = " << (1/a)*(1/a) << endl;  // here.
  cout << "Obvious flag waving generates the  ";
  raise(SIGFPE); }
```

Output

```
Testing coprocessor error signalling.

Enter  a = 0
FPE_ZERODIVIDE  signal. Bad input:  try again!
Enter  a = 1e-200
FPE_OVERFLOW  signal. Bad input:  try again!
Enter  a = 1e200
(1/a)² = 0
Obvious flag waving generates the  FPE_EXPLICITGEN  signal.
```

Figure 4.5.2 Testing coprocessor error signalling

The Figure 4.5.2 output shows that floating point division and overflow exceptions were generated and **FPError** handled them correctly. The input $a = 10^{200}$ results in *underflow*: $v = (1/a)^2 = 10^{-400}$, which is too small for a **double** value. This causes no exception, because Turbo C++ automatically *masks* underflow errors, as described under the next heading. Instead of signalling an exception, Turbo C++ uses $v = 0$.

If you change **a** to an **int** variable in the Figure 4.5.2 test program, you can test the response to the integer zero division exception.

Coprocessor Error Masking

It's possible to set the coprocessor (or the emulator) to handle many exceptions as best it can, by returning *NaN* (*Not a Number*) or infinite values. At the hardware level, this is done by setting certain bits in a coprocessor register called the *Control Word*. Bits set correspond to exceptions disabled, or *masked*. The **Float.H** function

```
unsigned _control87(unsigned NewCW, unsigned Mask)
```

does this for you. For each 1 bit in **Mask**, it sets the corresponding bit of the Control Word equal to the corresponding bit in **NewCW**. The function returns the previous value of the Control Word. (Thus, it's easy for you to reestablish the previous coprocessor behavior.) For your convenience, **Float.H** includes constant macros that specify the appropriate bits:

EM_INVALID	1	EM_UNDERFLOW	10
EM_DENORMAL	2	EM_INEXACT	20
EM_ZERODIVIDE	4		
EM_OVERFLOW	8	MCW_EM	3f

The last constant **MCW_EM** is the sum of all the others. For example, to disable both overflow and underflow exceptions, execute

```
unsigned CW = _control87(EM_OVERFLOW |
                    EM_UNDERFLOW, MCW_EM)
```

To restore the previous conventions, execute **_control87(CW, MCW_EM)**. By default, Turbo C++ masks *underflow* exceptions. To unmask them, execute **_control87(0,EM_UNDERFLOW)**. If you do this at the start of the test program in Figure 4.5.2, you'll see that the input $a = 10^{200}$ does cause an **SIGFPE** exception with code **FPE_UNDERFLOW**.

The test program and output in Figure 4.5.3 show some typical results of masking. It inputs a **double** argument a, then computes $1/a$, a^2, $\sqrt{a}$, and sin a. You can inspect the values computed for arguments that ordinarily would cause zero division, overflow, underflow, domain, and loss of significance exceptions. You must redefine function **matherr** as discussed earlier, to report that it has handled all

```
#include  "General.H"
#include    <Float.H>
#include    <StdIO.H>
#include    <Math.H>

int matherr(struct exception* e) {      // Disable _matherr
  return 1; }                           // messages.

void main() {
  clrscr();
  cout << "Testing coprocessor exception masking.\n";
  _control87(MCW_EM,MCW_EM);
  double a = 0;
  while (a != 666) {
    cout << "\nInput  a = ";  cin >> a;
    printf("1/a      = %g\n",1/a);
    printf("a²       = %g\n",a*a);
    printf("√a       = %g\n",sqrt(a));
    printf("sin a    = %g\n",sin(a)); }}
```

Selected Output

Input	a = 0		Input	a = -1e200		Input	a = 1e-200
1/a	= +INF		1/a	= -1e-200		1/a	= 1e+200
a²	= 0		a²	= +INF		a²	= 0
√a	= 0		√a	= +NAN		√a	= 1e-100
sin a	= 0		sin a	= +NAN		sin a	= 1e-200

Figure 4.5.3 Masking coprocessor exceptions

errors. Otherwise, when it returns to **_matherr**, the latter may display an error message and halt. (It's not clear where this error might originate — probably not from an arithmetic computation, but from an attempt to process an *NaN* or infinite result.)

If you mask exceptions this way, take care that you don't unwittingly send an *NaN* or infinite result to the coprocessor later as an operand. In that case you may cause an exception that can't be masked. See the Intel coprocessor manual, Reference [22], for details. Moreover, the Turbo C++ mathematical Library functions don't expect the coprocessor to mask errors, and don't expect *NaN* or infinite arguments. Computing mathematical functions under these conventions may require a major redesign.

Function **_control87** can also be used to select the coprocessor rounding method and some other options. See Section 4.2.

4.6   Using Complex Scalars

This book's MSP mathematical software package can use **double** scalars throughout a program, or **complex** scalars throughout. The device that permits this is simple: alternative **Scalar** modules. One of these modules defines the identifier **Scalar** to mean **double**; the other defines it to mean **complex**. The modules provide standard routines for displaying scalars, and take care of some other technical details. Although it would be desirable for a single program to be able to use some matrices, etc., with **double** entries and others with **complex** entries, this proved infeasible. Section 3.2 discussed why.

The Complex Class

Section 3.2 described the **double** version of **Scalar** in detail. On the optional diskette, that module is contained in header and source code files **ScDouble.H** and **ScDouble.CPP**. The current section is devoted to the **complex** version, files **ScCmplex.H** and **ScCmplex.CPP**. Unlike **double**, which is a C++ primitive type, **complex** is the name of a class defined in the Turbo C++ Library header file **Complex.H**. The class has two data components and two member functions that perform logical services:

```
class complex {
  private:
    double re;                  // Real part of a complex number.
    double im;                  // Imaginary part.
  public:
    complex( );                 // Default constructor.
    complex(double x,           // Construct the complex
            double y = 0);      // number x + yi .
  :
```

The default constructor builds the **complex** zero, $0 + 0i$. Most of the other functions related to this class are declared its *friends* — they're too numerous to list all at once. Friendship allows them to manipulate the real and imaginary parts of a **complex** value directly without invoking selector functions, but doesn't force on them the alien principal argument syntax. Most of the **Complex.H** functions are completely defined in the header file as inline functions.

Several of the nonmember **Complex.H** functions perform logical services. There are two selectors:

```
double real(complex& z); // Return the real part of z .
double imag(complex& z); // Return imaginary part of z .
```

You can also regard the first of these as a converter from type **complex** to type **double**. One of the constructors mentioned earlier is the opposite converter.

Next, there are two overloaded logical operators:

```
int operator= =(complex&, complex&);
int operator!= (complex&, complex&);
```

The first returns **True** just when both the real and the imaginary parts of the two operands agree.

Finally, there are two overloaded stream input/output operators:

```
istream& operator<<(istream&, complex&); // Stream input.
ostream& operator<<(ostream&, complex&); // Stream output.
```

With the standard output stream **cout**, the latter uses a default format something like "(%.6g, %.6g)". For example, if you set **complex** **z(sqrt(2),sqrt(3))** and execute **cout << z**, you'll see the display **(1.41421, 1.73205)**. These input/output operators don't enjoy **complex** friendship.

Since there are no pointer types among the **complex** data components, there's no need for a special destructor, nor for special copy and assignment operators. The built-in facilities work with **complex** as with any other **struct** types.

Complex Arithmetic

This paragraph gives a brief summary of the **complex** arithmetic features implemented as overloaded **inline** operator functions in Turbo C++ header file **Complex.H**. The more involved mathematical functions corresponding to those declared in header file **Math.H** are discussed in Section 4.7. Four singulary operators or functions are defined for arguments $z = x + yi$:

$$+z = z \qquad -z \qquad conj(z) = \bar{z} = x - yi \qquad abs(z) = \| z \| = \sqrt{x^2 + y^2} \ .$$

Three versions of the binary operators **+**, **−**, *****, and **/** are defined: for example, there are separate **+** operators for

complex + complex
complex + double
double + complex .

Finally, two versions of the replacement operators **+=**, **−=**, ***=**, and **/=** are defined: for example, there are separate **+** operators for

```
//*****************************************************************
//                          Scalar.H
//               complex version, also stored as   ScComplx.H

#ifndef   Scalar_H
#define   Scalar_H

#define   Complex_Scalar_H

#include "General.H"
#include <Complex.H>

#define Scalar complex

//*****************************************************************
//   Logical features

#define DefaultScalarFormat "(%.2g,%.2g)"     // Shortest formats.
#define DefaultRealFormat   "% -#9.2g"

char* ForShow(const complex& z,         // Convert  z  to a string
              const char* Format =      // for standard output.
              DefaultScalarFormat);     // Use  printf  Format .

int   Show   (const complex& z,         // Standard output; re-
              const char* Format =      // turn output length.
              DefaultScalarFormat);

//*****************************************************************
//   Mathematical features

double  Norm(complex z);                // Return  ‖z‖ .
complex Random();                       // Random  z  in unit square.

#endif
```

Figure 4.6.1 MSP header file Scalar.H: complex version

    complex + complex
    complex + double .

Scalar Module: Complex Version

The **complex** version of the MSP **Scalar.H** header file, **ScCmplex.H**, is shown in Figure 4.6.1. Its features parallel those of the **double** version described in Section 3.2 so closely that there's no need to show the source code here. You'll find that on the diskette. This discussion concentrates on the differences. First, when it's included, this header file defines an identifier **Complex_Scalar_H**. That will be sensed by the **Polynom.H** header and source code files, which must define a special constructor for the **complex** case only — see Section 3.7 for details.

The **ScCmplex.H** has a special **DefaultScalarFormat**. The double version is still available, now called **DefaultRealFormat**. Like the **double** version, **DefaultScalarFormat** produces very short numerals with two significant digits, mainly for use in checking for errors. Unlike the **double** version, these numerals aren't easily subjected to column alignment — that feature would have required too much screen space.

The **complex** versions of the display routines **ForShow** and **Show** differ from the **double** versions only in that they display both the real and imaginary parts of a **complex** value.

In the **double** version, function **Norm(x)** returns $|x|$. In the **complex** version, if $z = x + yi$, then **Norm(z)** returns

$$\| z \| \ = \sqrt{x^2 + y^2} \ .$$

Caution! The **Complex.H** function **norm(z)** returns $\| z \|^2$ — that use of the word *norm* contradicts conventional mathematical terminology!

In the complex version, function **Random( )** returns a random complex number $z = x + yi$ in the unit square: $0 \le x, y < 1$. If you need a random distribution of points z in the unit circle, use this function to compute x', y' in the unit square, and scale linearly to cover the square $-1 \le x', y' < 1$:

$$\begin{cases} x = 2x' - 1 \\ y = 2y' - 1 \ . \end{cases}$$

Then reject those points $z = x + yi$ for which $\| z \| \ge 1$.

Example Complex Programs

To illustrate the facility of MSP with **complex** computations, an example program is shown in Figure 4.6.2, with output in Figure 4.6.3. The program demonstrates the **complex** vector and matrix algebra routines by generating random vectors v and w and random matrices A and B and comparing the computed values $((v + w)A)B$ and $v(AB) + w(AB)$, which are theoretically equal. Then it divides the **complex** polynomial $F(x) = (x - i)^4 + x^2 + 1$ by $G(x) = (x - i)^2$ to obtain a quotient $Q(x)$ and remainder $R(x)$ such that

$$\frac{F(x)}{G(x)} = Q(x) + \frac{R(x)}{G(x)} \ .$$

It then tests to make sure this relation holds.

```
#include  "Matrix.H"
#include "Polynom.H"

void Test1() {
  clrscr();
  cout << "Testing complex vector and matrix algebra         \n"
          "v ,  w ,  A ,  B  are random vectors and matrices  \n"
          "v ,  w  are  1 x 2 .  A ,  B  are  2 x 3 ,  3 x 3 .\n"
          "Left = ((v + w)A)B  and  Right = v(AB) + w(AB) .  \n"
          "Left  should  =  Right.                         \n\n";
  Vector v(2), w(2);       v.MakeRandom();  w.MakeRandom();
  Matrix A(2,3), B(3,3);   A.MakeRandom();  B.MakeRandom();
  Vector Left  = ((v + w)*A)*B;
  Vector Right = v*(A*B) + w*(A*B);
  Vector Diff  = Left - Right;
  cout << " Left - Right  = ";  Diff.Show();
  cout << "‖Left - Right‖ = ";
    Show(MaxNorm(Diff),DefaultRealFormat); }

void Test2() {
  cout << "Testing complex polynomial algebra            \n"
          "F(x) = (x - i)^4 + x² + 1,  G(x) = (x - i)²   \n"
          "Divide  F(x)  by  G(x)  to get quotient       \n"
          "Q(x) = (x - i)² + 1 = -2ix + x²  and remainder  "
           "R(x) = 2 + 2ix .                              \n"
          "D(x) = F(x) - Q(x)G(x) - R(x)  should  = 0 .\n\n";
  complex i(0,1);
  Polynom x = xTo(1);
  Polynom F = ((x - i)^4) + (x^2) + 1;      // () are necessary!
  Polynom G = (x - i)^2;
  Polynom Q,R,D;  Divide( F,G,Q,R );  D = F - Q*G - R;
  Q.Show("",True,"Q(x)");
  R.Show("",True,"R(x)");
  D.Show("",True,"D(x)"); }

void main() {
  Test1();  cout << "\n\n\n";
  Test2(); }
```

Figure 4.6.2 Example program

This program was compiled with a project file that listed eight source code files:

CompTest.CPP	(the test program)	VectorM.CPP
General.CPP		MatrixL.CPP
Scalar.CPP	(complex version)	MatrixM.CPP
VectorL.CPP		Polynom.CPP

Counting the included Turbo C++ and MSP header files, this amounts to about 21 K lines of code! The linker complained that with the compact memory model the compiled code wouldn't fit in the single segment named _TEXT, so the large model was used. The size of the resulting executable file **CompTest.Exe** was 186 K.

```
Testing complex vector and matrix algebra
v , w , A , B are random vectors and matrices
v , w  are  1 x 2 .  A , B  are  2 x 3 ,  3 x 3 .
Left = ((v + w)A)B  and  Right = v(AB) + w(AB) .
Left  should    = Right.

 Left - Right  = (-4.4e-16,-4.4e-16) (-4.4e-16,-4.4e-16) (-2.2e-16,-2.2e-16)
‖Left - Right‖ = 6.3e-16


Testing complex polynomial algebra
F(x) = (x - i)^4 + x² + 1,  G(x) = (x - i)²
Divide  F(x)  by  G(x)  to get quotient
Q(x) = (x - i)² + 1 = -2ix + x²  and remainder  R(x) = 2 + 2ix .

D(x) = F(x) - Q(x)G(x) - R(x)  should  = 0 .

Q(x) :  (0,0)  (0,-2)  (1,0)
R(x) :  (2,0)  (-0,2)
D(x) :  ∅
```

Figure 4.6.3 Example program output

4.7 Complex Library Functions

Through overloading, the Turbo C++ Library extends to the **complex** domain all the **Math.H** functions described earlier:

exp	pow	sin	asin	sinh
log	sqrt	cos	acos	cosh
log10		tan	atan	tanh

These extended functions are prototyped in the Library header file **Complex.H**, so that both their arguments and values may be **complex**. They aren't so familiar as their real counterparts, so this section describes them and derives formulas for their real and imaginary components. The **Complex.H** Library functions are probably straightforward implementations of these formulas. (The source code is not readily available to check that.) For further information on the **complex** elementary functions, consult Reference [45, Chapter 15].

Polar Decomposition

Complex.H also provides three functions for handling **complex** numbers in polar form:

```
complex polar (double r,      // Construct
              double t = 0); // z = r cis t .
  double  abs  (complex& z);   // ‖z‖ .
  double  arg  (complex& z);   // Principal argument of z .
```

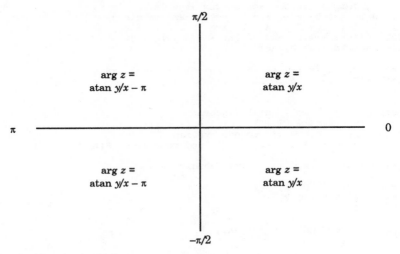

Figure 4.7.1 The principal argument of z = x + yi

Function **polar(r,t)** returns r cis $t = r(\cos t + i \sin t)$. Because of the initialization **t = 0**, you can also use it to convert **double** to **complex** values. Notice that

$$\| cis\ t \| = \sqrt{\cos^2 t + \sin^2 t} = 1 \ .$$

Thus, if $z = r$ cis t, then $\|z\| = |r|$.

The *polar decomposition* of a complex number $z \neq 0$ is the unique pair r, t such that $r > 0$, $-\pi < t \leq \pi$, and $z = r$ cis t. The polar decomposition of 0 is the pair $r = 0$, $t = 0$. Clearly, $r = \|z\|$; t is called the *principal argument* arg z. (This old terminology is inconsistent with other uses of the mathematical term *argument*.) The **Complex.H** functions **abs(z)** and **arg(z)** return these values r and t. The latter computes its value using the inverse tangent function **atan** (or its more basic coprocessor counterpart) according to Figure 4.7.1.

Exponential, Hyperbolic, and Trigonometric Functions

Using standard calculus techniques extended to the **complex** numbers, you can show that the power series

$$\exp z = \sum_{k=0}^{\infty} \frac{z^k}{k!}$$

converges for all complex z. The function exp that it defines is called the *complex exponential function* because for real z it agrees with the Maclaurin series for the real exponential function. It's easy to derive the *addition–multiplication rule* for the exponential function from the binomial expansion of powers of $z_1 + z_2$:

$$\exp(z_1 + z_2) = \sum_{j=0}^{\infty} \frac{(z_1 + z_2)^j}{j!} = \sum_{j=0}^{\infty} \frac{1}{j!} \sum_{j=k+l} \frac{j!}{k!\, l!} z_1^k z_2^l$$

$$= \sum_{j=0}^{\infty} \sum_{j=k+l} \frac{z_1^k}{k!} \frac{z_2^l}{l!} \left(\sum_{k=0}^{\infty} \frac{z_1^k}{k!} \right) \left(\sum_{l=0}^{\infty} \frac{z_2^l}{l!} \right) = \exp z_1 \exp z_2 \ .$$

Similarly, you can show that $\exp z$ is the sum of the two power series consisting of the even and odd powers. These also converge for all complex z. They define functions that are called the *complex hyperbolic cosine* and *sine* because for real z they agree with the Maclaurin series for the real hyperbolic cosine and sine functions:

$$\exp z = \cosh z + \sinh z$$

$$\cosh z = \sum_{k=0}^{\infty} \frac{z^{2k}}{(2k)!} \qquad \sinh z = \sum_{k=0}^{\infty} \frac{z^{2k+1}}{(2k+1)!} \ .$$

Clearly, $\cosh(-z) = \cosh z$ and $\sinh(-z) = -\sinh z$ for all complex z. By adding and subtracting series, you can see that

$$\cosh z = \frac{\exp z + \exp(-z)}{2} \qquad \sinh z = \frac{\exp z - \exp(-z)}{2} \ .$$

If you substitute $z = z_1 + z_2$ in these formulas, apply the addition–multiplication rule for the exponential function, and do the resulting algebra correctly, you'll get the *addition rules* for the hyperbolic cosine and sine functions:

$$\cosh(z_1 + z_2) = \cosh z_1 \cosh z_2 + \sinh z_1 \sinh z_2$$
$$\sinh(z_1 + z_2) = \sinh z_1 \cosh z_2 + \cosh z_1 \sinh z_2 \ .$$

For real z, the series expansions of $\cosh zi$ and $-i \sinh zi$ agree with the Maclaurin series for the trigonometric cosine and sine functions:

$$\cosh zi = \sum_{k=0}^{\infty} \frac{(zi)^{2k}}{(2k)!} = \sum_{k=0}^{\infty} (-1)^k \frac{z^{2k}}{(2k)!}$$

$$-i \sinh zi = -i \sum_{k=0}^{\infty} \frac{(zi)^{2k+1}}{(2k+1)!} = -i^2 \sum_{k=0}^{\infty} (-1)^k \frac{z^{2k+1}}{(2k+1)!} = \sum_{k=0}^{\infty} (-1)^k \frac{z^{2k+1}}{(2k+1)!} \quad .$$

Thus, you can use these formulas to define the *complex cosine* and *sine* functions:

cos z = cosh zi
sin z = $-i$ sinh zi .

Clearly, $\cos(-z)$ = cos z and $\sin(-z)$ = $-$ sin z for all complex z. If you substitute $z = z_1 + z_2$ in these formulas, apply the addition rules for the hyperbolic functions, and do the resulting algebra correctly, you'll get the *addition rules* for the cosine and sine functions:

$\cos(z_1 + z_2)$ = cos z_1 cos z_2 $-$ sin z_1 sin z_2
$\sin(z_1 + z_2)$ = sin z_1 cos z_2 + cos z_1 sin z_2 .

Now it's possible to find the real and imaginary parts of the complex exponentials, sines, and cosines. First, if x and y are real, and $z = x + yi$, then

exp yi = cosh yi + sinh yi = cos y $-$ (1/i) sin y
$\quad\quad$ = cos y + i sin y = cis y
exp z $\ $ = exp(x + yi) = exp x exp yi = e^x cos y + $i\,e^x$ sin y .

Next,

cosh z = cosh(x + yi) = cosh x cosh yi + sinh x sinh yi
$\quad\quad$ = cosh x cos y + sinh x[$-$(1/i) sin y]
$\quad\quad$ = cosh x cos y + i sinh x sin y .

You can perform similar manipulations, occasionally using the fact that the cosines and sines are even and odd functions, respectively, to derive the remaining formulas:

sinh z = sinh x cos y + i cosh x sin y
cos z $\ $ = cosh y cos x $-$ i sinh y sin x
sin z $\ $ = cosh y sin x + i sinh y cos x .

If necessary, you can work with the remaining **Complex.H** hyperbolic and trigonometric functions directly through their definitions:

$$\tanh z = \frac{\sinh z}{\cosh z} \qquad \tan z = \frac{\sin z}{\cos z}\ .$$

Square Root, Logarithms, and Powers

The **Complex.H** functions **sqrt** and **log** implement the complex *principal* square root and *principal* logarithm. Similar considerations lead to the definitions of these two functions. Square roots are considered first.

The *principal square root* of a **complex** number $z \neq 0$ is defined as the unique $w = r$ cis t such that $r > 0$, $-\pi/2 < t \leq \pi/2$, and $w^2 = z$. In fact,

$$r = \sqrt{\|z\|} \qquad t = \frac{1}{2}\arg z\ .$$

To validate this definition, you have to verify first that $w^2 = z$ with this r and t, and second, that only this r and t satisfy the requirements. The verification is simple:

$$w^2 = \|z\|\ \text{cis}^2 t = \|z\|\ (\exp ti)^2 = \|z\|\ \exp 2ti$$
$$= \|z\|\ \text{cis}\ 2t = \|z\|\ \text{cis arg}\ z = z\ .$$

To check uniqueness, suppose $r' > 0$, $-\pi/2 < t \leq \pi/2$, and $(r'$ cis $t')^2 = z$, so that r^2 cis$^2 t = r'^2$ cis$^2 t'$. Taking norms, you get $r^2 = r'^2$, hence $r = r'$. That implies cis $2t = $ cis$^2 t = $ cis$^2 t' = $ cis $2t'$, hence $2t$ and $2t'$ differ by a multiple of 2π. But that means t and t' differ by a multiple of π, hence $t = t'$: the pair r, t is indeed unique. As a special case, the principal square root of 0 is defined to be 0. Clearly, the principal square root of a real number $r \geq 0$ is $\sqrt{r}$, so it's appropriate to use the symbol $\sqrt{z}$ to denote the principal square root of any complex number z.

The *principal logarithm* of a complex number $z \neq 0$ is defined as the unique $w = u + vi$ such that u and v are real, $-\pi < v \leq \pi$, and $z = \exp w$. In fact,

$$u = \log \|z\| \qquad v = \arg z\ .$$

You can validate this definition following exactly the same steps as those in the previous paragraph. No principal logarithm is defined for 0. The principal logarithm of a positive real number u is clearly log u, so it's appropriate to use the symbol log z to denote the principal logarithm of any complex number z. *Caution!* The familiar algebraic rules like log ab = log a + log b don't necessarily hold for principal logarithms; you may have to adjust them by adding multiples of $2\pi i$ to one side. See Reference [45, Section 15.7] for details.

You can show by a recursive proof that for all complex z and all integers p, z^p = exp(p log z). For example, exp(2 log z) = (exp log z)^2 = z^2. Moreover, w = exp($\frac{1}{2}$ log z) is the same as $\sqrt{z}$: you can check that $w^2 = z$ and $-\pi/2 < $ arg $w \le \pi/2$. Thus, it's appropriate to define complex powers in general through the formula z^p = exp(p log z). This is implemented by the **Complex.H** function **pow**. *Caution!* Some of the usual algebraic rules for computation with powers don't hold for this definition, because of the difficulty with the logarithm discussed in the previous paragraph.

The complex *principal common logarithm* is defined as

$$\log_{10} z = \frac{\log z}{\log 10} .$$

Clearly, if $w = \log_{10} z$, then $10^w = z$. Conversely, if $10^w = z$, then w differs from $\log_{10} z$ by a multiple of $2\pi i$ / log 10. This function is rarely used, but it's implemented by **Complex.H** function **log10**. Take caution with ordinary algebra rules, just as remarked in the previous two paragraphs.

Inverse Trigonometric Functions

Section 4.4 derived a logarithmic formula for the inverse hyperbolic cosine function ArgCosh. Formulas exist for the other five inverse hyperbolic functions, too. When complex numbers are permitted, you can derive similar formulas for the inverse trigonometric functions. For example, if

$$z = \cos w = \frac{\exp wi + \exp(-wi)}{2} = \frac{(\exp wi)^2 + 1}{2 \exp wi}$$

then

$$(\exp wi)^2 - 2z \exp wi + 1 = 0 .$$

By the Quadratic Formula,

$$\exp wi = \frac{2z + \sqrt{4z^2 - 4}}{2} = z + \sqrt{z^2 - 1}$$

$$w = -i \log(z + \sqrt{z^2 - 1}) = \cos^{-1} z \ .$$

In this formula, the radical sign means *the principal square root plus a multiple of* πi and the symbol log means *the principal logarithm plus a multiple of* $2\pi i$. You can define the *principal inverse cosine* $\cos^{-1} z$ by using the *principal* square root and logarithm functions. You can check that this function agrees with the usual inverse cosine when z is real. It's implemented by the **Complex.H** function **acos**.

Through analogous manipulation, you can derive formulas for the complex principal inverse sine and tangent functions:

$$\sin^{-1} z = -i \log(z + \sqrt{1 - z^2}) \qquad \tan^{-1} z = \frac{i}{2} \log \frac{i + z}{i - z}$$

These are implemented by the **Complex.H** functions **asin** and **atan**.

Additional Functions

Several functions discussed in Section 4.4 and included in MSP module **RealFunc** have no **Complex.H** extensions:

cot	$\cot^{-1}$	coth	ArgCoth	ArgTanh
sec	$\sec^{-1}$	sech	ArgSech	ArgCosh
csc	$\csc^{-1}$	csch	ArgCsch	ArgSinh

and **root**. Since formulas are available, they should perhaps be included in an MSP **CplxFunc** module. But they appear so rarely that it doesn't seem worthwhile.

5

Solving Real and Complex Equations

Chapter 5 describes a set of high-level software tools for solving equations in a single scalar variable. It fills a practical need, for such equations are commonplace in scientific and engineering applications problems. At the same time, it provides a realistic test bed for much of the low-level MSP software introduced in Chapter 3. A variety of algorithms are implemented. They can be classified as general methods for finding roots of a function f, or specialized methods for use when f is a polynomial. Further, some of the methods work with either real or complex scalars, while others are limited to the real case.

Two connecting threads run through the discussion: the Bisection method and Fixpoint iteration. Bisection works with a very general class of real equations, but has limited efficiency and doesn't extend to complex equations or to multidimensional systems of equations. Fixpoint iteration is more general and flexible. Introduced first as a simple but inefficient method for solving a limited class of real equations, it's enhanced to yield the more general and faster Newton-Raphson technique, first for real equations, then for the complex case as well. Further enhancements incorporate Bisection features or step-size limitation to prevent the wild behavior that Newton-Raphson iteration exhibits in some situations. Later, in Chapter 7, Fixpoint methods are extended further, to solve systems of equations in several variables.

Chapter 5 culminates in two sections devoted to real and complex polynomial equations. First, Newton-Raphson iteration is adapted specifically for polynomials. Then the deflation technique is employed to build routines that compute *all* roots of a real or complex polynomial equation. A complementary function is provided to compute the roots' multiplicities. The complex routine is applied later, in Section 6.8, to compute matrix eigenvalues.

5.1   Preliminaries

Equate1 Module and Header File

The MSP functions for solving equations in a single variable constitute its **Equate1** module. Like the modules described earlier, this one has header and source code files **Equate1.H** and **Equate.CPP**. Much of the latter is displayed in this chapter, and it's included, of course, on the accompanying diskette. Unlike those of the earlier models, though, the **Equate1** header file is not particularly interesting: It consists only of function prototypes, which are reproduced in the source code file. Therefore, it's not shown here, but is displayed in Appendix A.3.

Trace Output

This chapter contains source code listings for many functions that solve equations $f(x) = 0$. Often they're accompanied by output listings that trace a function's execution. This output was *not* produced by the functions as listed, but by the versions on the diskette. The statements required to produce well-formatted intermediate output are usually elementary, but so long that they tend to overshadow more important parts of the routines. Therefore, those output features are purged from the code displayed in the text. Most of the **Equate1** functions have a parameter **int& Code = 0** that's used to convey an option code to the function and a status code back to the caller. If you invoke such a function with a nonzero **Code** value, you'll get intermediate "trace" output like that displayed in the text. Different nonzero **Code** values may produce different levels of detail; they're documented in the source code on the diskette. The source code displayed in the text simply omits many statements like **if (Code != 0)** { ... } where the dots represent very detailed output operations. As a result, the code displayed in the text is about half the size of that on the diskette, and is much easier to read and understand. Appendix

```
Boolean Bracket(double& xL,          // Find a bracketing in-
                double& xR,          // terval  [xL , xR]  of
                double  F(double),   // length  ≥ T  for  F
                double  T) {         // within the specified
   int S = Sign(F(xL));              // interval.  Return  True
   for (double dx = xR - xL;         // or  False  to report
              dx >= T;               // success or failure.
              dx /= 2) {             // dx = current interval
      for (double x = xL + dx;       // length.  Try intervals
                 x < xR;             // of this length.  You
                 x += 2*dx)          // already know that  F
         if (S != Sign(F(x))) {      // has sign  S  at half of
            xL = x - dx;  xR = x;    // the subdivision points.
            return True; }}
   return False; }
```

Figure 5.1.1 MSP function Bracket

A.4 displays an example of the source code, function **Bisect**, with provisions for intermediate output, listed from the diskette. You can compare that with the version purged of output code, in Figure 5.2.3.

The most detailed trace output options are designed for use with real scalars. To handle complex scalars, you'll have to modify the output formats.

Bracketing Intervals

When a function $f(x)$ is continuous on an interval $x_L \leq x \leq x_R$, and $f(x_L)$ and $f(x_R)$ differ in sign, then you know f has *at least* one root x in the interval: Its graph must cut the x axis somewhere there. Such an interval $[x_L, x_R]$ is called a *bracketing interval* for f. Finding a bracketing interval for f is often the first step in solving an equation $f(x) = 0$. MSP function **Bracket** will search a specified interval for a bracketing subinterval by checking the signs of f at its endpoints, dividing the interval into 2 parts, checking again, then into 4 parts, etc. It stops when it finds a sign change or when the next subinterval length would be smaller than a specified tolerance T. The code for **Bracket** is shown in Figure 5.1.1.

For example, executing **Bracket(xL,xR,cos,0.1)** with **xL** = 0 and **xR** = 6, returns **True** with **xL** = 0 and **xR** = 3; but **Bracket (0,1,cos,0.1)** returns **False**.

Checking Solutions

All equation-solving algorithms fail for some inputs. Various things can happen when a corresponding MSP function is invoked with such input. Ideal robust software would report all failures back to the caller, giving the client an opportunity to recover. Unfortunately, that's not generally possible. In some cases, failure is signaled by an exception in the floating point software/hardware system, like an attempted square root of a negative number. With enough attention to systems programming details, many such situations can be caught and analyzed before they disrupt the system. That's an extensive project, beyond the scope of this book. In other cases, it's not clear what constitutes an error in solving an equation $f(x) = 0$. Suppose an algorithm computes x such that $f(x)$ is small but different from zero. Is it close enough? A client might find it difficult or impossible to make such a decision in advance, as completely robust software would require. MSP puts the responsibility on the client: Some MSP functions may return a result x that's not an approximate solution of $f(x) = 0$. You must check x before using it, by evaluating $f(x)$.

5.2 Bisection Method

When a function $f(x)$ is continuous on an interval $x_L \leq x \leq x_R$, and $f(x_L)$ and $f(x_R)$ differ in sign, then you know f has *at least* one root x in the interval: Its graph must cut the x axis somewhere there. If you know such a bracketing interval $[x_L, x_R]$ and that there's *at most* one root in the interval, then you're in an ideal situation for solving the equation $f(x) = 0$. If you don't know a bracketing interval, but suspect there's one inside a specified interval $[x_L, x_R]$, you may be able to use MSP function **Bracket**, described in Section 5.1, to find one.

As an example, consider the cam in Figure 5.2.1, whose outline has polar equation

$$r = r(x) = \frac{1 + e^{-x/2\pi} \sin x}{2} .$$

Suppose you need to find the smallest positive angle x for which $r = 0.7$. From the graph in Figure 5.2.2, you can see that $f(x) = r(x) - 0.7$ is continuous on the interval $[x_L, x_R] = [0,1]$, changes sign, and has one root there. This *cam function f* is used as an example to demonstrate the MSP root finding routines described in this chapter.

The most general root finding technique is known as the *Bisection method*. First, you choose an error *tolerance T* — a small positive number. You'll accept any approximation within distance T of the root. Now, start with the known interval $[x_L, x_R]$, ascertain whether its left or right half contains the root, discard the other half, then

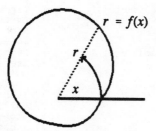

Figure 5.2.1 Outline of a cam

repeat this process with the remaining half. After each iteration, the length of the interval containing the root decreases by half, so eventually it will become smaller than T, and you can stop, accepting either interval endpoint as an approximation to the root.

Figure 5.2.3 shows MSP function **Bisect**, which implements the bisection method. As you'd expect, it has parameters corresponding to the function f, the left and right estimates x_L and x_R, and the tolerance T. In addition, **Bisect** uses a reference parameter **Code** to report the outcome of its computation: **Code** = 0 indicates that the iteration terminated satisfactorily with interval shorter than T, whereas **Code** = −1 signifies that the specified tolerance was unattainable. The routine begins operation by testing the interval length dx. If $dx \geq T$, then **Bisect** computes the interval midpoint x, and compares the signs of the function values y_L and y at the left end and midpoint. If they agree, there's no sign change in left half interval, so that's discarded and the midpoint becomes the new left end: $x_L = x$. If they disagree, the right half is discarded: $x_R = x$. The process iterates by returning back to the interval length test. For reasons explained later, the number of iterations is limited to 2049.

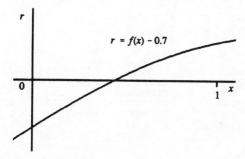

Figure 5.2.2 The cam function

```
double Bisect(double f(double),      // Find a root of  f .
              double xL,             // Left estimate.
              double xR,             // Right estimate.
              double T,              // Tolerance.
              int&   Code = 0) {     // Status code.
  int    n = 0;                      // Iteration number.
  double yL = f(xL);
  double dx,x,y;
  do {                               // Iterate.  If the inter-
     dx = xR - xL;                   // val is too long to
     if (dx >= T) {                  // accept, compute its
     x = (xL + xR)/2;  y = f(x);     // midpoint  x .  If  f
     if (Sign(yL) == Sign(y)) {      // doesn't change sign on
        xL = x;  yL = y; }           // the left half, discard
       else                         // it;  else discard the
          xR = x; }}                 // right half.  Do at most
  while (++n < 2049 && dx >= T);     // 2049  iterations.
  if (dx < T) Code = 0;              // Report success, or
    else Code = 1;                   // failure to converge.
  return xL; }                       // Return left end point.
```

Figure 5.2.3 MSP function Bisect

Figure 5.2.4 shows execution of function **Bisect** to locate the root of the cam function $f(x) = r(x) - 0.7$ of Figure 5.2.2. The Bisection method's efficiency can be estimated as in this table corresponding to Figure 5.2.4:

n	Length of nth interval
0	1
1	$\frac{1}{2}$
2	$\frac{1}{4} = \frac{1}{2}^2$
3	$\frac{1}{8} = \frac{1}{2}^3$
4	$\frac{1}{16} = \frac{1}{2}^4$
5	$\frac{1}{32} = \frac{1}{2}^5$

```
Finding a root of the cam function  f  by bisection

Left  estimate  xL :  0
Right estimate  xR :  1
Tolerance       T  :  0.05

Itera-
tion        xL            xR           f(xL)      xR - xL
    0    0.000000     1.000000       -0.20        1.0
    1    0.000000     0.5000000      -0.20        0.50
    2    0.2500000    0.5000000      -0.081       0.25
    3    0.3750000    0.5000000      -0.027       0.12
    4    0.4375000    0.5000000      -0.0024      0.062
    5    0.4375000    0.4687500      -0.0024      0.031

Root  x ≈  0.44
Code  =  0
```

Figure 5.2.4 Executing function Bisect

The initial interval $[x_L, x_R]$ had length 1 and the specified tolerance was 0.05. In that case, the interval length after the nth iteration is $1/2^n$; in general, it's $(x_R - x_L)/2^n$. The number of iterations required to achieve the desired accuracy is the first integer n such that the interval length is less than T. This can be reformulated in terms of logarithms as the first n such that

$$\frac{x_R - x_L}{2^n} < T,$$

i.e,

$$n > \log_2 \frac{x_R - x_L}{T}.$$

If the criterion for stopping the bisection process were simply $x_R - x_L < T$, the **do** loop in function **Bisect** would repeat forever if you specified the tolerance $T \leq 0$, or made it positive but so small that roundoff error prevented your computing $x_R - x_L$ accurately. To avoid that situation, **Bisect** enforces a limit on the number of iterations. The limit is the number required to reach an interval of the smallest possible size starting from one of maximum possible size. Since **double** values range in size from -2^{1023} to $+2^{1023}$ and the smallest positive **double** value is 2^{-1024}, the maximum number of iterations is

$$1 + \log_2 \frac{2^{1023} - (-2^{1023})}{2^{-1024}} = 2049$$

If function **Bisect** returns before achieving $x_R - x_L < T$, it sets the error signal **Code** = -1.

If you don't cause a roundoff problem by setting the tolerance too small, the Bisection method will succeed whenever function f is continuous on the interval $[x_L, x_R]$, has exactly one root there, and $f(x_L)$ and $f(x_R)$ differ in sign. What if f doesn't meet all these conditions? For instance, if there's no root, so that f doesn't change sign, Bisection will repeatedly discard the left half interval, and ultimately return a value between $x_R - T$ and x_R.

Figures 5.2.5–5.2.8 show four more situations where f fails to meet the Bisection conditions. Figure 5.2.5 shows a function with an initial interval [0,4] that contains five roots. Bisection discards the left half interval; the remaining interval [2,4] contains three roots. A second bisection yields the interval [3,4], which contains a single root. Further bisections will locate this root as precisely as desired. This is

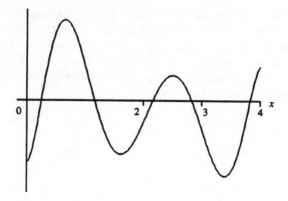

Figure 5.2.5 Function with five roots

typical: If there's an odd number of roots in the initial interval, the bisection method will locate one of them, but exactly which one depends on their position. If there's an even number of roots, bisection might locate one or not, as in Figures 5.2.6 and 5.2.7.

The Bisection method can also fail in various ways if the function f is discontinuous. For example, consider the function

$$f(x) = \begin{cases} \dfrac{x}{x^2 - 1} & \text{when } x \neq \pm 1 \\ \text{anything} \neq 0 & \text{when } x = \pm 1 \end{cases}$$

with the initial interval $[x_L, x_R] = [-2, +3]$, shown in Figure 5.2.8. The trace output in Figure 5.2.9 shows that function **Bisect** locates the pole $x = 1$ instead of the root $x = 0$!

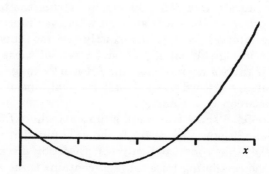

Figure 5.2.6 Bisection locates the left root in this example

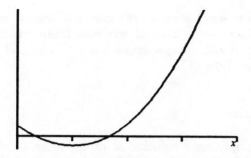

Figure 5.2.7 Bisection returns the right end point in this example

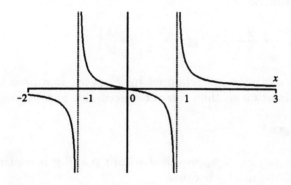

Figure 5.2.8 Here, Bisection locates a pole, not a root

```
Finding a root of   f(x) = x/(x²-1)   by Bisection

Left    estimate   xL :   -2
Right estimate    xR :    3
Tolerance         T  :    .1

Itera-
tion        xL                  xR              f(xL)     xR - xL
   0    -2.000000          3.000000            -0.67      5.0
   1     0.5000000         3.000000            -0.67      2.5
   2     0.5000000         1.750000            -0.67      1.2
   3     0.5000000         1.125000            -0.67      0.62
   4     0.8125000         1.125000            -2.4       0.31
   5     0.9687500         1.125000            -16.       0.16
   6     0.9687500         1.046875            -16.       0.078

Root   x ≈   0.97
Code     =   0
```

Figure 5.2.9 Here, Bisection locates a pole, not a root

Failures like these emphasize a principle that should govern your use of function **Bisect** — in fact, of any root finding routine: After you've used it to compute an approximation x to a root of a function f, *always verify* that $f(x) \approx 0$!

5.3   Fixpoint Iteration

The problem of computing a solution of an equation is often transformed into one of finding a *fixpoint* (fixed point) of a function g — that is, of solving a special kind of equation $x = g(x)$. For example, solving $x^2 = A$ for positive x and A is equivalent to solving $x = g(x)$ for any of the three functions

$$g(x) = \frac{A}{x} \qquad g(x) = \frac{x + A}{x + 1} \qquad g(x) = \frac{1}{2}\left[x + \frac{A}{x}\right] .$$

A fixpoint can sometimes be computed by *Fixpoint iteration*: Guess an initial approximation x_0, then compute successive approximations

$$x_1 = g(x_0), \ x_2 = g(x_1), \ \dots \ .$$

If the sequence $x_0, \ x_1, \ x_2, \ \dots$ approaches a limit p and g is continuous at p, then p is a fixpoint of g because

$$g(p) = g(\lim_{n \to \infty} x_n) = \lim_{x \to \infty} g(x_n) = \lim_{n \to \infty} x_{n+1} = \lim_{n \to \infty} x_n = p .$$

For the example functions and $A = x_0 = 2$, the fixpoint is $p = \sqrt{2} \approx 1.414214$. Fixpoint iteration yields the following approximations:

$g(x) = 2/x$		$g(x) = (x + 2)/(x + 1)$		$g(x) = \frac{1}{2}[x + A/x]$	
n	x_n	n	$x_n \approx$	n	$x_n \approx$
0	2	0	2.000000	0	2.000000
1	1	1	1.333333	1	1.500000
2	2	2	1.428571	2	1.416667
3	1	3	1.411765	3	1.414216
Bad!		Good!		Excellent!	

Apparently, proper choice of g is vital! This choice and its consequences are analyzed next.

Suppose the fixpoint p and initial approximation x_0 lie in a closed interval $I = [a, b]$. In order to apply g to the successive approxima-

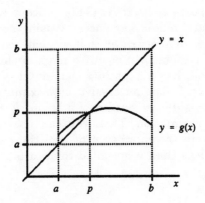

Figure 5.3.1 g maps interval [a,b] to itself

tions x_1, x_2, ... you may require that g map I into itself. Analysis of the convergence of the sequence x_n involves the idea of a *Lipschitz constant* for g on I: a number L such that

$$|g(x) - g(x')| < L\,|x - x'|$$

for all x and x' in I. (This concept can be defined for functions with vector, matrix, and complex arguments or values, too: Just replace the absolute value signs with appropriate norms.) Functions with Lipschitz constants are continuous, and Figure 5.3.1 shows that a continuous function g that maps I to itself has at least one fixpoint p there.

If $L < 1$, there can be only one fixpoint: If q were another, then $|p - q| = |g(p) - g(q)| < L|p - q| < |p - q|$, contradiction!

Now, define the *error* $\varepsilon_n = x_n - p$ of the approximation x_n. Then

$$|\varepsilon_{n+1}| = |x_{n+1} - p| = |g(x_n) - g(p)| \le L|\,x_n - p| = L|\varepsilon_n|$$

and applying this inequality repeatedly yields

$$|\varepsilon_n| \le L^n\,|\varepsilon_0|$$

for every n. If $L < 1$, then $\varepsilon_n \to 0$, hence $x_n \to p$. The type of convergence displayed here has a special name: If a sequence x_0, x_1, x_2, ... approaches a limit p and successive error terms $\varepsilon_n = x_n - p$ are related by an inequality $|\varepsilon_{n+1}| \le L|\varepsilon_n|$ with a constant $L < 1$, then x_n

is said to converge to p *linearly*. (This concept can be extended to vector, matrix, and complex sequences by using norms.)

This analysis has demonstrated that you can use Fixpoint iteration to approximate a fixpoint $p = g(p)$ if g maps a closed interval I containing p into itself, has a Lipschitz constant $L < 1$ there, and your initial guess lies in I. The successive approximations converge to p linearly. Moreover, suppose you know a bound $E > |\varepsilon_0|$ for the error in the initial approximation. Then you can use the inequality $|\varepsilon_n| \leq L^n |\varepsilon_0|$ to estimate the number n of iterations required to ensure that the error is less than a specified tolerance T: Stop when $L^n E < T$; i.e.,

$$n > \frac{\log(T/E)}{E \log L} .$$

This analysis partially explains the differences among the three functions g suggested at the beginning of this section to solve the equation $x^2 = A$. For the first one, $g(x) = A/x$, the required inequalities $g(a) \leq b$ and $a \leq g(b)$ would imply $A \leq ab \leq A$, hence $A = ab$ and $g(a) - g(b) = b - a$. Thus, there's no Lipschitz constant $L < 1$ for any interval $[a, b]$ that g maps to itself. The condition for using Fixpoint iteration fails, and the successive approximations don't converge. This function won't be considered further.

The difference between the good and excellent results given earlier for Fixpoint iteration with the other two functions

$$g(x) = \frac{x + 2}{x + 1} \qquad g(x) = \frac{1}{2}\left[x + \frac{A}{x} \right]$$

stems from the values of their derivatives at the fixpoint $p = \sqrt{A}$. If g' is continuous on the interval I under analysis and L is a number such that $|g'(\xi)| < L$ for all ξ in I, then L is a Lipschitz constant for g on I: for each x and x' in I, the Mean-Value theorem provides ξ between x and x' such that

$$|g(x) - g(x')| = |g'(\xi) (x - x')| \leq L |x - x'| .$$

In fact, a closer analysis — see Reference [10, Section 3.3] — shows that if g' is continuous at p and $|g'(p)| < L < 1$, then you can find some closed bounded interval I containing p that g maps into itself, for which L is a Lipschitz constant. Thus, you can use Fixpoint iteration to approximate a fixpoint $p = g(p)$, provided $|g'(p)| < 1$ and your initial approximation x_0 is close enough to p to lie in I.

(Unfortunately, this analysis doesn't tell how close you must be.) Further, you can use L with the inequality $|\varepsilon_n| \leq L^n |\varepsilon_0|$ to estimate the number of iterations required.

Here are the derivatives of the two functions g still under consideration:

$$g(x) = \frac{x + A}{x + 1} \qquad g(x) = \frac{1}{2}\left[x + \frac{A}{x}\right]$$

$$g'(x) = \frac{1 - A}{(1 + x)^2} \qquad g'(x) = \frac{1}{2}\left[1 - \frac{A}{x^2}\right]$$

$$g'(\sqrt{A}) = \frac{1 - \sqrt{A}}{1 + \sqrt{A}} < 1 \qquad g'(\sqrt{A}) = 0 .$$

For $A = 2$, the left-hand function has $g'(\sqrt{A}) \approx -0.17$; so $L = 1/5$ is a reasonable Lipschitz constant, and the error ε_n will decrease by at least a factor of 5 with each successive approximation. The right-hand function has $g'(\sqrt{A}) = 0$ for any A; hence, *any* positive L, no matter how small, can serve as a Lipschitz constant. This function is clearly the best choice for solving $x^2 = A$ by Fixpoint iteration. It displays a phenomenon called *quadratic* convergence, that will be considered in Section 5.4.

Implementing Fixpoint iteration requires a criterion for stopping the process. A client could find a Lipschitz constant and an initial error estimate and then determine the number of iterations required. But that's unrealistic, because these values are often difficult to estimate. The usual criterion is to stop when the distance between an approximation x and the corresponding function $g(x)$ becomes less than a specified tolerance T. Since that's not guaranteed to happen, the implementation must include an upper limit on the number of iterations.

The MSP implementation is function **Fixpoint**, shown in Figure 5.3.2. It has parameters corresponding to the function g, the initial approximation x, and the tolerance T. Parameters **g**, **x**, and the return value are given type **Scalar** because Fixpoint iteration works with complex functions as well as real. An additional reference parameter **Code** reports the outcome of the computation: **Code** = 0 indicates that the iteration terminated satisfactorily with $|x - g(x)|$ < T, whereas **Code** = −1 signifies that this condition was not attained even after one thousand iterations. (This upper limit was chosen arbitrarily.)

```
Scalar Fixpoint(Scalar g(Scalar),      // Find a fixpoint of  g .
                Scalar x,              // Initial estimate.
                double T,              // Tolerance.
                int&   Code = 0) {     // Status code.
    int    n = 0;                      // Iteration count.
    Scalar p,dx;
    do
        {p   = g(x);                            // Fixpoint itera-
         dx = x - p;                            // tion: do at most
         x . = p; }                             // 1000   steps.
       while (++n < 1000 && Norm(dx) >= T);
    if (Norm(dx) < T) Code = 0;                 // Report success,
       else Code = -1;                          // or failure to
    return x; }                                 // converge.
```

Figure 5.3.2 MSP function Fixpoint

As a more realistic example to demonstrate **Fixpoint**, consider the cam function $f(x)$ of Figure 5.2.2. The equation $f(x) = 0$ is equivalent to

$$\frac{1 + e^{-x/2\pi} \sin x}{2} = 0.7$$

$$e^{-x/2\pi} \sin x = 0.4$$
$$\sin x = 0.4 \, e^{x/2\pi}$$
$$x = \sin^{-1}(0.4 \, e^{x/2\pi}) = g(x) \quad .$$

Thus, the root of the cam function is the fixpoint of this function g. Figure 5.3.3 shows execution of function **Fixpoint** to locate it.

Notice that the ratios in Figure 5.3.3 of successive values of $x - g(x)$ are approximately constant, ≈ 0.075. There's a reason for that:

$$\lim_{n\to\infty} \frac{x_{n+1} - g(x_{n+1})}{x_n - g(x_n)} = \lim_{n\to\infty} \frac{g(x_n) - g(x_{n+1})}{x_n - x_{n+1}} = \lim_{n\to\infty} g'(\xi_n) = g'(p) \quad .$$

In this equation, ξ_n is a point (provided by the Mean-Value theorem) between the approximations x_{n+1} and x_n. Next, you can differentiate g, compute $g'(p) \approx 0.076$ for the fixpoint p, and thus explain the values of the ratios.

Earlier, you saw that one of the conditions for success of Fixpoint iteration is that $|g'(p)| < 1$, where $p = g(p)$ is the fixpoint. The following ratio limit, similar to the one just computed, shows what happens when $|g'(p)| > 1$. If g' is continuous in a neighborhood of p, then

```
Finding the fixpoint  x  of  g(x) = asin(.4 exp(x/2π))
by Fixpoint iteration

Initial estimate  x :  0
Tolerance         T :  .000001

Itera-
tion        x            g(x)         x - g(x)
   0    0.000000        0.41         -0.41
   1    0.4115168       0.44         -0.030
   2    0.4412554       0.44         -0.0022
   3    0.4434973       0.44         -0.00017
   4    0.4436669       0.44         -1.3e-05
   5    0.4436797       0.44         -9.7e-07

Fixpoint  x ≈  0.4436807
Code      = 0
```

Figure 5.3.3 Executing function Fixpoint

$$\lim_{n \to \infty} \frac{\varepsilon_{n+1}}{\varepsilon_n} = \lim_{n \to \infty} \frac{g(x_{n+1}) - p}{g(x_n) - p} = \lim_{n \to \infty} \frac{g(x_{n+1}) - g(p)}{x_{n+1} - p} = \lim_{n \to \infty} g'(\xi_n) = g'(p) \ .$$

Here, ξ_n lies between x_n and p. If $|g'(p)| > 1$, then $|\varepsilon_n|$ increases without bound: The sequence x_n diverges.

An inverse function g^{-1} has the same fixpoint as g: $p = g(p)$ if and only if $g^{-1}(p) = p$. If these functions are differentiable, then their derivatives at p are reciprocal. Except in the rare case when both have absolute value 1, one will have absolute value > 1, and the other, < 1. Thus, you'll be able to use Fixpoint iteration with *exactly one* of them to find p. For example, the inverse of the function g used in Figure 5.3.3 is $g^{-1}(x) = 2\pi \log(2.5 \sin x)$. If you perform Fixpoint iteration on g^{-1} starting with the final approximation $x_5 = 0.4436807$ in the figure, you'll just get the original values x_4, x_3, ... in reverse order. The sequence diverges.

5.4 Newton-Raphson Iteration

In Section 5.3 you saw how the problem of solving an equation $f(x) = 0$ for a root $x = p$ of a function f can be transformed in various ways into a problem of solving an equivalent equation $x = g(x)$ for a fixpoint $x = p$ of a related function g. If g' is continuous near p, $|g'(p)| \le L < 1$, and your initial approximation x_0 is close enough to p, then the successive approximations x_1, x_2, ... computed by Fixpoint iteration $x_{n+1} = g(x_n)$ converge linearly to p, and the approximation errors $\varepsilon_n = x_n - p$ satisfy the inequality $|\varepsilon_{n+1}| \le L|\varepsilon_n|$. Clearly, you should choose g so that $|g'(p)|$ is as small as possible. The example

$$A > 0 \qquad f(x) = x^2 - A \qquad p = \sqrt{A} \qquad g(x) = \frac{1}{2}\left[x + \frac{A}{x}\right] \qquad g'(p) = 0$$

indicated that very rapid convergence might result if you choose g' so that $g'(p) = 0$.

In fact, this is generally true. If g'' is continuous on a neighborhood N of p that g maps into itself, then

$$\frac{\varepsilon_{n+1}}{\varepsilon_n^2} = \frac{x_{n+1} - p}{(x_n - p)^2} = \frac{g(x_n) - g(p)}{(x_n - p)^2}$$

$$= \frac{g'(p)(x_n - p) + \frac{1}{2}g''(\xi)(x_n - p)^2}{(x_n - p)^2} = \frac{1}{2}g''(\xi) \quad .$$

Here, ξ is a number between x_n and p, provided by Taylor's theorem. If $g'(p) = 0$ and $|g''(\xi)| \le M$ for *all* ξ in N, then $|\varepsilon_{n+1}| \le \frac{1}{2}M|\varepsilon_n|^2$ in general. If the error terms ε_n of a convergent sequence $x_0, x_1, x_2, \ldots$ satisfy an inequality like this for any constant M, then the sequence is said to converge *quadratically* to p. (This concept can also be defined for vector, matrix, and complex sequences: Just replace the absolute values by appropriate norms.)

To achieve quadratic convergence, you need a way to transform functions f with roots p into functions g with fixpoints p such that $g'(p) = 0$. The most common method is to set

$$g(x) = x - \frac{f(x)}{f'(x)} \quad .$$

Then you can compute

$$g''(x) = \frac{f(x)f''(x)}{f'(x)^2}$$

$$g''(x) = \frac{f'(x)^2 f''(x) + f(x)f'(x)f'''(x) - 2f(x)f''(x)^2}{f'(x)^3}$$

hence, $g'(p) = 0$ and g'' is continuous near p provided $f'(p) \ne 0$ and f''' is continuous near p. Fixpoint iteration with this function g is called *Newton-Raphson* iteration. Under these assumptions, the successive approximations converge quadratically to p, provided your initial estimate x_0 is close enough to p. (A more precise analysis shows that only the continuity of f'' is required for this result: See Reference [20, Chapter 4].)

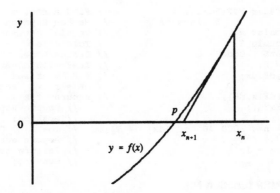

Figure 5.4.1 Newton-Raphson iteration

With $A > 0$ and $f(x) = x^2 - A$, the Newton-Raphson iteration function is

$$g(x) = x - \frac{f(x)}{f'(x)} = x - \frac{x^2 - A}{2x} = \frac{1}{2}\left[x + \frac{A}{x}\right] \ .$$

This is just the example given at the beginning of this section. It's known as *Newton's method* for computing square roots.

Newton-Raphson iteration has a vivid graphical representation, shown in Figure 5.4.1. Consider one of the successive approximations x_n to a root p of a function f. The tangent to the graph of $y = f(x)$ at the point $x, y = x_n, f(x_n)$ has equation $y - f'(x_n) = f'(x_n) (x - x_n)$. Set $y = 0$ and solve for the intercept x: you get

$$x = x_n - \frac{f(x_n)}{f'(x_n)} \ .$$

This is the next Newton-Raphson approximation x_{n+1}. Apparently, if x_n is close enough to p and the graph of $y = f(x)$ is sufficiently steep and smooth near $x = p$, the next approximation will be *much* closer to p.

The MSP implementation of Newton-Raphson iteration is function **NR**, shown in Figure 5.4.2. It has parameters **x** and **T** corresponding to the initial estimate x and the tolerance T, and a parameter corresponding to a C++ function **FdF** that computes values of both f and f'. **FdF** must have prototype

```
Scalar FdF(Scalar x, Scalar& dF) .
```

```
Scalar NR(Scalar FdF(Scalar x,        // Find a root of  f  by
                     Scalar& dF),     // Newton-Raphson method.
          Scalar x,                   // Initial estimate.
          double T,                   // Tolerance.
          int&   Code = 0) {          // Status code.
   int    n = 0;                      // Iteration count.
   Scalar Fx,dF,dx;                   // FdF must set
   do {                               // dF = f'(x)   and
      Fx = FdF(x,dF);                 // return  f(x) .
      dx = Fx/dF;                        // Newton-Raphson it-
      x -= dx; }                        // eration:  do at
   while (++n < 1000 && Norm(dx) >= T);  // most  1000  steps.
   if (Norm(dx) < T) Code = 0;          // Report success, or
      else Code = 1;                    // failure to
   return x; }                          // converge.
```

Figure 5.4.2 MSP function NR

It returns the value $f(x)$ after computing $\mathbf{dF} = f'(x)$. By packaging the code for both f and f' in a single C++ function, you can avoid duplicate computation of expressions common to f and f', as in the next example. Various parameters and variables in **NR** and **FdF** are given the type **Scalar** because this method works with complex as well as real equations. An additional **NR** reference parameter **Code** reports the outcome of the computation. **Code** = 0 indicates that the iteration terminated satisfactorily when the difference of two successive approximations became less than the tolerance T, whereas **Code** = 1 signifies that this condition was not attained even after one thousand iterations. (This upper limit was chosen arbitrarily.)

Figure 5.4.3 shows execution of function **NR** to locate the root of the cam function that was used in Figures 5.2.4 and 5.3.3. It also contains the code for the function **FdFforCam** used to evaluate the cam function and its derivative. You can see that expressions common to $f(x)$ and $f'(x)$ are computed only once.

The difference in accuracy between the three equation solving methods discussed so far is remarkable:

Method	$|x_5 - x_4|$	$|f(x_5)|$
Section 5.1 Bisection	$3.1 \cdot 10^{-2}$	$2.4 \cdot 10^{-3}$
Section 5.2 Fixpoint	$9.7 \cdot 10^{-7}$	$2.8 \cdot 10^{-8}$
Section 5.3 Newton-Raphson	$4.0 \cdot 10^{-17}$	$1.6 \cdot 10^{-17}$

(For the Fixpoint method, $|f(x_5)|$ was computed by hand.)

The rapid convergence of Newton-Raphson iteration for ideal cases like Figure 5.4.3 is attained at some cost: It is not so general, nor so predictable as the Bisection method. Is it ever as slow as that method? When does it fail altogether? Clearly, the iteration will halt with approximation x_n if $f'(x_n) = 0$ or fails to exist. Moreover, the

```
Finding a root  x  of the cam function  f  by Newton-Raphson
iteration

Initial estimate  x :  0
Tolerance         T :  1e-14

Itera-
tion         x            f(x)        f'(x)       dx
    0    0.000000       -0.20        0.50      -0.40
    1    0.4000000      -0.017       0.40      -0.043
    2    0.4429231      -0.00029     0.39      -0.00076
    3    0.4436805      -9.4e-08     0.39      -2.4e-07
    4    0.4436808      -9.6e-15     0.39      -2.5e-14
    5    0.4436808      -1.6e-17     0.39      -4.0e-17

Root  x ≈  0.44368077133345
Code    =  0
```

This function computed f(x) and f'(x) :

```
double FdFforCam(double x, double& dF) {
   double T = 2*M_PI;
   double E = .5*exp(-x/T);
   double S = sin(x);
   double C = cos(x);
   dF       = E*(C - S/T);
   return -.2 + E*S; }
```

Figure 5.4.3 Executing function NR with function FdFforCam

condition derived earlier for quadratic convergence requires that the initial estimate be sufficiently close to the root p, f'' be continuous near p, and $f'(p) \neq 0$. When the latter conditions fail, convergence slows. For example, if $f(x) = x^2$, so that $p = f(p) = f'(p) = 0$, then

$$x_{n+1} = x_n - \frac{x_n^2}{2x_n} = \frac{x_n}{2} \ .$$

Thus, in this case the ratio of successive approximation errors is always $1/2$, so the approximations converge linearly, not quadratically. This generally happens when $f'(p) = 0$ but the other conditions hold. If p is a root of order n, then the ratio is $1 - 1/n$. (See Reference [30, Section 2.3B].) For high-order roots, this ratio makes convergence so slow that numerical analysis software must sometimes use very special mathematical techniques.

A more serious failure can occur when the initial estimate is too far from p. The sequence of Newton-Raphson approximations may approach a different root. Or, if there's a local extremum at a point x

near p, the approximations may cycle indefinitely or at least "bounce around" for a while before converging. For example, execute **NR** with initial estimate $x = -12$ to find the root $p \approx 1.46$ (the only root) of the polynomial

$$f(x) = x^5 - 8x^4 + 17x^3 + 8x^2 - 14x - 20$$

shown in Figure 5.4.4. **NR** will iterate more than fifty times before settling down to converge rapidly to p. When an approximation x_n falls near the local maximum or minimum, x_{n+1} jumps far away, as shown by the solid tangent lines. Several steps are then needed to return to the region near the root. (The dotted line is referred to later.)

Figure 5.4.5 shows MSP function **NRBisect**, a hybrid root finder that combines features of the Newton-Raphson and Bisection methods to combat this "bouncing" problem. You invoke it like the Bisection method, with bracketing estimates x_L and x_R of a root p of a function f: $[x_L, x_R]$ must contain p and $f(x_L)$ and $f(x_R)$ must differ in sign. **NRBisect** uses the interval midpoint as an initial estimate x, and successively improves x by performing either Newton-Raphson or Bisection steps. After each step it adjusts x_L and x_R as in the Bisection method so that $[x_L, x_R]$ becomes a smaller bracketing interval, but doesn't necessarily shrink by half. If a Newton-Raphson iteration would throw the next approximation x outside the interval, **NRBisect** sets x equal to the interval midpoint. The iteration terminates when a Newton-Raphson step changes x by an amount less

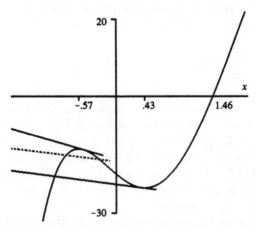

Figure 5.4.4 $f(x) = x^5 - 8x^4 + 17x^3 + 8x^2 - 14x - 20$

```
double NRBisect(double FdF(double,double&),  // Find a root of  f.
                double xL,                    // Left estimate.
                double xR,                    // Right estimate.
                double T,                     // Tolerance.
                int&   Code) {                // Status code.
Boolean Done;
int n = 0;                                    // Iteration count.
double x,h,yL,yLp,y,yp;
x = (xL + xR)/2;                              // The initial approxima-
h = x - xL;                                   // tion is the midpoint.
yL = FdF(xL,yLp);
do {                                          // Repeat until  h , the
    y = FdF(x,yp);                            // Newton-Raphson
    Done = (h < T);                           // correction or  ½  the
    if (!Done) {                              // current interval
        if (Sign(yL) == Sign(y)) {            // length, is  < T .
            xL = x;  yL = y; }
        else                                  // Adjust the bracketing
            xR = x;                           // interval.
        x -= (h = y/yp);                      // Try the Newton-Raphson
        h  = fabs(h);                         // correction.
        if (x < xL || xR < x) {               // If  x  would go out of
            x = (xL + xR)/2;                  // bounds, bisect instead.
            h = x - xL; }}}                   // Do at most  1000
    while (++n < 1000 && !Done);              // iterations, then set
Code = int(!Done);                            // Code  to report success
return x; }                                   // or failure.
```

Figure 5.4.5 MSP function NRBisect

than the specified tolerance T, or when a Bisection step yields the midpoint of a bracketing interval shorter than $2T$.

Figure 5.4.6 shows execution of **NRBisect** to find the root of the polynomial in Figure 5.4.4 that caused Newton-Raphson iteration to "bounce around" so much. The tabulated dx values are either the size of a Newton-Raphson step from the previous approximation, or the length of the current interval. **NRBisect** takes Newton-Raphson steps through Iteration 10. Convergence is somewhat slow because the graph is terribly steep and nonlinear. Then the hybrid function performs three bisections in a row, to avoid bouncing. After that, the approximation is close enough to the root for Newton-Raphson iteration to take over again and converge quickly.

Another device for avoiding "bouncing" is simply to limit the size of the Newton-Raphson steps, relative to the size of the current approximation. That is particularly appropriate for complex polynomial equations, and is implemented in Section 5.6 as function **NRHStep**. Operating on the polynomial shown in Figure 5.4.6 with the same initial estimate, it required 21 iterations — a few more than **NRBisect**.

```
Finding a root of the bouncing function  f
by the hybrid Newton-Raphson bisection method

Left   estimate  xL :  -26
Right estimate  xR :    2
Tolerance       T  :  .01
```

Itera-tion	xL	x	xR	f(x)	dx
0	-26.00000	-12.00000	2.000000	-4.4e+05	14.
1	-12.00000	-9.334385	2.000000	-1.4e+05	2.7
2	-9.334385	-7.215922	2.000000	-4.7e+04	2.1
:	:	:	:	:	:
9	-1.311093	-0.9262393	2.000000	-20.	0.38
10	-0.9262393	-0.4665007	2.000000	-14.	0.46
11	-0.4665007	0.7667497	2.000000	-21.	1.2
12	0.7667497	1.383375	2.000000	-3.3	0.62
13	1.383375	1.466876	2.000000	0.087	0.084
14	1.383375	1.464772	1.466876	4.9e-05	0.0021

```
Root  x ≈  1.465
Code    =  0
```

Figure 5.4.6 Executing function NRBisect

One disadvantage of the Newton-Raphson method and its hybrid is their requirement for a value of the derivative $f'(x_n)$ at each approximation x_n of the root p of f. That might be difficult or impossible to provide, especially if values of f are given only by a table, or by the solution of some other substantial problem like a differential equation or a multiple integral. One way to avoid that problem is to replace $f'(x_n)$ in the Newton-Raphson iteration formula

$$x_{n+1} = x_n - \frac{f(x_n)}{f'(x_n)}$$

by its approximation

$$f'(x_n) \approx \frac{f(x_n) - f(x_{n-1})}{x_n - x_{n-1}}$$

You can check that the resulting expression

$$x_{n+1} = x_n - \frac{x_n - x_{n-1}}{f(x_n) - f(x_{n-1})} f(x_n)$$

is the formula for the x intercept of the secant line through points x, $y = x_{n-1}, f(x_{n-1})$, and $x_n, f(x_n)$. For this reason, the resulting root finding algorithm is called the *Secant method*. This method requires *two* initial estimates x_0 and x_1. They need not bracket the root.

```
Scalar Secant(Scalar f(Scalar),       // Find a root of  f .
               Scalar x0,              // Initial
               Scalar x1,              // estimates.
               double T,               // Tolerance.
               int&   Code) {          // Status code.
    int    n  = 0;                     // Iteration count.
    Scalar dx = x1 - x0;
    Scalar y0 = f(x0);
    Scalar y1,dy;
    do {                               // Secant method
        y1  = f(x1);                   // iteration.  Do at most
        dy  = y1 - y0;                 // 1000  steps.
        dx  = -y1*dx/dy;
        x0  = x1;   y0  = y1;
        x1 += dx; }
    while (Norm(dx) >= T && ++n < 1000);
    if (Norm(dx) < T) Code = 0;        // Report success, or
    else Code = 1;                     // failure to
    return x1; }                       // converge.
```

Figure 5.4.7 MSP function Secant

The Secant method attains greater generality than the Newton-Raphson method at a cost. Two initial estimates are required, and convergence is somewhat slower. Its behavior in difficult situations is sometimes problematic, as shown in the next paragraph. Its convergence conditions are similar to those of Newton-Raphson iteration, but the rate of convergence falls between linear and quadratic: If p is a simple root, then the approximation errors ε_1, ε_2, ε_3, ... satisfy the equation

$$\lim_{n\to\infty} \frac{\varepsilon_{n+1}}{\varepsilon_n^r} = K \qquad r = \frac{1 + \sqrt{5}}{2} \approx 1.6$$

for some constant K. (See Reference [20, Section 4.2].)

While the Secant method is conceptually similar to Newton-Raphson iteration, its implementation involves an extra complication: You need two initial estimates and you must keep two approximations current. You can see how this is done by inspecting the MSP implementation, function **Secant**, shown in Figure 5.4.7. Executing it to find the root of the cam function as in Figure 5.4.3 produces results comparable to the Newton-Raphson method: With initial estimates 0 and 1, or 0 and 0.1, the Secant method achieves the same accuracy with five or six steps. With the troublesome polynomial f of Figure 5.4.4, the results are mixed. With initial estimates −12 and 5 bracketing the root, **Secant** attains the accuracy 0.01 after only seven iterations. But with initial estimates −12 and −11 and tolerance 0.01 it falsely reports a root $x \approx -0.34$ after 16 iterations, even though $f(-0.34) \approx -15$. This happens because two successive approximations x_{14} and x_{15} straddle the local maximum, so that $f(x_{14})$ ≈ $f(x_{15})$. The resulting secant — the dotted line in Figure 5.4.4 — is nearly horizontal. Thus, x_{16} jumps away from the region shown and $f(x_{16})$ is so large that the secants determined by x_{15} and x_{16} and by x_{16} and x_{17} are nearly vertical. Their intercepts x_{17} and x_{18} are closer than the tolerance, so **Secant** terminates successfully and returns x_{18} even though it's not close to the root. With the smaller tolerance 10^{-6} this anomaly disappears, though the computation takes longer: **Secant** computed the root appropriately after 27 iterations.

Some variations on the Secant method are easy to consider. First, you can construct its hybrid with the Bisection method, analogous to function **NRBisect**. Second, you can remove the need for two initial estimates of the root of function f by selecting x_1 close to x_0, but so that $f(x_0)$ and $f(x_1)$ aren't too close. (However, this would prevent you from using bracketing estimates, which might be safer, if you have them at hand.)

5.5   Real Polynomial Roots

The problem of finding a root of a polynomial $F(x)$ is common enough that you'll want to modify the MSP root finding functions already considered, using a parameter F of type **Polynom** instead of defining a function specifically to evaluate F and perhaps its derivative. Three such modifications are required for this section: function **Bracket**, and the Newton-Raphson routines **NR** and **NRBisect**. To use the versions presented earlier to solve arbitrary equations $F(x) = 0$ a client must write one of the functions

```
Scalar F(double t)
Scalar FandDF(Scalar t, Scalar& DF) .
```

The first returns $F(t)$; the second returns $F(t)$ after setting **DF** = $F'(t)$. The Newton-Raphson routines have a corresponding parameter of the same type. For polynomial equations, however, you only need to use a constant reference parameter F of type **Polynom**.

The new version of **Bracket** is named **BracketPoly**. Here's its prototype:

```
Boolean BracketPoly(double&  xL,
                    double&  xR,
               const Polynom& F,
                    double   T) .
```

No further changes are necessary, because the syntax for polynomial evaluation is the same as that for functions. The source code for **BracketPoly** is on the diskette. You can modify MSP functions **Bisect**, **Fixpoint**, and **Secant** to handle polynomial equations in exactly the same way.

It's more interesting to modify **NR** and **NRBisect**, because they use values of both the function F and its derivative F'. Instead of executing **y = FdF(t,yp)** to evaluate $y = F(t)$ and **yp** $= F'(t)$, you can use MSP function **Horner**:

```
Polynom Q;
y   = Horner(Q,F,t);
yp = Q(t);
```

The first invocation divides the polynomial $F(x)$ by $x - t$, computing the quotient polynomial $Q(x)$ and returning the remainder $y = F(t)$. It was shown in Section 3.7 that $Q(t) = F'(t)$; thus, the third statement computes the derivative as claimed. With this modification, the routines **NR** and **NRBisect** described in Section 5.4 become

```
Scalar NRH(                   double NRBH(
   const Polynom& F,             const Polynom& F,
         Scalar   x,                   double   xL,
                                       double   xR,
         double   T,                   double   T,
         int&     Code)                int&     Code) .
```

Because only these few changes were required, there's no need to display the source code for **NRH** or **NRBH**. You'll find it on the diskette.

Function **NRBH** is the basic MSP tool for solving polynomial equations. But it requires an initial bracketing interval and finds only one root at a time. What do you do with polynomials like x^2, that don't have bracketing intervals — *i.e.*, whose value doesn't change sign at a root? When a bracketing interval exists, how do you find it? How do you find several roots in succession? How do you know when you've found them all? The rest of this section is devoted to answering these questions, in turn. Each one requires some theoretical discussion.

The first theoretical tool is *Taylor's theorem* for polynomials: let $F(x)$ be any polynomial, $n = $ degree(F), and t be any scalar. Then there are unique scalars $a_0, \ldots, a_n$ such that

$$F(x) = \sum_{k=0}^{n} a_k (x - t)^k \quad.$$

Moreover, $a_k = F^{(k)}(t)/k!$ for $k = 0, \ldots, n$.

From Taylor's theorem you can see that the following three conditions on a positive integer $m \leq n$ are equivalent:

- $F(x)$ is divisible by the polynomial $(x - t)^m$,

- $F(x) = \sum_{k=m}^{n} a_k (x - t)^k$,

- $F^{(k)}(t) = 0$ for $k < m$.

When $(x - t)^m$ divides $F(x)$ but $(x - t)^{m+1}$ does not, t is called a root of *multiplicity* m. Thus, t is a root of multiplicity m if the values of f and its first $m - 1$ derivatives at t are zero but $f^{(m)}(t) \neq 0$.

Let $t_1, \ldots, t_l$ denote all the roots of F, with orders $m_1, \ldots, m_l$, and consider a prime decomposition

$$f(x) = q(x) \prod_{j=1}^{l} (x - t_j)^{m_j}$$

where $q(x)$ is a product of prime factors of f that have no roots. From this equation it's apparent that

$$\sum_{j=1}^{l} m_j \leq n \quad.$$

That is, $F(x)$ has *at most* n roots, counted by multiplicity. Of course, some polynomials, like $x^2 + 1$, have no roots at all. There are some theorems that indicate when polynomials must have roots. The only simple one states that any polynomial $F(x)$ of odd degree must have some root (because it's continuous and its values for sufficiently large x have opposite signs).

$F(x)$ doesn't change sign at a root t of even multiplicity m: If x is sufficiently close to t, the term $a_m x^m$ is so much larger than the others that $F(x)$ has the same sign as a_m on both sides of t. Thus, if F has only roots of even multiplicity, it will never change sign, and there's no bracketing interval.

To use function **NRBH** to approximate a root t of a polynomial $F(x)$ for which there may be no bracketing interval, you must replace $F(x)$ by a related function that does change sign at t. You can accomplish that by dividing $F(x)$ by a greatest common divisor $G(x)$ of $F(x)$ and $F'(x)$. Such a $G(x)$ is computed by the function **GCD** described in Section 3.7. Why does this work? In a prime decomposition of $F(x)$, each linear factor $x - t_j$ has exponent m_j. In the decomposition of $F'(x)$, this factor has exponent $m_j - 1$. Therefore, each factor $x - t_j$ also occurs in the decomposition of $G(x)$ with exponent $m_j - 1$. When you divide $F(x)$ by $G(x)$, you get a quotient $Q(x)$ with linear factors $x - t_j$, each with exponent 1. Finally, $Q(x)$ has no further roots: Since $F(x) = G(x)Q(x)$, any root of $Q(x)$ is a root of $F(x)$. Thus, $Q(x)$ has the same roots as $F(x)$, but they all have order 1.

Using the GCD idea of the last paragraph, you can convert any polynomial into one for which all roots have bracketing intervals. MSP function **Bracket**, described in Section 5.1, can then help you find the intervals. However, it will only find a bracketing interval that's inside an initially specified interval. How can you select an initial interval that's guaranteed to be large enough? The following theorem is the tool you need: All real roots of the nth degree polynomial $F(x) = a_0 + a_1 x + \cdots + a_n x_n$ lie in the interval $[-C, C]$ where

$$C = 1 + \max_{k=0}^{n} \left| \frac{a_k}{a_n} \right| .$$

You can find a simple proof of this result in Reference [20, Section 2.2]; it's based on the triangle inequality and geometric series. (The theorem holds even for complex roots of complex polynomials: Just use the norm instead of absolute value, and the disk with radius C centered at the origin in place of interval $[-C, C]$.) C is called the *Cauchy bound* for F. Here's an MSP function that computes it:

```
double CauchyBound(const Polynom& F) { // Return Cauchy's
   int n = Degree(F);                  // upper bound for
   if (n <= 0) return 1;               // the norms of the
   double M = Norm(F[0]);              // roots of F .
   for (int k = 1; k < n; ++k)
     M = fmax(M,Norm(F[k]));
   return 1 + M/Norm(F[n]); }
```

Thus, to find a bracketing interval for a root of polynomial $F(x)$, you can compute the Cauchy bound C and then apply function **BracketPoly** to the initial interval $[-C, C]$.

The question remains, how to find several roots of $F(x)$ in succession, and how to determine when you've found them all. Here's the most common technique:

1. If $F(x)$ is linear, use elementary algebra to find a root.
2. If $F(x)$ is quadratic, use the Quadratic formula to find a root or decide that there's none.
3. Otherwise, use **CauchyBound**, **Bracket**, and **GCD**, if necessary, to find a bracketing interval, then **NRBH** to find a root t. **Bracket** may report that there's none.
4. Use **Horner** to divide $F(x)$ by $x - t$, obtaining a quotient polynomial $Q(x)$.
5. Apply the previous steps recursively to find the roots of $Q(x)$.

Step (4) is called *Deflation*. *Caution:* Subtraction of nearly equal quantities in the Quadratic formula numerator can cause loss of accuracy. You may want to incorporate some safeguards described in Reference [16].

Figure 5.5.1 contains MSP function **RealRoots**, which implements the Deflation technique to approximate all roots of a polynomial $F(x)$. The corresponding parameter **F** is passed by value because it's used to store the successive deflations of F. Since it uses **NRBH** to calculate the approximations, **RealRoots** has a parameter **T** for specifying the tolerance, and a reference parameter **Code** for requesting intermediate output and reporting success or failure. (See Appendix A.4 for a discussion of intermediate output. The dual nature of the **Code** parameter requires its awkward manipulation with **RealRoots** variables C and C1.) Since it uses **BracketPoly** to find a bracketing interval, **RealRoots** also has a parameter **S** for specifying the root separation: It won't search intervals shorter than **S** for a sign change. There's one further awkward programming point: When it can make a reasonable estimate of the number of roots, **RealRoots** allocates a vector **Root** for storing them, and uses a variable **k** to count them. When it's finished, **Root** may not be full, so its first **k** entries are copied to a new vector for return to the caller. This awkwardness stems from the fact that an MSP **Vector** object isn't quite the appropriate data structure for accumulating roots.

The mathematical aspects of **RealRoots** are straightforward. It follows the outline of the algorithm except in one small detail. With each recursive step the polynomial F changes; hence, its Cauchy bound changes. But the roots don't change, so **RealRoots** always uses the smallest Cauchy bound computed so far, to keep **BracketPoly** from wasting time.

```
Vector RealRoots(Polynom F,       // Return a vector consisting
                 double  S,       // of all the roots of  F , as
                 double  T,       // approximated by  NRBH .
                 int&    Code) {  // Ignore any two roots
  int n = Degree(F);              // separated by a distance
  if (n <  0) {                   // < S .  Use parameters  T
    Code = 0;                     // and  Code  like  NRBisect .
    Vector V = 0;                     // Return one root  0  for
    return V; }                       // the zero polynomial.
  if (n == 0) {                       // Nonzero constant poly-
    Code = 0;                         // nomials have no roots:
    Vector V(0);   return V; }        // return an empty vector.
  for (int k = 0;  F[k] == 0;  ++k);  // Compute the multiplici-
  F /= xTo(k);                        // ty  k  of the root  0 .
  n = Degree(F);                      // Deflate if appropriate.
  double  B = CauchyBound(F);
  Polynom D = Deriv(F);           // Divide by  GCD(F,F')  to
  Polynom G = GCD(F,D,T);         // discard duplicate roots.
  F /= G;
  n = Degree(F);  if (k > 0) ++n; // There are  ≤ n  roots.  If a
  Vector Root(n);                 // zero root was discovered
  if (k > 0) {                    // earlier, report it first.
    k = 1;  Root[k] = 0; }        // From now on,  k  counts the
  Boolean Done = False;           // roots.
  int C, C1 = 0;                  // C  and  C1 handle the  Code
  while (!Done) {                 // parameter.
    if (n > 2) {
      B = fmin(B,CauchyBound(F));            // The Cauchy bound
      double xL = -B;  double xR =  B;       // may decrease
      if (n%2 == 0 &&                        // through deflation.
        !BracketPoly(xL,xR,F,S))             // Quit if  F  never
        Done = True;                         // changes sign.
      if (!Done) {
        C = Code;                            // Find, record,
        Root[++k] = NRBH(F,xL,xR,T,C);       // and count a
        C1 |= C;                             // root, then
        Polynom Q;  Horner(Q,F,Root[k]);     // deflate.
        F = Q;       n = Degree(F); }}
    else {                                   // Elementary
      Done = True;                           // algebra.
      if (n == 2) {
        double D = F[1]*F[1] - 4*F[2]*F[0];  // Discriminant.
        if (D >= 0) {                        // No root if
          double S  = sqrt(D);               // D < 0 .
          double T  = 2*F[2];
          Root[++k] = (-F[1] + S)/T;         // Quadratic
          Root[++k] = (-F[1] - S)/T; }}      // formula.
        else                                 // k  counts roots!
          Root[++k] = -F[0]/F[1]; }}         // Linear equation.
  Code = C1;
  Vector V(k);                    // k  is the number of roots.
  V.Copy(1,Root,1,k);             // Copy them into a vector  V
  return V; }                     // of length  k  and return it.
```

Figure 5.5.1 MSP function RealRoots

The Legendre polynomials L_n, introduced in Section 3.7, provide a useful test of function **RealRoots**, because their roots play a significant role in approximating integrals. L_n has n distinct roots, which all lie in the open interval $(-1, 1)$. Since L_n is either odd or even, the roots are located symmetrically about zero, and zero is a root if n is odd. At right are the root approximations that result from executing the code at left:

Separation = 0.01	$-.973907$	$+.973907$
Tolerance = 1e–3;	$-.865063$	$+.865063$
RealRoots (Legendre(10),	$-.679410$	$+.679412$
Separation,	$-.433393$	$+.433385$
Tolerance,	$-.148884$	$+.148889$
Code)		

Root estimates $t_1, \ldots, t_m$ computed later in the Deflation process tend to be less accurate than those produced at early stages, because the coefficients of the deflated polynomials are the results of long sequences of calculations depending on all earlier steps. Roundoff error can grow quite noticeably. Therefore, it's usually prudent to *polish* the estimates after deflation. The simplest method is to compute new root approximations using Newton-Raphson iteration with the original (not deflated) polynomial and the initial approximations $t_1, \ldots, t_m$. This process is implemented by MSP function **Polish**:

```
void Polish(Vector& Root,        // Root contains approxi-
       const Polynom& F,         // mations to roots of
              double  T,         // F . Improve them,
         int&    Code) {         // using NRH .
   int C; int C1 = 0;            // For handling Code .
   for (int k = Root.LowIndex( );
           k <= Root.HighIndex( ) && F(Root[k]) != 0; ++k) {
     C = Code; Root[k] = NRH(F,Root[k],T,C); C1 |= C; }
   Code = C1; }
```

Polish operates on a vector **Root** of root approximations like the vector computed by **RealRoots**. Its remaining parameters are just like those of **NRH**.

Function **Polish** was tested by applying it to the vector $[r_1, \ldots, r_{10}]$ of root approximations computed earlier for the Legendre polynomial L_{10}. The largest value of $L_{10}(r_j)$ was $4.0 \cdot 10^{-5}$. With the same tolerance 10^{-3}, polishing required one Newton-Raphson iteration; the polished approximations are denoted by $[s_1, \ldots, s_{10}]$. The largest value of $L_{10}(s_j)$ was 1.9×10^{-10}, which represents a slight improvement. The largest adjustment in a single root was $r_j - s_j \approx 1.5 \times 10^{-5}$. Here are the original and polished root estimates, side by side:

original	polished	original	polished
−.973907	−.973907	+.973907	+.973907
−.865063	−.865063	+.865063	+.865063
−.679410	−.679410	+.679412	+.679410
−.433393	−.433395	+.433385	+.433395
−.148884	−.148874	+.148889	+.148874

To compute the roots of a polynomial f, function **RealRoots** divides f by the greatest common divisor of f and f', to ensure that all the roots are simple. This loses some information about them: their multiplicities. To regain that, MSP provides function

```
Vector Multiplicities(Vector x,    // Return the vector m
                      Polynom P,   // of multiplicities of
                      double E);   // the x entries as
                                   // roots of P .
```

This routine simply evaluates $P(x)$, $P'(x)$, ..., counting the number of zeroes. Since most computations are inexact, **Multiplicities** regards as zero any number z with **Norm(z)** less than the specified tolerance E. The source code is shown in Figure 5.5.2.

5.6 Complex Equations and Roots

Some applications problems lead to equations for which you must find complex solutions. One of the more familiar examples is an nth order linear homogeneous ordinary differential equation (ODE) with constant real coefficients a_0, ..., a_n:

$$a_0 \, y + a_1 \, y' + a_2 \, y'' + \cdots + a_n \, y^{(n)} = 0.$$

You may ask, for what values λ does the function $y = \exp \lambda x$ satisfy the ODE? Since $y^{(k)} = \lambda^k y$ for $k = 0$, ..., n,

$$(a_0 + a_1\lambda + a_2\lambda^2 + \cdots + a_n\lambda^n) \, y = 0,$$

i.e.,

$$a_0 + a_1\lambda + a_2\lambda^2 + \cdots + a_n\lambda^n = 0.$$

The real solutions $y = \exp \lambda x = e^{\lambda x}$ occur just when λ is a real root of the polynomial with coefficients a_0, ..., a_n. When $\lambda = a + bi$ is a

```
Vector Multiplicities(Vector    x,         // Return a vector  m
                      Polynom P,           // such that for each
                      double   E) {        // j , m[j]  is the
    if (Degree(P) == -1) {                 // multiplicity of
      x.AllEntries(-1);  return x; }       // x[j]  as a root
    for (int j  = x.LowIndex();            // of  P . Regard
              j <= x.HighIndex(); ++j) {   // as zero any
      Polynom Q = P;                                // scalar with
      for (int m = 0; Norm(Q(x[j])) < E; ++m) {     // Norm < E .
        Q = Deriv(Q); }
      x[j] = m; }
    return x; }
```

Figure 5.5.2 MSP function Multiplicities

complex root, $y = \exp \lambda x = u(x) + v(x)i$ is a complex solution of the ODE, where

$$u(x) = e^{ax}\cos bx \qquad v(x) = e^{ax}\sin bx.$$

But then

$$0 = a_0 y + a_1 y' + a_2 y'' + \cdots + a_n y^{(n)}$$
$$= (a_0 u + a_1 u' + a_2 u'' + \cdots + a_n u^{(n)}) + (a_0 v + a_1 v' + a_2 v + \cdots + a_n v^{(n)}) i$$
$$a_0 u + a_1 u' + a_2 u'' + \cdots + a_n u^{(n)} = 0 = a_0 v + a_1 v' + a_2 v'' + \cdots + a_n v^{(n)}.$$

Thus, the single complex root λ yields *two* real ODE solutions $y = e^{ax} \cos bx$ and $y = e^{ax} \sin bx$.

Some of the equation solving methods described earlier in this chapter work for complex equations, some do not. Those that involve the Bisection method are based on the *ordering* of scalars; they cannot be directly extended to complex equations.

(A method known as Lehmer's is a kind of extension of the Bisection method for complex polynomials. It uses a theoretical criterion for the existence of a root within a circle of given center and radius. One certainly exists within the circle centered at 0 with the Cauchy bound as radius, because the Cauchy bound theorem — see Section 5.5 — is valid for complex as well as real polynomials. When a circle is determined to contain a root, it is covered by seven circles with smaller radii, and the same criterion is repeated until a smaller circle is found to contain a root. This process continues recursively until the radius of the enclosing circle is smaller than a specified tolerance. As you see, the idea is simple enough to describe in a paragraph. But the details of the algorithm are too involved to present here. See Reference [20, Section 2.7].)

The Secant and Newton-Raphson methods do apply to complex equations, because the mathematics that underlies their convergence properties generalizes to complex functions. You can check that functions **Secant** and **NR** described in Section 5.5 work with **complex** scalars as well as **double**. (If you want either method to converge to a nonreal root, you'll have to start with a nonreal initial estimate, else the algebra will result only in successive real approximations.) Because most complex equations that you'll encounter involve polynomials, the discussion in the present section is confined to that case. Moreover, the considerations for the Secant method are like those for Newton-Raphson, so only the latter are included.

Newton-Raphson Iteration for Complex Polynomials

Numerical analysts have learned from experience that in complex applications, Newton-Raphson iteration frequently *overshoots*. That is, in correcting an approximation x_n to the desired root x of a function f, the derivative can be so small that the next approximation

$$x_{n+1} = x_n - \delta x_n = x_n - \frac{f(x_n)}{f'(x_n)}$$

becomes huge, relative to the size of the root. This results in overflow, or at least requires many iterations to get back to an approximation near x. A possible remedy is to ensure that the norm $\| \delta x_n \|$ of the correction doesn't exceed $\| x \|$, by dividing the correction by $\| x \|$ if necessary. This idea is implemented by function **NRHStep**, shown in Figure 5.6.1. It's intended for use with **complex** scalars, but works as well with **double**. Executing it on the Section 5.4 "bouncing" polynomial

$$f(x) = x^5 - 8x^4 + 17x^3 + 8x^2 - 14x - 20$$

with tolerance $T = 0.01$ produces these results:

Initial Estimate	Iterations	Root
−12	21	1.465
10 + 10i	10	3.969 + 1.430i
10 − 10i	10	3.969 − 1.430i
−10 + 10i	12	−0.701 + 0.524i
−10 − 10i	12	−0.701 − 0.524i

The results illustrate the theorem that the complex roots of a real polynomial occur in conjugate pairs. Section 5.4 reported that the

```
Scalar NRHStep(               // Return an approximation to a
   const Polynom& F,          // root of  F , computed by
           Scalar   x,        // Newton-Raphson iteration.
           double   T,        // Use the initial estimate  x ,
           int&     Code) {   // correct it for each succes-
   int      nMax = 100;       // sive approximation, and stop
   Scalar Fx,dF,dx;           // when the distance to the next
   int    n = 0;              // estimate is  < T ,  or the
   do {                                // number of itera-
        Polynom Q;   Fx = Horner(Q,F,x);   // tions reaches the
        dF = Q(x);   dx = Fx/dF;           // limit  nMax .
        double N = Norm(x);               // Insure that the
        if (x != 0 && Norm(dx) > N) dx /= N;  // step size  ≤ ‖x‖ .
        x -= dx; }                        // Set  Code = 0  to
     while (++n < nMax && Norm(dx) >= T); // report success,
   if (Norm(dx) < T) Code = 0;            // or  = 1  if the
     else Code = 1;           // desired accuracy is not
   return x; }                // achieved after  nMax  steps.
```

Figure 5.6.1 MSP function NRHStep

unmodified Newton-Raphson routine **NR** required more than 50 iterations to reach the root 1.465 from the initial estimate −12, and the hybrid Newton-Raphson/Bisection routine **NRBisect** required 14. Overstep limitation seems reasonably successful in this case.

Function **NRHStep** is the basis for MSP routine

```
Vector Roots(Polynom F,   // Return a vector consisting
             double T,    // of all the roots of F ,
             int& Code);  // approximated by NRHStep .
```

This routine computes all the complex roots of a complex polynomial. (It will work with **double** scalars as well.) **Roots** operates much like the Section 5.5 routine **RealRoots**, which computes all the real roots of a real polynomial. However, to begin the process of approximating each root r, the earlier routine used the Cauchy bound and function **BracketPoly** to find an interval containing r, then employed a hybrid Newton-Raphson/Bisection algorithm to insure that r is ultimately captured inside an interval whose length is smaller than the tolerance T. The Bisection hybrid is not available for complex polynomials, so **Roots** uses another, less reliable, starting device. First, an initial estimate $x_0 + y_0 i$ for Newton-Raphson iteration is chosen randomly so that $0 \leq x_0, y_0 < 1$. If **NRHStep** doesn't achieve convergence within the specified tolerance after 100 iterations, **Roots** tries another random initial estimate. It makes up to 10 such attempts before returning the last approximation — which is probably incorrect — and setting parameter **Code = 1**. The source code for **Roots** is shown in Figure 5.6.2.

Before beginning Newton-Raphson iteration to approximate a root of a polynomial f, **RealRoots** divided f by the greatest common

```
Vector Roots(Polynom F,        // Return a vector consisting
             double  T,        // of all the roots of  F ,  as
             int&    Code) {   // approximated by NRHStep .
  int n = Degree(F);           // Use  parameters  T  and
  if (n <  0) {                // Code  like  NRHStep .
    Code = 0;                      // Return one root  0  for
    Vector V = 0;  return V; }     // the zero polynomial.
  if (n == 0) {                    // A nonzero nonconstant
    Code = 0;                      // polynomial has no root:
    Vector V(0);  return V; }      // return an empty vector.
  for (int k = 0;  F[k] == 0;  ++k);  // Compute the multiplici-
  F /= xTo(k);                   // ty  k  of the root  0 .
  n = Degree(F);                 // Deflate if appropriate.
  if (k > 0) k = 1;              // k = number of zero
  if (n > 1) {                   // roots.  Divide by
    Polynom D = Deriv(F);        // GCD(F,F') to discard
    Polynom G = GCD(F,D,T);      // duplicate nonzero
    F /= G;  n = Degree(F); }    // roots.  n + k =  number
  Vector Root(n+k);              // of roots.  If  0  is a
  if (k == 1) Root[1] = 0;       // root, report it.
  int CodeOut = 0;               // Code  output parameter.
  while (n > 2) {                // Deflation loop, for
    int m = 0;  Scalar x;  int C;   // nontrivial cases.  Do
    do { x = Random();  C = Code;   // NRHStep  m ≤ 10  times
         x = NRHStep(F,x,T,C); }    // with random initial
      while (C != 0 && ++m < 10);   // estimates.  Record the
    Root[++k] = x;                  // root, setting CodeOut
    if (C != 0) CodeOut = 1;        // if it's unreliable.
    Polynom Q;  Horner(Q,F,x);      // Deflate.
    F = Q;        n = Degree(F); }
  if (n == 2) {
    Scalar D  = F[1]*F[1] - 4*F[2]*F[0];   // Quadratic formula.
    Scalar S  = sqrt(D);
    Scalar U  = 2*F[2];
    Root[++k] = (-F[1] + S)/U;
    Root[++k] = (-F[1] - S)/U; }
  if (n == 1)
    Root[++k] = -F[0]/F[1];                // Linear equation.
  Code = CodeOut;
  Vector V(k);                   // k  is the number of roots.
  V.Copy(1,Root,1,k);            // Copy them into a vector  V
  return V; }                    // of length  k  and return it.
```

Figure 5.6.2 MSP function Roots

divisor (GCD) of f and f'. This ensured that the root has multiplicity 1, so that **BracketPoly** could detect a sign change to determine the initial interval. Although that step is unnecessary for complex polynomials, **Roots** includes it anyway, because it eliminates the problem of extremely slow convergence to multiple roots. It's conceivable that the extra computations required to compute the GCD could cause accuracy problems with some polynomials f. You may want to modify **Roots** slightly, so that, for example, an input value 2 for the **Code** parameter would cause it to bypass the GCD computation.

MSP functions **Polish** and **Multiplicities**, already discussed in Section 5.5, can be used unaltered with vectors returned by **Roots** to polish approximate roots of complex polynomials and determine their multiplicities.

6

Matrix Computations

Systems of linear equations are found everywhere in scientific and engineering applications problems; hence, they constitute one of the most important branches of numerical analysis. This chapter is devoted to two algorithms: solution of a linear system through Gauss elimination and computation of its eigenvalues by Leverrier's method. The Gauss elimination algorithm is implemented first in Section 6.2 in its simplest form. In later sections it's enhanced to include

- maximal column pivoting,
- computation of the determinant,
- LU decomposition,
- matrix inversion,
- Gauss-Jordan elimination to compute the reduced echelon form of a nonsquare or singular matrix.

Leverrier's algorithm first computes the coefficients of the characteristic polynomial, then finds its roots through Newton-Raphson iteration and deflation. You can then use Gauss-Jordan elimination to study the eigenvectors for each eigenvalue. All these algorithms and their implementations work with either real or complex scalars.

6.1 Systems of Linear Equations

Everywhere in applications of mathematics, you'll find systems of linear equations. Here's just one. Consider a square metal plate with

6.	5.	4.	3.	2.	1.	0.
5.	x_{21}	x_{22}	x_{23}	x_{24}	x_{25}	1.
4.	x_{16}	x_{17}	x_{18}	x_{19}	x_{20}	2.
3.	x_{11}	x_{12}	x_{13}	x_{14}	x_{15}	3.
2.	x_6	x_7	x_8	x_9	x_{10}	4.
1.	x_1	x_2	x_3	x_4	x_5	5.
0.	1.	2.	3.	4.	5.	6.

Figure 6.1.1 Temperature distribution on a metal plate

edge 7 cm. Suppose some heating elements keep the temperatures along its edges at fixed values ranging from 0° to 6° as shown in Figure 6.1.1. For measurement, the plate is divided into 1 cm square cells, and the temperature is regarded as constant within each cell. The edge cells have fixed temperatures, but the interior cells have variable temperatures x_1, ..., x_{25} as shown. If no other heat sources are applied, the interior cell temperatures will approach steady state values. To compute these you can assume that in the steady state each of x_1, ..., x_{25} is the average of the temperatures in its four neighboring cells. Thus, you can write a system of 25 linear equations, including

$$
\begin{cases}
x_1 = \dfrac{1}{4}\cdot 1 + \dfrac{1}{4}\cdot 1 + \dfrac{1}{4}x_2 + \dfrac{1}{4}x_6 \\[2mm]
x_2 = \dfrac{1}{4}\cdot 2 + \dfrac{1}{4}x_1 + \dfrac{1}{4}x_3 + \dfrac{1}{4}x_7 \\[2mm]
\vdots \\[2mm]
x_7 = \dfrac{1}{4}x_2 + \dfrac{1}{4}x_6 + \dfrac{1}{4}x_8 + \dfrac{1}{4}x_{12} \\[2mm]
\vdots
\end{cases}
$$

These can be rearranged as follows:

$$
\begin{cases}
x_1 - \dfrac{1}{4}x_2 \quad - \dfrac{1}{4}x_6 \qquad\qquad\qquad = \dfrac{1}{2} \\[2mm]
-\dfrac{1}{4}x_1 + x_2 - \dfrac{1}{4}x_3 \quad - \dfrac{1}{4}x_7 \qquad\qquad = \dfrac{1}{2} \\[2mm]
-\dfrac{1}{4}x_2 \quad - \dfrac{1}{4}x_6 + x_7 - \dfrac{1}{4}x_8 - \dfrac{1}{4}x_{12} = 0 \\[2mm]
\vdots
\end{cases}
$$

The solution x_1, ..., x_{25} of this system of 25 equations is the steady state temperature distribution. Clearly, this method can be adapted for an arbitrarily shaped plate, and the system would become much larger if smaller cells were required for finer temperature resolution.

Most of this chapter is concerned with the general problem of solving a system of m linear equations

$$\begin{cases} a_{11}x_1 + \cdots + a_{1n}x_n = b_1 \\ \vdots \qquad\qquad \vdots \qquad \vdots \\ a_{m1}x_1 + \cdots + a_{mn}x_n = b_m \end{cases}$$

in n unknowns x_1, ..., x_n, where the coefficients a_{ij} and b_j are known scalars. (m and n can be any positive integers, not necessarily equal.) Matrix and vector algebra notation is generally used to abbreviate this system as $A\xi = \beta$, where A is an $m \times n$ matrix, and ξ and β are n × 1 and m × 1 column vectors:

$$A = \begin{bmatrix} a_{11} & a_{12} & \cdots & a_{1n} \\ a_{21} & a_{22} & \cdots & a_{2n} \\ \vdots & \vdots & & \vdots \\ a_{m1} & a_{m2} & \cdots & a_{mn} \end{bmatrix} \quad \xi = \begin{bmatrix} x_1 \\ x_2 \\ \vdots \\ x_n \end{bmatrix} \quad \beta = \begin{bmatrix} b_1 \\ b_2 \\ \vdots \\ b_m \end{bmatrix}.$$

A linear system might have no solution at all, or exactly one, or infinitely many. For example, the system

$$\begin{cases} x_1 + 2x_2 = 3 & [1] \\ 4x_1 + 5x_2 = 6 & [2] \end{cases}$$

has a unique solution, determined as follows:

$$\begin{cases} x_1 + 2x_2 = 3 & [3] \\ -3x_2 = -6 & [4] = [2] - 4 \cdot [1] \end{cases}$$

$$\begin{cases} x_2 = 2 & [5] = [4] \text{ solved} \\ x_1 = -1 & \text{Substitute [5] into [3] and solve .} \end{cases}$$

Systems with unique solutions are called *nonsingular*. Next, the system

$$\begin{cases} x_1 + 2x_2 = 3 & [6] \\ 4x_1 + 8x_2 = 12 & [7] \end{cases}$$

has more than one solution — for example, x_1, x_2 = 0, 3/2, or 1, 1. In fact, any solution of [6] also satisfies [7], so there are infinitely many solutions. Finally, this system obviously has no solution:

$$\begin{cases} x_1 + 2x_2 = 3 & [8] \\ 4x_1 + 8x_2 = 13 & [9] \end{cases}.$$

Section 6.2 presents the Gauss elimination method for solving non-singular square systems. Section 6.4 implements this method using this book's MSP software. Section 6.5 discusses singular or non-square systems in detail.

6.2   Gauss Elimination

The main algorithm considered in this chapter for solving linear systems $A\xi = \beta$ is called *Gauss elimination*. Its basic strategy is to replace the original system step by step by equivalent simpler ones until the resulting system can be analyzed very easily. Two systems are called *equivalent* if they have the same sets of solution vectors ξ. Just two kinds of operations are used to produce the simpler systems:

1.   interchange two equations;
2.   subtract from one equation a scalar multiple of another.

Obviously, operation (1) doesn't change the set of solution vectors: It produces an equivalent system. Here's an application of operation (2), from the example in Section 6.1:

$$\begin{cases} x_1 + 2x_2 = 3 & [1] \\ 4x_1 + 5x_2 = 6 & [2] \end{cases}$$

$$-3x_2 = -6 \quad [4] = [2] - 4 \cdot [1] \ .$$

In general, this operation has the following appearance:

$$\begin{cases} a_{i1} x_1 + \cdots + a_{in} x_n = b_i & [1] \\ a_{j1} x_1 + \cdots + a_{jn} x_n = b_j & [2] \end{cases}$$

$$(a_{ji} - ca_{i1}) x_1 + \cdots + (a_{jn} - ca_{in}) x_n = b_j - cb_i \quad [3] = [2] - c \cdot [1] \ .$$

(1)   for ($k = 1$; $k < \min(m,n)$; ++ k) {
(2)   for ($i = k$; $a_{ik} == 0$ && $i \leq m$; ++i);
(3)   if ($i \leq m$) {
(4)   if ($i > k$) { Interchange Equations i and k; }
(5)   for ($i = k + 1$; $i \leq m$; ++i) {
(6) $M = a_{ik}/a_{kk}$;
(7)   Subtract M times Equation k from Equation i; } } }

Figure 6.2.1 Pseudocode for the downward pass

Clearly, any solution x_1, ..., x_n of [1] and [2] satisfies [3]. On the other hand, [2] = [3] + $c \cdot$ [1]; hence, any solution of [1] and [3] also satisfies [2]. Thus, operation (2) doesn't change the solution set; it produces an equivalent system.

Downward Pass

The first steps of Gauss elimination, called the *downward pass*, convert the original system

$$\begin{cases} a_{11}x_1 + \cdots + a_{1n}x_n = b_1 \\ \vdots \qquad\qquad \vdots \quad\; \vdots \\ a_{m1}x_1 + \cdots + a_{mn}x_n = b_m \end{cases}$$

into an equivalent upper triangular system

$$\begin{cases} a_{11}x_1 + a_{12}x_2 + \cdots + a_{1m-1}x_{m-1} + a_{1m}x_m + \cdots + a_{1n}x_n = b_1 \\ \qquad\quad a_{22}x_2 + \cdots + a_{2m-1}x_{m-1} + a_{2m}x_m + \cdots + a_{2n}x_n = b_2 \\ \qquad\qquad\qquad\qquad\qquad \vdots \qquad\qquad \vdots \qquad\qquad \vdots \quad \vdots \\ \qquad\qquad\qquad\qquad a_{m-1m-1}x_{m-1} + a_{m-1m}x_m + \cdots + a_{m-1n}x_n = b_{m-1} \\ \qquad\qquad\qquad\qquad\qquad\qquad\qquad a_{mm}x_m + \cdots + a_{mn}x_n = b_m \end{cases}.$$

A linear system is called *upper triangular* if $a_{ij} = 0$ whenever $i > j$.

Figure 6.2.1 contains pseudocode for the downward pass. The algorithm considers in turn the diagonal coefficients a_{11}, ..., $a_{n-1\,n-1}$, called *pivots*. Lines 2 to 4 ensure that each pivot is nonzero, if possible. That is, if a diagonal coefficient is zero, you search downward for a nonzero coefficient; if you find one, you interchange rows to make it the pivot. If you don't, then you proceed to the next equation.

Nonzero pivots a_{kk} are used in Lines 6 and 7 to eliminate the unknown x_k from all equations below Equation k. This process clearly produces an equivalent upper triangular system.

Here's an example downward pass to convert a system of five equations in six unknowns x_1, ..., x_6 into an equivalent upper triangular system:

$$
\begin{cases}
7x_1 + 3x_2 + 8x_3 \quad\quad - 15x_3 - 12x_6 = -18 & [1] \\
7x_1 + 3x_2 + 8x_3 - 2x_4 - 10x_5 - 9x_6 = -15 & [2] \\
-14x_1 - 6x_2 - 16x_3 - 4x_4 + 30x_5 + 18x_6 = 28 & [3] \\
-7x_1 \quad\quad -6x_3 - 2x_4 + 15x_5 + 10x_6 = 13 & [4] \\
14x_1 + 3x_2 + 14x_3 + 4x_4 - 40x_5 - 31x_6 = -41 & [5]
\end{cases}
$$

$$
\begin{cases}
7x_1 + 3x_2 + 8x_3 \quad\quad - 15x_5 - 12x_6 = -18 & [6] = [1] \\
\quad\quad - 2x_4 + 5x_5 + 3x_6 = 3 & [7] = [2] - [1] \\
\quad\quad - 4x_4 \quad\quad - 6x_6 = -8 & [8] = [3] + 2 \cdot [1] \\
3x_2 + 2x_3 - 2x_4 \quad\quad - 2x_6 = -5 & [9] = [4] + [1] \\
-3x_2 - 2x_3 + 4x_4 - 10x_5 - 7x_6 = -5 & [10] = [5] - 2 \cdot [1]
\end{cases}
$$

$$
\begin{cases}
7x_1 + 3x_2 + 8x_3 \quad\quad - 15x_5 - 12x_6 = -18 & [11] = [6] \\
3x_2 + 2x_3 - 2x_4 \quad\quad - 2x_6 = -5 & [12] = [9] \\
\quad\quad - 4x_4 \quad\quad - 6x_6 = -8 & [13] = [8] \\
\quad\quad - 2x_4 + 5x_5 + 3x_6 = 3 & [14] = [7] \\
- 3x_2 - 2x_3 + 4x_4 - 10x_5 - 7x_6 = -5 & [15] = [10]
\end{cases}
$$

$$
\begin{cases}
7x_1 + 3x_2 + 8x_3 \quad\quad - 15x_5 - 12x_6 = -18 & [16] = [11] \\
3x_2 + 2x_3 - 2x_4 \quad\quad - 2x_6 = -5 & [17] = [12] \\
\quad\quad - 4x_4 \quad\quad - 6x_6 = -8 & [18] = [13] \\
\quad\quad - 2x_4 + 5x_5 + 3x_6 = 3 & [19] = [14] \\
\quad\quad 2x_4 - 10x_5 - 9x_6 = -10 & [20] = [15] + [12]
\end{cases}
$$

$$
\begin{cases}
7x_1 + 3x_2 + 8x_3 \quad\quad - 15x_5 - 12x_6 = -18 & [21] = [16] \\
3x_2 + 2x_3 - 2x_4 \quad\quad - 2x_6 = -5 & [22] = [17] \\
\quad\quad - 4x_4 \quad\quad - 6x_6 = -8 & [23] = [18] \\
\quad\quad - 2x_4 + 5x_5 + 3x_6 = 3 & [24] = [19] \\
\quad\quad - 5x_5 - 6x_6 = -7 & [25] = [20] + [19] \; .
\end{cases}
$$

You can assess this algorithm's efficiency by counting the number of scalar arithmetic operations it requires. They're all in Lines 6 and 7 of the pseudocode in Figure 6.2.1. When these are executed for particular values of k and i, one division is needed to evaluate M, then $n - k + 1$ subtractions and as many multiplications to subtract M times Equation k from Equation i. (While the equations have

$n + 1$ coefficients, the first k coefficients of the result of the subtraction are known to be zero.) Thus, the total number of scalar operations is

$$\sum_{k=1}^{m-1} \sum_{i=k+1}^{m} [1 + 2(n - k + 1)] = \sum_{k=1}^{m-1} (m - k)(2n + 3 - 2k)$$

$$= \sum_{k=1}^{m-1} [m(2n + 3) - (2m + 2n + 3)k + 2k^2]$$

$$= m(m - 1)(2n + 3) - (2m + 2n + 3) \sum_{k=1}^{m-1} k + 2 \sum_{k=1}^{m-1} k^2$$

$$= m(m - 1)(2n + 3) - (2m + 2n + 3) \frac{m(m-1)}{2} + 2 \frac{m(m-1)(2m-1)}{6}$$

$$= m^2 n - \frac{1}{3}m^3 + \text{lower order terms} \quad .$$

In particular, for large $m = n$, about $\frac{2}{3} n^3$ operations are required.

This operation count has two major consequences. First, solving large linear systems can require an excessive amount of time. For example, computing the steady state temperature distribution for the problem at the beginning of this section required solving a system of 25 equations, one for each interior cell. The result will be only a coarse approximation, because each cell is one square centimeter. To double the resolution — to use cells with edge 0.5 cm — requires four times as many cells and equations, hence $4^3 = 64$ times as many operations. Second, solving large linear systems can require a huge number of scalar operations, each of which depends on the preceding results. This can produce excessive roundoff error. For example, computing the temperature distribution just mentioned for a 0.5 cm grid requires about 700,000 operations.

These large numbers justify spending considerable effort to minimize the use of Gauss elimination in numerical analysis applications. Unfortunately, there are few alternatives. Linear systems of special form — where nonzero coefficients are rare and occur in symmetric patterns — can sometimes be solved by special algorithms that are more efficient. For systems of general form there are algorithms that are somewhat more efficient than Gauss elimination, but only for extremely large systems. They are considerably more difficult to implement in software. Thus, roundoff error in solving linear systems is often unavoidable. This subject has been studied in detail, particularly by Wilkinson. (See Reference [42].)

Upward Pass for Nonsingular Square Systems

When you apply Gauss elimination to a system of m linear equations in n unknowns $x_1, \ldots, x_n$, the downward pass always yields an equivalent upper triangular system. This system may have a unique solution, infinitely many, or none at all. In one situation, you can easily determine a unique solution: namely, when $m = n$ and none of the diagonal coefficients of the upper triangular system is zero. Such a system is called *nonsingular*. For example, if the upper triangular system has the form

$$
\left\{
\begin{array}{ll}
a_{11}x_1 + a_{12}x_2 + a_{13}x_3 + a_{14}x_4 = b_1 & [1] \\
\quad\quad a_{22}x_2 + a_{23}x_3 + a_{24}x_4 = b_2 & [2] \\
\quad\quad\quad\quad a_{33}x_3 + a_{34}x_4 = b_3 & [3] \\
\quad\quad\quad\quad\quad\quad a_{44}x_4 = b_4 & [4]
\end{array}
\right.
$$

with $a_{11}, a_{22}, a_{33}, a_{44} \neq 0$, then you can solve [4] for x_4 and substitute this value into [3], then solve that equation for x_3. You can substitute the x_3 and x_4 values into Equation [2], and solve that for x_2. Finally, Equation [1] would yield a value for x_1. This process is called the *upward pass* of Gauss elimination. In pseudocode, it has the form

$$
\text{for } (k = n; \ k \geq 1; \ --k)
$$

$$
x_k = \frac{b_k - \sum\limits_{j=k+1}^{n} a_{kj}\,x_j}{a_{kk}} \ .
$$

For $k = n$ to 1, the assignment statement in the upward pass requires $n - k$ subtractions, $n - k$, multiplications, and one division. Thus, the total number of scalar arithmetic operations required is

$$
\sum_{k=1}^{n} \left(2(n-k) + 1 \right) = 2\sum_{k=1}^{n} (n-k) + n = 2\sum_{k=0}^{n-1} k + n = 2\frac{(n-1)n}{2} + n
$$

$$
= n^2 + \text{lower order terms} \ .
$$

Notice two facts about nonsingular square systems. First, their solutions are unique: Each iteration of the for-loop in the upward pass pseudocode *determines* the value of one entry of the solution vector.

Second, the nonsingularity criterion (no zero among the diagonal coefficients of the upper triangular system) doesn't involve the right
hand sides of the equations. Here's a summary of the preceding discussion of the downward and upward passes:

Consider a square linear system

$$\begin{cases} a_{11}x_1 + \cdots + a_{1n}x_n = b_1 \\ \quad \vdots \qquad\qquad \vdots \quad\ \vdots \\ a_{n1}x_1 + \cdots + a_{nn}\,x_n = b_n \end{cases},$$

that is, $A\xi = \beta$ with

$$A = \begin{bmatrix} a_{11} & a_{12} & \cdots & a_{1n} \\ a_{21} & a_{22} & \cdots & a_{2n} \\ \vdots & \vdots & & \vdots \\ a_{n1} & a_{n2} & \cdots & a_{nn} \end{bmatrix} \quad \xi = \begin{bmatrix} x_1 \\ x_2 \\ \vdots \\ x_n \end{bmatrix} \quad \beta = \begin{bmatrix} b_1 \\ b_2 \\ \vdots \\ b_n \end{bmatrix}.$$

Suppose the downward pass of Gauss elimination yields an upper
triangular system

$$\begin{cases} a'_{11}x_1 + \cdots + a'_{1n}x_n = b'_1 \\ \qquad\qquad\qquad \vdots \qquad \vdots \\ \qquad\qquad\quad a'_{nn}x_n = b'_n \end{cases}$$

with no zero among the diagonal coefficients a_{kk}'. Then this situation will occur for *any* coefficient vector β on the right-hand side,
and each of these systems has a unique solution ξ. Each solution
may be computed by the upward pass, executed after the downward pass. For large n, the downward pass requires about $2/3\,n^3$
scalar arithmetic operations; the upward pass, about $1/2\,n^2$.

6.3 Determinants

To every square matrix A corresponds a scalar det A, its *determinant*. For a 2×2 matrix A, the definition is simple:

$$\det \begin{bmatrix} a_{11} & a_{12} \\ a_{21} & a_{22} \end{bmatrix} = a_{11}a_{22} - a_{12}a_{22}.$$

You may recall a slightly more complicated equation that defines the
determinant of a 3×3 matrix. For $n \times n$ matrices in general, the
definition is more complicated:

$$\det A = \sum_{\pi} \text{sign}(\pi)\, a_{1\pi_1} \cdots a_{n\pi_n} .$$

The sum extends over all $n!$ permutations π of the index set $\{1, ..., n\}$. For example, if $n = 2$, there are 2 permutations: The first is the identity, with $\pi_1 = 1$ and $\pi_2 = 2$; the second is the transposition, with $\pi_1 = 2$ and $\pi_2 = 1$. Any permutation can be constructed as a succession of transpositions; while you can do it in many ways, for a given permutation π, you'll always use an even number of transpositions, or always use an odd number. $\text{sign}(\pi)$ is defined to be 1 or −1 in these two cases. Thus, the $n \times n$ definition agrees with the earlier 2×2 definition.

Determinants find many applications in mathematics, particularly in evaluating the effects of coordinate changes on areas, volumes, etc. In n dimensions, they appear as Jacobian determinants in the substitution rule for multiple integrals. And for a nonsingular system $A\xi = \beta$, *Cramer's rule* gives an explicit formula for the entries of the solution vector ξ:

$$x_i = \frac{\det A_i}{\det A}$$

where A_i is the matrix obtained from A by replacing column i by B. (Although perhaps familiar from elementary algebra, Cramer's rule is an inefficient method for computing solutions, as you'll see later.)

The definition of a determinant provides no practical method for computing $n \times n$ determinants in general, because it requires $n(n! - 1)$ scalar arithmetic operations. For $n = 25$, this amounts to 3.9×10^{26} operations. On the author's 33 MHz 80386 machine (with no coprocessor), a **double** operation requires about 3.7×10^{-5} second, so a 25×25 determinant would take about 5×10^{14} years to compute following the definition!

Although the theory of determinants is perhaps the hardest part of elementary linear algebra, some of its results yield a simple method for computing the determinant of an $n \times n$ matrix A:

1. interchanging two rows of A changes the sign of det A;
2. subtracting a scalar multiple of one row of A from another leaves det A unchanged;
3. the determinant of an upper triangular matrix A is the product of its diagonal entries.

(See Reference [14, Chapter 5].) Since the downward pass of Gauss elimination uses a sequence of steps of types (1) and (2) to convert A to upper triangular form, you can compute det A during that process:

- initialize a variable $D = 1$;
- each time you interchange rows of A, execute $D = -D$;
- when the downward pass is complete and A is upper triangular, multiply D by the product of the diagonal entries of A.

The resulting value of D is the determinant of the original matrix.

You saw in Section 6.2 that for large n the downward pass requires about $\frac{2}{3} n^3$ scalar arithmetic operations. Computing the determinant during that process only adds $n - 1$ more multiplications, so the total remains approximately $\frac{2}{3} n^3$. On the author's machine, the 25×25 determinant considered earlier would require less than 0.01 second.

Even with this fast method for computing determinants, Cramer's rule is inefficient: It computes $n + 1$ determinants, each of which requires about $\frac{2}{3} n^3$ scalar operations — hence, it requires about $\frac{2}{3} n^4$ operations in all. But Gauss elimination only requires about $\frac{2}{3} n^3$.

In Section 6.2, a square matrix was defined as singular if its diagonal contained a zero after the downward pass. Since the determinant is ± the product of these diagonal entries, a square matrix is singular just in case its determinant is zero.

Another property of determinants that's used occasionally in later discussions is its relationship with matrix multiplication: For any $n \times n$ matrices A and B, det AB = det A det B.

6.4 Gauss Elimination Software

The Gauss elimination software described in this chapter forms MSP module **GaussEl**. As usual, it consists of two files, header file **GaussEl.H** and source code file **GaussEl.CPP**. The header file is listed in Appendix A.3, and you'll find both on the diskette.

This section presents first a basic Gauss elimination routine **GaussElim**, then some enhancements. Incorporating these into the software requires considerable modification of **GaussElim**, and the routine is split into two functions, **Down** and **Up**, corresponding to the two passes of Gauss elimination. The section concludes with a

(1)   for $(k = 1; k < m);$ ++ $k)$ {
(2)   for $(i = k; a_{ik} = = 0$ && $i \leq m;$ ++$i)$;
(3)   if $(i \leq m)$ {
(4)   if $(i > k)$ { Interchange Equations i and k; }
(5)   for $(i = k + 1; i \leq m;$ ++$i)$ {
(6) $M = a_{ik}/a_{kk}$;
(7)   Subtract M times Equation k from Equation i; } } }
(8)   for $(k = m);$ k $\geq 1; --k)$

$$(9) \quad x_k = \frac{b_k - \sum\limits_{j=k+1}^{m} a_{kj} x_j}{a_{kk}}$$

Figure 6.4.1 Gauss elimination pseudocode

discussion of the LU factorization of a square matrix, a theoretical result that parallels the software organization.

Basic Gauss Elimination Routine

In Section 6.2 you saw pseudocode for the downward and upward passes of the Gauss elimination method for solving linear systems $A\xi = \beta$. That code is combined in Figure 6.4.1 and specialized to the square case: A is $m \times m$; β and ξ are $m \times 1$.

This pseudocode is implemented in function

```
Vector GaussElim(Matrix A,      // Return the solution  X
                 Vector B,      // of the linear system
                 int& Code) { // AX = B . Set status
                                report Code.
```

GaussElim uses the status report parameter **Code** as follows:

Code	Status report
−1	X was computed, and an interchange was required.
0	X was computed without interchanging any equations.
1	A is singular.
2	The dimensions of **A** and **B** don't match. In this case, GaussElim also sets the MSP error signal.

The interchange status is reported because for some considerations — particularly LU factorization — it is useful information. The

```
Vector GaussElim(Matrix A,           // Return the solution  X  of
                 Vector B,           // the  mxn  system  AX = B .
                 int&   Code) {      // Set  Code  as follows:
    int Low = A.LowIndex();          //    2  index error,
    int m   = A.HighRowIndex();      //    1  A  is singular,
    Vector X;                        //    0  solved with no swap,
    if (Low != B.LowIndex()  ||      //   -1  solved with a swap.
        m   != B.HighIndex()  ||
        m   != A.HighColIndex())) {  // Check dimensions.
      Code = 2;  SetError(IndexError);
      return X; }                    // Return  X  empty.
    Boolean Swapped = False;         // A  is singular until
    Code = 1;                        // proved otherwise.
    int k,i,j;
    for (k = Low; k < m; ++k) {                // Downward
      for (i = k; A[i][k] == 0 && i <= m; ++i);   // pass.
      if (i <= m) {
        if (i > k) {                           // Swap
          Swapped    = True;                   // Equa-
          Vector T = A[i];  A[i] = A[k];  A[k] = T;   // tions
          Scalar t = B[i];  B[i] = B[k];  B[k] = t; } // i & k .
        for (i = k+1; i <= m; ++i) {
          Scalar M = A[i][k] / A[k][k];        // Subtract  M  times
          A[i] -= A[k] * M;                    // Equation  k  from
          B[i] -= B[k] * M; }}                 // Equation  i .
      else
        return X; }                // Singular!    Return
    if (A[m][m] == 0) return X;     // Singular!    X  empty.
    Code = (Swapped ? -1 : 0);      // Nonsingular.
    X.SetUp(m,Low);
    for (k = m; k >= Low; --k) {    // Upward pass.
      Scalar S = B[k];
      for (j = k+1; j <= m; ++j)
        S -= A[k][j] * X[j];
      X[k] = S / A[k][k]; }
    return X; }
```

Figure 6.4.2 Basic Gauss elimination routine GaussElim

GaussElim source code is listed in Figure 6.4.2. It adheres to the pseudocode except in three aspects: It sets **Code**, it accommodates an arbitrary lower index bound (0 is common), and it returns an empty vector **X** immediately when it detects that **A** is singular.

Pivoting

In solving an $m \times m$ linear system $A\xi = \beta$, the basic Gauss elimination function **GaussElim** must sometimes interchange equations to ensure that a pivot a_{kk} is not zero. For $k = 1$ to $m - 1$, it searches for the first nonzero entry on or below the diagonal, and interchanges equations, if necessary, to make that the diagonal entry. It's generally good practice to search instead for the entry *of largest norm* on or below the diagonal: If the diagonal entry happens to be nonzero but very small, the subsequent division in pseudocode Step (6) could greatly magnify any roundoff errors already present. Using the pivot of largest possible norm tends to minimize this problem. This technique is called *maximal column pivoting*.

As an example, consider this 2×2 system $A\xi = \beta$:

$$\begin{cases} 10^{-14}x_1 + x_2 = 1 \\ \quad x_1 + x_2 = 2 \end{cases}.$$

Its exact solution is

$$\begin{cases} x_1 = \dfrac{10^{14}}{10^{14} - 1} = 1.\overline{000\ 000\ 000\ 000\ 01} \\ x_2 = \dfrac{10^{14} - 2}{10^{14} - 1} = 1.\overline{999\ 999\ 999\ 999\ 98} \end{cases}.$$

(The overlines signify repeating decimals.) Because the pivot $a_{11} = 10^{-14}$ is so small, **GaussElim** returns the inaccurate solution

$$x_1 = 0.999\ 2... \qquad\qquad x_2 = 0.999\ 999\ 999\ 999\ 99 \ .$$

If you reverse the order of the equations, implementing maximal column pivoting in this one instance, **GaussElim** returns the solution

$$x_1 = 1.000\ 000\ 000\ 000\ 00 \qquad x_2 = 0.999\ 999\ 999\ 999\ 99 \ ,$$

which is as accurate as possible. Of course, this example is artificially generated — it's due essentially to George Forsythe (Reference [16]). But comparable situations frequently occur in practice, so maximal column pivoting is generally recommended.

Unfortunately, the problem of roundoff error in solving linear systems is not this simple. For example, if you multiply the first equation in Forsythe's system by 10^{15}, you get the equivalent system

$$\begin{cases} 10x_1 + 10^{15}x_2 = 10^{15} \\ \quad x_1 + x_2 = 2 \end{cases}.$$

Maximal column pivoting doesn't interchange the equations of this system, and **GaussElim** returns the inaccurate solution listed in the previous paragraph. However, if you reverse the order of the equations — *contrary* to maximal pivoting strategy — then **GaussElim** returns the most accurate solution possible! Thus, maximal column pivoting *could* make results worse. Further consideration of pivoting strategy is beyond the scope of this book; consult the book by For-sythe & Moler (Reference [15]) for more information.

In view of the preceding two paragraphs, the basic Gauss elimination routine **GaussElim** should be enhanced to permit, but not to require, maximal column pivoting. This is simple to do: to Steps (2, 3) of the pseudocode in Figure 6.4.1, provide an alternative, Steps (2.1, ..., 2.5) as follows:

(2.1) $Max = |a_{kk}|$; $i = k$;
(2.2)   for $(j = k+1; j \le m; ++j)$ {
(2.3) $N = |a_{jk}|$;
(2.4)   if $(N > Max)$ { $Max = N$; $i = j$; }}
(2.5)   if $(Max > 0)$ {

These steps will be built into the enhanced routine **Down** considered later.

Using a Row Finder

Later, you'll need to solve in succession several systems $A\xi = \beta$ with the same $m \times m$ matrix A but different vectors β. (Sometimes each β depends on the solution ξ of the previous system.) Most of the downward pass of Gauss elimination doesn't involve β. It would be unfortunate if you had to repeat for each β in succession the computations involving only A. In fact, you can avoid that. In the Figure 6.4.1 pseudocode, all the downward pass computations involving β are in Step (7): subtracting a multiple of one equation from another. The multipliers M are computed in Step (6). If the multipliers — for indices $k = 1, ..., m - 1$ and $i = k + 1, ..., m$ — were saved somewhere, then all computations dependent only on A could be done once and for all, and the β computations postponed until the beginning of the upward pass. Where could you save the multipliers? There's an ideal place: After you've computed M in Step (6), entry a_{ik} in the lower triangular part of A is never used again. Therefore, you could add to Step (6) the statement $a_{ik} = M$, and move the computations from Step (7) to the upward pass.

There's still one reference to β in the downward pass. It's involved in Step (4): interchanging equations. To move those manipulations to the upward pass, you have to keep a record of the interchanges, to perform them later on β. This problem is solved as a byproduct of an efficiency enhancement to be considered next.

Interchanging equations in routine **GaussElim** is inefficient. Doing it for every pivot would require $n + 1$ **Scalar** assignments for each of $n - 1$ equations: a total of $n^2 - 1$ assignments. It's much more efficient to use a *row finder*: a vector $[r_1, ..., r_m]$ of indices of rows of A. Each entry r_k indicates where the row now regarded as row k is actually stored. You initialize $r_k = k$ for each k. Instead of interchanging Equations i and k in pseudocode Step (4), you interchange r_i and r_k. You never actually *move* the rows of A nor, later, the entries of B.

To incorporate a row finder into the Gauss elimination routine, you must construct and initialize $\mathbf{R} = [r_1, ..., r_m]$, replace the statements interchanging equations by statements interchanging row finder entries, then replace all references to entries a_{kj} or b_k as follows:

$$a_{kj} \to a_{r_k j} \quad \text{and} \quad b_k \to b_{r_k} \ ,$$

that is, A[k][j] → A[R[k]][j] and B[k] → B[R[k]].

That would be fairly simple, except for two complications:

- the row finder **R** isn't an MSP vector, because its entries are integers, not scalars;
- if **R** were merely a C++ array, its indices would have to start at 0, whereas MSP permits arbitrary index bounds.

The solution is to define a new MSP **RowFinder** class like **Vector**, but with array entries of type **int**. Since **RowFinder** objects will be used only with Gauss elimination routines, the **RowFinder** components can be limited to just those absolutely necessary for the task at hand.

Figure 6.4.3 shows the definition of class **RowFinder**, from header file **GaussEl.H**. The member functions operate exactly like their **Vector** counterparts described earlier in Section 3.3, except that **SetUp** constructs a row finder $\mathbf{R} = [r_1, ..., r_m]$, then *initializes* it so that $r_k = k$ for each k. (**R** can have an arbitrary index lower bound, just like a vector.) Source code for the member functions is listed in Appendix A.5.

Downward Pass

The basic Gauss elimination routine **GaussElim** can now be enhanced according to the previous discussions and split into two parts, **Down** and **Up**. Given an $m \times m$ matrix **A** and an $m \times 1$ vector **B**,

```
class RowFinder {
  private:
    int  Low;                       // Index bounds for
    int  High;                      // row finder entries.
    int* Array;                     // Storage for entries.
  public:
    int& operator [](int k) const;  // Entry selector.
    RowFinder& SetUp(int Hi,        // Set the index bounds
                     int Lo = 1);   // and allocate storage.
    RowFinder();                    // Default constructor.
    ~RowFinder();                   // Destructor.
    void Swap(int i,                // Interchange entries
              int j); };            // i  and  j .
```

Figure 6.4.3 Class RowFinder

GaussElim returned a solution vector **X** for the linear system **AX** = **B**. The new downward pass routine **Down** operates only on matrix **A**. It transforms **A** to upper triangular form using a row finder, optionally employing maximal column pivoting. It stores the multipliers in the lower triangular part of **A**, and returns **A** and the row finder for later use by the upward pass routine. **Down** also returns the determinant of **A** as function value. Thus, **Down** has prototype

```
Scalar Down(Matrix& A,      // Downward pass on A . Max.
            RowFinder& Row, // col. pivoting if Code = 0 .
            int& Code       // Return det A , A with
            = 0);           // stored multipliers, and row
                            // finder. Set status Code .
```

The source code for **Down** is listed in Figure 6.4.4.

For your convenience, MSP includes a function that merely returns the determinant:

```
Scalar det(Matrix A) {      // Return det A . This sets
  RowFinder R; int C;       // the error signal and returns
  return Down(A,R,C); }     // 0 if A isn't square.
```


Upward Pass

The Gauss elimination process for solving an $m \times m$ linear system $A\xi = \beta$, where ξ and β are $m \times 1$ column vectors, has now been split into two passes. The downward pass routine transforms A into a lower triangular matrix using a row finder $\rho = [r_1, ..., r_m]$, and preserves the multipliers and ρ for later use by the upward pass. All

```
Scalar Down(Matrix& A,              // Downward pass on  A .  Max.
            RowFinder& Row,         // col. pivoting if  Code = 0 .
                 int& Code) {       // Return  det A ,  A  with
    int Low = A.LowIndex();         // stored multipliers, and row
    int m   = A.HighRowIndex();     // finder. Set status  Code .
    if (m  != A.HighColIndex()) {
      Code  = 2;  SetError(IndexError);   // Check that  A  is
      return 0; }                   // square.
    Row.SetUp(m,Low);               // Initialize row finder.
    Boolean MCPivot = (Code == 0);
    Boolean Swapped = False;        // A  is singular until
    Code = 1;                       // proved otherwise.
    Scalar Mik, Det = 1;            // Multiplier, determinant.
    double Max,N;                   // Temp. storage for norms.
    int   k,i,j;
    for (k = Low; k < m; ++k) {
      if (MCPivot) {
        Max = Norm(A[Row[k]][k]);  i = k;        // Maximal
        for (j = k+1; j <= m; ++j) {             // column
          N = Norm(A[Row[j]][k]);                // pivoting.
          if (N > Max) { Max = N;  i = j; }}
          if (Max == 0) return 0; }              // Singular!
        else {
          for (i = k; A[Row[i]][k] == 0 && i <= m ; ++i);
          if (i > m) return 0; }                 // Singular!
        if (i > k) {
          Swapped = True;                        // Interchange
          Row.Swap(i,k);                         // rows  i
          Det = -Det; }                          // and  k .
        Det *= A[Row[k]][k];
        for (i = k+1; i <= m; ++i) {
          Mik = A[Row[i]][k] / A[Row[k]][k];     // Subtract  Mik
          for (j = k+1; j <= m; ++j)             // times  row  k
            A[Row[i]][j] -= Mik * A[Row[k]][j];  // from row  i .
          A[Row[i]][k] = Mik; }}                 // Store  Mik .
    Det *= A[Row[m]][m];
    if (Det == 0) return 0;                      // Singular!
    Code = (Swapped ? -1 : 0);                   // Nonsingular.
    return Det; }
```

Figure 6.4.4 Downward pass function Down

computations involving β have been deferred to the upward pass. Here is the resulting pseudocode for the upward pass:

$$\text{for } (k = 1; \ k < m; \ ++k)$$
$$\quad \text{for } (i = k + 1; \ i \leq m; \ ++i)$$
$$\quad\quad b_{r_i} = b_{r_i} - M b_{r_k};$$
$$\text{for } (k = m; \ k \geq 1; \ --k)$$

$$x_k = \frac{b_{r_k} - \displaystyle\sum_{j=k+1}^{m} a_{r_k j} \, x_j}{a_{r_k k}} \quad ;$$

The first three lines of pseudocode represent the β computations from the earlier version of the downward pass. M is the multiplier that the downward pass stored earlier in $a_{r,k}$.

This code can be adapted easily to solve matrix equations $AX = B$, where A is $m \times m$ and B and X are $m \times n$. Just solve n separate systems $A\xi^{(l)} = \beta^{(l)}$, where $\beta^{(l)}$ is column l of B. Construct X with columns $\xi^{(1)}, \ldots, \xi^{(n)}$. Then $AX = B$ because, for each l,

(column l of AX) = A(column l of X) = $A\xi^{(l)}$ = $\beta^{(l)}$ = column l of B.

This amounts to enclosing the entire Figure 6.4.4 pseudocode in a loop using

for $(l = 1;\ l \le n;\ ++l)$ { ... } .

Header file **GaussEl.H** includes the prototype for the enhanced upward pass routine:

```
Matrix Up(const Matrix& A,      // Upward pass on AX = B :
                   Matrix& B,   // return X . A is mxm
          const RowFinder& Row) {  // and X , B are mxn .
                                 // A and Row have been
                                 // prepared by Down .
```

This function assumes that **A** and **Row** have been prepared properly by the downward pass routine **Down** described under the previous heading. It sets the MSP error signal if the dimension of **A** doesn't agree with the number of rows of **B**. After the upward pass, it returns the solution **X** as function value. The matrix **B** is destroyed in the process, so if you need it later, you'll have to make a copy before calling **Up**. The source code for **Up** is listed in Figure 6.4.5.

You'll usually want to execute **Down** and **Up** in immediate succession to solve a single linear system **AX = B**, where **A** is $m \times m$ and **B** is $m \times n$. This facility is provided by MSP function

```
Matrix Solve(Matrix A,      // Return X such that AX =
             Matrix B,      // B , where A is mxm and
             int& Code);    // X and B are mxn . Use
                            // Code as in Down .
```

Its straightforward source code is in Figure 6.4.6.

```
Matrix Up(const Matrix& A,                // Upward pass on  AX = B :
             Matrix& B,                   // return  X .  A  is  mxm ,
      const RowFinder& Row) {             // X  and  B  are  mxn .
  Matrix X;                               // A  and  Row  have been
  int m     = A.HighRowIndex();           // prepared by  Down .
  int n     = B.HighColIndex();
  int Low = A.LowIndex();
  X.SetUp(m,n,Low);
  int      L,k,i,j;                       // L  indexes the columns
  Scalar  S;                              // of  X .
  for (L = Low; L <= n;  ++L) {
    for (k = Low;  k < m;  ++k)           // This  B  computation
      for (i = k+1; i <= m;  ++i)         // was originally in the
        B[Row[i]][L] -=                   // downward pass of
          A[Row[i]][k] * B[Row[k]][L];    // GaussElim .
    for (k = m; k >= Low;  --k) {
      S = B[Row[k]][L];                   // Original upward pass
      for (j = k+1; j <= m;  ++j)         // from  GaussElim .
        S -= A[Row[k]][j] * X[j][L];
      X[k][L] = S / A[Row[k]][k]; }}
  return X; }
```

Figure 6.4.5 Upward pass routine Up

LU Factorization

Previous headings described the downward pass of the Gauss elimination method for converting a linear system $A\xi = \beta$ with matrix A to an equivalent upper triangular system with matrix U. The algorithm was enhanced by storing the multipliers in entries of A not needed for further computations, so that all computations involving the right-hand side B could be done *after* U is computed. When the downward pass can be completed without interchanging rows, this process is called *LU factorization*, for the following reason. First, call a matrix *unit lower triangular* if it has diagonal entries 1 and entries 0 above or to the right of the diagonal. If L is the unit lower triangular matrix containing the multipliers, then LU is the original matrix

```
Matrix Solve(Matrix A,                    // Return  X  such that  AX =
               Matrix B,                   // B , where  A  is  mxm  and
               int&  Code) {              // X  and  B  are  mxn .  Use
  RowFinder Row;                           // Code  as in  Down .
  Matrix   X;
  Down(A,Row,Code);                        // Downward pass.
  if (Code > 0) return X;                  // Singular or dimension error:
  int Low  = A.LowIndex();                 // return  X  empty.
  int m    = A.HighRowIndex();
  if (Low != B.LowIndex()
    || m  != B.HighRowIndex()) {
    Code = 2;  SetError(IndexError);       // Dimension error:
    return X; }                            // return  X  empty.
  return X = Up(A,B,Row); }                // Upward pass.
```

Figure 6.4.6 Function Solve

A. In fact, if the downward pass of Gauss elimination on a square matrix *A* can be completed without interchanging rows, then *A* has a *unique* factorization as a product of a unit lower triangular matrix *L* and an upper triangular matrix *U*. The proof of this result is not difficult: See Reference [8, Section 6.6].

The condition that the downward pass be completed without row interchanges is often expressed differently. The *principal minors* of a matrix *A* are the square submatrices in its upper left corner. By considering the effect of the downward pass on larger and larger principal minors of *A* in succession, you can see that the downward pass on *A* can be completed without row interchanges just in case *all principal minors of A are nonsingular*.

LU factorization is implemented by the MSP function

```
Scalar LU(Matrix& L,    // Return det A, and the LU
          Matrix& U,    // factorization of A if all
          Matrix A,     // its principal minors are non-
          int& Code);   // singular. Set Code like
                        // GaussElim .
```

This is easy to write: just construct a row finder **Row**, execute **Down(A,Row,Code)**, then construct upper triangular and unit lower triangular matrices U and L from the entries of A. The source code is included on the diskette.

6.5 Rectangular Systems in General

Nonsquare or Singular Systems

The discussion of Gauss elimination in Sections 6.2 and 6.4 applied only to square nonsingular systems. What about nonsquare systems or square ones with one or more diagonal zeroes in the equivalent upper triangular system? Systems equivalent to the last type are called *singular*. Instead of proceeding with the upward pass, you can perform further elimination operations (interchanging equations or subtracting a multiple of one equation from another) to convert the upper triangular system to an equivalent *reduced echelon* system. Such a system has two defining properties:

1. if a_{ij} is the first nonzero coefficient in Equation i, then $a_{kl} = 0$ whenever $k > i$ and $l \leq j$, or $k < i$ and $l = j$;
2. any equations whose a coefficients are all zero come last.

To construct an equivalent system satisfying (1), just use the diagonal coefficient in each equation in turn, if it's not zero, to eliminate the corresponding variable from all preceding equations. Here's pseudocode for that process:

```
for (k = 1; k ≤ min(m,n); ++k)
  if (a_kk ≠ 0)
    for (i = 1; i < k; ++i)
      { M = a_ik / a_kk;
        Subtract M times Equation k from Equation i; }
```

To meet criterion (2), reorder equations as necessary. Sometimes, criterion (1) is strengthened by requiring that the first nonzero coefficient in any equation be 1. That's easy to achieve by dividing the equation by the coefficient.

The process of eliminating unknowns above the diagonal as well as below is called *Gauss-Jordan elimination*. This could be carried out during the downward pass, simply by altering the loop in Line (5) of the pseudocode in Figure 6.2.1 for Gauss elimination. However, because it's used here only for nonsquare or singular systems, the Gauss-Jordan step is treated separately. Now, as an example, it's applied to the upper triangular system considered earlier in Section 6.2:

$$
\begin{cases}
7x_1 + 3x_2 + 8x_3 \quad\quad - 15x_5 - 12x_6 = -18 \\
\quad\quad 3x_2 + 2x_3 - 2x_4 \quad\quad - 2x_6 = -5 \\
\quad\quad\quad\quad - 4x_4 \quad\quad - 6x_6 = -8 \\
\quad\quad\quad\quad - 2x_4 + 5x_5 + 3x_6 = 3 \\
\quad\quad\quad\quad\quad - 5x_5 - 6x_6 = -7
\end{cases}
\quad
\begin{aligned}
&[21] = [16] \\
&[22] = [17] \\
&[23] = [18] \\
&[24] = [19] \\
&[25] = [20] + [19]
\end{aligned}
$$

$$
\begin{cases}
7x_1 \quad\quad + 6x_3 + 2x_4 - 15x_5 + 10x_6 = -13 \\
\quad 3x_2 + 2x_3 - 2x_4 \quad\quad - 2x_6 = -5 \\
\quad\quad\quad - 4x_4 \quad\quad - 6x_6 = -8 \\
\quad\quad\quad - 2x_4 + 5x_5 + 3x_6 = 3 \\
\quad\quad\quad\quad - 5x_5 - 6x_6 = -7
\end{cases}
\quad
\begin{aligned}
&[26] = [21] - [22] \\
&[27] = [22] \\
&[28] = [23] \\
&[29] = [24] \\
&[30] = [25]
\end{aligned}
$$

$$
\begin{cases}
7x_1 \quad\quad + 6x_3 \quad\quad - 10x_5 - 7x_6 = -10 \\
\quad 3x_2 + 2x_3 \quad\quad - 5x_5 - 5x_6 = -8 \\
\quad\quad\quad\quad - 10x_5 - 12x_6 = -14 \\
\quad\quad\quad - 2x_4 + 5x_5 + 3x_6 = 3 \\
\quad\quad\quad\quad - 5x_5 - 6x_6 = -7
\end{cases}
\quad
\begin{aligned}
&[31] = [26] + [29] \\
&[32] = [27] - [29] \\
&[33] = [28] - 2 \cdot [29] \\
&[34] = [29] \\
&[35] = [30]
\end{aligned}
$$

$$\begin{cases} 7x_1 & + 6x_3 & & + 5x_6 = & 4 & \quad [36] = [31] - 2 \cdot [35] \\ & 3x_2 + 2x_3 & & + \ x_6 = & -1 & \quad [37] = [32] - [35] \\ & & & 0 = & 0 & \quad [38] = [33] - 2 \cdot [35] \\ & & - 2x_4 & - 3x_6 = & -4 & \quad [39] = [34] + [35] \\ & & - 5x_5 & - 6x_6 = & -7 & \quad [40] = [35] \ . \end{cases}$$

To satisfy requirement (2) for a reduced echelon system, just move the 0 = 0 equation [38] to the end.

Equations like [38] of the form 0 = 0 can be called *nonrestrictive*, since they have no effect on the solutions. But you should realize that the occurrences of the two zeroes are almost accidental. For example, a slight change in the right-hand sides of the original equations would have yielded instead of [38] an equation

$$0 = b \qquad [38^*]$$

where $b \neq 0$. Since no values of the unknowns can satisfy a system containing [38*], neither the reduced echelon nor the original system would have any solution. They would be *inconsistent*.

However, when no equation of the form [38*] occurs in the reduced echelon system, you can find a solution. This process is best described in terms of the "new" unknowns that you see in each equation, as you climb from bottom to top through the reduced echelon system. Here are the "new" unknowns in the equations of the reduced echelon example just considered:

[36] x_1
[37] x_2, x_3
[39] x_4
[40] x_5, x_6 .

Except for the equations 0 = 0, each equation will have at least one new unknown. To construct a solution, proceed from bottom to top, skipping the equations 0 = 0. If an equation has more than one new unknown, assign arbitrary values to all but one of them, and solve the equation for the remaining one. This process is also called an *upward pass*. Here, then, is a solution for the earlier example:

$$\begin{cases} 7x_1 & + 6x_3 & & + 5x_6 = & 4 & \quad [41] = [36] \\ & 3x_2 + 2x_3 & & + \ x_6 = & -1 & \quad [42] = [37] \\ & & - 2x_4 & - 3x_6 = & -4 & \quad [43] = [39] \\ & & - 5x_5 & - 6x_6 = & -7 & \quad [44] = [40] \\ & & & 0 = & 0 & \quad [45] = [38] \end{cases}$$

[44] x_6 = arbitrary value

$$x_5 = \frac{-7 + 6x_6}{-5} = \frac{7}{5} - \frac{6}{5} x_6$$

[43] $x_4 = \frac{-4 + 3x_6}{-2} = 2 - \frac{3}{2} x_6$

[42] x_3 = arbitrary value

$$x_2 = \frac{-1 - 2x_3 - x_6}{3} = -\frac{1}{3} - \frac{2}{3} x_3 - \frac{1}{3} x_6$$

[41] $x_1 = \frac{4 - 6x_3 - 5x_6}{7} = \frac{4}{7} - \frac{6}{7} x_3 - \frac{5}{7} x_6$.

Here's a summary of the preceding discussion of the solution of nonsquare or singular systems:

Suppose that the downward pass of Gauss elimination, then Gauss-Jordan elimination, have been performed on a linear system, resulting in a reduced echelon system. If an equation of the form $0 = b$, where b is not zero, occurs in the reduced echelon system, then it and the original system are inconsistent: They have no solution. On the other hand, if no equation of that form occurs, then the system has at least one solution, and perhaps infinitely many, which can be computed by an upward pass.

Function GaussJordan

For completeness, MSP contains routine **GaussJordan** for computing reduced echelon forms:

```
int GaussJordan     // Return rank A and the reduced echelon
  (Matrix& A,       // form of system AX = B. A is mxn and
   Vector& B,       // X , B are nx1 . Scalars with norm < T
   double  T,       // are regarded as zero. Set status Code =
   int&    Code);   // 2 : index error,   1 : many solutions,
                    // 0 : one solution, -1 : no solution.
```

The *rank* of a matrix is the number of nonzero rows in its reduced echelon form. The tolerance parameter is necessary to recognize

```
int GaussJordan(Matrix& A,        // Return  rank A  and the re-
                Vector& B,        // reduced form of the system
                double  T,        // system  AX = B.  A  is  mxn
                int&    Code) {   // and  X , B  are  nx1 .  Sca-
    int Low = A.LowIndex();       // lars with norm  < T  are re-
    int m   = A.HighRowIndex();   // garded as zero.  Set status
    int n   = A.HighColIndex();   // Code =
    if (Low != B.LowIndex()       //    2 :  index error,
       || m != B.HighIndex()) {   //    1 :  many solutions,
      Code = 2;                   //    0 :  one solution,
      SetError(IndexError);       //   -1 :  no solution.
      return -1; }
    Code = (m < n ? 1 : 0);
    for (int k = Low; k <= min(m,n); ++k) {          // Downward
      for (int i = k; i <= m && A[i][k] == 0; ++i);  // pass.
      if (i <= m) {
        if (i > k) {                                 // Swap
          Vector T = A[i];  A[i] = A[k];  A[k] = T;   // Eqs.
          Scalar t = B[i];  B[i] = B[k];  B[k] = t; } // i & k .
        for (i = Low; i <= m; ++i) if (i != k) {
          Scalar M = A[i][k] / A[k][k];       // Gauss-Jordan
          A[i] -= A[k] * M;                   // elimination.
          B[i] -= B[k] * M; }}
      else Code = 1; }
    int Rank  = 0;                  // 0 on diagonal.
    int Old_m = m;                  // Rank  will be the
    for (k = Low; k <= m; ++k) {    // number of nonzero
      int L = Low - 1;              // rows A[k] .  L
      for (int j = k; j <= n; ++j) {  // will indicate the
        if (Norm(A[k][j]) < T) A[k][j] = 0;   // first nonzero
        else if (L < Low) L = j; }            // A[k] entry.  If
      if (L >= Low) {               // there is one, in-
        ++Rank;                     // crement  Rank  and
        Scalar t = 1/A[k][L];       // divide Eq. k by
        A[k] *= t;                  // A[k][L]  to nor-
        B[k] *= t; }                // malize it.  If
      else {                        // not, move  Eq. k
        Scalar Bk = B[k];           // to the end.  If
        if (Norm(Bk) < T) {         // it's inconsistent,
          Bk = 0;  L = Old_m; }     // report that with
        else {                      // Code  and use
          Code = -1;  L = m; }      // Old_m  and  L  to
        for (int i = k; i < L; ++i) {  // make it precede
          A[i] = A[i+1];            // any  0 = 0  equa-
          B[i] = B[i+1]; }          // tions.  Arrange to
        A[L].MakeZero();            // avoid reprocessing
        B[L] = Bk;                  // any  equation just
        --k;  --m; }}               // moved, and to redo
    return Rank; }                  // Eq. k  if a new
                                    // one was moved up.
```

Figure 6.5.1 Function GaussJordan

unrestrictive rows of the form $0 = 0$ and inconsistent rows of the form $0 = b$ where $b \ne 0$. The source code for **GaussJordan** appears in Figure 6.5.1. The code resembles that of the basic Gauss elimination routine **GaussElim** through the downward pass: There's a minor adjustment to implement Gauss-Jordan elimination. Since only the reduced echelon form is computed, not the solution itself, there's no upward pass. However, some messy code is required to inspect and process the equation to get the rank and the final form of the output. Here are the high points:

- After the elimination steps are complete, coefficients with norm < T are replaced by zeroes. (The appropriate tolerance for roundoff error may change from one application to another, so the client is given control.)
- Equations corresponding to nonzero rows of **A** are normalized by dividing by their first nonzero coefficients. This makes it easier to construct the solutions from the reduced echelon form. At the same time, the number of these equations is tallied to get the rank of **A**.
- Equations are shuffled so that nonrestrictive 0 = 0 equations come last, preceded by any inconsistent equations.

Homogeneous Linear Systems

One type of linear system is particularly important in theoretical considerations, needed later. A *homogeneous* linear system has the form $A\xi = 0$: that is,

$$\begin{cases} a_{11}x_1 + \cdots + a_{1n}x_n = 0 \\ \vdots \qquad\qquad \vdots \quad \vdots \\ a_{m1}x_1 + \cdots + a_{mn}x_n = 0 \end{cases}.$$

A homogeneous system always has the trivial solution $x_1 = x_2 = \ldots = x_n = 0$. To search for nontrivial solutions, perform the downward pass of Gauss elimination. Suppose $m < n$, or $m = n$ and a zero falls on the diagonal of the resulting equivalent upper triangular system. Now perform Gauss-Jordan elimination. In these two cases, the resulting reduced echelon system will contain at least one equation with more than one "new" unknown — that is, more than one unknown that does not occur in lower equations. Solution of that equation during the upward pass involves at least one arbitrary choice. Therefore, the system has infinitely many solution vectors. In summary,

Every homogeneous system of m linear equations in n unknowns $x_1, \ldots, x_n$ has at least one solution, the trivial one $x_1 = \ldots = x_n = 0$. If $m < n$, or if $m = n$ and a zero falls on the diagonal of the upper triangular system resulting from the downward pass of Gauss elimination, then the system has infinitely many solutions.

6.6   Matrix Inverses

Many applications of linear systems involve the concept of an inverse matrix. An *inverse* of a square matrix A is a matrix J such that $AJ = JA = I$, an identity matrix. If A has an inverse, it's said to be *invertible*. You'll see later that when A has an inverse, it has only one, so it's valid to speak of *the* inverse of A, which is denoted by A^{-1} when it exists.

Inverse matrices facilitate describing solutions of linear systems: for example, if A is invertible, then $X = A^{-1}B$ is the solution of the linear system or matrix equation $AX = B$, because $AX = A(A^{-1}B) = (AA^{-1})B = IB = B$. This idea is neat, but not always practical, because if A is $m \times m$ and B is $m \times 1$, then computing X directly via Gauss elimination generally takes only $1/m$ of the time that it takes to compute A^{-1}. On the other hand, if you need to compute solutions X for many different B vectors, it may be very helpful to compute A^{-1} first, so that each solution requires merely the matrix multiplication $A^{-1}B$. This is particularly beneficial when A and A^{-1} represent mutually inverse coordinate transformations.

What matrices are invertible? The identity I is self inverse since $II = I$. The zero matrix O is not invertible since $OJ = O \neq I$ for any matrix J. Many nonzero matrices fail to be invertible, too: For example,

$$\begin{bmatrix} 1 & 0 \\ 0 & 0 \end{bmatrix} \begin{bmatrix} a & b \\ c & d \end{bmatrix} = \begin{bmatrix} a & b \\ 0 & 0 \end{bmatrix} \neq \begin{bmatrix} 1 & 0 \\ 0 & 1 \end{bmatrix}$$

for any scalars a, b, c, and d; hence, the matrix on the left has no inverse.

If A is a nonsingular matrix, then you can solve the equation $AX = I$ to obtain a solution $X = R$, which satisfies half the criterion for an inverse: $AR = I$. What about the other equation, $RA = I$? Arbitrarily chosen matrices A and R almost never satisfy the equation $AR = RA$. But these two aren't arbitrary: You know $AR = I$. In fact, that equation entails the other one, $RA = I$; but the argument, based on the last result in Section 6.5 about homogeneous linear systems, is delicate. First, remember that the transposition operator ˜ reverses the order of matrix multiplication, so $I = I\tilde{} = (AR)\tilde{} = R\tilde{}A\tilde{}$. This equation implies that no linear system of the form $A\tilde{}X = B$ can have more than one solution. *Proof*: If $A\tilde{}X_1 = B$ and $A\tilde{}X_2 = B$, then $X_1 = IX_1 = (R\tilde{}A\tilde{})X_1 = R\tilde{}(A\tilde{}X_1) = R\tilde{}B = R\tilde{}(A\tilde{}X_2) = (R\tilde{}A\tilde{})X_2 = IX_2 = X_2$. Therefore, $A\tilde{}$ must be nonsingular, since otherwise the homogeneous system $A\tilde{}X = O$ would have more than one solution. Thus, you can solve the system $A^-X = I$ to obtain a solution $X = S$, so that $A^-S = I$. Transpose again: $I = I^- = (A^-S)^- = S^-A^{--} = S^-A$. Finally, $R = IR = (S^-A)R = S^-(AR) = S^-I = S^-$; hence, $RA = I$. This paragraph has shown that every nonsingular matrix is invertible.

You can argue the converse as well: If A is invertible, then it must be nonsingular. *Proof*: If A were singular, then the homogeneous system $AX = O$ would have distinct solutions X_1 and X_2; but then $X_1 = IX_1 = (A^{-1}A)X_1 = A^{-1}(AX_1) = A^{-1}O = A^{-1}(AX_2) = (A^{-1}A)X_2 = IX_2 = X_2$.

Speaking of *the* inverse of a matrix A is justified by two propositions. First: If $AX = I$, then $X = A^{-1}$. *Proof*: $X = IX = (A^{-1}A)X = A^{-1}(AX) = A^{-1}I = A^{-1}$. Second: If $XA = I$, then $X = A^{-1}$. You can prove that for yourself.

Here's a summary of the previous paragraphs:

- a matrix is invertible just in case it's nonsingular;
- you can compute an inverse $X = A^{-1}$ by solving the system $AX = I$;
- A^{-1} is the only matrix X that satisfies either of the equations $AX = I$ or $XA = I$.

These results imply some others about invertible matrices A and B:

- since $A^{-1}A = I$, A^{-1} is invertible and its inverse is A;
- since $A^-(A^{-1})^- = (A^{-1}A)^- = I^- = I$, A^- is invertible and its inverse is $(A^{-1})^-$;
- since $(AB)(B^{-1}A^{-1}) = I$, AB is invertible and its inverse is $B^{-1}A^{-1}$.

MSP includes a simple routine for computing matrix inverses:

```
Matrix Inverse(Matrix A) {        // Return A inverse
   int m = A.HighColIndex( );      // if it exists, else
   int Low = A.LowIndex( );        // an empty matrix.
   Matrix I(m,m,Low);
   I.MakeIdentity( );
   int Code = 0;                    // Use maximal column
   Matrix X = Solve(A,I,Code);     // pivoting.
   return X; }
```

The next section describes a means of testing this routine.

Integral powers of matrices occur frequently in applications. MSP overloads the ^ operator to compute them, using for nonnegative powers the same algorithm that it employed in Section 3.7 for polynomials, and inverting the result to get negative powers. *Danger!*

```
Matrix operator^(Matrix A,        // Return Aⁿ , if it exists,
                 int n) {          // else an empty matrix.
   int m = A.HighRowIndex();
   if (m != A.HighColIndex()) {    // Error if A isn't square.
      SetError(IndexError);
      Matrix Empty;  return Empty; }
   if (n < 0)                      // If n < 0 ,
      A = Inverse(A^(-n));         // then Aⁿ = (A^(-n))^(-1) .
      else if (n == 0)
      A.MakeIdentity();            // A° = identity.
      else if (n % 2 == 1)         // If n is odd,
      A *= A^(n-1);                // then Aⁿ = A·A^(n-1) .
      else {                       // If n is even,
      A ^= n/2;  A *= A; }         // then Aⁿ = A^(½n) } .
   return A; }
```

Figure 6.6.1 Matrix power operator

Operator ^ has lower precedence than accorded exponentiation in conventional mathematical notation. For example, to get $(A^\wedge m) + B$ you *must* use the parentheses! The source code is in Figure 6.6.1. (The code in Section 3.7 for the corresponding polynomial operator is briefer, because it places return statements inside the conditional. That doesn't work in this case. Some versions of Turbo C++ evidently suffer a bug that prevents proper destruction of multiple temporary variables on returning from a function. The briefer version failed for the matrix operator, so the author followed Borland's suggestion to avoid that situation.) MSP also implements the corresponding replacement operator ^=.

6.7 Testing with Hilbert Matrices

Every software development project needs a set of problems with known solutions for testing. At least some test problems should not have been developed specifically for that purpose, and some should be really difficult.

A simple but not very challenging test would be to generate an $n \times n$ random matrix H with entries h in the range $0 \le h < 1$, and compute $D = \det H$ and $A = H^{-1}$ using MSP software. Then you can check how close are the approximations $HA \approx I$ and $AH \approx I$ by evaluating the row norms $\|HA - I\|$ and $\|AH - I\|$. Next you can compute $\det A$ and the L, U factorization of A, and check how close are the approximations $\det A \approx 1/D$ and $LU \approx A$ by evaluating $|\det A - 1/D|$ and $\|LU - A\|$. (The principal minors of a random matrix are usually nonsingular, so you should expect $LU \approx A$.)

Finally, you can compute $X = A^{-1}$ and check how close is the approximation $X \approx H$ by evaluating $\| X - H \|$. Using MSP scalars of type **double**, all of these tests come out about the same, depending on the size of n. For example,

$$
\begin{array}{ll}
n & \text{error norms} \approx \\
6 & 10^{-15} \\
13 & 10^{-14}
\end{array}
$$

But randomly selected problems generally don't provide severe enough tests. Moreover, you don't know the *exact* solutions, so there's uncertainty in analyzing the results. On the other hand, the *Hilbert* matrices

$$
H^{(n)} = \begin{bmatrix}
1 & \dfrac{1}{2} & \dfrac{1}{3} & \cdots & \dfrac{1}{n} \\
\dfrac{1}{2} & \dfrac{1}{3} & \dfrac{1}{4} & \cdots & \dfrac{1}{n+1} \\
\dfrac{1}{3} & \dfrac{1}{4} & \dfrac{1}{5} & \cdots & \dfrac{1}{n+2} \\
\vdots & \vdots & \vdots & & \vdots \\
\dfrac{1}{n} & \dfrac{1}{n+1} & \dfrac{1}{n+2} & \cdots & \dfrac{1}{2n-1}
\end{bmatrix}
$$

for $n = 1, 2, 3, \ldots$ provide classic linear algebra software test problems, whose solutions are known exactly. They appear naturally in many areas of mathematics, and even for moderately sized n are very *ill-conditioned*: Roundoff errors build up rapidly when you attempt to invert them, and the errors can dwarf the entries of the exact results. Linear algebra algorithms and software implementations are sometimes compared on the basis of how accurately they perform calculations on Hilbert matrices. MSP includes a simple function to generate Hilbert matrices:

```
Matrix Hilbert(int n) {         // Return the nxn
  Matrix H(n,n);                // Hilbert matrix
  int i,j;                      // matrix H .
  for (i = 1; i <= n; ++i)
    for (j = 1; j <= n; ++j)    // Convert to
      H[i][j] = 1.0/(i + j - 1); // double!
  return H; }
```

Algebraic formulas are available for the determinant det $H^{(n)}$ and for the k,lth entry $a_{kl}^{(n)}$ of the inverse $A^{(n)}$ of $H^{(n)}$.

$$\det H^{(n)} = \frac{\prod_{i<j} (i-j)^2}{\prod_{i,j} (i+j-1)}$$

$$a_{kl}^{(n)} = \frac{\prod_{i} (i+k-1) \prod_{j \neq k} (l+j-1)}{\prod_{i \neq l} (i-1) \prod_{i \neq k} (i-k)}$$

$$= (-1)^{k+l} (k+l-1) \binom{n+k-1}{n-l} \binom{n+l-1}{n-k} \binom{k+l-2}{k-1}^2 .$$

(See Reference [9], and the literature cited there.) For example, here's $A^{(5)} = (H^{(5)})^{-1}$:

$$\begin{bmatrix} 25 & -300 & 1050 & -1400 & 6300 \\ -300 & 4800 & -18900 & 26880 & -12600 \\ 1050 & -18900 & 79380 & -117600 & 56700 \\ -1400 & 26880 & -117600 & 179200 & -88200 \\ 630 & -12600 & 56700 & -88200 & 44100 \end{bmatrix} .$$

Most of the work in deriving these formulas lies in the determinant computation; the last two come from the first through straightforward algebra. The first formula shows that the determinant is not zero, so the matrix is invertible. The last one shows that all entries of the inverse matrix are integers, and its factor $(-1)^{k+l}$ produces the alternate ± pattern.

The first formula is the basis for MSP function

```
Matrix InvHilbert(int n);   // Return the inverse of the
                            // nxn Hilbert matrix.
```

This simply computes the entries $a_{kl}^{(n)}$ according to the formula; its source code is on the diskette. The inverse provides better test problems than the Hilbert matrix itself: its entries are all integers; hence, for moderately sized n, they can be entered with no roundoff error. Errors in the results of test computations are due to roundoff in the computation, not in the input.

Proceeding in analogy to the earlier test with random matrices, the $n \times n$ Hilbert matrix H and its inverse A were generated for $n = 1, 2, 3, \ldots$ using routines **Hilbert** and **InvHilbert**. Then $D \approx \det A$

n	6	8	10	12	13
$\|A\|$	1×10^7	1×10^{10}	1×10^{-13}	1×10^{-16}	4×10^{17}
$\det A$	2×10^{17}	4×10^{32}	5×10^{52}	4×10^{77}	4×10^{91}
$|D - \det A|$	1×10^5	1×10^{24}	2×10^{47}	3×10^{75}	3×10^{91}
$\|HA - I\|$	2×10^{-10}	2×10^{-7}	2×10^{-4}	2×10^{-1}	8×10^1
$\|AH - I\|$	3×10^{-10}	4×10^{-7}	3×10^{-4}	3×10^{-1}	2×10^2
$\|LU - A\|$	9×10^{-10}	6×10^{-7}	1×10^{-3}	8×10^{-1}	3×10^2
$\|AX - I\|$	2×10^{-10}	2×10^{-7}	1×10^{-4}	1×10^{-1}	2×10^2
$\|XA - I\|$	3×10^{-7}	2×10^{-3}	8×10^{-2}	7×10^6	4×10^9
$\|X - H\|$	4×10^{-12}	6×10^{-9}	2×10^{-6}	2×10^{-4}	4×10^0

Figure 6.7.1 Experimental results with Hilbert matrices

and the L, U factorization of A were computed with routine LU. (Since the principal minors of a Hilbert matrix are just smaller Hilbert matrices, they're nonsingular, so you should expect $LU \approx A$.) Finally, an approximation $X \approx H$ to A^{-1} was computed using routine **Inverse**. The resulting error norms are substantially different from those reported earlier for random test matrices H. To condense the resulting data, selected norms are tabulated in Figure 6.7.1. These show that determinants of the inverse matrices A are huge compared to the size of their entries: for $n = 13$, $\det A \approx 4 \times 10^{91}$, whereas $\|A\| \approx 4 \times 10^{17}$. This means that the determinant of a Hilbert matrix H is tiny compared to the size of its entries, so it's nearly singular; hence, A is nearly singular, too.

For even the moderately large n values tabulated, most of the results are very inaccurate. Accuracy of $\det A$ drops to about five significant digits at $n = 10$: $\det A \approx 5 \times 10^{52}$, but the error is about 2×10^{47}. For the computations HA, AH, $AX \approx I$ the results are about the same. XA loses accuracy much faster, falling to five significant digits even when $n < 8$. On the other hand, X is a better approximation to H, falling to five significant digits somewhat after $n = 10$. And the approximation $LU \approx A$ is quite accurate: For $n = 13$, the norm of the error is only about 3×10^2, whereas $\|A\| \approx 4 \times 10^{17}$.

These tests show that even when you're using high-precision software like the Turbo C++ double arithmetic routines, *you must take extreme care with ill-conditioned linear algebra problems.* See Reference [15] for further information.

6.8 Eigenvalues and Complex Linear Systems

An *eigenvalue* of an $n \times n$ matrix A is a scalar t such that $tI - A$ is singular, where I is the $n \times n$ identity matrix. Eigenvalue problems arise from diverse applications, usually after considerable mathematical analysis. The entries of A are usually real scalars, but to perform the analysis, you must allow t and $tI - A$ to be complex. This section implements Leverrier's algorithm for computing eigenvalues. It's not the most common one, because it requires more arithmetic operations than some others. For that reason, it's also sometimes less accurate. But it's completely general, it's based on general mathematical principles that are easy to describe, and it's implemented with standard MSP software tools.

MSP routines involved with computing eigenvalues are contained in module **Eigenval**. Like other modules, this one consists of header and source code files **Eigenval.H** and **Eigenval.CPP**. You'll find both on the accompanying diskette. For convenient reference, the header file is listed in Appendix A.3. The source code for all the routines is displayed and discussed later in this section.

Example Application: Compartmental Analysis

As an example application, consider a system of compartments C_k for $k = 1, ..., n$, each filled with liquid containing a solute; the solute concentrations $y_k(t)$ vary with the time t, but are often written simply as y_k. Suppose some compartments are adjacent, and the rate of solute diffusion from C_j to C_k is proportional to the difference $y_j - y_k$ of their concentrations; call the proportionality constant c_{jk}. Set $c_{jk} = 0$ if the corresponding compartments aren't adjacent. Finally, suppose that if any compartment C_k were isolated from its neighbors, the concentration y_k would grow or decrease exponentially with rate $c_{kk}y_k$. (Thus, the total amount of solute in the system could grow or decrease.) The concentrations satisfy the system of n linear ordinary differential equations (ODE)

$$y_j' = c_{jj} y_j + \sum_{k \neq j} c_{jk} (y_j - y_k) = \sum_{k=1}^{n} a_{jk} y_k$$

for $j = 1, ..., n$. If you assemble the resulting coefficients a_{jk} into a matrix A and the functions $y_1, ..., y_n$ and $y_1', ... y_n'$ into columns η and η', the ODE system can be written $\eta' = A\eta$ or $\eta'(t) = A\eta(t)$. A solution of the system is determined once you specify the value $\eta(t_0)$ at any initial time t_0. Clearly, one solution is the column $\eta(t)$ of functions with constant value zero. The system is called *asymptotically stable* if every solution approaches that one as $t \to \infty$. That means

$$\lim_{t \to \infty} \| \eta \| = 0$$

for some vector norm $\| \eta \|$. On the other hand, the system is called *unstable* if

$$\lim_{t \to \infty} \| \eta \| = \infty \ .$$

In an asymptotically stable system, the concentrations all decrease to zero; in an unstable system, some concentration increases without limit. It can be shown that the system is asymptotically stable if all eigenvalues of matrix A have negative real part, and unstable if any eigenvalue has positive real part. Oscillating solutions are possible if some eigenvalues are purely imaginary but none has positive real part. Thus, complex eigenvalue computations can play an important role even in applications problems that, on the surface, involve neither eigenvalues nor complex numbers.

Characteristic Polynomial

In Section 6.3 you saw that a matrix is singular just in case its determinant is zero. Thus, the eigenvalues of an $n \times n$ matrix A are the scalars t such that $\det(tI - A) = 0$ — that is, the roots of the function $p_A(x) = \det(xI - A)$. This determinant is the sum of signed products of n entries, one from each row of $xI - A$, and exactly one of these products is the product of all the diagonal entries $x - a_{kk}$. Thus, $p_A(x)$ is an nth degree polynomial, called the *characteristic polynomial* of A:

$$p_A(x) = x^n + p_{n-1}x^{n-1} + \cdots + p_1 x + p_0.$$

Clearly, $p_0 = p_A(x) = \det(-A) = (-1)^n \det A$. Moreover, each of the signed products that make up the determinant contains exactly one factor from each row of $xI - A$, so none contains exactly $n - 1$ diagonal terms $x - a_{kk}$. Thus, the x^{n-1} term in the characteristic polynomial is the same as the corresponding term in the product

$$\prod_{k=1}^{n} (x - a_{kk}) \quad .$$

That is,

$$p_{n-1} = - \sum_{k=1}^{n} a_{kk} = - \operatorname{tr} A \quad .$$

The sum $\operatorname{tr} A$ of the diagonal entries of a matrix A is called its *trace*.

Factor the characteristic polynomial to display its roots $t_1, \ldots, t_n$ — the eigenvalues of A. (Some of the t_k may coincide.) Then you can express the coefficients p_0 and p_{n-1} another way:

$$p_A(x) = \prod_{k=1}^{n} (x - t_k) \qquad p_0 = (-1)^n \prod_{k=1}^{n} t_k \qquad p_{n-1} = \sum_{k=1}^{n} t_k \quad .$$

More complicated formulas for the other coefficients will be derived later.

Leverrier's algorithm requires you to relate the eigenvalues $t_1, \ldots, t_n$ of A to those of powers A^m for $m = 0, 1, \ldots$. Most linear algebra texts show that $t_1^m, \ldots, t_n^m$ are eigenvalues of A^m, but that result isn't sufficient: It doesn't say anything about *all* the eigenvalues of A^m, nor about their multiplicity. Gantmacher (Reference [17, Section 4]) includes the following stronger and more general result: For any polynomial g with degree m,

$$p_{g(A)}(x) = \prod_{k=1}^{n} (x - g(t_k))$$

This equation says that when you expand the product on the right, you get a polynomial with the same coefficients as $p_{g(A)}(x)$. In this equation and its proof, you must interpret g on the right as a polynomial over the complex numbers, and on the left as a polynomial over complex matrices. For example, if $g(x) = x^m - 3x + 2$, then $g(A) = A^m - 3A + 2I$. The proof strategy is to show that

$$p_{g(A)}(t) = \prod_{k=1}^{n} (t - g(t_k))$$

for an arbitrary scalar t. Then, since the values of the two nth degree polynomials coincide for more than n arguments, their coefficients must all agree. First, Gantmacher factors the mth degree polynomial $g(x) - t$ completely:

$$g(x) - t = \prod_{j=1}^{m} (x - u_j) \quad .$$

Then the desired result follows if you regard both sides as matrix polynomials, evaluate them at $x = A$, and take determinants:

$$g(A) - tI = \prod_{j=1}^{m} (A - u_j I)$$

$$\det\left(g(A) - tI\right) = \prod_{j=1}^{m} \det\left(A - u_j I\right)$$

$$(-1)^n p_{g(A)}(t) = \prod_{j=1}^{m} (-1)^n p_A(u_j) = \prod_{j=1}^{m} \left((-1)^n \prod_{k=1}^{n} (u_j - t_k)\right)$$

$$= \prod_{k=1}^{n} \prod_{j=1}^{m} (t_k - u_j) = \prod_{k=1}^{n} (g(t_k) - t) = (-1)^n \prod_{k=1}^{n} (t - g(t_k)) \quad .$$

Newton's Formula

Leverrier's algorithm also requires you to use Newton's formula, which relates the coefficients of a polynomial to the sums of powers of its roots. Detailed treatment of such a general result doesn't really belong in a discussion of eigenvalue computations, but it plays a crucial role, and is used nowhere else in this book. Moreover, although it's mentioned in most algebra texts, it's rarely proved, and in fact is sometimes misstated. The treatment here is adapted from Uspensky (Reference [40], Section 11.2).

For a positive integer n, let $t_1, \ldots, t_n$ and $p_0, \ldots, p_n$ be scalars such that

$$\sum_{j=0}^{n} p_j x^j = p_n \prod_{k=1}^{n} (x - t_k) \quad .$$

Then *Newton's formula*

$$-m p_{n-m} = \sum_{j=0}^{m-1} p_{n-j} s_{m-j}$$

relates the coefficients p_j to the sums

$$s_m = \sum_{k=1}^{n} \lambda_k^m \ .$$

To prove the formula, first differentiate $p(x)$:

$$p'(x) = \sum_{k=1}^{n} \prod_{j \neq k} (x - t_j) \qquad \frac{p'(x)}{p(x)} = \sum_{k=1}^{n} \frac{1}{x - t_k}$$

$$p'(x) = \sum_{k=1}^{n} \frac{p(x)}{x - t_k} = \sum_{k=1}^{n} q_k(x) \ .$$

You can find the coefficients of the $(n-1)$st degree quotient polynomial $q_k(x)$ by using Horner's method to evaluate $p(t_k)$:

$$q_k(x) = q_{k0} + q_{k1} x + \cdots + q_{k,n-1} x^{n-1}$$

$$q_{k,n-1} = 1$$

$$q_{k,n-l-1} = p_{n-1} + q_{k,n-l} t_k \qquad \text{for } l = 1, \ldots, n-1 \ .$$

Newton's formula results if you consider the coefficient of x^{n-m-1} in the previous equation for $p'(x)$:

$$(n-m)p_{n-m} = \sum_{k=1}^{n} q_{k,n-m-1} = \sum_{k=1}^{n} \sum_{j=0}^{m} p_{n-j} t_k^{m-j}$$

$$= \sum_{j=0}^{m} p_{n-j} \sum_{k=1}^{n} t_k^{m-j} = \sum_{j=0}^{m} s_{m-j} p_{n-j}$$

$$= \sum_{j=0}^{m-1} s_{m-j} p_{n-j} + n p_{n-m} \ .$$

Computing Characteristic Polynomials

MSP function **CharPoly(const Matrix& A)** returns the characteristic polynomial of **A**. If **A** isn't square, it sets the error signal and returns the empty polynomial 0. **CharPoly** is declared in header file **Eigenval.H,** and its source code, listed in Figure 6.8.1, is contained in file **Eigenval.CPP** on the diskette. **CharPoly** implements *Leverrier's algorithm*, which is based on the mathematics covered in the previous two headings. First, it allocates memory for the

```
Polynom CharPoly(const Matrix& A) {      // Return the characteris-
  Polynom p;                             // tic polynomial  p  of
  int m = A.LowIndex();                  // A .  Set the error
  int n = A.HighRowIndex();              // signal and return empty
  if (n != A.HighColIndex()) {           // if  A  isn't square.
    SetError(IndexError);   return p; }
  n -= m - 1;  p.SetUp(n);  p[n] = 1;    // n = Degree(p) .
  Matrix Am = A;                         // Am  will be  A^m .
  Vector s(n);                           // s[m]  will contain
  for (m = 1; m <= n; ++m) {             // Trace(Am) = sum of
    s[m] = Trace(Am);                    // the  mth  powers
    Scalar Sum = 0;                      // of the roots
    for (int j = 0; j <= m-1; ++j)       // of  p .
      Sum += s[m-j]*p[n-j];
    p[n-m] = -Sum/m;                     // Newton's formula.
    if (m < n) Am *= A; }
  return p; }
```

Figure 6.8.1 MSP function CharPoly

coefficients p_0, ..., p_n of the characteristic polynomial, for a matrix **Am** that will contain A^m for $m = 1$, ..., n, and for the array s_1, ..., s_n of sums of powers of the eigenvalues of A. Each entry s_m is the sum of the mth powers, hence the sum of the eigenvalues of **Am**, and it can be computed as the trace of **Am**. **CharPoly** initializes $p_n = 1$ and **Am** $= A$, then executes a loop for indices $m = 1$, ..., n. The mth iteration calculates $s_m = $ tr **Am** and uses previously computed values s_k and p_{n-k} with Newton's formula to calculate the coefficient p_{n-m}.

Computing Eigenvalues

You can now compute all real eigenvalues of a real matrix A by using first **CharPoly**, then **RealRoots**, compiled with the **double** version of the **Scalar** module. Or you can find *all* eigenvalues, real or complex, by using the **complex** version of **Scalar** and function **Roots**. You can use function **Polish** to polish eigenvalues, and function **Multiplicities** to ascertain their multiplicities. The MSP **Eigenval** module includes this function:

```
Vector Eigenvalues(        Vector& M,       // Return a vec-
                    const Matrix& A,         // tor consisting
                          double  T,         // of the eigen-
                          int&    Code) {    // values of A ;
  Polynom p = CharPoly(A);                   // enter their
  Vector V = Roots(p,T,Code);                // multiplicities
  if (Code = = 0) Polish(V,p,T,Code);        // in vector M .
  M = Multiplicities(V,p,T);                 // Use Code and
  return V; }                                // T as in Roots .
```

```
void main() {
  cout << "Enter an nxn matrix A .\nn = ";
  int n;  cin >> n;
  Matrix A(n,n);  A.KeyIn("A");
  A.Show("","A");
  cout << "\nCoefficients of characteristic polynomial:\n";
  CharPoly(A).Show();
  cout << "\nEigenvalues, with multiplicities:\n";
  int Code = 0;  Vector M;
  Eigenvalues(M,A,1e-10,Code).Show();
  M.Show("%-13g");  }
```

Output

```
A[1] :  (0,0)   (0,0)   (0,0)   (-1,0)
A[2] :  (1,0)   (0,0)   (0,0)   (-2,0)
A[3] :  (0,0)   (1,0)   (0,0)   (-2,0)
A[4] :  (0,0)   (0,0)   (1,0)   (-2,0)

Coefficients of characteristic polynomial:
(1,0)   (2,0)   (2,0)   (2,0)   (1,0)

Eigenvalues, with multiplicities:
(-1,-1.4e-25)   (5.7e-18,-1)   (2.2e-17,1)
2               1              1
```

Figure 6.8.2 Test program for function Eigenvalues, with sample output

Figure 6.8.2 contains a test program that exercises **Eigenvalues**, with sample output. The matrix shown has characteristic polynomial

$$x^4 + 2x^3 + 2x^2 + 2x + 1 = (x + 1)^2(x + i)(x - i) \ .$$

Eigenvectors and Eigenspaces

If t is an eigenvalue of a matrix A, then $tI - A$ is singular, so $(tI - A)\,\xi = 0$ for some nonzero vector ξ, *i.e.*, $A\xi = t\xi$. A nonzero vector ξ with this property is called an *eigenvector* of A corresponding to t. If s is any scalar and ξ is an eigenvector, then so is $s\xi$, because $A(s\xi) = s(A\xi) = s(t\xi) = t(s\xi)$. If ξ and η are eigenvectors corresponding to t, then so is $\xi + \eta$, because $A(\xi + \eta) = A\xi + A\eta = t\xi + t\eta = t(\xi + \eta)$. Thus, the eigenvectors of A that correspond to t constitute a linear space, called the *eigenspace* of t.

Some applications need information about the eigenspace corresponding to an eigenvalue t of a matrix A: perhaps a single eigenvector, or the dimension m of the space, or even a basis consisting of m linearly independent eigenvectors corresponding to t. You can use function **GaussJordan** in module **GaussEl** to provide this data. For example, the test program displayed with sample output in Figure 6.8.3 analyzes matrix

```
#include "Eigenval.H"
#include  "GaussEl.H"

void main() {                                          // Program to
  cout << "Enter an  nxn  matrix  A .  n = ";          // demonstrate
  int n;              cin >> n;                         // GaussJordan
  Matrix A(n,n);      A.KeyIn("A");                     // eigenspace
  cout << "A :\n";    A.Show();                         // analysis.
  Matrix I(n,n);      I.MakeIdentity();
  Vector O(n);        O.MakeZero();
  double T = 1e-10;   int Code = 0;                     // T  is used as
  Vector M, L = Eigenvalues(M,A,T,Code);               // tolerance in
  for (int k = 1; k <= L.HighIndex(); ++k) {           // Eigenvalue
    cout << "\nEigenvalue  t = " << L[k]               // and as zero
         << " :\nMultiplicity  = " << real(M[k]);      // level in
    Matrix C = I*L[k] - A;   Code = 0;                 // GaussJordan .
    int Rank = GaussJordan(C,O,T,Code);
    cout << " .\nEigenspace of  t  has dimension  " << n - Rank
         << " .\nReduced echelon form of  C = tI - A :\n\n";
    C.Show("(%2g,%2g)"); }}
```

Output

```
A :
(3,0)  (2,0)  (1,0)  (0,0)
(0,0)  (1,0)  (0,0)  (1,0)
(0,0)  (2,0)  (1,0)  (0,0)
(0,0)  (0,0)  (0,0)  (1,0)

Eigenvalue  t = (1, 0) :
Multiplicity  = 3 .
Eigenspace of  t  has dimension  1 .
Reduced echelon form of  C = tI - A :

( 1,-0)  (-0,-0)  (0.5,-0)  (-0,-0)
(-0,-0)  ( 1,-0)  (-0,-0)   (-0,-0)
(-0,-0)  (-0,-0)  (-0,-0)   ( 1,-0)
( 0, 0)  ( 0, 0)  ( 0, 0)   ( 0, 0)

Eigenvalue  t = (3, 0) :
Multiplicity  = 1 .
Eigenspace of  t  has dimension  1 .
Reduced echelon form of  C = tI - A :

( 0, 0)  ( 1, 0)  ( 0, 0)  ( 0, 0)
( 0, 0)  ( 0, 0)  ( 1, 0)  ( 0, 0)
( 0, 0)  ( 0, 0)  ( 0, 0)  ( 1, 0)
( 0, 0)  ( 0, 0)  ( 0, 0)  ( 0, 0)
```

Figure 6.8.3 Eigenspace analysis with function GaussJordan

$$A = \begin{bmatrix} 3 & 2 & 1 & 0 \\ 0 & 1 & 0 & 1 \\ 0 & 2 & 1 & 0 \\ 0 & 0 & 0 & 1 \end{bmatrix}.$$

It finds eigenvalues $t_1 = 1$ and $t_2 = 3$ with multiplicities 3 and 1. The reduced echelon form of $t_1 I - A$ is

$$\begin{bmatrix} 1 & 0 & 0.5 & 0 \\ 0 & 1 & 0 & 0 \\ 0 & 0 & 0 & 1 \\ 0 & 0 & 0 & 0 \end{bmatrix},$$

hence the components x_1, ..., x_4 of the corresponding eigenvectors are determined by the equations

$$\begin{cases} x_1 = -0.5x_3 \\ x_2 = 0 \\ x_4 = 0 \end{cases}.$$

The eigenspace has dimension 1 and consists of all multiples of the vector with components $x_1, x_2, x_3, x_4 = -0.5, 0, 1, 0$. You can interpret the second reduced echelon form similarly.

Complex Linear Systems

The test program in Figure 6.8.3 used function **GaussJordan** with a **complex** matrix. In fact, all the routines in module **GaussEl** work with complex matrices if you compile them with the **complex** version of the **Scalar** module.

Iterative Solution of Systems of Equations

Let D be a set of n-tuples of scalars. Often it's convenient to gather n scalar valued functions g_1, ..., g_n on D into a single vector valued function

$$\gamma(\xi) = \begin{bmatrix} g_1(\xi) \\ \vdots \\ g_n(\xi) \end{bmatrix} \qquad \xi = \begin{bmatrix} x_1 \\ \vdots \\ x_n \end{bmatrix}$$

defined for all vectors ξ in D. A vector α in D is called a *fixpoint* of γ if $\gamma(\alpha) = \alpha$.

Fixpoints arise naturally in many applications, often through differential equations. For example, consider the second order boundary value problem (BVP)

$$y'' = f(t, y, y') \qquad\qquad y(a) = y_0 \qquad\qquad y(b) = y^* .$$

Given the function f, interval endpoints a and b, and boundary values y_0 and y^*, the problem is to find a function y that's defined for all t in the interval $a \le t \le b$ and satisfies those three equations. A common solution technique, known as *Liebmann's method*, approximates the differential equation by a fixpoint problem. First, you divide the interval into n subdivisions:

$$a = t_0 < t_1 < \ldots < t_n = b,$$

$$t_k = z + kh \quad \text{for} \quad k = 0, \ldots, n, \qquad h = \frac{b-a}{n}.$$

For $j = 1, \ldots, n - 1$ let y_k denote an approximation to $u(t_k)$, where $y = u(t)$ is the exact solution of the differential equation. The problem is to find good approximations $y_1, \ldots, y_{n-1}$. For notational convenience, let $y_n = y^*$. Now, consider two ways to approximate the derivative y' in the BVP by differential quotients:

$$y'(t_j) \approx \frac{y_j - y_{j-1}}{h} \qquad y'(t_j) \approx \frac{y_{j+1} - y_{j-1}}{2h}$$

for $j = 1, \ldots, n$. At the end of Section 7.1, you'll see that the left-hand formula isn't appropriate for Liebmann's method; the symmetric difference formula on the right is used instead. But the left-hand formula, applied three times, does yield a good approximation of the second derivative:

$$y''(t_j) \approx \frac{y'(t_{j+1}) - y'(t_j)}{h} \approx \frac{1}{h}\left[\frac{y_{j+1} - y_j}{h} - \frac{y_j - y_{j-1}}{h}\right] = \frac{y_{j+1} - 2y_j + y_{j-1}}{h^2}$$

for $j = 1, \ldots, n - 1$. The BVP is then approximated by this difference equation:

$$\frac{y_{j+1} - 2y_j + y_{j-1}}{h^2} = f\left(t_j, y_j, \frac{y_{j+1} - y_{j-1}}{2h}\right).$$

You can rewrite the difference equation as

$$y_j = \frac{1}{2}y_{j+1} + \frac{1}{2}y_{j-1} - \frac{h^2}{2}f\left(t_j, y_j, \frac{y_{j+1} - y_{j-1}}{2h}\right) = g_j(y_1, \ldots, y_{n-1})$$

for $j = 1, \ldots, n - 1$. Thus, the original boundary value problem is approximated first by the difference equation, then by the fixpoint problem

$$\eta = \gamma(\eta) = \begin{bmatrix} g_1(\eta) \\ \vdots \\ g_{n-1}(\eta) \end{bmatrix} \qquad \eta = \begin{bmatrix} y_1 \\ \vdots \\ y_{n-1} \end{bmatrix}.$$

Remember, the constants a, b, y_0, y^*, and n are all involved in this problem, as well as the original function f.

If the boundary value problem is linear—that is, if

$$f(t, y, y') = p(t) + q(t) y + r(t) y'$$

for some functions p, q, and r, then the fixpoint equations $y_k = g_k(y_1, ..., y_{n-1})$ can be rewritten as a linear system. Linear problems are simpler than the general case, and are considered in Section 7.2. In Section 7.1, fixpoint iteration software is developed for the general case, and demonstrated with a typical nonlinear boundary value problem. Performance is poor, and motivates an analysis of the approximation error.

What's involved in the error analysis? Make two assumptions: there exist unique solutions $y = u(t)$ of the BVP, and $y_1, ..., y_{n-1}$ of the difference equation. (You can find in the literature conditions that guarantee existence and uniqueness of solutions.) There are two separate error questions:

- How well do $y_1, ..., y_{n-1}$ approximate $u(t_1), ..., u(t_{n-1})$?
- How accurately can you compute $y_1, ..., y_{n-1}$?

These questions are related. The answer to the first generally involves the number n of subdivisions—the more, the better. But large n values yield large systems of fixpoint equations, which can require much time and space for accurate solution. If your application must limit the size of n, there will be a limit on the accuracy: No matter how accurately you compute $y_1, ..., y_{n-1}$, they'll remain a certain distance from the true solution values $u(t_1), ..., u(t_{n-1})$. (For details of this analysis, see [8, Sections 11.1–11.4] and the literature cited there.)

For this reason, extreme accuracy is often not important in solving multidimensional fixpoint problems. In Section 7.1, single dimensional Fixpoint iteration is modified to fit the new situation, and demonstrated both with a simple example, and with a typical nonlinear second order boundary value problem. You'll see that speed is even more of a problem than it was with single dimensional Fixpoint iteration. That will motivate an analysis of the rate of convergence, which explains the problem.

In Section 7.3, the Newton-Raphson method is generalized to multidimensional problems. It can speed up computations considerably.

7.1   Multidimensional Fixpoint Iteration

The topics in this section involve some concepts from advanced calculus that may not be familiar to you. A few are needed even to discuss the introductory material that will motivate or facilitate the more detailed study later. These are the notions of limit, continuity, and open, closed, and convex sets in n dimensional space $\mathbf{R}^n$.

First, *convergence* of a sequence of n dimensional vectors $\xi^{(0)}$, $\xi^{(1)}$, $\xi^{(2)}$, ... can be expressed in two equivalent ways:

$$\alpha = \lim_{k \to \infty} \xi^{(k)} \longleftrightarrow \lim_{k \to \infty} \| \xi^{(k)} - \alpha \| = 0 \longleftrightarrow a_j = \lim_{k \to \infty} x_j^{(k)} \text{ for } j = 1, ..., n .$$

That is, $\xi^{(k)}$ approaches α if, and only if, the max norm $\| \xi^{(k)} - \alpha \|$ approaches 0, and that happens just in case each component $x_j^{(k)}$ of $\xi^{(k)}$ approaches the corresponding component a_j of α. A set D of vectors is called *closed* if it contains the limit of any convergent sequence of vectors in D.

Vector limits are compatible with vector and matrix algebra, just as in the single dimensional case. For example, these equations hold for any convergent sequences of vectors $\xi^{(k)}$ and $\kappa^{(k)}$, any scalar t, and any matrix A :

$$\lim_{k \to \infty} (\xi^{(k)} + \eta^{(k)}) = \lim_{k \to \infty} \xi^{(k)} + \lim_{k \to \infty} \eta^{(k)}$$

$$\lim_{k \to \infty} (t \xi^{(k)}) = t \lim_{k \to \infty} \xi^{(k)}$$

$$\lim_{k \to \infty} (A \, \xi^{(k)}) = A \lim_{k \to \infty} \xi^{(k)} .$$

An *open cube* centered at an n dimensional vector α is a subset of $\mathbf{R}^n$ of the form $N = \{ \, \xi : \| \xi - \alpha \| < r \, \}$ for some constant $r > 0$. (This definition uses the max norm.) A set D is called *open* if each member of D is the center of an open cube entirely within D. Any open set containing a set S of vectors is called a *neighborhood* of S. It's easy to show that a set D is open just in case its complement $\mathbf{R}^n - D$ is closed. A subset of the form $\{ \, \xi : \| \xi - \alpha \| \le r \, \}$ is closed; it's called a *closed cube*.

Consider a function $\gamma : D \to \mathbf{R}^m$, where D is a neighborhood of an n dimensional vector α. γ is said to be *continuous* at α if $\gamma(\xi^{(k)})$ approaches $\gamma(\alpha)$ whenever a sequence $\xi^{(0)}$, $\xi^{(1)}$, ... in D approaches α. You can show that γ is continuous in this sense just when each component function g_j is continuous at α.

A vector η is said to lie *between* two vectors ξ and ζ if $\eta = t\xi + (1 - t)\zeta$ for some t in the unit interval. Finally, a subset D of $\mathbf{R}^n$ is called *convex* if it contains every vector η that lies between two members of D. For example, open and closed cubes are convex.

All the n dimensional concepts just described can be extended, if necessary, to apply to complex vectors. This general terminology is used next to introduce the basic multidimensional Fixpoint iteration, and to show the need for detailed study of related convergence problems.

Implementing the Multidimensional Fixpoint Algorithm

In this chapter's introduction, you saw how a fixpoint problem—solving the equation

$$\xi = \gamma(\xi) = \begin{bmatrix} g_1(\xi) \\ \vdots \\ g_n(\xi) \end{bmatrix} \qquad \xi = \begin{bmatrix} x_1 \\ \vdots \\ x_n \end{bmatrix}$$

for a fixpoint $\xi = \alpha$ — can arise naturally in applications, especially through differential equations. The equation's form suggests the following *multidimensional Fixpoint iteration* algorithm: Start with an initial estimate $\xi^{(0)}$ of α, then compute

$$\xi^{k+1} = \gamma(\xi^{(k)}) = \begin{bmatrix} g_1(\xi^{(k)}) \\ \vdots \\ g_n(\xi^{(k)}) \end{bmatrix} \qquad \xi^{(k)} = \begin{bmatrix} x_1^{(k)} \\ \vdots \\ x_n^{(k)} \end{bmatrix}$$

for $k = 0, 1, \dots$. If the sequence $\xi^{(0)}, \xi^{(1)}, \xi^{(2)}, \dots$ converges, then the desired solution should be

$$\alpha = \lim_{k \to \infty} \xi^{(k)} .$$

That is, the equation

$$\gamma(\alpha) = \gamma\left(\lim_{k \to \infty} \xi^{(k)} \right) = \lim_{k \to \infty} \gamma(\xi^{(k)}) = \lim_{k \to \infty} \xi^{(k+1)} = \alpha$$

will hold if γ is continuous on a closed set D containing your initial estimate $\xi^{(0)}$, and Fixpoint iteration yields a convergent sequence of vectors $\xi^{(1)}, \xi^{(2)}, \dots$ in D.

This algorithm is easy to implement. But before rushing to do so, pause a moment to question the validity of what you're doing:

- Can you predict whether a solution exists?
- If the sequence converges to a fixpoint, is that necessarily the solution you're looking for? (There might be more than one fixpoint.)
- What conditions ensure convergence?
- How fast can you expect the sequence to converge?

You may want to be sure that a fixpoint exists before attempting to compute one. Section 5.3 presented a condition that guarantees existence in the single dimensional case $n = 1$: If a continuous function g maps a nonempty closed interval $I = \{ x : a \leq x \leq b \}$ into itself, then g has a fixpoint in I. That was easy to see by considering the graph of g. An analogous result—called the *Brouwer Fixpoint theorem*—is true for any dimension n: If a continuous function γ maps a closed cube I into itself, then γ has a fixpoint in I. Unfortunately, there's no clear picture to illustrate that, and the theorem is hard to prove. (Usually, it's found in books on combinatorial topology.) In practical applications it's hard to find the appropriate cube; fortunately, however, the existence of a fixpoint is usually apparent from the problem setting. The main question is whether you can use Fixpoint iteration to compute it.

Later in this section, conditions are presented that guarantee convergence of Fixpoint iteration, provided your initial estimate is close enough to the desired fixpoint. Unfortunately, you usually don't know how close that must be until you execute the algorithm. Often, multidimensional functions have multiple fixpoints, and Fixpoint iteration can lead you to an unanticipated solution, not the one you want. You must analyze situations like that individually.

As in the single dimensional case of Section 5.3, the theory that leads to a convergence criterion can also predict the rate of convergence.

Figure 7.1.1 contains the source code for MSP function **Fixpoint2**, an implementation of the multidimensional Fixpoint algorithm. It's structured exactly like the single dimensional function **Fixpoint** shown in Figure 5.3.2. Along with other routines that implement algorithms for solving systems of equations, function **Fixpoint2** is included in MSP module **Equate2**. You'll find its prototype in header file **Equate2.H** on the optional diskette, and the source code in file **Equate2.CPP**. For your convenience, the former is listed in Appendix A.3. The two fixpoint functions are distinguished by their prototypes:

```
Vector Fixpoint2(Vector G(Vector),    // Find a fixpoint of  G .
                 Vector X,            // Initial estimate.
                 double T,            // Tolerance.
                 int&    Code) {      // Status code.
   int n = 0;  double M;              // n  counts iterations.
   do {
       Vector P = G(X);               // Fixpoint iteration:
       M = MaxNorm(X - P);            // do at most  1000
       X = P; }                       // steps.
     while (++n < 1000 && M >= T);
   Code = (M < T ? 0 : -1);           // Report success, or
   return X; }                        // failure to converge.
```

Figure 7.1.1 MSP function Fixpoint2

Equate1 function

```
Scalar
  Fixpoint(Scalar g(double),
           Scalar x,
           double T,
           int&    Code = 0)
```

Equate2 function

```
Vector
  Fixpoint2(Vector G(Vector),
            Vector X,
            double T,
            int&    Code = 0)
```

The only differences in source code consist in changing **Scalar** parameters to **Vector**, using the max norm instead of the absolute value, and in using upper case identifiers for vectors.

Examples: The Need for Error Analysis

As a first example of multidimensional Fixpoint iteration, consider the nonlinear system

$$\begin{cases} x = \sin(x + y) \\ y = \cos(x - y) \end{cases}.$$

From its graph in Figure 7.1.2 you can see that it has a solution near the point $x, y = 1, 1$. The solution is a fixpoint of the function

$$\gamma(\xi) = \begin{bmatrix} \sin(x + y) \\ \cos(x - y) \end{bmatrix} \quad \xi = \begin{bmatrix} x \\ y \end{bmatrix}.$$

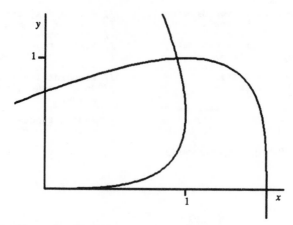

Figure 7.1.2 The curves x = sin(x + y), y = cos(x – y)

The fixpoint was computed by a test program shown in Figure 7.1.3; its execution is described in Figure 7.1.4. With tolerance $T = 10^{-6}$, function **Fixpoint2** required nine iterations. That's comparable with the single dimensional example in Figure 5.3.3. (Like several MSP routines in Chapter 5, **Fixpoint2** is really implemented with additional code for intermediate output like Figure 7.1.4. That code is not shown in Figure 7.1.1, because it obscures the structure of the program. You'll find the version that produced the output on the optional diskette. The test program is there, too, in file **Equ2Test.CPP**.)

The Liebmann method for second order boundary value problems (BVP), described in the introduction to this chapter, provides many example fixpoint problems. A BVP

```
Vector G(Vector X) {
  Vector Y(2);
  Y[1] = sin(X[1] + X[2]);
  Y[2] = cos(X[1] - X[2]);
  return Y; }

void main() {
  cout << "Solving  x = sin(x + y)  by Fixpoint iteration\n"
       "          y = cos(x - y)                     \n\n";
  double T = 1e-6;  int Code = 2;
  cout << "Tolerance  = ";  Show(T);
  Vector X(2);  X.AllEntries(1);
  X.Show(""     ,True,"\nInitial estimate  x y" );
  X = Fixpoint2(G,X,T,Code);
  X.Show("%.6f",True,"Solution  x y");
  cout << "Code = " << Code; }
```

Figure 7.1.3 Fixpoint2 test program

```
Solving  x = sin(x + y)  by Fixpoint iteration
         y = cos(x - y)

Tolerance  =  1.0e-06
Initial estimate  x y :   1.0        1.0

Itera-
tion       ‖ X - G(X) ‖
 0           0.091
 1           0.034
 2           0.010
 3           0.0027
 4           0.00069
 5           0.00016
 6           3.8e-05
 7           8.6e-06
 8           1.9e-06
 9           4.0e-07

Solution  x y :   0.935082   0.998020
Code = 0
```

Figure 7.1.4 Fixpoint2 test program output

$$y'' = f(t, y, y') \qquad\qquad y(a) = y_0 \qquad\qquad y(b) = y^*$$

leads to the equation $\eta = \gamma(\eta)$, where

$$\gamma(\eta) = \begin{bmatrix} g_1(\eta) \\ \vdots \\ g_{n-1}(\eta) \end{bmatrix} \qquad \eta = \begin{bmatrix} y_1 \\ \vdots \\ y_{n-1} \end{bmatrix} \qquad y_n = y^*$$

$$g_j(\eta) = \frac{1}{2} y_{j+1} + \frac{1}{2} y_{j-1} - \frac{h^2}{2} f\left(t_j, y_j, \frac{y_{j+1} - y_{j-1}}{2h} \right) .$$

Liebmann's method is tested by the MSP client program shown in Figure 7.1.5. You'll find that code in file **BVP.CPP** on the diskette. Function **main** first calls **BVPSetUp** to set up vectors **T** and **U** consisting of $t_1, \ldots, t_{n-1}$ and the corresponding values $u_1, \ldots, u_{n-1}$ of the exact solution $y = u(t)$. It also sets up the initial estimate $Y = \eta^{(0)}$ for the Fixpoint iteration: This vector consists of values of the linear function that satisfy the boundary conditions. Then **main** calls **Fixpoint2** to compute a solution vector **Y** and compares that with the vector **U** of exact solution values.

As an example, consider the nonlinear second order boundary value problem

$$y'' = \frac{2}{y' + 1} \qquad y(1) = \frac{1}{3} \qquad y(4) = \frac{20}{3} .$$

```
#include "Equate2.H"      // Solving      y" = f(t,y,y')
#include    <Math.H>      //              y(a) = y0  y(b) = y*

double  a,b,y0,yStar;     // t takes  n  steps of size  h  from  a
int n;  double T;         // to  b .  T = Tolerance. The initial
double  h,k;              // estimate  Y  is linear, with step size
Vector  t,U,Y;            // k .  U  is the exact BVP solution.

double f(double t, double y, double yp) {    // Compute the  ODE's
  return 2/(yp + 1);                          // right hand side.

double u(double t) {                          // Return the exact
  return t*(4*sqrt(t)/3 - 1); }               // solution of the
                                              // ODEBVP .

void BVPSetUp() {
  h = (b - a)/n;   k = (yStar - y0)/n;        // Set up the  t
  t.SetUp(n-1);    Y.SetUp(n-1);              // steps, the linear
  U.SetUp(n-1);                               // initial estimate
  for (int j = 1; j <= n-1; ++j) {            // Y , and the exact
    t[j] = a  + j*h;                          // solution  U .
    Y[j] = y0 + j*k;
    U[j] = u(t[j]); }}

Vector G(Vector Y) {                          // Fixpoint function
  int    m = Y.HighIndex();                   // for Liebmann's
  Vector V(m);  double Dummy;                 // method.
  for (int k = 1; k <= m; ++k) {
    double Ykm1 = (k == 1 ? y0    : Y[k-1]);  // Y[0] = y0 .
    double Ykp1 = (k == m ? yStar : Y[k+1]);  // Y[n] = y* .
    double Ypk  = (Ykp1 - Ykm1)/(2*h);        // Ypk = y'
    V[k] = (Ykp1 + Ykm1                       // at  t[k] .
      - h*h*f(t[k],Y[k],Ypk,Dummy,Dummy))/2; }
  return V; }

void main() {
  a = 1;    y0 = 1./3.;     b = 4;  yStar = 20./3.;
  cout << "Solving      y\"  = 2/(y' + 1)      \n"
          "            y(1) = 1/3  y(4) = 20/3\n\n"
          "by Fixpoint      iteration         \n";
  cout << "Number of subdivisions: ";  cin >> n;
  cout << "Tolerance: ";               cin >> T;
  BVPSetUp();   int Code = 1;
  Y = Fixpoint2(G,Y,T,Code);
  cout << "‖Y - U‖ = ";  Show(MaxNorm(Y - U)); }
```

Figure 7.1.5 Testing Liebmann's method

Its solution is the function

$$u(t) = \frac{4}{3} t^{3/2} - t .$$

To compute an approximate solution η via Liebmann's method, the program in Figure 7.1.5 defines

```
double f(double t, double y, double yp) { return 2/(yp + 1); }
double a = 1;  double y0    = 1/3.;
double b = 4;  double yStar = 20/3.;
```

and inputs the number **n** of subdivisions and the **Fixpoint2** tolerance parameter **T**. For this example, the program was executed with T = 0.0001 and several **n** values, yielding the following results:

Number of Subdivisions	Number of Iterations	Error
5	36	.0017
10	122	.0022
20	375	.0083

The tabulated Error value is the max norm of the error vector $Y - U$. As you can see, there was no point in using such a small tolerance T, because the solution of the fixpoint equation is evidently farther than that distance from the true solution of the BVP. Moreover, if you only need a few evenly spaced solution values, there's no point in making a finer subdivision, because in this case the accuracy decreases as the number of subdivisions grows.

As a final example, consider the linear second order BVP $y'' = 2y' - y - 3$, $y(0) = -3$, $y(2) = 1$. Its exact solution is $u(t) = -3 + 2te^{t-2}$. Although you might expect a linear problem to be more tractable, similar phenomena occur:

Number of Subdivisions	Number of Iterations	Error
5	42	.073
10	137	.016
17	331	.00081
20	431	.0037

To obtain these results, the Figure 7.1.5 functions **main, f,** and **u** were adapted for this problem, then run with the same tolerance T = 0.0001.

These examples show the need for error analysis, to predict the behavior of problems for which true solutions are not known, and to suggest methods for arranging fixpoint problems so that the iterations converge more quickly. The analysis has two aspects, corresponding to these questions:

• How well does the true solution to the fixpoint equation approximate that of the BVP?
• How accurately can you compute the solution to the fixpoint equation?

The first of these is a deep problem in the numerical analysis of differential equations, beyond the scope of this book. The second will be discussed under later headings in this section.

Jacobians

Another advanced calculus concept that's needed for this error analysis is the Jacobian. It often plays the role of a multidimensional derivative. Consider a function $\gamma : D \to \mathbf{R}^m$, where D is a set in $\mathbf{R}^n$:

$$\gamma(\xi) = \begin{bmatrix} g_1(\xi) \\ \vdots \\ g_m(\xi) \end{bmatrix} \qquad \xi = \begin{bmatrix} x_1 \\ \vdots \\ x_n \end{bmatrix} .$$

Suppose all the partial derivatives of the components g_j of γ exist at a point ξ. Then the *Jacobian* of γ at ξ is the matrix

$$J\gamma(\xi) = \begin{bmatrix} \dfrac{\partial g_1}{\partial x_1} & \cdots & \dfrac{\partial g_1}{\partial x_n} \\ \vdots & & \vdots \\ \dfrac{\partial g_m}{\partial x_1} & \cdots & \dfrac{\partial g_m}{\partial x_n} \end{bmatrix} .$$

For example, consider a linear function $\gamma(\xi) = A\xi + \beta$, where A is an $m \times n$ matrix and an n dimensional vector. The components γ of and their partials are given by the equations

$$g_j(\xi) = \sum_{k=1}^{n} a_{jk} x_k + b_j \qquad \frac{\partial g_j}{\partial x_k} = a_{jk} .$$

That is, the Jacobian of a linear function $\gamma(\xi) = A\xi + \beta$ is the constant A.

Another familiar example occurs when $m = 1$. In that case, $\gamma(\xi)$ has just the single component $g_1(\xi)$, and its Jacobian is just the row of partial derivatives:

$$J\gamma(\xi) = \begin{bmatrix} \dfrac{\partial g_1}{\partial x_1}, & \cdots, & \dfrac{\partial g_1}{\partial x_1} \end{bmatrix} .$$

This row is usually called the *gradient* $\nabla\gamma(\xi)$.

Jacobians are particularly handy for stating the multidimensional *Chain Rule*, as follows. Suppose

- $\gamma : D \to \mathbf{R}^m$, where D is an open set in $\mathbf{R}^n$, and all partial derivatives of γ exist and are continuous there;
- $\phi : \gamma[D] \to \mathbf{R}^l$, and all partial derivatives of ϕ exist and are continuous in $\gamma[D]$.

Let η denote the composition of ϕ and γ : That is, $\phi(\gamma(\xi)) = \eta(\xi)$ for all vectors ξ in D. Then

- all the partial derivatives of η exist and are continuous at all vectors ξ in D, and $J\eta(\xi) = J\phi(\gamma(\xi)) \cdot J\gamma(\xi)$.

The entries of $J\phi(\gamma(\xi))$ are the partial derivatives of the components of the function ϕ evaluated at points

$$\gamma(\xi) = \begin{bmatrix} g_1(\xi) \\ \vdots \\ g_m(\xi) \end{bmatrix}$$

and are often written

$$\frac{\partial f_i}{\partial g_j} \; .$$

With that notation, the entries of $J\eta(X)$ take the familiar form

$$\frac{\partial h_i}{\partial x_k} = \sum_{j=1}^{m} \frac{\partial f_i}{\partial g_j} \frac{\partial g_j}{\partial x_k} \; .$$

A Multidimensional Mean-Value Theorem

The Mean-Value theorem played a major role in the error analysis for single dimensional Fixpoint iteration. For the multidimensional theory, you need an analogous result that may be unfamiliar to you:

Suppose a real valued function g is defined on an open convex subset D of $\mathbf{R}^n$ and has continuous partial derivatives there, and suppose ξ and ζ are vectors in D. Then

$$g(\xi) - g(\zeta) = \nabla g(\eta)(\xi - \zeta)$$

for some vector η between, but different from ξ and ζ.

(Here the gradient $\nabla g(\eta)$ is an n dimensional row and $\xi - \zeta$ is an n dimensional column.) The theorem is simple to prove. Define a function $\lambda : \mathbf{R} \to \mathbf{R}^n$ and a real valued function f on the unit interval I by setting

$$\lambda(t) = \zeta + t(\xi - \zeta) \qquad\qquad f(t) = g(\lambda(t)) .$$

Since λ is linear, $J\lambda(t) = \xi - \zeta$. By the Chain Rule, f has a continuous derivative on I, hence

$$g(\xi) - g(\zeta) = f(1) - f(0) = f'(t)(1 - 0) = f'(t)$$

for some t such that $0 < t < 1$, by the single dimensional Mean-Value theorem. Again, by the Chain Rule,

$$f'(t) = Jg(\lambda(t)) \cdot J\lambda(t) = \nabla g(\zeta)(\xi - \zeta)$$

where $\zeta = \lambda(t)$.

This Mean-Value theorem is often used to estimate the difference in values of a function $\gamma : D \to \mathbf{R}^m$, where D is an open convex subset D of $\mathbf{R}^n$:

Suppose all components of γ have continuous partials in D; then for any vectors ξ and ζ in D, there's a vector η in D such that

$$\| \gamma(\xi) - \gamma(\zeta) \| \le \| J\gamma(\eta) \| \ \ \| \xi - \zeta \| \ .$$

All the norms here are matrix row norms; since the vectors are columns, their row norms are the same as max norms.

The proof is simple: For some index j^*,

$$\| \gamma(\xi) - \gamma(\zeta) \| \ = \ \max_{j=1}^{m} |g_j(\xi) - g_j(\zeta)| \ = \ |g_j \cdot (\xi) - g_j \cdot (\zeta)|$$

$$= \ |\nabla g_j \cdot (\eta)(\xi - \zeta)| \ \le \ \| \nabla g_j \cdot (\eta) \| \ \ \| \xi - \eta \|$$

$$= \left[\sum_{k=1}^{n} \left| \frac{\partial g_j}{\partial x_k} \right| \right] \| \xi - \eta \|$$

$$\le \ \| J\gamma(\eta) \| \ \ \| \xi - \zeta \| \ .$$

(At one step here, the row norm inequality $\| AB \| \le \| A \| \ \| B \|$ was used; it's valid for any matrices A and B that you can multiply.)

Convergence Condition, Speed of Convergence

As in the single dimensional discussion in Section 5.3, the inequality just demonstrated is used to obtain a Lipschitz constant, which will indicate whether and how fast multidimensional Fixpoint iteration converges. Consider a function $\gamma : D \to \mathbf{R}^m$, where D is a subset D of $\mathbf{R}^n$. A *Lipschitz constant* for γ on D is a number L such that

$$\| \gamma(\xi) - \gamma(\zeta) \| \le L \| \xi - \zeta \|$$

for all vectors ξ and ζ in D. Suppose D is open and convex and all components of γ have continuous partials there. By the previous inequality, any number $L \ge \| J\gamma(\eta) \|$ for all η in D is a Lipschitz constant. (In this paragraph, the vector norms are max norms, and the matrix norm is a row norm.)

Now it's possible to state a condition that guarantees convergence of Fixpoint iteration:

Suppose $\gamma : D \to D$, where D is an open convex subset D of $\mathbf{R}^n$ containing a fixpoint α of γ. Suppose γ has a Lipschitz constant $L < 1$ on D. Then D contains only one fixpoint, and Fixpoint iteration $\xi^{(0)}$, $\xi^{(1)}$, $\xi^{(2)}$, ... with $\xi^{(k+1)} = \gamma(\xi^{(k)})$ converges to α for any initial estimate $\xi^{(0)}$ in D.

The proof is the same as that for the single dimensional case: The *error vectors* $\varepsilon^{(k)} = \xi^{(k)} - \alpha$ satisfy the inequalities

$$\| \varepsilon^{(k+1)} \| \le L \| \varepsilon^{(k)} \| \qquad \| \varepsilon^{(k)} \| \le L^k \| \varepsilon^{(0)} \|$$

for all k. Convergence of this sort is called *linear*, as in the single dimensional case.

You can use these error inequalities to study the convergence of the Fixpoint iterations considered earlier in this section. In the first example,

$$\gamma(\xi) = \begin{bmatrix} \sin(x + y) \\ \cos(x - y) \end{bmatrix} \qquad \xi = \begin{bmatrix} x \\ y \end{bmatrix}$$

and the row norm of the Jacobian is $J = 2 \max(|\sin(x + y)|, |\cos(x - y)|)$. At the fixpoint x, $y \approx 0.935$, 0.998 and $J \approx 0.708$, so you can use the Lipschitz constant $L = 0.71$. From Figure 7.1.2 you can see that $\| \varepsilon^{(0)} \| \le 0.1$ with the initial estimate x, $y = 1, 1$. By the error inequality, $\| \varepsilon^{(k)} \| \le L^k \| \varepsilon^{(0)} \| \le 0.1 L^k$, hence $\| \varepsilon^{(k)} \|$ will be less than the tolerance $T = 10^{-6}$ if $0.1 \ L^k \leq T$. You can solve this inequality to get $k \geq 34$. The example iteration actually converged much faster (9 iterations in Figure 7.1.4) than this analysis predicts.

The boundary value problems (BVP)

$$y'' = f(t, y, y') \qquad\qquad y(a) = y_0 \qquad\qquad y(b) = y^*$$

considered earlier were approximated by fixpoint problems

$$\eta = \gamma(\eta) = \begin{bmatrix} g_1(\eta) \\ : \\ g_{n-1}(\eta) \end{bmatrix} \qquad \eta = \begin{bmatrix} y_1 \\ : \\ y_{n-1} \end{bmatrix} \qquad y_n = y^*$$

$$h = \frac{b-a}{n}, \qquad t_j = a + jh \ \text{ for } \ j = 0, ..., n$$

$$g_j(\eta) = \frac{1}{2} y_{j+1} + \frac{1}{2} y_{j-1} - \frac{h_2}{2} f\left(t_j, y_j, \frac{y_{j+1} - y_{j-1}}{2h}\right) \quad \text{for } j = 1, ..., n-1 \ .$$

A solution η of the fixpoint problem should approximate the solution u of the BVP: $y_j \approx u(t_j)$ for $j = 1, ..., n-1$. The behavior of the Fixpoint iteration $\eta^{(k+1)} = \gamma(\eta^{(k)})$ is related to the value $\|J\gamma\|$ of the row norm of the Jacobian near the solution. That's not difficult to analyze. The j,kth entry of $J\gamma$ is

$$\frac{\partial g_j}{\partial j_k} = 0 \ \text{ unless } \ k = j - 1, j, \text{ or } j + 1$$

$$\frac{\partial g_j}{\partial y_{j-1}} = \frac{1}{2} + \frac{h}{4} \frac{\partial f}{\partial y'} \qquad \frac{\partial g_j}{\partial y_j} = -\frac{h^2}{2} \frac{\partial f}{\partial y} \qquad \frac{\partial g_j}{\partial y_{j+1}} = \frac{1}{2} - \frac{h}{4} \frac{\partial f}{\partial y'}$$

The row norm $\|J\gamma\|$ is the largest of the sums

$$\left|\frac{\partial g_1}{\partial y_1}\right| + \left|\frac{\partial g_1}{y_2}\right|$$

$$\left|\frac{\partial g_1}{\partial y_{j-1}}\right| + \left|\frac{\partial g_1}{\partial y_1}\right| + \left|\frac{\partial g_1}{\partial y_{j+1}}\right| \qquad \text{for } j = 2, ..., n-2$$

$$\left|\frac{\partial g_{n-1}}{\partial y_{n-2}}\right| + \left|\frac{\partial g_{n-1}}{\partial y_{n-1}}\right| \ .$$

The f partials in these equations are evaluated at

$$t_j, y_j, \frac{y_{j+1} - y_{j-1}}{2h} .$$

Assuming that the f partials are bounded in the region under study, the top and bottom sums approach $\frac{1}{2}$ as n increases. The middle sums have the form

$$\left| \frac{1}{2} + x \right| + \left| \frac{1}{2} - x \right| + \frac{h^2}{2} \left| \frac{\partial f}{\partial y} \right| \qquad x = \frac{h}{4} \frac{\partial f}{\partial y'}$$

You can verify that

$$\left| \frac{1}{2} + x \right| + \left| \frac{1}{2} - x \right| \geq 1$$

for all x, hence $\| \mathcal{J}\gamma \| > 1$ for all h. In general, the Liebmann method applies Fixpoint iteration in a borderline situation where convergence cannot be guaranteed; you should expect it to diverge sometimes, and converge sometimes, but never very fast.

Had the asymmetric formula

$$\frac{y_k - y_{k-1}}{h}$$

been used to approximate the derivative $y'(t_k)$ in deriving the Liebmann difference equation from the BVP, the component functions g_j and their partials would have formulas

$$g_j(\eta) = \frac{1}{2} y_{j+1} + \frac{1}{2} y_{j-1} - \frac{h^2}{2} f\left(t_j, y_j, \frac{y_j - y_{j-1}}{h} \right)$$

$$\frac{\partial g_j}{\partial y_{j-1}} = \frac{1}{2} + \frac{h}{2} \frac{\partial f}{\partial y'} \qquad \frac{\partial g_j}{\partial y_j} = -\frac{h^2}{2} \frac{\partial f}{\partial y} - \frac{h}{2} \frac{\partial f}{\partial y'} \qquad \frac{\partial g_j}{\partial y_{j+1}} = \frac{1}{2} .$$

The row norms of the first and last rows of the Jacobian $\mathcal{J}\gamma$ would still approach 1/2 as n increases. But the norms of the middle rows have the form

$$\left| \frac{1}{2} + 2x \right| + | 2x | + \frac{1}{2} + \frac{h^2}{4} \left| \frac{\partial f}{\partial y} \right| \qquad x = \frac{h}{2} \frac{\partial f}{\partial y'} .$$

You can verify that

$$\left| \frac{1}{2} + 2x \right| + |2x| + \frac{1}{2} \geq \left| \frac{1}{2} + x \right| + \left| \frac{1}{2} - x \right|$$

for all x. Thus, using the asymmetric differential quotient to approximate the first derivative in Liebmann's method would generally yield a Jacobian with a larger row norm. The symmetric quotient is more appropriate.

7.2   Iterative Solution of Linear Systems

This section is concerned with the solution of linear systems by linear Fixpoint iteration. Given an $n \times n$ matrix A and an n dimensional vector β, you'll convert equations $A\xi = \beta$ to an equivalent form $\xi = \gamma(\xi) = C\xi + \delta$, make an initial estimate $\xi^{(0)}$, then construct a sequence of successive approximations using the scheme $\xi^{(k+1)} = \gamma(\xi^{(k)})$. According to Section 7.1, the approximations will converge to a unique solution $\xi = \alpha$ if $\|C\| = \|J\gamma(\xi)\| < 1$. In fact, $\|C\|$ is a Lipschitz constant for γ, and the error vectors $\varepsilon^{(k)} = \xi^{(k)} - \alpha$ satisfy the inequalities

$$\| \varepsilon^{(k+1)} \| \leq \| C \| \ \| \varepsilon^{(k)} \| \qquad \| \varepsilon^{(k)} \| \leq \| C \|^k \| \varepsilon^{(0)} \| \ .$$

Thus, to solve a system $A\xi = \beta$ you'll want to find an equivalent fixpoint problem $\xi = C\xi + \delta$ with $\|C\|$ as small as possible, and in particular < 1.

Jacobi Iteration

Given an $n \times n$ linear system $A\xi = \beta$, *Jacobi's method* constructs an equivalent linear fixpoint problem $\xi = C\xi + \delta$ as in the following 3×3 example: Convert the equations

$$\begin{cases} a_{11}x_1 + a_{12}x_2 + a_{13}x_3 = b_1 \\ a_{21}x_1 + a_{22}x_2 + a_{23}x_3 = b_2 \\ a_{31}x_1 + a_{32}x_2 + a_{33}x_3 = b_3 \end{cases}$$

to the fixpoint problem

$$\begin{cases} x_1 = & - \dfrac{a_{12}}{a_{11}} x_2 - \dfrac{a_{13}}{a_{11}} x_3 + \dfrac{b_1}{a_{11}} \\[2ex] x_2 = - \dfrac{a_{21}}{a_{22}} x_1 & - \dfrac{a_{23}}{a_{22}} x_3 + \dfrac{b_2}{a_{22}} \\[2ex] x_3 = - \dfrac{a_{31}}{a_{33}} x_1 - \dfrac{a_{32}}{a_{33}} x_2 & + \dfrac{b_3}{a_{33}} \end{cases},$$

that is,

$$\xi = C\xi + D^{-1}\beta \qquad\qquad C = -D^{-1}A + I,$$

where D is the diagonal matrix extracted from A. Of course, this process assumes that there's no zero on the diagonal of A. You can verify in general that this last equation is equivalent to $A\xi = \beta$: It holds just in case

$$\xi = -D^{-1}A\xi + \xi + D^{-1}\beta$$
$$0 = -D^{-1}A\xi + D^{-1}\beta$$
$$0 = -A\xi + \beta.$$

What criterion should A satisfy, to ensure that $\|C\| < 1$? The row norm $\|C\| = \|-D^{-1}A + I\|$ is the largest sum

$$\sum_{j=1}^{n} |c_{ij}| \quad,$$

hence, each of these sums must be < 1. But

$$c_{ii} = 0, \qquad c_{ij} = \frac{a_{ii}}{a_{ij}} \text{ when } j \neq i \;,$$

so A should satisfy the inequality

$$\sum_{\substack{j=1 \\ j \neq i}}^{n} \left| \frac{a_{ij}}{a_{ii}} \right| < 1$$

i.e.,

$$\sum_{\substack{j=1 \\ j \neq i}}^{n} |a_{ij}| < |a_{ii}| \;.$$

```
Vector Jacobi(const Matrix& A,                    // Solve  AX = B  by
                 const Vector& B,                 // Jacobi iteration.
                        Vector  X,                // Initial estimate.
                        double  T,                // Tolerance.
                        int&    Code) {           // Status code.
   int m = A.HighRowIndex();                      // n  counts
   int n = 0;  double M;                          // iterations.
   do {
       Vector P = B;                              // Fixpoint
       for (int i = 1; i <= m; ++i) {             // iteration:
         for (int j = 1; j <= m; ++j)             // do at most
           if (j != i) P[i] -= A[i][j]*X[j];      // 1000  steps.
         P[i] /= A[i][i]; }
       M = MaxNorm(P - X);
       X = P; }
     while (++n < 1000 && M >= T);
   Code = (M < T ? 0 : -1);                       // Report success, or
   return X; }                                    // failure to converge.
```

Figure 7.2.1 MSP function Jacobi

for each i. Such a matrix A is called *strictly diagonally row dominant*. Note that $\|C\|$ approaches 1; hence, convergence deteriorates as the two sides of this inequality get closer.

If you carry out the entire multidimensional fixpoint analysis with column norms in place of row norms, you'll get a corresponding result. Jacobi iteration also converges if A is strictly diagonally *column* dominant: For each j,

$$\sum_{\substack{i=1 \\ i \neq j}}^{n} \left| \frac{a_{ij}}{a_{ii}} \right| < 1$$

i.e.,

$$\sum_{\substack{i=1 \\ i \neq j}}^{n} |a_{ij}| < |a_{ii}| \ .$$

Strict diagonal dominance implies nonsingularity: If A is strictly diagonally row or column dominant, then $\|C\| < 1$ for the row or column norm; hence, Jacobi iteration converges to a unique fixpoint of the function $\gamma(\xi) = C\xi + \delta$. This implies that the equations $A\xi = \beta$ have a unique solution for any β, hence A is nonsingular.

MSP function **Jacobi** implements this method. Shown in Figure 7.2.1, it's structured like the Section 7.1 function **Fixpoint2**. **Jacobi** will be demonstrated later in this section.

```
Vector Seidel(const Matrix& A,          // Solve  AX = B  by
              const Vector& B,          // Gauss-Seidel iteration.
              Vector   X,               // Initial estimate.
              double   T,               // Tolerance.
              int&     Code) {          // Status code.
   int m = A.HighRowIndex();            // n  counts
   int n = 0;  double M;                // iterations.
   do {
      Vector P = X;                                    // Fixpoint
      for (int i = 1; i <= m; ++i) {                   // iteration:
         X[i] = B[i];                                  // do at most
         for (int j = 1; j <= m; ++j)                  // 1000  steps.
            if (j != i) X[i] -= A[i][j]*X[j];
         X[i] /= A[i][i]; }
      M = MaxNorm(P - X); }
   while (++n < 1000 && M >= T);
   Code = (M < T ? 0 : -1);             // Report success, or
   return X; }                          // failure to converge.
```

Figure 7.2.2 MSP function Seidel

Gauss-Seidel Iteration

To compute $\xi^{(k+1)} = \gamma(\xi^{(k)})$ by Jacobi's algorithm, you use

- entry $x_1^{(k)}$ in calculating $x_2^{(k+1)}$, ..., $x_n^{(k+1)}$,
- entries $x_1^{(k)}$, $x_2^{(k)}$ in calculating $x_3^{(k+1)}$, ..., $x_n^{(k+1)}$,
- and so on.

It might seem better to use

- $x_1^{(k+1)}$ in place of $x_1^{(k)}$ in calculating $x_2^{(k+1)}$,
- $x_1^{(k+1)}$, $x_2^{(k+1)}$ in place of $x_1^{(k)}$, $x_2^{(k)}$ in calculating $x_3^{(k+1)}$,
- and so on,

because the approximations $x_1^{(k+1)}$, $x_2^{(k+1)}$, ... are supposedly more accurate than their predecessors. It's easy to make this modification. The resulting algorithm is called *Gauss-Seidel* iteration; it's implemented by MSP function **Seidel**, shown in Figure 7.2.2.

In the Jacobi algorithm, each component $x_i^{(k+1)}$ is a linear combination of the components $x_1^{(k)}$, ..., $x_n^{(k)}$; hence, the same is true when $x_1^{(k+1)}$, ..., $x_i^{(k+1)}$ are used in place of $x_1^{(k)}$, ..., $x_i^{(k)}$ in computing $x_{i+1}^{(k+1)}$ in the Gauss-Seidel method. Thus, Gauss-Seidel iteration is also a special case of linear Fixpoint iteration $\xi^{(k+1)} = C\xi^{(k)} + \delta$ with C and δ computed from the matrix and vector of the original system $A\xi = \beta$. Convergence of Gauss-Seidel iteration can be analyzed in the same way as the Jacobi algorithm, and the same result applies: Gauss-

```
#include "Equate2.H"
#include "GaussEl.H"

void main() {
   cout << "Solving a  20x20  system  AX = B                    \n"
           "by Jacobi  [1]  or Gauss-Seidel  [2]  iteration.\n"
           "Select method      [1/2] : ";  int     M;  cin >> M;
   cout << "Enter diagonal entry  d :  ";  double d;  cin >> d;
   cout << "B  and the other entries of  A  are random.  \n\n";
   int       n = 20;   double T = 1e-4;
   Vector    X(n);      X.MakeZero();
   Vector    B(n);      B.MakeRandom();
   Matrix    A(n,n);    A.MakeRandom();
   for (int i = 1; i <= n; ++i) A[i][i] = d;
   Vector    a = Solve (A, ¯B,     0);
   if (M == 1) X = Jacobi(A, B,X,T,1);
   if (M == 2) X = Seidel(A, B,X,T,1);
   cout << " ‖Aα - ß‖ = ";   Show(MaxNorm(A*a-B));   cout << endl
        << " ‖AX - ß‖ = ";   Show(MaxNorm(A*X-B));   cout << endl
        << " ‖ X - α‖ = ";   Show(MaxNorm( X-a));    cout << endl; }
```

Figure 7.2.3 Testing Jacobi and Gauss-Seidel iteration

Seidel iteration converges if the matrix A is strictly diagonally row or column dominant. Moreover, it usually converges faster than Jacobi iteration. (See Reference [8, Section 7.3] and the literature cited there.) However, it's possible for either method to converge but not the other, and even for either method to be faster when they both converge (see Reference [41].)

Example: A Random System

As a first example, the MSP client program in Figure 7.2.3 tests Jacobi and Gauss-Seidel iteration and shows how their rates of convergence depend on the degree of diagonal dominance. You'll find its source code on the optional diskette in file **Equ2Test.CPP**. For a given value d, the program constructs an $n \times n$ matrix A with diagonal entries d. Its other entries, and those of an n dimensional vector β, are selected at random from the unit interval. Using Gauss elimination, the program next computes an "exact" solution $\xi = \alpha$ of the system $A\xi = \beta$. Then it computes approximate solutions ξ by Jacobi or Gauss-Seidel iteration, using the zero vector as initial estimate, and a tolerance of 0.0001. It displays the number of iterations and the error measures $\| A\xi - \beta \|$ and $\| \xi - \alpha \|$. Here are some results for $n = 20$:

d	Jacobi's Method			Gauss-Seidel Method		
	Iterations	$\|A\xi - \beta\|$	$\|\xi - \alpha\|$	Iterations	$\|A\xi - \beta\|$	$\|\xi - \alpha\|$
8	Diverges			7	9×10^{-5}	1×10^{-5}
10	152	9×10^{-4}	5×10^{-5}	6	1×10^{-4}	1×10^{-5}
15	15	7×10^{-4}	3×10^{-5}	5	5×10^{-5}	4×10^{-6}

The error measure $\|A\xi - \beta\|$ for the "exact" solution $\xi = \alpha$ is about 2 $\times 10^{-16}$. Since the sum of the nondiagonal entries of any row of A is about $(n - 1) \times 0.5 = 9.5$, the input $d = 8$ should lead to a matrix that's not diagonally row dominant; hence, you can't expect either method to converge. Jacobi's method is the more sensitive to this criterion: It diverges. Jacobi's method converges when $d = 10$ and A is just barely row dominant. Both methods converge faster as A becomes more dominant.

As shown in Section 6.2, Gauss elimination requires about $\frac{2}{3} n^3 \approx$ 5000 operations to solve the system $A\xi = \beta$. Each step of an iterative method requires n additions and n multiplications for each row, hence, $2n^2$ operations in all. The most rapidly convergent example tabulated required 5 iterations, hence, about 4000 operations. Thus, if extreme accuracy is not important and an iterative method is known to converge very rapidly, you may save time by using that rather than Gauss elimination.

You could also save time if matrix A is sparse and your algorithm for computing the successive approximations avoids operating with its zero entries, so that substantially fewer than $2n^2$ operations are required per iteration. That possibility is not illustrated here, because it requires implementation of a new data structure for sparse matrices.

Example: PDE Boundary Value Problem

The heat conduction problem that introduced Section 6.1 provides a more practical test for Jacobi and Gauss-Seidel iteration. A square metal plate is divided by an evenly spaced grid into n^2 square cells, whose center temperatures $w_{11}, ..., w_{nn}$ are studied. (The relationship between this notation and that in Section 6.1 will become clear soon.) The top, bottom, left, and right boundary cell temperatures w_{1k}, w_{nk}, w_{j1}, and w_{jn} for $j, k = 1, ..., n$ are held at known constant values, and the other w_{jk} are given the initial temperature zero. The plate is then allowed to reach an equilibrium temperature distribution, in which each interior temperature w_{jk} is the average of the four neighboring cell temperatures:

$$4\,w_{jk} - w_{j-1,\,k} - w_{j+1,\,k} - w_{j,\,k-1} - w_{j,\,k+1} = 0.$$

The equations for the interior cell temperatures, together with the boundary cell equations w_{jk} = constant, constitute an $n^2 \times n^2$ linear system $A\omega = \beta$.

This example is actually a *partial* differential equation BVP. Start with the equation

$$\frac{\partial^2 f}{\partial x^2} + \frac{\partial^2 f}{\partial y^2} = 0$$

that governs the equilibrium heat distribution $w = f(x, y)$. Introduce coordinate axes parallel to the cell boundaries, so that the temperatures w_{jk} are measured at the n^2 intersections of evenly spaced grid lines $x = x_j$ and $y = y_k$ for $j,\ k = 1, \ldots, n$. Thus, $w_{jk} = f(x_j, y_k)$. Now approximate the second partials by difference quotients, as in the Liebmann method discussed earlier. You get the same system of linear equations for the unknown w_{jk} values:

$$\frac{\partial^2 f}{\partial x^2}\bigg|_{x_j,\,y_k} \approx \frac{w_{j-1,\,k} - 2w_{jk} + w_{j+1,\,x}}{h^2} \qquad \frac{\partial^2 f}{\partial y^2}\bigg|_{x_j,\,y_k} \approx \frac{w_{j,\,k-1} - 2w_{jk} + w_{j,\,k+1}}{h^2}$$

$$0 = \frac{\partial^2 f}{\partial x^2} + \frac{\partial^2 f}{\partial y^2} \approx \frac{w_{j-1,\,k} + w_{j+1,\,k} + w_{j,\,k-1} + w_{j,\,k+1} - 4w_{jk}}{h^2}\ .$$

To describe this system, you'll need a way to correlate doubly indexed cell temperatures w_{jk} with singly indexed ω entries w_i. The scheme

$$i = j + (n - 1)k = \mathrm{sub}(j, k) \qquad w_i = w_{jk}$$

is shown in Figure 6.1.1. The boundary cell equations have the simple form w_i = the constant boundary cell temperature. That is,

• if j or $k = 1$ or n, and $h = \mathrm{sub}(j, k)$, then $a_{hh} = 1$ and b_h = constant.

```
#include "Equate2.H"

int n = 7;
int sub(int j, int k) { return j + (k - 1)*n; }

void main() {
  cout << "Solving the heat BVP for an  nxn  plate      \n"
          "by Jacobi  [1] or Gauss-Seidel iteration  [2]\n";
  cout << "Select the method  [1/2] :  ";   int M;   cin >> M;
  double T = .01;   int h,i,j,k,n2 = n*n;
  Vector X(n2);      X.MakeZero();  {          // A , B are
  Matrix A(n2,n2);   A.MakeZero();             // declared in
  Vector B(n2);      B.MakeZero();             // this block,
  for (k = 1; k <= n; ++k) {                   // so they die
    h = sub(1,k);    A[h][h] = 1;  B[h] = n - k;  // before  W is
    h = sub(n,k);    A[h][h] = 1;  B[h] = k - 1;  } // constructed.
  for (j = 2; j < n; ++j) {
    h = sub(j,1);    A[h][h] = 1;  B[h] = n - j;
    h = sub(j,n);    A[h][h] = 1;  B[h] = j - 1;
    for (k = 2; k < n; ++k) {
      h = sub(j,k);       A[h][h] =  4;
      i = sub(j-1,k);     A[h][i] = -1;
      i = sub(j+1,k);     A[h][i] = -1;
      i = sub(j,k-1);     A[h][i] = -1;
      i = sub(j,k+1);     A[h][i] = -1; }}
  if (M == 1) X = Jacobi(A,B,X,T,1);
  if (M == 2) X = Seidel(A,B,X,T,1);
  cout << "‖AX - β‖ = ";  Show(MaxNorm(A*X-B)); }
  Matrix W(n,n);
  for (j = 1; j <= n; ++j)
    for (k = 1; k <= n; ++k) {
      i = sub(j,k);  W[j][k] = X[i]; }
  cout << endl << endl;  W.Show(); }
```

Figure 7.2.4 Program to solve the heat conduction problem

The interior cell equations have the form shown earlier: for other indices j and k,

- if $h = \text{sub}(j, k)$, then $a_{hh} = 4$;
- if $i = \text{sub}(j - 1, k)$, $\text{sub}(j + 1, k)$, $\text{sub}(j, k - 1)$, or $\text{sub}(j, k + 1)$, then $a_{hi} = -1$.

All unmentioned entries a_{hi} and b_h are zero.

The MSP client program in Figure 7.2.4 sets up matrix A and vector β for $n = 7$ according to this scheme, using the Figure 6.1.1 boundary cell temperatures. Then it computes a solution vector ω by Jacobi or Gauss-Seidel iteration with tolerance $T = 0.01$, and outputs the error measure $\| A\omega - \beta \|$. Finally, it outputs the solution in array form compatible with Figure 6.1.1. You'll find the source code for this program in file **Equ2Test.CPP** on the optional diskette. Here are its results:

6.0	5.0	4.0	3.0	2.0	1.0	0.0
5.0	4.3	3.7	3.0	2.3	1.7	1.0
4.0	3.7	3.3	3.0	2.7	2.3	2.0
3.0	3.0	3.0	3.0	3.0	3.0	3.0
2.0	2.3	2.7	3.0	3.3	3.7	4.0
1.0	1.7	2.3	3.0	3.7	4.3	5.0
0.0	1.0	2.0	3.0	4.0	5.0	6.0

Figure 7.2.5 Solution of the heat conduction problem

Method	Iterations	$\|A\omega - \beta\|$
Jacobi	31	0.036
Gauss-Seidel	19	0.019

Actually, matrix A isn't *strictly* diagonally row dominant: The absolute values of most of its diagonal entries are *equal to*, not greater than, the sums of the absolute values of the remaining entries in their rows. The iterative methods converge nevertheless, but slowly. Cutting the tolerance T to 0.001 increased the iteration counts to 47 and 27, respectively, and cut the error measures by a factor of 10. The computed solution is displayed in Figure 7.2.5.

The Gauss-Seidel method required $2(n^2)^2$ operations per iteration times 19 iterations, or about 90,000 operations to compute this solution; Gauss elimination would have required about $\frac{2}{3}(n^2)^3 \approx 80,000$ operations. Thus, even if this large a tolerance is appropriate, the iterative methods are slower. You can only save time with the iterative methods if you can cut down the number of operations per iteration by avoiding arithmetic on the zero entries. In fact, that's quite simple with this example, but you lose the advantage of the ready-prepared iteration functions.

Example: Second Order Linear ODEBVP

Earlier in this chapter you saw how to use the Liebmann method to convert a second order ODE boundary value problem (BVP) into a difference equation suitable for solution by multidimensional Fix-point iteration. Starting with the problem

$$y'' = f(t, y, y') \qquad\qquad y(a) = y_0 \qquad\qquad y(b) = y^*,$$

you divide the interval $a \le t \le b$ into n subdivisions of length h:

$$h = \frac{b-a}{n} \qquad t_j = a + jh \text{ for } j = 0, ..., n \ .$$

Then you set $y_n = y^*$ and introduce approximations y_j to the solution $u(t)$ at $t = t_j$ for $j = 1, ..., n - 1$. These satisfy the difference equation

$$\frac{y_{j+1} - 2y_j + y_{j-1}}{h^2} = f\left(t_j, y_j, \frac{y_{j+1} - y_{j-1}}{2h}\right)$$

obtained when you approximate derivatives in the ODE by differential quotients. If f is linear with constant coefficients—that is,

$$f(t, y, y') = py' + qy + r$$

for some constants p, q, and r — the difference equation is also linear:

$$\frac{y_{j+1} - 2y_j + y_{j-1}}{h^2} = p \frac{y_{j+1} - y_{j-1}}{2h} + qy_j + r \ .$$

Remember that y_0 and $y_n = y^*$ are constants specified in the problem. This equation can be rewritten as an $(n - 1) \times (n - 1)$ linear system $A\eta = \beta$, where A and β have entries

$$\begin{cases} a_{jk} = 0 & \text{unless } k = j - 1, j, \text{ or } j + 1 \\ a_{j,j-1} = \frac{1}{h^2} + \frac{p}{2h} & a_{jj} = -q - \frac{2}{h^2} \quad a_{j,j+1} = \frac{1}{h^2} - \frac{p}{2h} \end{cases}$$

$$\begin{cases} b_1 = q - a_{10} y_0 \\ b_j = q & \text{unless } j = 1 \text{ or } n - 1 \\ b_{n-1} = q - a_{n-1,n} y_n \ . \end{cases}$$

A is called a *tridiagonal* matrix: All its nonzero entries lie on the diagonal, or immediately above or below it. You can solve a tridiagonal system $A\eta = \beta$ by Gauss elimination, by a special elimination algorithm for tridiagonal systems, or by the iterative methods introduced in this section. The special algorithm for tridiagonal systems is simply Gauss elimination, with the formulas adjusted to mention only the nonzero entries of A (see Reference [8, Section 6.7]). With that method, you can use a variant of the **Matrix** data structure that stores the superdiagonal, diagonal, and subdiagonal entries of A in vectors. That technique avoids wasting space storing the zero entries, and saves time by avoiding arithmetic operations with the zeroes in the matrix. It's the most efficient way to handle problems of this type, but is not covered further in this book because the tridiagonal matrix data type is not implemented here.

Success of the iterative methods depends on the diagonal row dominance of matrix A. In particular, when $1 < j < n - 1$, you want the condition

$$|a_{jj}| > |a_{j,j-1}| + |a_{j,j+1}|$$

$$\left| q + \frac{2}{h^2} \right| > \left| \frac{1}{h^2} + \frac{p}{2h} \right| + \left| \frac{1}{h^2} - \frac{p}{2h} \right|$$

to hold for small positive h values. If $h < |2/p|$, the right-hand side of this inequality is just $2/h^2$. If $q < 0$, the inequality is false for sufficiently small h values. If $q > 0$, it's true for all h, but only barely, unless q is enormous. Thus, you should expect the iterative methods to converge very slowly, if at all.

Figure 7.2.6 shows an MSP client program that compares the solutions of a linear ODEBVP obtained via the Gauss elimination, Jacobi, and Gauss-Seidel methods. Function **main** lets the user select the method, and inputs the number n of subdivisions and the tolerance T (if required). It calls **BVPSetUp** to set up the linear system corresponding to the linear BVP considered earlier in Section 7.1:

$y'' = pu' - qu - r$	$y(a) = y_0$	$y(b) = y^*$
$p = 2$	$q = -1$	$r = -3$
$a = 0$	$y_0 = -3$	
$b = 2$	$y^* = 1$	

BVPSetUp builds the vector U whose entries are the exact solution values $u(t) = -3 + 2t\, e^{t-2}$ for $t = t_1, \ldots, t_{n-1}$. These correspond to the computed approximations $y_1, \ldots, y_{n-1}$. **BVPSetUp** constructs their initial estimates for the iterative methods. The initial entries of the solution vector Y are the values of the linear function that satisfies the boundary conditions; they're updated by each iteration. After computing the approximate solution Y, the program reports the error $\|Y - U\|$. You'll find this source code in file **LnearBVP.CPP** on the optional diskette.

```
#include "GaussEl.H"              // Solving the ODEBVP
#include "Equate2.H"              //     u" = pu' + qu + r
#include    <Math.H>              // y(a) = y0    y(b) = yStar*

double p = 2;   double q    = -1;  double r = -3;
double a = 0;   double y0   = -3;
double b = 2;   double yStar = 1;   // n =  no. of subdivisions.
int    n;       double T;           // T = Tolerance.  h , k =
double h,k;                         // t step, linear  y  step.
Matrix A;                  // AY = B is the linear system.  U is
Vector B,Y,U;              // the exact BVP solution, to be compared
                           // with the approximate solution  Y .

double u(double t) {                     // Exact solution.
  return -3 + 2*t*exp(t-2); }

void BVPSetUp() {
  h = (b - a)/n;      k = (yStar - y0)/n;
  double Subdiagonal   = (1/h + p/2)/h;     // Set up the linear
  double Diagonal      = -q - 2/(h*h);      // system.
  double Superdiagonal = (1/h - p/2)/h;
  A.SetUp(n-1,n-1).MakeZero();
  for (int i = 1; i <= n-1; ++i) {
    if (i > 1) A[i][i-1]   = Subdiagonal;
    A[i][i]             = Diagonal;
    if (i < n-1) A[i][i+1] = Superdiagonal; }
  B.SetUp(n-1,1).AllEntries(r);
  B[1]    -= Subdiagonal *y0;                // Set up the linear
  B[n-1]  -= Superdiagonal*yStar;            // initial estimate
  Y.SetUp(n-1,1);  U.SetUp(n-1,1);           // Y , and the exact
  for (i = 1; i <= n-1; ++i) {               // solution  U , to
    Y[i]     = y0 + i*k;                     // be compared with
    double t =  a + i*h;                     // the approximate
    U[i]     = u(t);  }}                      // solution  Y .

void main() {
  clrscr();
  cout << "Solving   y\" = 2y' - y - 3      \n"
       "           y(0) = -3  y(2) = 1\n   \n"
       "by Gauss Elimination      [1]  \n"
       "or Jacobi iteration       [2]  \n"
       "or Gauss-Seidel iteration [3]\n\n"
       "Enter method number [1/2/3] :  ";
  int M;   cin >> M;
  cout << "n = number of subdivisions  :  ";   cin >> n;
  if (M > 1) { cout <<   "Tolerance T :  ";   cin >> T; }
  BVPSetUp();   int Code = 1;
  if (M == 1) Y = GaussElim(A,B,   Code);      // Compute  Y ,
  if (M == 2) Y = Jacobi  (A,B,Y,T,Code);      // compare with
  if (M == 3) Y = Seidel  (A,B,Y,T,Code);      // exact
  cout << "\n||Y - U|| = ";  Show(MaxNorm(Y - U));  }  // solution.
```

Figure 7.2.6 Testing GaussElim, Jacobi, and Seidel with a linear second order boundary value problem

Figure 7.2.7 shows the results from the program in Figure 7.2.3. Clearly, the iterative methods are inappropriate. This is predictable because $q < 0$: the matrix is not diagonally row dominant. However, even if you change the problem to one with a positive q — for

No. of Subdivisions	Gauss Elimination	Jacobi's Method		Gauss-Seidel Method	
	Error	Iterations	Error	Iterations	Error
8	.028	92	.027	49	.028
16	.0069	298	.0021	165	.0046
32	.0017	905	.019	519	.0086

Figure 7.2.7 Test results

example, $y'' = y' + 2y + 3$ — the results change little, because A becomes only slightly row dominant.

Because numerical solution of linear boundary value problems is so important in applications, several other versions of linear Fixpoint iteration, comparable to the Gauss-Seidel method, have been investigated. These apply to particular types of differential equations, and are described in more specialized texts. (See Reference [8, Section 7.3] and the literature cited there.)

7.3   Multidimensional Newton-Raphson Iteration

In Section 7.1 you saw that Fixpoint iteration $\xi^{(k+1)} = \gamma(\xi^{(k)})$ converges if

- $\gamma : D \to \mathbf{R}^n$ for some open set D of $\mathbf{R}^n$ containing a fixpoint $\alpha = \gamma(\alpha)$ and your initial estimate $\xi^{(0)}$,
- all components $g_j(\xi)$ of $\gamma(\xi)$ have continuous partial derivatives in D, and
- there's a Lipschitz constant $L < 1$ such that $\| J\gamma(\xi) \| \leq L$ for all in D.

Moreover, the error vectors $\varepsilon^{(k)} = \xi^{(k)} - \alpha$ satisfy the inequalities $\| \varepsilon^{(k+1)} \| \leq L \| \varepsilon^{(k)} \|$ and $\| \varepsilon^{(k)} \| \leq L^k \| \varepsilon^{(0)} \|$. This suggests that—as in the single dimensional case—you should be able to expedite the solution of an n dimensional system of equations $\phi(\xi) = 0$, where $\phi : D \to \mathbf{R}^n$, by finding an equation $\gamma(\xi) = \xi$ with the same solution α, such that $\| J\gamma(\xi) \|$ is as small as possible for ξ near α. That is, you want $J\gamma(\alpha) = 0$. Under rather general conditions this is in fact possible, and convergence will be *quadratic*: You can find M such that $\| \varepsilon^{(k+1)} \| \leq M \| \varepsilon^{(k)} \|^2$. This result, and a precise statement of its conditions, is derived under the next two headings.

Quadratic Convergence

Close analysis of the convergence of the iteration $\xi^{(k+1)} = \gamma(\xi^{(k)})$ to approximate a fixpoint α where $J\gamma(\alpha) = 0$ requires use of a *multivariable Taylor theorem*:

> Suppose g is a real valued function defined on an open convex subset D of $\mathbf{R}^n$, with continuous second partials. Then for any vectors α and β in D,

$$g(\beta) = g(\alpha) + \nabla g(\alpha)(\beta - \alpha) + \frac{1}{2} \sum_{i,j=1}^{n} \frac{\partial^2 g}{\partial x_i \, \partial x_j} \Big|_{\xi} (b_i - a_i)(b_j - a_j)$$

> where

$$\begin{bmatrix} a_1 \\ : \\ a_n \end{bmatrix} = \alpha \qquad \begin{bmatrix} b_1 \\ : \\ b_n \end{bmatrix} = \beta$$

> and ξ is between, but distinct from, α and β.

To prove this, define functions η and f from the unit interval to $\mathbf{R}^n$ and $\mathbf{R}$ by setting

$$\eta(t) = \alpha + t(\beta - \alpha) = \begin{bmatrix} h_1(t) \\ : \\ h_n(t) \end{bmatrix} \qquad f(t) = g(\eta(t))$$

so that

$$f'(t) = Jf(T) = Jg(\eta(t)) \, J\eta(t) = \nabla g(\eta(t))(\beta - \alpha) = \sum_{j=1}^{n} \frac{\partial g}{\partial x_j} \Big|_{\xi = \eta(t)} (b_j - a_j)$$

$$f''(t) = \sum_{j=1}^{n} \left[\frac{d}{dt} \frac{\partial g}{\partial x_j} \Big|_{\xi = \eta(t)} \right] (b_j - a_j) = \sum_{j=1}^{n} \left[\sum_{i=1}^{n} \frac{\partial^2 f}{\partial x_i \partial x_j} \Big|_{\xi = \eta(t)} h_i'(t) \right] (b_j - a_j)$$

$$= \sum_{i,j=1}^{n} \frac{\partial^2 g}{\partial x_i \partial x_j} \Big|_{\xi = \eta(t)} (b_i - a_i)(b_j - a_j) \ .$$

Now use the single variable Taylor theorem on function f:

$$g(\beta) = f(1) = f(0) + f'(0) + \tfrac{1}{2} f''(t) = g(\alpha) + \nabla g(\alpha)(\beta - \alpha) + \tfrac{1}{2} f''(t)$$

for some t between, but different from 0 and 1.

You can apply the multidimensional Taylor theorem to consider Fixpoint iteration $\xi^{(k+1)} = \gamma(\xi^{(k)})$ when $J\gamma(\xi) = 0$ at the fixpoint $\xi = \alpha$.

Suppose $\gamma : D \to D$ and its components have bounded continuous second partials in a convex neighborhood D of α:

$$g(\xi) = \begin{bmatrix} g_1(\xi) \\ \vdots \\ g_n(\xi) \end{bmatrix} \qquad \xi = \begin{bmatrix} x_1 \\ \vdots \\ x_n \end{bmatrix} \qquad \left| \frac{\partial^2 g}{\partial x_1\, \partial x_j} \right| \leq M$$

for a constant M and all ξ in D. Moreover, suppose $J\gamma(\alpha) = 0$. Then Fixpoint iteration converges quadratically to α if its initial estimate lies in D. Moreover, the error vectors $\varepsilon^{(k)}$ satisfy the inequality

$$\| \varepsilon^{(k+1)} \| \leq \tfrac{1}{2} n^2 M \| \varepsilon^{(k)} \|^2 \ .$$

To prove this, note that for each m, the mth row of $J\gamma(\alpha)$ is zero: $\nabla g_m(\alpha) = 0$. The desired inequality is then the result of a straightforward, if tedious, estimation of $\varepsilon^{(k+1)}$, using the multidimensional Taylor theorem:

$$\| \varepsilon^{(k+1)} \| = \| \xi^{(k+1)} - \alpha \| = \| \gamma(\xi^{(k)}) - \gamma(\alpha) \|$$

$$= \max_{m=1}^{n} \left| g_m(\xi^{(k)}) - g_m(\alpha) \right| = \left| g_m(\xi^{(k)}) - g_m(\alpha) \right| \qquad \text{for some } m$$

$$= \left| \nabla g_m(\alpha)\,(\xi^{(k)} - \alpha) + \frac{1}{2} \sum_{i,j=1}^{n} \frac{\partial^2 g_m}{\partial x_i\, \partial x_j} \bigg|_{\xi} (x_i^{(k)} - \alpha_i)\,(x_j^{(k)} - a_j) \right| \qquad \text{for some } \xi$$

$$= \frac{1}{2} \left| \sum_{i,j=1}^{n} \frac{\partial^2 g_m}{\partial x_i\, \partial x_j} \bigg|_{\xi} (x_i^{(k)} - \alpha_i)\,(x_j^{(k)} - a_j) \right| \leq \frac{1}{2} \sum_{i,j=1}^{n} \left| \frac{\partial^2 g_m}{\partial x_i\, \partial x_j} \right|_{\xi} \left| x_i^{(k)} - \alpha_i \right| \left| x_j^{(k)} - a_j \right|$$

$$\leq \frac{1}{2} \sum_{i,j=1}^{n} M \| \varepsilon^{(k)} \|^2 \leq \frac{1}{2} n^2 M \| \varepsilon^{(k)} \|^2 \ .$$

Newton-Raphson Formula

Now the question is, how can you convert an n dimensional system of equations

$$\phi(\xi) = 0 \qquad \phi(\xi) = \begin{bmatrix} f_1(\xi) \\ \vdots \\ f_n(\xi) \end{bmatrix} \qquad \xi = \begin{bmatrix} x_1 \\ \vdots \\ x_n \end{bmatrix}$$

with solution $\xi = \alpha$ into an equivalent fixpoint form $\gamma(\xi) = \xi$ with the same solution, so that $J\gamma(\alpha) = 0$ and Fixpoint iteration with function γ will converge quadratically? In the analogous single dimensional case, the Newton-Raphson method converts the equation $f(x) = 0$ to the fixpoint form $g(x) = x$, where

$$g(x) = x - \frac{f(x)}{f'(x)} = x - f'(x)^{-1} f(x) \ .$$

That suggests setting

$$\gamma(\xi) = \xi - J\phi(\xi)^{-1} \phi(\xi) \ .$$

Of course, you must assume that the components of $\phi(\xi)$ have first partials and the Jacobian $J\phi(\xi)$ is nonsingular for ξ near the solution α. If $\phi(\xi) = 0$ then clearly $\gamma(\xi) = \xi$; and if $\gamma(\xi) = \xi$ then $J\phi(\xi)^{-1}\phi(\xi) = 0$, and you get $\phi(\xi) = 0$ after multiplying by $J\phi(\xi)$. Thus, the equations $\phi(\xi) = 0$ and $\gamma(\xi) = \xi$ have the same solutions.

For the rest of this discussion, assume additionally that the components of ϕ have bounded, continuous first, second, and third partials in a convex open set D containing the solution α and your initial estimate $\xi^{(0)}$. Then the first and second partials of the components of $\gamma(\xi)$ are continuous and bounded on D because they are rational functions of $x_1, ..., x_n, f_1(\xi), ..., f_n(\xi)$ and their first, second, and third partials. To verify that $J\gamma(\alpha) = 0$, note first that

$$J\phi(\xi)\gamma(\xi) = J\phi(\xi)\xi - \phi(\xi) \ .$$

The kth entry of this vector is

$$\nabla f_k(\xi)\, \gamma(\xi) \ = \ \nabla f_k(\xi)\xi - f_k(\xi)$$

$$\sum_{j=1}^{n} \frac{\partial f_k}{\partial x_j} g_j(\xi) = \sum_{j=1}^{n} \frac{\partial f_k}{\partial x_j} x_j - f_k(\xi) \ .$$

Differentiating with respect to x_i and using the product rule, you get

$$\sum_{j=1}^{n} \frac{\partial^2 f_k}{\partial x_i\, \partial x_j} g_j(\xi) + \sum_{j=1}^{n} \frac{\partial f_k}{\partial x_j} \frac{\partial g_j}{\partial x_i} = \sum_{j=1}^{n} \frac{\partial^2 f_k}{\partial x_i\, \partial x_j} x_j + \frac{\partial f_k}{\partial x_i} - \frac{\partial f_k}{\partial x_i} = \sum_{j=1}^{n} \frac{\partial^2 f_k}{\partial x_i\, \partial x_j} x_j \ .$$

Evaluate this expression at $\xi = \alpha$ to get

$$\sum_{j=1}^{n} \frac{\partial^2 f_k}{\partial x_i\, \partial x_j}\bigg|_{\xi=\alpha} a_j + \sum_{j=1}^{n} \frac{\partial f_k}{\partial x_j}\bigg|_{\xi=\alpha} \frac{\partial g_j}{\partial x_i}\bigg|_{\xi=\alpha} = \sum_{j=1}^{n} \frac{\partial^2 f_k}{\partial x_i\, \partial x_j}\bigg|_{\xi=\alpha}$$

$$\sum_{j=1}^{n} \frac{\partial f_k}{\partial x_j}\bigg|_{\xi=\alpha} \frac{\partial g_j}{\partial x_i}\bigg|_{\xi=\alpha} = 0$$

But this is the k,ith entry of $J\phi(\alpha)J\gamma(\alpha)$, hence $J\phi(\alpha)J\gamma(\alpha) = 0$. Finally, $J\gamma(\alpha) = 0$ because $J\phi(\alpha)$ is nonsingular.

A more detailed analysis beyond the scope of this book will show that if the components of ϕ have bounded, continuous first, second, and third partials in a convex neighborhood D of α, and $J\phi(\alpha)$ is nonsingular, then $\gamma : D' \rightarrow D'$ for some convex neighborhood D' of α contained in D. (See Reference [8, Section 10.2].) Therefore, Newton-Raphson iteration

$$\xi^{(k+1)} = \xi^{(k)} - J\phi(\xi^{(k)})^{-1}\phi(\xi^{(k)})$$

will converge quadratically to α if you select an initial estimate $\xi^{(0)}$ in D'. (Unfortunately, you usually don't know how small D' is — i.e., how close you must start to the solution.)

For Newton-Raphson iteration, it's not necessary to calculate the inverse of $J\phi(\xi^{(k)})$. You can save time by carrying out each iteration in several steps:

- compute $A = J\phi(\xi^{(k)})$;
- compute $\beta = \phi(\xi^{(k)})$;
- solve the linear system $A\delta = \beta$ for δ;
- compute $\xi^{(k+1)} = \xi^{(k)} - \delta$.

Complex Newton-Raphson Iteration

You've already seen examples of *two* dimensional Newton-Raphson iteration, perhaps without realizing it. In Section 5.6 the single dimensional Newton-Raphson formula was extended to solve an equation $f(z) = 0$ for a complex root $z = a$. No justification was given earlier, other than a remark that the calculus principles on which the method was based can be extended to apply to complex functions. The complex extension is justified here on the basis of the results just derived for two dimensional real Newton-Raphson iteration. For these problems you may assume that f is a complex valued function defined on a convex neighborhood of a, $f'(a) \neq 0$, and $f'''(z)$ exists and is continuous and bounded in D. Given an initial estimate z_0, the single dimensional Newton-Raphson formula yields the sequence z_1, z_2, ... of successive approximations to a, where

$$z_{j+1} = z_j - \Delta z \qquad \Delta z = \frac{f(z_j)}{f'(z_j)} \ .$$

If you write

$$z = x + iy , \quad f(z) = u(x, y) + iv(x, y),$$

then you can compute $f'(z)$ two ways using the partials of u and v:

$$f'(z) = \lim_{\Delta x \to 0} \left[\frac{u(x + \Delta x, y) - u(x,y)}{\Delta x} + i\,\frac{v(x + \Delta x, y) - v(x,y)}{\Delta x} \right] = \frac{\partial u}{\partial x} + i\,\frac{\partial v}{\partial x}$$

$$= \lim_{\Delta y \to 0} \left[\frac{u(x, y + \Delta y) - u(x,y)}{i\,\Delta y} + i\,\frac{v(x, y + \Delta y) - v(x,y)}{i\,\Delta y} \right] = -i\,\frac{\partial u}{\partial y} + \frac{\partial v}{\partial y} \ .$$

(In both calculations, $\Delta z = \Delta x + i\,\Delta y$. In the first, you keep $\Delta y = 0$; in the second, $\Delta x = 0$.) These two equations also yield the *Cauchy-Riemann equations*:

$$\frac{\partial u}{\partial x} = \frac{\partial u}{\partial y} \qquad\qquad \frac{\partial u}{\partial y} = -\,\frac{\partial v}{\partial x}$$

Now reconsider the Newton-Raphson formula:

$$z_{j+1} = z_j + \Delta z, \qquad\qquad z_j = x_j + iy_j,$$

$$\Delta z = \Delta x + i\,\Delta y = \frac{f(z_j)}{f'(z_j)} = \frac{u + iv}{\dfrac{\partial u}{\partial x} + i\dfrac{\partial v}{\partial x}} = \frac{(u + iv)\left(\dfrac{\partial u}{\partial x} - i\dfrac{\partial v}{\partial x}\right)}{D},$$

$$D = \left(\frac{\partial u}{\partial x}\right)^2 + \left(\frac{\partial v}{\partial x}\right)^2$$

$$\Delta x = \frac{u\dfrac{\partial u}{\partial x} + v\dfrac{\partial v}{\partial x}}{D} \qquad \Delta y = \frac{v\dfrac{\partial u}{\partial x} - u\dfrac{\partial v}{\partial x}}{D}$$

In these equations, u and v and their partials are evaluated at x_j, y_j. Using the Cauchy-Riemann equations, you get

$$D = \frac{\partial u}{\partial x}\frac{\partial v}{\partial y} - \frac{\partial v}{\partial x}\frac{\partial u}{\partial y} = \det\begin{bmatrix} \dfrac{\partial u}{\partial x} & \dfrac{\partial u}{\partial y} \\[2ex] \dfrac{\partial v}{\partial x} & \dfrac{\partial v}{\partial y} \end{bmatrix}$$

$$\Delta x = \frac{u\dfrac{\partial u}{\partial y} - v\dfrac{\partial u}{\partial x}}{D} = \frac{1}{D}\det\begin{bmatrix} u & \dfrac{\partial u}{\partial y} \\[2ex] v & \dfrac{\partial v}{\partial y} \end{bmatrix} \qquad \Delta y = \frac{v\dfrac{\partial u}{\partial x} - u\dfrac{\partial v}{\partial x}}{D} = \frac{1}{D}\det\begin{bmatrix} \dfrac{\partial u}{\partial y} & u \\[2ex] \dfrac{\partial v}{\partial y} & v \end{bmatrix}.$$

These equations show that Δx and Δy are the solutions of the 2×2 linear system

$$\begin{bmatrix} \dfrac{\partial u}{\partial x} & \dfrac{\partial u}{\partial y} \\[2ex] \dfrac{\partial v}{\partial x} & \dfrac{\partial v}{\partial y} \end{bmatrix}\begin{bmatrix} \Delta u \\ \Delta y \end{bmatrix} = \begin{bmatrix} u \\ v \end{bmatrix}.$$

The left-hand matrix is exactly the Jacobian $Jf(z_j)$ that you get when you regard $f(z)$ as a function

$$f(z) = \begin{bmatrix} u(z) \\ v(z) \end{bmatrix} \qquad z = \begin{bmatrix} x \\ y \end{bmatrix}.$$

That is, the single dimensional complex Newton-Raphson formula is the same as the corresponding two dimensional real formula.

MSP Function NR2

The multidimensional Newton-Raphson algorithm is implemented by
MSP function **NR2**, shown in Figure 7.3.1. Its prototype is

```
Vector NR2 (Vector FJF (Vector& X,    // Find a root of F by
                        Matrix& JF),  // Newton-Raphson iteration.
            Vector X,                 // Initial estimate.
            double T,                 // Tolerance.
            int&   Code);             // Status code.
```

To find a solution to an n dimensional system of equations

$$\phi(\xi) = 0 \qquad \phi(\xi) = \begin{bmatrix} f_1(\xi) \\ : \\ f_n(\xi) \end{bmatrix} \qquad \xi = \begin{bmatrix} x_1 \\ : \\ x_n \end{bmatrix}$$

you must provide a function

```
Vector FJF (Vector& X, Matrix& JF).
```

Given a vector $\mathbf{X} = \xi$, **FJF** must calculate the entries of the Jacobian
matrix $\mathbf{JF} = J\phi(\xi)$, then return the vector $\phi(\xi)$. You specify an initial
estimate $\mathbf{X}$ and a tolerance $\mathbf{T}$ just as for the functions **Fixpoint2**,
Jacobi, and **Seidel** described in Sections 7.1 and 7.2. Like those
functions, **NR2** returns a status **Code** variable. The version of **NR2**
on the optional diskette also includes statements to provide intermediate output: Not just the number of iterations if you set **Code** = 1
on entry, but also a report of $\| \phi(\xi^{(k)}) \|$, det $J\phi(\xi)$, and $\| \xi^{(k+1)} - \xi^{(k)} \|$
for each iteration if you set **Code** = 2. These statements were omit-
ted from Figure 7.3.1 because they obscure the structure of the function, which exactly matches that of the implementations of fixpoint
methods introduced earlier in this chapter and in Chapter 5.

  NR2 performs Gauss Elimination through the statements

```
F = FJF (X,JF);
Det = Down (JF,R);
dX = Vector (Up (JF,~F,R));
```

The first computes $\mathbf{F} = \phi(\xi)$ and $\mathbf{JF} = J\phi(\xi)$. The second performs the
downward pass on the matrix $\mathbf{JF} = J\phi(\xi)$, returning the determinant
Det and preparing **JF** and the **RowFinder R** for the upward pass.
While the determinant isn't used by the **NR2** version displayed in

```
Vector NR2(Vector FJF(Vector& X,          // Find a root of  F  by
                      Matrix& JF),        // Newton-Raphson iteration.
           Vector X,                      // Initial estimate.
           double T,                      // Tolerance.
           int&   Code) {                 // Status code.
  Vector F,dX;  Matrix JF;                // JF  is the Jacobian.
  Scalar Det;   RowFinder R;              // Det  is the determinant.
  double M;     int n = 0;                // n  counts iterations.
  do {
       F   = FJF(X,JF);                   // Solve the linear system
       Det = Down(JF,R);                  // JF(X) dX = F(X)
       dX  = Vector(Up(JF,~F,R));         // to get  dX .
       M   = MaxNorm(dX);
       X -= dX; }                         // Set  Code = 0  to report
    while (++n < 1000 && M >= T);         // success, or  -1  if the
  Code = (M < T ? 0 : -1);                // desired accuracy is not
  return X; }                             // achieved after  n = 1000 .
```

Figure 7.3.1 MSP multidimensional Newton-Raphson function NR2

Figure 7.3.1, it's an optional intermediate output in the version on the diskette. (An extremely large or small determinant could reveal that a Jacobian is nearly singular, which could explain poor convergence properties in some examples.) The third statement performs the upward pass, solving the linear system $A\delta = \beta$ with $A = J\phi(\xi)$ and $\beta = \phi(\xi)$, returning the solution $\delta = \mathbf{dX}$. Because MSP function **Up** was written to solve systems of the form $AY = B$ with matrices Y and B, it's necessary to cast vector **F** to type **Matrix**, and the return value back to type **Vector**. Because MSP **Vector** objects are regarded as rows, the first cast is performed by the transpose operator ~.

Besides the desirability of the determinant as an intermediate output, there's another reason to split the downward and upward passes in the Newton-Raphson algorithm. Often, the Jacobian doesn't vary much from one step to the next, so you can speed up execution by using the same matrix in the system $A\delta = \phi(\xi)$ for several steps in succession. That saves the time required for several downward passes. You may want to experiment with that: For example, perform the downward pass only when the iteration count n is even.

Examples

The nonlinear system considered earlier in Section 7.1 provides a good test for Newton-Raphson iteration: finding a root of the function

$$\phi(x) = \begin{bmatrix} x - \sin(x + y) \\ y - \cos(x - y) \end{bmatrix} \qquad \xi = \begin{bmatrix} x \\ y \end{bmatrix} .$$

The components of ϕ and its Jacobian

$$J\phi(\xi) = \begin{bmatrix} 1 - \cos(x + y) & -\cos(x + y) \\ \sin(x - y) & 1 - \sin(x - y) \end{bmatrix}$$

are computed by the routine

```
Vector FJF(Vector& X,                // Compute function value
           Matrix& JF) {             // F(X) and Jacobian
   Vector F(2); JF.SetUp(2,2);       // JF(X) for Newton-
   F[1] = X[1] - sin(X[1] + X[2]);   // Raphson test.
   F[2] = X[2] - cos(X[1] - X[2]);
   JF[1][2] = - cos(X[1] + X[2]);
   JF[1][1] = 1 + JF[1][2];
   JF[2][1] = sin(X[1] - X[2]);
   JF[2][2] = 1 - JF[2][1];
   return F; }
```

The solution was computed by an MSP client program like the one in Figure 7.1.1 that tested Fixpoint iteration. Their only essential difference is in the statements

```
X = Fixpoint2(G ,X,T,Code)    \\ Fixpoint iteration
X = NR2      (FJF,X,T,Code)    \\ Newton-Raphson iteration
```

You'll find the code in file **Equ2Test.CPP** on the optional diskette. It used the same initial estimate $x = y = 1$ and tolerance $T = 10^{-6}$, but required only 3 iterations to compute the same solution, compared with 9 for Fixpoint iteration.

The Liebmann method for second order boundary value problems (BVP), described earlier in this chapter, also provides a good test. The BVP

$$y'' = f(t, y, y') \qquad y(a) = y_0 \qquad y(b) = y^*$$

leads to the equations $\psi(\eta) = 0$, where

$$\psi(\eta) = \begin{bmatrix} p_1(\eta) \\ : \\ p_{n-1}(\eta) \end{bmatrix} \qquad \eta = \begin{bmatrix} y_1 \\ : \\ y_{n-1} \end{bmatrix} \qquad y_n = y^*$$

$$h = \frac{b-a}{n} \qquad\qquad t_j = a + jh \qquad\qquad \text{for } j = 0, ..., n$$

$$p_j(\eta) = y_{j+1} - 2y_j + y_{j-1} - h^2 f\left(t_j, y_j, \frac{y_{j+1} - y_{j-1}}{2h}\right) \quad \text{for } j = 1, ..., , n-1 .$$

Liebmann's method is tested by an MSP client program like the one in Figure 7.1.5 that tested Fixpoint iteration. They differ in the statements

```
X = Fixpoint2(G,X,T,Code)    \\ Fixpoint iteration
X = NR2     (PJP,X,T,Code)    \\ Newton-Raphson iteration
```

You'll find its code in file **BVP.CPP** on the optional diskette. **NR2** requires a routine **Vector PJP(Vector& X, Matrix& JP)** to compute the components of $\psi(\eta)$ and the Jacobian $J\psi(\eta)$. The latter is the matrix whose i,jth entry is

$$\frac{\partial p_j}{\partial y_k} = 0 \quad \text{unless } k = j-1, j, \text{ or } j+1$$

$$\frac{\partial p_j}{\partial y_{j-1}} = 1 + \frac{h}{2}\frac{\partial f}{\partial y'} \qquad \frac{\partial p_j}{\partial y_j} = -2 - h^2\frac{\partial f}{\partial y} \qquad \frac{\partial p_j}{\partial y_{j+1}} = 1 - \frac{h}{2}\frac{\partial f}{\partial y'} .$$

The f partials in these equations are all evaluated at

$$t_j, \; y_j, \; \frac{y_{j+1} - y_{j-1}}{2h} \quad .$$

PJP must in turn call a function

```
double f(double t, double y, double yp,
   double& dfdy, double& dfdyp)
```

to return the right-hand side $f(t, y, y')$ of the ODE and compute its partials **dfdy** = $\partial f/\partial y$ and **dfdyp** = $\partial f/\partial y'$. The code for function **PJP** is shown in Figure 7.3.2.

The Section 7.1 example ODE

$$y'' = f(t, y, y') = \frac{2}{y' + 1}$$

```
Vector PJP(Vector& Y,                    // Newton-Raphson function
           Matrix& JP) {                 // for Liebmann's method.
    int m = Y.HighIndex();
    Vector P(m);  JP.SetUp(m,m).MakeZero();       // Jacobian  JP
    for (int k = 1; k <= m; ++k) {                // is sparse.
        double Ykm1 = (k == 1 ? y0    : Y[k-1]);  // Y[0] = y0 .
        double Ykp1 = (k == m ? yStar : Y[k+1]);  // Y[n] = y* .
        double Ypk = (Ykp1 - Ykm1)/(2*h);         // Ypk = y'
        double dfdy,dfdyp;                         // at  t[k] .
        P[k] = Ykp1 - 2*Y[k] + Ykm1               // Compute the
            - h*h*f(t[k],Y[k],Ypk,dfdy,dfdyp);    // entries of  P
        if (k > 1) JP[k][k-1] = 1 + h*dfdyp/2;    // and the non-
        JP[k][k] = -2 - h*h*dfdy;                 // zero entries
        if (k < m) JP[k][k+1] = 1 - h*dfdyp/2; }  // of the
    return P; }                                    // Jacobian.
```

Figure 7.3.2 Function PJP for Liebmann's method

is implemented by the code

```
double f(double t, double y, double yp,    // Compute the right-
         double& dfdy, double& dfdyp) {    // hand side of the
    double d = yp + 1;                      // ODE , and its
    dfdy = 0; dfdyp = -2/(d*d);             // partials dfdy
    return 2/d; }                           // and dfdy' .
```

Executed with the same boundary values, tolerance $T = 0.0001$ and linear initial estimate as the earlier Fixpoint test, the Liebmann program with Newton-Raphson iteration yielded these results:

Number of Subdivisions	Number of Iterations	Error
5	3	.0012
10	2	.00032
20	2	.00008

The improvement is astounding!

Appendix:
Selected Source Code

This Appendix contains some excerpts from the MSP source code that seemed inappropriate for the main part of the text, yet too important to relegate to the accompanying diskette. Each excerpt is discussed to some extent in the cited section of the text, and detailed commentary is provided in the source code itself.

The last section of the appendix describes the optional diskette that contains all the MSP source code files and many test routines.

A.1   Vector and Matrix Display Output Functions

The **Vector** module display output function **Show** is described in Section 3.3. Like most display functions that provide neat row and/or column output, its source code is uninstructively complicated, so it was not included in the main text. Because of its utility, however, it's shown here. It uses Library functions **strlen**, **gettextinfo**, and the data type **textinfo**, which are declared in header files **String.H** and **ConIO.H**. While **strlen** is a standard C feature, the other functions are specific to Turbo C++.

```
Vector& Vector::Show(                    // Standard output using
    char*   Format,                      // printf Format string.
    Boolean RowFormat,                   // Row or column format?
    char*   Name) const {                // Name to display.  For
  if (Low > High) {                      // an empty vector, print
    if (!StrEmpty(Name))                 // the name and the empty
      cout << Name << " :  ";            // set symbol φ .  Treat
    cout << 'φ'; }                       // an empty  Format  as
  if (StrEmpty(Format))                  // a default.  NumL  and
    Format = DefaultScalarFormat;        // L0  will be the max
```

```
int NumL, L0 = strlen(Name);          // width of index  i  and
if (L0 != 0) {                         // the left margin width.
  L0 += 4;                             // If the margin contains
  if (!RowFormat) {                    // Name , it also con-
    int DL = Digits(Low);             // tains 4  characters
    int DH = Digits(High);            // " : " .  In column
    NumL   = max(DL,DH);              // format, it contains
    L0     += NumL + 2; }}            // numeral i and 2
text_info T;  gettextinfo(&T);         // characters "[ ]" .
Boolean NL = False;
int    L = L0;                         // L  is the number of
for (int i = Low; i <= High;) {        // characters output.
  if (NL) {                            // Does this iteration
      cout << endl;                    // start a new line (with
      L = L0; }                        // left margin)?
    else                               // If not, assume the next
      NL = True;                       // one does.
  if (L0 !=0 &&
    (!RowFormat || i == Low)) {        // If required, write
      cout << Name;                    // Name , and perhaps the
      if (!RowFormat)                  // index, in the left
        cout << '[' <<                 // margin.
          setw(NumL) << i << ']';
      cout << " : "; }
    else if (L == L0)                  // Otherwise, if at margin
      cout << setw(L0) << "";          // fill it with blanks.
  char* S = ForShow(This[i],Format);   // Prepare output.  This
  if (GetError( )) return This;        // allocates S  storage.
  if (!RowFormat) {                    // In column format, out-
      cout << S;  ++i; }               // put a vector entry.
    else {                             // In row format,
      int dL = strlen(S);
      if (L + dL < T.screenwidth) {    // if there's room,
          cout << S;  ++i;             // output a vector entry.
          if (i <= High) {             // For each output except
            L += dL;                   // the last,
            if (L + 2
              < T.screenwidth) {       // if there's room,
                cout << "  ";          // write two blanks, and
                L += 2;                // prepare to continue on
                NL = False; }}}}       // the same line.
    delete S; }                        // Release S  storage.
  cout << endl;
  return This; }
```

The **Matrix** module display output function **Show**, described in Section 3.5, is based on the analogous **Vector** function just displayed. It also uses Library functions **strcpy**, **strcat**, and **sprintf** which are declared in header files **String.H** and **StdIO.H**. Here's its source code:

```
Matrix& Matrix::Show(              // Standard output using
    char* Format,                  // printf Format string.
    char* Name) const {
  if (Low > HighRow) {             // For an empty matrix,
    if (!StrEmpty(Name))           // print the name and the
      cout << Name << " : ";       // empty set symbol  φ .
    cout << 'φ'; }
  int L = Digits(Low);             // m = the maximum number
  int H = Digits(HighRow);         // of digits necessary for
  int m = max(L,H);                // the row index.
  char* S = new char[7];                // Index numeral.
  char* T = new char[strlen(Name) + m + 3];  // Row caption.
  for (int i = Low; i <= HighRow; ++i) {     // If  Name  is
    strcpy(T,Name);                          // specified,
    if (!StrEmpty(T)) {                      // construct for
      strcat(T,"[" );                        // each row a
      sprintf(S,"% d",i);                    // caption
      for (int j = 1; j <= m - strlen(S); ++j)  // containing
        strcat(T," ");                       // Name  and
      strcat(T, S);                          // index.
      strcat(T,"]" ); }
    This[i].Show(Format,True,T); }  // True  means row format.
  delete S;  delete T;
  return This; }
```

A.2 Vector and Matrix Stream Input/Output Operators

The **Vector** module stream input/output operators are described in Section 3.3, along with the MSP file format. The code for the output operator **<<** defines the file format. Before it selects scientific notation, it saves the previous format settings. It restores them after outputting the vector. For formatting details, see the Turbo C++ *Programmer's Guide* (Reference [5]) and Lippman's book (Reference [29, Appendix A]. The logic of the input operator is like that of the assignment operator discussed in Section 3.3: **>>** deletes the target vector array, reads new index bounds, sets up a new array, then reads its entries. If there is insufficient memory for the new array, it returns without inputting.

```
ostream& operator<<(ostream& Target,      // Output the source
                const Vector& Source) {    // vector to the
  int OldFormat = Target.setf(             // target stream:
    ios::scientific,ios::floatfield);      // overload << .
  int OldPrecision = Target.precision( );  // Select 15 digit
  Target.precision(14);                    // scientific nota-
  int Low  = Source.LowIndex( );           // tion and save old
  int High = Source.HighIndex( );          // format settings.
  Target << Low  << endl;
  Target << High << endl;                  // Write the index
  for (int i = Low; i <= High; ++i)        // bounds, then the
    Target << Source[i] << endl;           // entries, followed
  Target.precision(OldPrecision);          // by newlines.
  Target.setf(OldFormat,ios::floatfield);  // Restore the old
  return Target; }                         // format settings.

istream& operator>>(istream& Source,       // Input the target vector
                Vector& Target) {          // from the source stream:
  delete Target.Array;                     // overload >> .
  int Low,High;                            // Delete the old array,
  Source >> Low >> High;                   // read the new index
  Target.SetUp(High,Low);                  // bounds, and set up the
  if (GetError( )) return Source;          // new array.  Quit if out
  for (int i = Low; i <= High; ++i)        // of memory.  When all
    Source >> Target[i];                   // set up, read the vector
  return Source; }                         // entries, one by one.
```

The **Matrix** module stream input/output operators, described in Section 3.5, are based on the analogous **Vector** module operators just displayed. Again, the code for the output operator << defines the matrix file format. Here is the source code; it's very similar to that of the **Vector** operations:

```
ostream& operator<<(ostream& Target,       // Output the source
                const Matrix& Source) {     // matrix to the
  int Low     = Source.LowIndex( );         // target stream:
  int HighRow = Source.HighRowIndex( );     // overload << .
  int HighCol = Source.HighColIndex( );
  Target << Low     << endl;                // Write the index
  Target << HighRow << endl;                // bounds,
  Target << HighCol << endl;
```

```
for (int i = Low; i <= HighRow; ++i)        // then each row, in
  Target << Source[i];                      // turn, followed by
return Target; }                            // newlines.


istream& operator>>(istream& Source,        // Input the target
                    Matrix& Target) {       // matrix from the
int m = Target.HighRow-Target.Low+1;        // source stream:
delete [m] Target.Row;                      // overload >> .
int Low,HighRow,HighCol;                    // Delete  m  old
Source >> Low >> HighRow >> HighCol;        // rows.  Read new
Target.SetUp(HighRow,HighCol,Low);          // index bounds, set
if (GetError( )) return Source;             // up the new rows.
for (int i = Low; i <= HighRow; ++i)        // Quit if out of
  Source >> Target[i];                      // memory.  When set
return Source; }                            // up, read each row.
```

A.3 Selected MSP Header Files

Some MSP header files are listed and described in detail in the text.
Others are less instructive because they contain only function prototypes. There's no need to list them in the text. However, they provide
a good index to the accompanying diskette, so they're listed here, in
alphabetical order.

Eigenval.H

```
//****************************************************************
//                      Eigenval.H
#ifndef Eigenval_H
#define Eigenval_H
#include "GaussEl.H"
#include "Polynom.H"
#include "Equate1.H"
Polynom CharPoly(            // Return the characteristic poly-
  const Matrix& A);          // nomial of  A .  Signal error and
                             // return empty if  A  isn't square.

Vector Eigenvalues(          // Return a vector consisting of the
        Vector& M,           // eigenvalues of  A  and enter
  const Matrix& A,           // their multiplicities in vector
        double  T,           // M .  Use  T  and  Code  as in
        int&    Code);       // Roots .
#endif
```

Equate1.H

```
//******************************************************************
//                        Equate1.H
#ifndef Equate1_H
#define Equate1_H
#include "Polynom.H"
#include    <Math.H>
Boolean Bracket(double& xL,              // Find a bracketing in-
                double& xR,              // terval [xL,xR] of
                double  F(double),       // length ≥ T within
                double  T);              // the specified one.
                                         // Return  True  to
                                         // report success.
double Bisect(double f(double),          // Return an approximation
              double xL,                 // x  to a root of  f ,
              double xR,                 // computed by the
              double T,                  // bisection method.
              int&   Code = 0);
Scalar Fixpoint(Scalar g(double),        // Return an approxima-
                Scalar x,                // tion to a fixpoint of
                double T,                // g ,  computed by
                int&   Code = 0);        // fixpoint iteration.
Scalar NR(Scalar FdF(Scalar   x,         // Return an approximation
                     Scalar& dF),        // to a root of  f ,
          Scalar x,                      // computed by Newton-
          double T,                      // Raphson iteration.
          int&   Code = 0);
double NRBisect(double f(double,double&),    // Return an approxi-
                double xL,                   // mation to a root
                double xR,                // of  f  computed by the
                double T,                 // hybrid Newton-Raphson
                int&   Code = 0);         // Bisection method.
Scalar Secant(Scalar f(Scalar),          // Return an approximation
              Scalar x0,                 // to a root of  f ,
              Scalar x1,                 // computed by the Secant
              double T,                  // method.
              int&   Code = 0);
Boolean BracketPoly(double&  xL,         // Find a bracketing in-
                    double&  xR,         // terval [xL,xR] of
                    const Polynom& F,    // length ≥  T within
                    double   T);         // the specified one.
                                         // Return  True  to
                                         // report success.
```

```
Scalar NR(const Polynom& F,         // Return an approximation
              Scalar   x,           // to a root of  f ,
              double   T,           // computed by Newton-
              int&     Code = 0);   // Raphson iteration.
double NRBH(const Polynom& F,       // Return an approximation
              double   xL,          // to a root of  F ,
              double   xR,          // computed by the hybrid
              double   T,           // Newton-Raphson
              int&     Code);       // Bisection method.
double CauchyBound(const Polynom& F); // Return Cauchy's bound
                                    // for the roots of  P .
Vector RealRoots(Polynom F,         // Return a vector of all
              double   S,           // the real roots of  F ,
              double   T,           // approximated by  NRBH .
              int&     Code);       // Ignore any two roots
                                    // separated by <  S .
void Polish(Vector&  Root,          // Root  contains approxi-
         const Polynom& F,          // mations to roots of
              double   T,           // F .  Improve them,
              int&     Code);       // using  NRH .
Vector Multiplicities(Vector   x,   // Return a vector consis-
                   Polynom P,       // ting of the multiplici-
                   double  E);      // ties of the  x[i]  as
                                    // roots of  P .  Regard
                                    // z = 0  if  ||z|| <  E .
Scalar NRHStep(const Polynom& F,    // Return an approximation
              Scalar   x,           // to a root of  F ,  com-
              double   T,           // puted by Newton-Raphson
              int&     Code);       // iteration, controlling
                                    // overstep.
Vector Roots(Polynom F,             // Return a vector of all
              double   T,           // the roots of  F ,  as
              int&     Code);       // approximated by
                                    // NRHStep .

#endif
```

Equate2.H

```
//*************************************************************
//                         Equate2.H
#ifndef Equate2_H
#define Equate2_H
#include "Matrix.H"
Vector Fixpoint2(Vector G(Vector),      // Return an approxima-
                 Vector X,              // tion to a fixpoint of
                 double T,              // G , computed by fix-
                 int&   Code);          // point iteration.
Vector Jacobi(const Matrix& A,          // Return an approximation
              const Vector& B,          // to a solution of  AX =
                    Vector  X,          // B , computed by Jacobi
                    double  T,          // iteration.
                    int&    Code);
Vector Seidel(const Matrix& A,          // Return an approximation
              const Vector& B,          // to a solution of  AX =
                    Vector  X,          // B , computed by Gauss-
                    double  T,          // Seidel iteration.
                    int&    Code);
Vector NR2(Vector FJF(Vector& X,        // Return an approximation
                      Matrix& JF),      // to a root of  F ,
           Vector X,                    // computed by Newton-
           double T,                    // Raphson iteration.
           int&   Code);
#endif
```

GaussEl.H

```
//*************************************************************
//                         GaussEl.H
#ifndef GaussEl_H
#define GaussEl_H
#include "Matrix.H"
class RowFinder {
  private:
    int  Low;                           // Index bounds for
    int  High;                          // row finder entries.
    int* Array;                         // Storage for entries.
  public:
    int& operator [ ](int k) const;     // Entry selector.
```

```
    RowFinder& SetUp(int Hi,          // Set the index bounds
                   int Lo = 1);       // and allocate storage.
    RowFinder( );                     // Default constructor.
   ~RowFinder( );                     // Destructor.
    void Swap(int i,                  // Interchange entries
             int j); };               // i  and  j .
```

//***
// Gauss elimination routines

```
Vector GaussElim(Matrix A,            // Return the solution  X  of
                 Vector B,            // the linear system  AX = B .
                 int&  Code);         // Set status report  Code .
Scalar Down(Matrix& A,                // Downward pass on  A . Max.
            RowFinder& Row,           // col. pivoting if  Code = 0 .
            int& Code = 0);           // Return  det A ,  A  with
                                      // stored multipliers, and row
                                      // finder. Set status  Code .
Scalar det(Matrix A);                 // Determinant of  A .
Matrix Up(const Matrix& A,            // Upward pass on  AX = B :
               Matrix& B,             // return  X .  A  is  mxm ,
          const RowFinder& Row);      // X  and  B  are  mxn .
                                      // A  and  Row  have been
                                      // prepared by  Down .
Matrix Solve(Matrix A,                // Return  X  such that  AX =
             Matrix B,                // B ,  where  A  is  mxm  and
             int&  Code);             // X  and  B  are  mxn .  Use
                                      // Code  as in  Down .
Scalar LU(Matrix& L,                  // Return  det A,  and the  L, U
          Matrix& U,                  // decomposition of  A  if all its
          Matrix  A,                  // principal minors are nonsingular.
          int&  Code);               // Set  Code  like  GaussElim .
int GaussJordan                       // Return  rank A  and the reduced echelon
   (Matrix& A,                        // form of system  AX = B .  A  is  mxn  and
    Vector& B,                        // X , B  are  nxl .  Scalars with norm <  T
    double  T,                        // are regarded as zero. Set status  Code =
    int&  Code);                      // 2 :  index error,   1 :  many solutions,
                                      // 0 :  one solution,  -1 :  no solution.
Matrix Inverse(Matrix A);             // Return  A  inverse if it exists,
                                      // else an empty matrix.
Matrix operator^(Matrix A,            // Return  A^n.
               int  n);
Matrix& operator^=(Matrix& A,         // Raise  A  to the  nth power.
                 int   n);
```

```
Matrix Hilbert(int n);          // Return the  nxn  Hilbert matrix.
Matrix InvHilbert(int n);       // Return the inverse of the  nxn
                                // Hilbert matrix.

#endif
```

RealFunc.H

```
//*****************************************************************
//                          RealFunc.H
#ifndef    RealFunc_H
#define    RealFunc_H
#include   "Scalar.H"
long double Factorial (int n)    // n!
double Binomial(double x,        // Binomial coefficient  x
                int   m);        // over  m .
double Root(double b,            // b^(1/r) .
            double r);
double logbase(double b,         // Base  b  logarithm of  x .
               double x);
double coth(double x);           // Hyperbolic cotangent.
double sech(double x);           // Hyperbolic secant.
double csch(double x);           // Hyperbolic cosecant.
double ArgSinh(double x);        // Inverse hyperbolic sine.
double ArgCosh(double x);        // Inverse hyperbolic cosine.
double ArgTanh(double x);        // Inverse hyperbolic tangent.
double ArgCoth(double x);        // Inverse hyperbolic cotangent.
double ArgSech(double x);        // Inverse hyperbolic secant.
double ArgCsch(double x);        // Inverse hyperbolic cosecant.
double cot(double x);            // Cotangent.
double sec(double x);            // Secant.
double csc(double x);            // Cosecant.
double acot(double x);           // Inverse cotangent.
double asec(double x);           // Inverse secant.
double acsc(double x);           // Inverse cosecant.
#endif
```

A.4   Example Mathematical Function with Intermediate Output

The text often displays intermediate output from MSP functions to demonstrate convergence of iterative processes, failure of various methods, etc. The code required to produce intermediate output is elementary, but often so long that it overshadows more important

aspects of the MSP functions. Therefore, the intermediate output features have been purged from source code shown in the text. The
versions on the accompanying diskette, however, contain all those
features. To show how they're constructed from those shown in the
text, the diskette version of function **Bisect** is displayed here. You
can compare it with the version displayed in Section 5.2.

```
double Bisect(double f(double),     // Return an approximation
              double xL,            // x  to a root  p  of  f
              double xR,            // such that  xL ≤ x ≤ xR
              double T,             // and  |x - p| < T ,
              int&   Code) {        // computed by the
  if (Code > 1)                     // bisection method. If
    cout << " \nItera- \ntion    " // Code > 1 ,  display
      "xL            xR         "   // intermediate results,
      " f(xL)    xR - xL\n";        // with a heading. If
  char* Form = "% - #15.7g";        // Code = 1 ,  report the
  int   n    = 0;                   // number  n  of itera-
  double yL  = f(xL);               // tions. Set  Code = 0
  double dx,x,y;                    // to report success, or
  do {                              // = -1  if the desired
    dx = xR - xL;                   // accuracy is not
    if (Code > 1) {                 // achieved after  2049
      cout << setw(5) << n << " "; // iterations.
      Show(xL,Form);   Show(xR,Form);
      Show(f(xL));     cout << " ";
      Show(dx);        cout << endl; }
    if (dx >= T) {                  // xM is the interval
      x = (xL + xR)/2;  y = f(x);   // midpoint. If  f
      if (Sign(yL) = = Sign(y)) {   // doesn't change sign on
        xL = x;  yL = y; }          // the left half, discard
      else                         // it;  else discard the
        xR = x; }}                  // right half. Do at most
    while (++n < 2049 && dx >= T); // 2049  iterations.
  if (Code > 1) cout << endl;       // Report the number
    else if (Code = = 1) cout <<    // n  of iterations,
      setw(4) << n << " iterations\n";// if requested.
  if (dx < T) Code = 0;             // Report success, or
    else Code = 1;                  // failure to converge.
  return xL; }                      // Return left endpoint.
```

The most detailed intermediate output format is designed for use
with real scalars. To handle complex scalars, you may want to
change the formats.

A.5   RowFinder Class Member Functions

Since the **RowFinder** class member functions, described in Section
6.4, behave almost exactly like their Section 3.3 **Vector** counterparts, it seemed unnecessary to include their source code in the text
proper. However, such basic code should be accessible, so the functions are listed here. It's contained in file **GaussEl.CPP**, on the
diskette. Their prototypes are in header file **GaussEl.H**, already
listed in Section A.3.

```
//*************************************************************
//  RowFinder  member functions

int& RowFinder::operator[ ] (int k)     // Entry selector:  over-
    const {                             // load  [ ] .  Adjust for
    return Array[k-Low]; }              // lower index  != 0 .
RowFinder& RowFinder::SetUp(int Hi,     // Set index bounds and
                     int Lo) {          // allocate storage.
  Low = Lo;  High = Hi;
  int n = High - Low + 1;              // Allocate  n  entries.
  Array = new int[n];                  // If free memory is ex-
  if (n > 0 && Array = = NULL) {       // hausted, set the error
    SetError(OutOfMemory);             // signal and set up an
    Low = 0;  High = -1; }             // empty vector.
  for (int i = Low; i <= High; ++i)    // Initialize row finder
    This[i] = i;                       // to identity
  return This; }                       // permutation.
RowFinder::RowFinder( ) {              // Default constructor:
  Low  = 0;                            // initialize an empty
  High = -1;                           // row finder.
  Array = NULL; }
RowFinder::~RowFinder( ) {             // Destructor.
  int n = High - Low + 1;
  delete [n] Array; }
void RowFinder::Swap(int i,            // Interchange entries  i
                 int j) {              // and  j .
  int  T  = This[i];
  This[i] = This[j];  This[j] = T; }
```

A.6   Optional Diskette

This appendix contains a list of the files on the optional diskette
with label **MSP&Tests** that accompanies this book. Subdirectory
MSP contains the MSP header and source code files. All routines

listed in the book are here, and quite a few which were not listed there for reasons of space or redundancy. Subdirectory **Tests** contains many routines that test or demonstrate various MSP features. A few of these were mentioned explicitly, or even listed, in the text. Most, however, were used during MSP development to check out its individual routines. All code on the diskette is documented, or self-documenting, in the style used in the text. Individual .CPP files generally contain source code for many routines.

To obtain the diskette, fill out the coupon at the end of the book and send it directly to the author.

Volume MSP&Tests

Subdirectory MSP

Eigenval.H	Eigenval.CPP
Equate1 .H	Equate1 .CPP
Equate2 .H	Equate2 .CPP
GaussEl .H	GaussEl .CPP
General .H	General .CPP
Matrix .H	MatrixL .CPP
	MatrixM .CPP
	Polynom .CPP
Polynom .H	RealFunc.CPP
RealFunc.H	ScCmplex.CPP
ScCmplex.H	ScDouble.CPP
ScDouble.H	VectorL .CPP
Vector .H	VectorM .CPP

Subdirectory Tests

BVP .CPP	GausTest.In3	PolyTst2.CPP
CompTest.CPP	GenTest .CPP	RealFTst.CPP
EigenTst.CPP	Legendre.CPP	ScaTest .CPP
Equ1Test.CPP	LnearBVP.CPP	SinTest .CPP
Equ2Test.CPP	Masking .CPP	SqrtTest.CPP
FPError .CPP	MathErr .CPP	Timing .CPP
GausTest.CPP	MatTestL.CPP	VecTestL.CPP
GausTest.In	MatTestM.CPP	VecTestM.CPP
GausTest.In2	PolyTest.CPP	VecTstL2.CPP

References

[1]   Blaise Computing Inc., *C ASYNCH MANAGER Serial Communications Support, Version 3.0: Reference Manual,* 1987.

[2]   Blaise Computing Inc., *Turbo C TOOLS Function Support for Turbo C, Version 6.00: Reference Manual,* 1990.

[3]   Borland International, Inc., *Turbo Assembler, Version 2.0: Reference Guide, Quick Reference Guide, User's Guide,* 1990.

[4]   Borland International, Inc., *Turbo C 1.5 Run-Time Library Support,* 1988. This is also available for Turbo C++.

[5]   Borland International, Inc., *Turbo C++, Version 1.00: Getting Started, Programmer's Guide, Reference Guide, User's Guide,* 1990.

[6]   Borland International, Inc., *Turbo Debugger, Version 2.0: User's Guide,* 1990.

[7]   Borland International, Inc., *Turbo Profiler, Version 1.0: User's guide,* 1990.

[8]   Richard L. Burden and J. Douglas Faires, *Numerical Analysis,* 3rd ed., Prindle, Weber and Schmidt, 1985.

[9]   Choi Man-Duen, "Tricks or Treats with the Hilbert Matrix," *American Mathematical Monthly,* XC (1983), 301-312.

[10] S. D. Conte and Carl de Boor, *Elementary Numerical Analysis: An Algorithmic Approach,* 3rd ed., McGraw-Hill, 1980.

[11] R. Courant, *Differential and Integral Calculus,* Vol. 2, 2nd ed., trans. E. J. McShane, Interscience, 1936–1937.

[12] Ray Duncan, *Advanced MS-DOS,* Microsoft Press, 1986.

[13] Margaret A. Ellis and Bjarne Stroustrup, *The Annotated C++ Reference Manual,* Addison-Wesley Publishing Company, 1990.

[14] Daniel T. Finkbeiner II, *Introduction to Matrices and Linear Transformations,* 3rd ed., Freeman, 1978.

[15] George E. Forsythe and Cleve B. Moler, *Computer Solution Of Linear Algebraic Systems,* Prentice-Hall, 1967.

[16] George E. Forsythe, "Pitfalls in Computation, or Why a Math Book Isn't Enough," *American Mathematical Monthly*, LXXVII (1970), 931–955.

[17] F. R. Gantmacher, *The Theory of Matrices*, Vol. I, Chelsea, 1977.

[18] Samuel P. Harbison and Guy L. Steele, Jr., *C: A Reference Manual*, 3rd ed., Prentice-Hall, 1991.

[19] Einar Hille, *Analysis*, Vol. 2, Blaisdell, 1964–1966.

[20] A. S. Householder, *The Numerical Treatment of a Single Non-linear Equation*, McGraw-Hill, 1970.

[21] Institute for Electrical and Electronics Engineers (IEEE), *An American National Standard: IEEE Standard for Binary Floating-Point Arithmetic*, IEEE, 1985.

[22] Intel Corporation, *iAPX 286 Programmer's Reference Manual Including the IAPX 286 Numeric Supplement*, Intel Corporation, 1984.

[23] International Business Machines Corporation, *Disk Operating System 4.00*, several volumes, 1988.

[24] International Business Machines Corporation, *IBM Personal Computer Hardware Personal Reference Library Technical Reference*, 1982. There's a different manual for each PC model.

[25] Eugene Isaacson and Herbert Bishop Keller, *Analysis of Numerical Methods*, Wiley, 1966.

[26] Richard Karpinski, "Paranoia: A Floating-Point Benchmark," *Byte*, February 1985, 223-235.

[27] Brian W. Kernighan and Dennis M. Ritchie, *The C Programming Language*, Prentice-Hall, 2nd ed., 1988.

[28] Donald E. Knuth, *The Art of Computer Programming*, Vol. 1: *Fundamental Algorithms* (2nd ed.), Vol. 2: *Seminumerical Algorithms*, Addison-Wesley, 1973.

[29] Stanley B. Lippman, *C++ Primer*, Addison-Wesley, 1989.

[30] Melvin J. Maron and Robert J. Lopez, *Numerical analysis: A Practical Approach*, 3rd ed., Wadsworth, 1991.

[31] David B. Meredith, *Calculus Calculator*, Prentice-Hall, 1991.

[32] Microsoft Corporation, *The MS-DOS Encyclopedia*, ed. Ray Duncan, 1988.

[33] Peter Norton, *Inside the IBM PC*, Rev. and enl. ed., Brady, 1986.

[34] Peter Norton, *Programmer's guide to the IBM PC*, Microsoft Press, 1985.

[35] William H. Press, *et al.*, *Numerical Recipes in C: The Art of Scientific Computing*, Cambridge, 1989.

[36] Murray Sargent III and Richard Shoemaker, *The IBM Personal Computer from the Inside Out*, 2nd ed., Addison-Wesley, 1986.

[37] James T. Smith, *Advanced Turbo C*, Intertext/McGraw-Hill, 1989.

[38] James T. Smith, *Programmer's Guide to the IBM PC AT*, Prentice-Hall, 1986.

[39] Bjarne Stroustrup, *The C++ Programming Language*, Addison-Wesley, 1986.

[40] J. V. Uspensky, *Theory of Equations*, McGraw-Hill, 1948.

[41] Stewart Venit, "The Convergence of Jacobi and Gauss-Seidel Iteration," *Mathematics Magazine*, XLVIII (1975), 163–167.

[42] J. H. Wilkinson, *Rounding Errors in Algebraic Processes*, Prentice-Hall, 1963.

[43] Wolfram Research, Inc., *Mathematica, for 386-Based MS-DOS systems: Users guide*, 1989.

[44] Stephen Wolfram, *Mathematica: A System for Doing Mathematics by Computer*, Addison-Wesley, 1988.

[45] C. Ray Wylie, *Advanced Engineering Mathematics*, 4th ed., McGraw-Hill, 1975.

Index

A diskette containing software for the book *C++ for Scientists and Engineers* is available directly from the author. It includes all source code for the Mathematical Software Package (MSP) described in the book, as well as many MSP test programs. To order your copy, fill out and mail this card.

Yes, please send me a copy of the diskette accompanying *C++ for Scientists and Engineers,* by James T. Smith. I enclose a check or money order for $20 plus 7% sales tax in California.

We're sorry that we can't accept credit card orders.

Name   _____

Firm   _____

Address   _____

City   _____ State _____ ZIP_____

- -

James T. Smith
Mathematics Department
San Francisco State University
1600 Holloway Avenue
San Francisco, CA 94132